MATTERS OF JUSTICE

THE MEXICAN EXPERIENCE | William H. Beezley, series editor

MATTERS OF JUSTICE

Pueblos, the Judiciary, and Agrarian Reform in Revolutionary Mexico

Helga Baitenmann

UNIVERSITY OF NEBRASKA PRESS | Lincoln

© 2020 by the Board of Regents of the University of Nebraska. Portions of chapter 3 first appeared in "Zapata's Justice: Land and Water Conflict Resolution in Revolutionary Mexico (1914–16)," *Journal of Latin American Studies* 51, no. 4 (2019): 801–28, https://doi.org/10.1017/S0022216X19000634.

All rights reserved. ∞

Library of Congress Control Number: 2019041551

Set in Lyon Text by Laura Buis.

To Kevin

A Mariel

CONTENTS

List of Illustrations   ix

Acknowledgments   xi

Introduction: Hidden Histories of Revolutionary Agrarian Reform   1

1. The Inherent Difficulties of Winning Pueblo Land and Water Suits in Nineteenth-Century Mexico   25

2. Pueblo Land and Water Claims during the Madero Administration, 1911–1913   53

3. The Zapatista Land Reform, 1911–1916   76

4. The Constitutionalist Land Reform in the Absence of the Judiciary, 1914–1917   108

5. The Return of the Judiciary in Uncertain Times, 1917–1924   135

6. The Morelos Laboratory, 1920–1924   162

Epilogue: Zapatista and Constitutionalist Agrarian Reforms Compared   191

Glossary   201

Notes   207

Bibliography   275

Index   303

ILLUSTRATIONS

1. Map of eight Sierra de Juárez pueblos (Oaxaca)   43
2. Map of Santa María del Monte, Tehuacán (Puebla)   43
3. Yurécuaro (Michoacán) petition to Madero   60
4. Zapatista restitution map of San Miguel Huajintla (Morelos)   92
5. Minutes from the Tlatenchi (Morelos) Zapatista restitution   96 & 97
6. Representatives of Cuecillos Ranch (Tlaxcala) in charge of restitution   114
7. Venustiano Carranza and the Puebla Agrarian Commission overseeing land grant   129
8. Justices of the First Revolutionary Supreme Court, 1917   138
9. Land grant map of Tepexpan and Tequisistlán (Mexico State)   154
10. Merced of San Miguel Anenecuilco, Morelos, 1853   178
11. Land grant map for San Gabriel Amacuzac (Morelos)   189

ACKNOWLEDGMENTS

This book has been long in the making, and many people have been helpful at various times.

William Roseberry at the New School for Social Research has been the single most influential person in my academic life. I would not have become a historical anthropologist had it not been for Bill's inspiring writings and teachings. I wish I could thank Bill as a colleague, but sadly he passed away soon after I finished my dissertation and so he will forever remain my advisor. I hope a little part of his spirit lives on in this book.

Emilio H. Kourí was the first historian to read my manuscript and make important comments and a few vital corrections. He greatly helped me conceptualize my central arguments, and he invited me to develop one part of this book as a dossier he put together for *Historia Mexicana*. His ongoing, generous, and expert feedback has been a guiding light for this project; nowhere have I learned more than during our many long and enjoyable conversations. Gracias, Emilio.

Anyone studying the Mexican Revolution has read Alan Knight's work. I had the pleasure of meeting him at a seminar in Michoacán in 1994, and since moving to London many years ago, I have had the good fortune to count him and Lidia as friends. Although not a formal reviewer, Alan took the time to write detailed comments about my manuscript, and he persuaded me to take a more decisive stand in some of my arguments. Thank you, Alan.

Christopher Boyer and John J. Dwyer reviewed my manuscript for the University of Nebraska Press. They were both very generous and constructive reviewers. Chris's comments led me to spend many months rethinking broader questions, which I believe greatly improved my introduction and overall framework. Jay wrote long and detailed comments on all matters, large and small. I am confident this is a better book because of his contributions.

Jonathan Fox and Kevin J. Middlebrook, both *politólogos*, have for a long time kept me focused on the larger questions. Fernando Franco González Salas on many occasions helped me understand the workings of the judiciary in Mexico. Ann Varley and Horacio Mackinlay taught me the importance of studying agrarian law with care and depth. Antonio Azuela de la Cueva and Juan Carlos Pérez Castañeda helped me understand many legal matters. Victoria Chenaut's pioneering legal anthropological work always reminds me why I remain an anthropologist. I am most fortunate that all the above have also been very dear, long-time personal friends.

My work originally focused on agrarian reform in twentieth-century Mexico. When, many years ago, Emilio Kourí suggested I transcend the customary 1910 divide and I began studying nineteenth-century agrarian history, I had the great fortune to be received with open arms by a large group of experts on the subject. The main organizer of this academic group was Antonio Escobar Ohmstede, who generously invited me to participate in numerous conferences, seminars, and book projects, and who has also become a close friend. At these conferences, I have had the opportunity to learn from such great scholars as Diana Birrichaga, Romana Falcón, Eric Leonard, Daniela Marino, Edgar Mendoza, Emilia Velázquez, and others. Gracias a todas y a todos.

Parts of chapter 3 were first published in the *Journal of Latin American Studies*. I thank the journal's reviewers—particularly Sam Brunk—for their insightful comments, which helped me interpret the Zapatista movement with greater nuance.

Living in the United Kingdom, where libraries have limited collections of rare books on Mexico, I often had to rely on Luis Espinoza, owner of the digital bookshop Tardes en la Alameda. He is a master at scouring old bookstores in Mexico City for obscure material.

The Archivo de Terrenos Nacionales repeatedly declined my petition to conduct research there, making me even more grateful to all other archives that do welcome scholars. I especially wish to thank the directors and staff at the Archivo Central de la Suprema Corte de Justicia, the Archivo General de la Nación, the Archivo General Agrario (especially director Regina Tapia Chávez and archivist Jeovani Montaño Pineda, who went out of their way to assist researchers), and the Archivo Histórico del Agua. I also thank Linda Arnold for generously sharing with me her digitalized copies of archival material.

I relied on the assistance of several magnificent researchers. I thank Regina Henríquez Morales and Diego Marañón Henríquez for their help during the early phases of this project. I am also grateful to Beatriz Montes Rojas and Karen Verdejo Ramírez for their invaluable support; I could not have written this book without their exceptional public relations skills, their determined archival searches, their patience with tedious transcripts, and their creativity in taking photographs of archival material in less than ideal conditions. This book is theirs, too.

At the University of Nebraska Press, Emily Wendell received my manuscript with enthusiasm and guided the process with extreme ease and efficiency, and Elizabeth Zaleski patiently worked with me before and during the copyediting stage. One could not hope for better editors. I would also like to thank copy editors Elizabeth Brown, who edited the manuscript with great humor and thoughtfulness, and Wayne K. Larsen, who caught many mistakes and made the text more fluid.

Finally, I thank Brett Kahr for many years of kind and patient guidance in crafting historical narratives, personal and otherwise. Thank you also to my family—Edna, Erika, Vicky & Davia, and Reni—for always being there; to Patrick & Francine, for our renewed bond; and to Angie, Pat (Breslin), and Peg for the many years of friendship. Gracias a Fernanda, Luz y Sandra, por ser nuestra familia en Londres, a Gisela & Yoli por nuestra amistad originaria y eterna y a "las ángeles de la guarda"—Adriana, Birgit, Claudia y Sabine—por su amistad tan antigua y tan presente.

I dedicate this book to Kevin, my dear *companero* for so many years, and to Mariel, our wonderful daughter—who is an anthropologist and an educator in her own right. Both had to live with this book in all its versions. I thank Kevin and Mariel for their unconditional support throughout the years and their unwavering faith that—someday—I would finish. Our common interests and shared values have made family life deeply rewarding. Their company has been life's greatest gift.

MATTERS OF JUSTICE

Introduction

Hidden Histories of Revolutionary Agrarian Reform

> Like the New World, agrarianism existed long
> before it was discovered by newcomers.
> —Alan Knight, *The Mexican Revolution*, vol. 2

Studies of land reform in twentieth-century Mexico tend to project onto the past concepts that were created in the 1930s and 1940s, bestowing the early revolutionary agrarian reforms with meanings they did not have. This book is a study of the two main agrarian reform programs in revolutionary Mexico—the Zapatista and the Constitutionalist projects—as they were implemented in practice at the local level and then reconfigured in response to unanticipated inter- and intravillage conflicts.[1] What archival documents show is that neither of these agrarian projects intended to create what we now know as the twentieth-century *ejido*—that is, population centers with their own patrimony, juridical standing, and administrative and representative organs under the tutelage of the federal executive, and operating parallel to autonomous municipal governments.[2] This book is about what the architects of these programs actually sought to achieve and what in fact happened on the ground.

Both land reform programs were first and foremost responses to *pueblo* representatives' petitions for the restitution of their ancestral communal lands and water resources. When meeting with revolutionary leader Francisco I. Madero in Mexico City on 8 June 1911, Emiliano

Zapata famously told him, "My soldiers—the armed farmers and all the people in the villages—demand that I tell you, with full respect, that they want the restitution of their lands to be got under way right now."[3] That same year, feeling betrayed by Madero, Zapata issued his Plan de Ayala, which allowed pueblos and citizens with titles to fields, woodlands, and water resources unjustly appropriated by landlords, *científicos* (advisers to the ousted dictator Porfirio Díaz), or *caciques* (local or regional strongmen) to immediately reclaim their property and defend it, arms in hand.[4] Similarly, Venustiano Carranza's 6 January 1915 law began by stating, "One of the most general causes for the unrest and discontent of the agricultural populations of this country has been the dispossession of their communal lands ... granted to them by the colonial government as a means to assure the existence of the Indian class." The law therefore promised the restitution of usurped pueblo lands and water resources.[5]

Because restituting usurped pueblo properties often proved unfeasible for a variety of reasons, both the Zapatista and Constitutionalist (Carrancista) revolutionary factions also promised to grant pueblos land and water resources from expropriated haciendas. The Plan de Ayala promised to distribute a third of all large landholdings to impoverished Mexican pueblos and citizens; the 6 January 1915 law proposed granting needy pueblos enough land to satisfy their basic needs.

Frank Tannenbaum's *The Mexican Agrarian Revolution* (1929), which is widely considered to be the first comprehensive study of revolutionary agrarian reform in Mexico, tellingly noted a crucial shift in the Constitutionalists' justification for land reform: in little more than a decade, the architects of the Constitutionalist project (which would prevail throughout most of the twentieth century) changed the focus from the restitution of pueblo lands to the granting of expropriated lands to needy villages. He explained that under the 6 January 1915 agrarian law,

> restitution occupied the most prominent place both in the law and in the reasons given for the legislation. In Article 27 restitution and

donation were more nearly on parity with each other, with restitution still occupying first place.... But now donation comes first and restitution is subordinate. That is, the law has moved from an attempt to undo an injustice by returning lands to communities that had illegally been deprived of them—an attempt that was beset with innumerable and almost insurmountable legal difficulties—to a clear recognition of the equal right of all communities to land.[6]

Tannenbaum's observation accurately described the relationship between restitutions and donations (*dotaciones*, or grants), and it remains central to understanding land reform in revolutionary Mexico. In fact, the shift from restitutions to dotaciones has probably been the single most misunderstood element of the country's twentieth-century redistribution of land, woodlands, and water resources. Moreover, and despite its foundational importance, restitutions remain the least studied of all agrarian concepts.

What exactly were restitutions? Why did they face, as Tannenbaum pointed out, innumerable and insurmountable legal difficulties? Why did revolutionary governments' failed attempts to undo an injustice end up as land grants to impoverished villagers for subsistence agriculture? Why and how did the Constitutionalists' restitutions and grants become the vehicle for the redistribution of landed property in Mexico, even though they were not originally designed to do so? And what does this mean for the historical narrative of the Mexican Revolution and for studies of postrevolutionary state formation? In addressing these questions, and as the title of the book indicates, this work introduces two subjects not generally considered part of the history of agrarian reform in Mexico: the role of the judiciary, and villagers' agency in promoting and shaping revolutionary land reform.

Scholars have not studied the role of the judiciary in revolutionary agrarian reform even though restitutions normally are judicial matters. Restitution (the restoration of lands and water resources granted to Indian pueblos by the Spanish crown) was not a revolutionary concept to restore pueblo lands. Rather, it was a legal procedure created in the sixteenth century to allow Indian pueblo representatives to take to court—oftentimes generations after the illegal seizure had occurred—those who invaded or seized their landholdings and water resources. With national independence and the closure of the Indian courts, the judicial branch of government took over all restitution suits. During the Revolution (1910–20), however, with the judicial system shut down by insurgent factions because of its association with the overthrown regime of dictator Porfirio Díaz (1876–80, 1884–1911, the period known as the Porfiriato), both Zapatistas and Constitutionalists created administrative offices that assumed court responsibilities for pueblo land and water restitutions. The Zapatistas were the first revolutionary faction to take on land restitutions in any systematic way, not as legend has it (granting villages total autonomy in land distribution) but by creating a ministry of agriculture with the authority to resolve all land claims administratively. A few years later, Constitutionalists also sidestepped the courts, granting judicial functions to the National Agrarian Commission at the federal level and local agrarian commissions at the state level. Therefore, one transformative aspect of Mexico's twentieth-century land reform (in both its Zapatista and Constitutionalist versions) was that revolutionaries employed a state of exception (public officials' ability to transcend the rule of law in the name of the public good) to justify transferring the legal underpinnings of land reform to the executive branch. Paradoxically, the justices of the first two reinstated Supreme Courts granted the Constitutionalists executive-branch jurisdiction over contentious land matters. Lucio Cabrera Acevedo, the most distinguished historian of the Mexican Supreme Court, writes that the Supreme Court rulings between 1917 and 1922 "made agrarian reform possible."[7] In fact, they did so even though this action violated several articles of the 1917 Constitution guaranteeing the separation of powers and due process.[8] Supreme Court justices allowed for this anomaly, in part, because restitutions and dotaciones were not intended to be legal or procedural tools for a long-lasting redistribution of landed property in Mexico.

Scholars have also neglected to study village agency in Mexico's revolutionary agrarian reform, even though it was key in promoting and then shaping the reform process. This was the case in both the Zapatista region of influence, where scholars have always assumed (despite little empirical knowledge of how) villagers played a role, and in territories controlled by the Constitutionalist forces.[9] In fact, the research for this book reveals a sharp difference between what most historians conclude (namely, that Carranza's overarching conservatism made him reluctant to distribute land) and what is reflected in the pioneering work of Berta Ulloa: active and widespread participation by both villagers and Carrancista officials in the early implementation of agrarian reform.[10]

Village representatives (often democratically elected and representing dozens and even hundreds of residents, but sometimes acting only for an interested minority) and their followers actively participated in shaping Mexico's sui generis agrarian reform not only by rising up in arms but also by exerting legal pressure on those who held power.[11] This involvement should come as no surprise because, in the last two decades or so, legal anthropologists and social historians of nineteenth-century Mexico have found village representatives actively employing all available courts, and appealing to whatever laws best legitimated their position, in the pursuit of their claims.[12]

Throughout the nineteenth century in much of the country, attorneys, elected officials, and spokespersons for pueblos—whether Indian, multiethnic, or mestizo—brought to the courts land and water claims against encroaching landowners, municipal authorities, caciques, and neighboring pueblos.[13] Pueblo attorneys filed *amparo* suits at the district level and at the Supreme Court to challenge "political and judicial dispositions they found arbitrary, illegal, or unfair,"[14] and they used Liberal laws intended to privatize communal lands to recover usurped pueblo lands and water resources, to legalize properties without titles, and to bring boundary suits against neighboring towns.[15] When judges and justices failed to restore usurped lands and water resources, villagers repeatedly tried to sidestep the judiciary by petitioning the executive to address their unresolved claims. They did so in particular during regime changes—and they did so in multitudes when Madero ousted the Díaz regime. Villagers, individually and collectively, never stopped exerting pressure on the revolutionary leadership—not even in the Zapatista regions, where hundreds of them signed petitions directed to Zapata's General Headquarters. And as the Constitutionalists gradually became the only national alternative (outside the Zapatista stronghold of Morelos), thousands of village leaders throughout the country sent their appeals and complaints to the newly established agrarian commissions.

Village representatives and their followers also shaped revolutionary agrarian reforms through their inter- and intravillage disputes. Most histories of revolutionary agrarian reform focus exclusively on village-hacienda relations, when in fact much of what determined the future shape of land reform in postrevolutionary Mexico were conflicts within and between pueblos.[16] In the nineteenth century, at least half of all restitution suits involved conflicts between or among neighboring pueblos or between the *cabecera* (municipal head town) and its *barrios* (cabecera wards or quarters) or *sujeto* villages (smaller towns within the cabecera's jurisdiction).[17] Such conflicts did not cease during the revolutionary period.

Zapatistas soon realized that hacienda land takeovers caused or revived intervillage boundary disputes. As villagers recovered what they believed to be their ancestral lands and water resources, they often trespassed on what neighboring pueblos considered to be their properties. As a result, when the Zapatista Ministry of Agriculture and Colonization ran into problems defining boundaries based on colonial titles, the Zapatista leadership created the *reparto provisional*, or temporary land distribution, which privileged need and equality over ancestral land rights.[18]

Carrancistas decided early on that the executive branch would not have jurisdiction over intervillage conflicts, which would be left to the judiciary. But the ways in which they responded to intravillage complaints about corruption and abuse of power in the management of restituted and granted lands and water resources would be the single most important precedent for the post-1934 ejido. By creating the *comité particular administrativo*, a temporary form of local governance and justice parallel to municipal authorities, the Constitutionalists also laid the groundwork for what would become the twentieth-century ejido.[19]

Historiographical Gaps in the Literature on Mexico's Agrarian Reform

Although Mexico's agrarian reform has long constituted the focus of voluminous scholarship in the fields of political economy, political science, history, anthropology, and legal studies, until now no scholar has investigated in detail and with archival sources the historical construction of pueblo land restitution or the role of the judiciary in agrarian matters.[20] This section identifies some of the reasons for these gaps in the literature.

Agrarian Reform and the Judiciary in Revolutionary Mexico

Because both the 1857 and the 1917 constitutions forbade special courts outside judicial purview (except for military tribunals) and established a division of powers among the executive, legislative, and judicial branches of government to create political checks and balances, Carranza's 1915 land reform program that gave the presidency judicial faculties should have been suspect. Early on, however, most legal scholars welcomed the imbalance of powers regarding land reform because they saw the judiciary as a symbol of the Díaz dictatorship: conservative, corrupt, and weak in its defense of pueblo lands. In 1916, for instance, the National Agrarian Commission published a booklet justifying the exclusion of the judiciary from pueblo land restitutions. Written by lawyer and politician Fernando González Roa, the booklet argued, "A long-sustained doctrine has been that a trial is necessary to recover the communal property of the pueblos, but this doctrine is mistaken because it is contrary to the precedents and practices of colonial legislation." González Roa explained how colonial laws had allowed kings, viceroys, and governors to inspect the titles of those suspected of having seized pueblo lands, to conduct surveys based on these titles, and to return usurped lands. Therefore, following colonial precedent, it was the executive's prerogative to decide which of the opposing parties (pueblo or property owners) was in the right. According to González Roa, the Díaz government was responsible for taking away the executive's right to rule over these matters—in order to favor land speculators. Therefore, Carranza's 6 January 1915 law was simply restoring an old principle that gave the executive the rightful authority to determine the outcome of land disputes.[21]

In the 1920s, the party line for legal experts was not to challenge the executive's authority over litigious land matters but rather to fashion a legal language that could justify the peculiarities of the postrevolutionary state. Legal scholar Narciso Bassols, for example, coined the term "agrarian administrative trial" (*proceso administrativo agrario*) to describe court proceedings in land matters judged by the executive branch—one of the many terms that normalized the idiosyncrasies of the agrarian program. Bassols went to great lengths to show that the agrarian reform based on the Constitutionalist 6 January 1915 law followed the same proceedings as a civil suit: it provided for hearings at a lower court and a superior court (the governor in the first instance and the president in the second); it presented a rationale for the decision; and it rendered a final judgment. The "agrarian administrative trial" thus fulfilled constitutional guarantees to private property; there was no reason, therefore, why agrarian tribunals could not operate outside the judicial branch. By good fortune, Bassols concluded, the National Agrarian Commission had the Supreme Court's absolute support on this question.[22]

To justify these special tribunals, government officials in the 1930s embraced the belief that the judiciary was to blame for pueblo land losses.[23] According to the preamble of the 1931 reforms to Constitutional article 27, for instance, it was "beyond doubt that the 1917 Constitutional Convention delegates, as faithful interpreters of the sentiments of the popular masses for whom the revolution is reconquering their rights, in redacting article 27 of the Constitution set out to exclude judicial authorities from all intervention in agrarian matters, given that our one hundred years of independent life demonstrated that . . . in all the lawsuits that the pueblos took to the courts to defend their rights, a great percentage invariably were condemned to lose their lands." The reason villagers systematically lost their court claims, as stated in the preamble, was that during the Diaz dictatorship landlords had excessive influence over judges.[24]

Landowners filing for amparo protection against the agrarian administration in the 1920s and the 1930s continually reminded judges of the due-process guarantees found in the Constitution's article 14, and legal scholars carried on providing language to justify the anomaly.[25] For example, in his 1934 book titled *El problema agrario de México desde su origen hasta la época actual*, lawyer and public official Lucio Mendieta y Núñez explained that agrarian procedures began with a restitution or dotación petition, which was considered the initial filing of the suit (*demanda inicial del juicio*). Landowners had the right to be informed of the suit through its publication in the official state newspaper. Those who believed they held rights to lands affected by pueblo petitions for restitution or dotación could go to the state agrarian commission while the case file was being processed (and before the ruling was issued) to make claims and present corroborating evidence (*alegatos y pruebas*) in support of them. "This way," Mendieta y Núñez argued, "even though it is not precisely the classic form of a trial, the agrarian procedures preserved the essential formalities of article 14 of the Constitution."[26]

That the executive had taken over "the classic form of a trial" to implement land reform entirely escaped most historians and social scientists. For instance, Tannenbaum stated that "the grant of lands is declared to proceed as a matter of public utility and therefore comes under administrative rather than judicial authority." He did not, however, explain why the grant did not follow conventional expropriation rules or why, in the case of restitutions, the executive branch of government would preside over contentious land matters.[27] At the time, delving into such questions was usually viewed as upholding landowners' rights, and most foreign scholars studying Mexico's land reform were largely supportive of what they saw as the state's efforts to benefit the rural classes. The idea that the imbalance of power between the executive and the judiciary could also affect land beneficiaries or small property holders was virtually unimaginable at the time.

Moreover, some scholars openly supported the complete exclusion of the judiciary from agrarian matters. In his book *The Ejido: Mexico's Way Out* (1937), Eyler N. Simpson lamented the Supreme Court's powers to award amparo protection to landowners. He believed that "one of the worst blunders of the decree of 1915 was the insertion of the provision recognizing the right of injured parties to have recourse to the ordinary courts against the actions of the government."[28] In fact, *not* questioning why or how Mexico's land reform had become a matter of executive jurisdiction, and instead condemning the Supreme Court's judicial review powers (a related but separate matter), became the common trend in the literature. For example, in his book *Rural Mexico* (1948), Nathan L. Whetten explained that Carranza's law "gave landowners recourse to the courts in case they felt they were being unduly injured by any expropriation proceedings. Affected landlords, accordingly, resorted to court injunctions whenever threatened, and they succeeded in delaying the program and making it ineffective through long-drawn-out legal disputes, which usually ended in their favor."[29]

For jurists at the time, following the Institutional Revolutionary Party (Partido Revolucionario Institucional, or PRI) line meant providing legal language to justify the executive's judicial faculties. In 1963, for example, legal scholar Héctor Fix Zamudio observed that there was yet no "scientifically structured agrarian procedural law"—the rules by which a court hears and determines what happens in a lawsuit.[30] To fill this void, Martha Chávez Padrón published the first of a series of textbooks on "agrarian procedural law." This work, which would become de rigueur reading for all law students interested in agrarian law, produced a new academic discipline called *derecho social*, or social law. This new social law was based on the idea of a "delegated judicial branch" (*poder judicial delegado*), with agrarian authorities who "without being part of the judiciary were real judges."[31]

There were, of course, several jurists who challenged the constitutionality of the delegated judicial branch. In several national law congresses during the 1950s and 1960s, legal scholars questioned the existence of this parallel judicial system within the executive branch of government.[32] For example, legal expert Raúl Cervantes Ahumada published an article in 1964 noting the urgent need to organize an "ejido justice system." He suggested creating regional ejido tribunals that would rule on all contentious matters between land reform beneficiaries and complaints against the agrarian administration. To do so, he proposed adding a third chamber to the Supreme Court—one specifically for agrarian matters.[33] In the 1970s, legal scholar Antonio de Ibarrola observed "with great anguish" that agrarian proceedings were being conducted by agrarian officials without formal legal training. He went farther than most legal scholars at the time by adding that "the resolution of agrarian matters evaded the jurisdiction of the judiciary, which is unconstitutional and inexplicable."[34] These voices upholding the constitutional right to a fair trial (something that affected agrarian beneficiaries as much as landowners) and demanding that the agrarian administration be accountable for its actions were easily dismissed by agrarian officials as conservative, pro-landowner, and counterrevolutionary.

Social scientists and historians working on agrarian reform in Mexico did not engage in this important debate because, at the time, they took for granted the executive's judicial powers over contentious land matters. In the 1950s, Jesús Silva Herzog criticized the 6 January 1915 law for its vagueness on matters such as the form and times of compensation payments to landowners, but he did not question the executive's judicial functions.[35] In the 1960s, Moisés T. de la Peña confused Luis Cabrera's proposals regarding the reconstitution of communal lands with land restitutions (a difference explained in detail in chapter 4), altogether avoiding the question of the balance of power between the executive and the judiciary.[36] And, in the 1970s, the 1,174-page volume written by Sergio Reyes Osorio, Rodolfo Stavenhagen, Salomón Eckstein, and others on agrarian reform in Mexico did not once mention the executive overstepping its constitutional limits.[37]

Most surprisingly, even in the 1970s and 1980s when critics of the postrevolutionary regime began questioning Mexican authoritarianism from several angles (including the inordinate power of the federal executive), these authors did not focus on how the executive took over judicial functions and powers in the design of the revolutionary land reform. Adolfo Gilly, for instance, found fault with the executive-led reform because pueblo petitions for land restitution had been processed not through officials elected by the pueblos—as he believed the Zapatistas had done—but by governors or military chiefs. He concluded, "This was the leg on which stood a gigantic operation of land appropriation by the Constitutionalist generals and high officials, functionaries, and politicians, who were the most direct beneficiaries of the 'agrarian reform' and enriched themselves with a voracity comparable to that of the bourgeoisie of the great French revolution."[38] His focus was more on corruption and lack of village autonomy than on the executive becoming judge and jury over agrarian matters and how this anomaly affected land beneficiaries. Similarly, Arnaldo Córdova ignored the executive's judicial functions or questions about constitutional checks and balances and, instead, focused on the populist nature of the Mexican state.[39]

The "metaconstitutional faculties" that the Constitutionalists granted the executive, and which the first two revolutionary Supreme Courts ratified, not only became fully institutionalized in a land reform program that would constitute one of the pillars of the long-ruling PRI regime, but were also greatly expanded in the 1930s to include the settling of thousands of individual agrarian-rights claims by land beneficiaries and hundreds of intervillage boundary conflicts. The magnitude of the executive's involvement in not only administering land reform but also resolving contentious land and water matters was hard to conceptualize until 1992, when President Carlos Salinas de Gortari (1988–94) overhauled the entire agrarian reform sector and created a new agrarian court system.[40] It was only when these new tribunals became flooded with thousands of pending case files that scholars could begin to comprehend the enormity of the executive's involvement in conflict resolution between or among beneficiaries, between beneficiary populations and their neighbors, and between individual and collective beneficiaries and the agrarian administration.[41] The agrarian administration had become a massive parallel court system, at once judge and jury, in which officials who were neither lawyers nor judges, nor accountable to the judiciary, ruled on hundreds of thousands of contentious matters, usually with decades-long delays.

Restitutions and Dotaciones

Given that restitutions were the founding justification for revolutionary land reform, it is surprising that there are no studies on the topic. One possible explanation for this void is that an understanding of the concept of restitution requires two related conceptual shifts. First, scholars must transcend the 1910 historiographical divide ("before" and "after" the 1910 Revolution) to study nineteenth-century pueblo court cases.[42] Second, studies must focus on the relationship between villagers and the judiciary, both in the nineteenth century as well as in revolutionary Mexico. These shifts are difficult because for years scholars studying agrarian reform have begun with the 1910 Revolution and focused solely on the role of the executive branch.

In the absence of archival research on pueblo land restitutions, most historians and social scientists adopt Mexican anthropologist Arturo Warman's characterization of the difference between restitutions and dotaciones. In his influential 1976 book on Morelos, ... *Y venimos a contradecir*, Warman shows that after the revolution the government granted few restitutions in Morelos; on that basis, he concludes: "Agrarian reform was not going to legitimize the historical right of villages to the land nor strengthen their autonomy; it was not going to carry out acts of justice.... On the contrary, it was going to distribute land as a unilateral concession from the State."[43] In what would serve as the basis for a critique of the postrevolutionary authoritarian regime, Warman turns the restitution into a symbol of village justice and autonomy and reduces the dotación to a mechanism of state clientelism and a tool for peasant co-optation.

Most studies of agrarian reform published in the 1980s and 1990s adopt the Warman position without critique. Linda Hall, for example, relies on it to characterize President Obregón's 1920–24 land reform, explaining that the dotación "procedure was followed principally because it was easier to grant land than to prove earlier legal title and thus restore it, but it had the added effect of converting the campesinos into clients of the Obregón administration, dependent on government largesse rather than on their own ancient claims to the land."[44] Similarly, Dana Markiewicz expresses the conviction that restitutions failed because neither the Madero administration nor succeeding governments could recognize peasants' claims. "To do so," she maintains, "would call into question the validity of many a landlord's seemingly legal titles and, ultimately, the validity of all private property, a danger illustrated by Zapatismo's expropriation of the sugar mills as well as the land supplying them."[45] Counter to Hall and Markiewicz, Susan Walsh Sanderson correctly notes that the difficulties involved in resolving restitution claims were primarily due to the plaintiff's burden of proof: "Some villages were able to preserve documentation proving their right to traditional landholdings, but these were rare. Many villages had incomplete documentation, sufficient to give them hope but insufficient to meet the rigorous scrutiny of agrarian officials." But, having read Warman, Sanderson then adopts jargon that obscures her own empirical findings in Morelos. For instance, she finds it ironic that "in the center of peasant revolution the peasants who fought a 10-year battle for the restoration of village lands were denied them by the federal government and were instead given outright grants.... The government claimed to be paternalistically and generously giving out land, rather than acceding to peasants' prior rights."[46]

The Warman opposition between restitutions as a form of autonomy and ejidos as a form of state co-optation was such an expedient shortcut for explaining the history of agrarian reform that it became the hallmark of theories of peasant resistance to the state published in the 1990s and thereafter. For example, in her important book on revolutionary movements in the state of Michoacán, Jennie Purnell states, "Whereas a restitution constituted recognition by the state of a community's claim of legitimate ownership and unjust dispossession, a dotación was simply a grant bestowed by a paternalist state, with a good many strings attached at that."⁴⁷ Similarly, in his agrarian history of the Chihuahuan town of Namiquipa, Daniel Nugent observes, "The distinction between *restitución* and *dotación* is extremely important for understanding community-state relations in Mexico generally after the revolution.... Securing a restitution was justice, while securing a dotación was an insult, a matter of the state posturing as a *patrón*."⁴⁸ Nugent and Ana María Alonso further develop this idea in their chapter on land reform in the highly influential *Everyday Forms of State Formation: Revolution and Negotiation of Rule in Modern Mexico*. They argue that "petitions for *restitución* of lands were routinely negated; but sometimes the very same territory was granted to the community as a dotación. When finally an *ejido* was granted, in other words, it was to figure as a gift from the state; a gift for which peasants were expected to express their gratitude, demonstrating their indebtedness by becoming the loyal subjects of the state." In their view, this logic explains why Namiquipa peasants resisted the state's agrarian project.⁴⁹

Studies published in the twenty-first century continued to uphold Warman's oppositional categories. For example, Raymond Craib's book on the history of cartography in Mexico maintains that pueblos insisted on restitution "rather than allowing themselves to be portrayed as the submissive recipients of state grace in the form of dotación."⁵⁰ Similarly, John Gledhill writes that "the ejido granted by dotación rather than by restitution ... strengthen[ed] the clientelist content of the new relationship between state and peasants."⁵¹ Finally, in one of the first efforts to understand restitutions based on material from the new Archivo General Agrario, Guillermo Palacios also concludes his essay with a Warman variant. He maintains that the term *restitution* comes from Spanish legislation applied to minors under age twenty-five who could have been harmed by their tutors or representatives. The *Novísima Recopilación de Indias* would extend that concept to include Indian pueblos, which were also seen as minors who had to be represented by tutors. The architects of the revolutionary agrarian reform, according to Palacios, kept the term restitution, even though they probably did not know its legal history. "But the paternalist attitude of the revolutionary authorities towards campesinos and Indians fit the context well."[52]

One problem with the Warman dichotomy is that it rests on a misconception of the nature of land reform in postrevolutionary Mexico: the idea that restituted lands belonged to the villages, whereas granted lands became property of the nation or the federal state. Antonio Azuela de la Cueva has questioned why so many social scientists have believed incorrectly that land granted in the form of the twentieth-century ejido became national property.[53] The misunderstanding likely stems from the rule that whereas population centers after 1934 became corporate owners of land, individual beneficiaries had conditional use-rights to a land parcel or to communal lands—conditional because "agrarian subjects" could not sell them; they could only bequeath their rights to their spouses or offspring. Moreover, if they broke agrarian law, they could lose their use-rights altogether. This condition, however, applied to *both* restitutions and dotaciones. In fact, dotaciones and restitutions did not differ in terms of fundamental property rights and conditions.[54]

Of course, many villagers would have preferred a restitution to a dotación. Recognizing old colonial boundaries often meant restoring more land (sometimes considerably more land) than what they would receive in the form of a dotación. Also, many town leaders did strongly believe that restitutions were a matter of justice, the resolution of longstanding disputes with nearby haciendas, neighboring villages, and the local elite that had legally and illegally purchased communal lands during the nineteenth century. But to the extent that different forms of agrarian property and local organization served as means of embedding state clientelism and a tool for peasant co-optation, such problems arose equally in beneficiary groups receiving restitutions and dotaciones.[55]

Organization of the Book

Venustiano Carranza's famous 6 January 1915 law, and the historiography it influenced, rested on two somewhat contradictory ideas about

Mexico during the second half of the nineteenth-century.[56] On the one hand, the story goes, pueblos lost their right to represent themselves in court, and therefore they could not defend their communal lands, woodlands, or water resources against encroaching haciendas. On the other hand, Carranza's law implies, when pueblo representatives took their claims to court, corrupt and biased judges systematically ruled in favor of landowners. So the question becomes, were pueblo representatives able or unable to take their claims to court?

Chapter 1 shows that hundreds of pueblo representatives and attorneys did indeed file restitution and other suits in the civil courts, even when Supreme Court justices interpreted article 27 of the 1857 Constitution as the pueblos' loss of juridical standing to pursue litigation over communal lands. Moreover, substantial evidence suggests that some judges and justices acted with a degree of fairness—enough for pueblo representatives to conclude that taking their claims to court was worth the effort, time, and expense. Furthermore, restitution claims were not always filed against hacienda owners; there were probably as many boundary suits against municipal governments and neighboring towns as against the landed elite.

If pueblo representatives had been able to be heard in court more often than previously acknowledged, why did so few of them manage to recover their old colonial lands and water resources? Chapter 1 explains in depth why restitution and boundary suits were inherently difficult to win in court. No doubt many judges favored the landed elite in a corrupt and authoritarian system that allowed such bias. Even in cases that perhaps should have been clear wins for pueblos, however, one key problem remained: many pueblos did not possess the deeds that would hold up in civil court, even though most of them did have some kind of ancient document they could call a "primordial title."[57] Moreover, it was often difficult to determine which contesting party held the strongest evidence in a country with a long history of diverse and overlapping land possession, use, and ownership rights, and where, throughout decades and even centuries, legitimate property transactions blended with fraudulent ones.[58] As a result executive branch officials (municipal officials, district prefects or political chiefs, governors, and even the president) attempted at various times and in diverse ways to resolve these conflicts outside the judicial system, and village authorities frequently tried to sidestep the judiciary by petitioning the executive to resolve their land conflicts administratively. As soon as defendants demanded their constitutional right to be heard in court, however, the judiciary often sided with them by upholding the constitutional separation of powers and thus protecting its jurisdiction.

On the eve of the revolution, hundreds of pueblo representatives were engaged in old and new land suits against other pueblos, municipal governments, local caciques, and landowners; they employed all available laws, including Liberal privatization and federal public lands laws, in their efforts to regain or expand pueblo lands; and they strategically pitted one branch of government against another. As chapter 2 shows, at the outbreak of the Madero revolution, this broad and profoundly litigious rural sector would play a key role in urging the executive to intervene in judicial matters, alongside those who rose up in arms, many of whom had also experienced decades of litigation.

When the 1910 Revolution broke out, hundreds of pueblo representatives throughout the country, many with long histories as plaintiffs and defendants, would use their legal expertise to exert pressure on the various revolutionary governments to resolve their old (and new) land and water claims outside the court system. To appease these claimants, in early 1912 Madero's Ministry of Development, Colonization, and Industry (Secretaría de Fomento, Colonización e Industria) issued two circulars based on federal public lands laws intended to privatize the pueblos' ejidos.[59] The hope was that during the survey of the pueblos' colonial boundaries, ministry officials could resolve boundary disputes by arbitration. Chapter 2 shows that village leaders saw these circulars as the Madero administration's efforts to restitute seized pueblo lands outside the courts, and they proceeded to challenge boundaries with neighboring haciendas. Fomento's surveys failed repeatedly when landowners demanded their constitutional right to a fair trial. Madero's agrarian policies thus clearly exposed the executive's limited ability to resolve land and water conflicts outside the judiciary, and in response the more radical members of Congress proposed sidestepping the 1857 Constitution's separation of powers to enable the executive to assume court functions. However, with a functioning judiciary still in place, the idea of expanding executive authority over contentious land matters remained a largely untenable proposition.

While the Madero administration unsuccessfully sought to resolve village land claims by administrative means using federal public land laws, villagers in Morelos were taking land and water restitution into their own hands. Chapter 3 focuses on the famous but largely unstudied Zapatista agrarian reform, which began as a takeover of disputed lands that villagers had been repeatedly unable to reclaim in state and federal courts. When revolutionary leader Emiliano Zapata and his supporters first invaded hacienda lands, they were reappropriating what they regarded as their ancestral pueblo lands—thus reversing the burden of proof and forcing landowners to take their claims to the special courts they planned to set up "after the Revolution's triumph."[60]

As the movement spread and Zapatista chiefs distributed hacienda lands, the Zapatista repartos triggered widespread intervillage conflict. Pueblo titles often overlapped or were too ambiguous to enable surveyors to mark precise boundaries between two or more neighboring towns, thus provoking relentless intervillage disputes. Moreover, the distribution of confiscated hacienda lands was tainted by nepotism, corruption, and conflicts between rebel factions. Consequently—and in response to hundreds of complaints—the Zapatista land reform became an ongoing effort to control and regulate repartos. In the same way that Samuel Brunk's research focuses on Zapata's efforts to bring order to an undisciplined army, this chapter examines the Zapatista leadership's efforts to create administrative offices capable of resolving contentious land matters. One way of resolving conflicts and uncertainties was to distribute land in temporary repartos. Agricultural lands were distributed in individual and soon to be titled parcels, while woodlands, pasturelands, and water resources were left undivided for common or public use.

Chapter 4 shows that as the Zapatistas were adapting their land-reform procedures to reflect realities on the ground, Carranza—seeking to control autonomous land-reform efforts and indefinitely postpone comprehensive land redistribution—signed the 6 January 1915 law that essentially reduced land reform to the restitution of pueblo lands by executive fiat. The authors of the 1915 law well knew, however, that the agrarian administration would be unable to grant favorable decisions in a property system in which many land seizures and unlawful sales had already been legalized. Therefore, to compensate for failed restitutions, Carranza's law allowed villagers to petition for lands in the form of a dotación: land and water resources granted from expropriated neighboring haciendas to impoverished villages for their subsistence.

What the Constitutionalist land reform meant in practice was shaped by negotiations among town representatives, surveyors, and agrarian officials, both at the state level and in Mexico City. Depending on each village's circumstances, Constitutionalists essentially made three types of grants. First, some dotaciones were designed to compensate for failed restitutions. Second, dotaciones were "ejido" grants to impoverished villages with landless resident farmers. This could mean granting either one or several *sitios de ganado mayor* (1,755.61 hectares each) or enough land to satisfy all landless heads of family residing in a village. Third, and quite accidentally, dotaciones legalized communal lands not privatized during the nineteenth or early twentieth century.

Of crucial importance was how the justices of the new 1917 Supreme Court would react to the executive's appropriation of judicial authority over land issues. As Timothy M. James suggests in his work, and as chapter 5 explores in depth, until 1924 the Supreme Court unconditionally backed and encouraged the executive's extended jurisdiction over agrarian matters on the grounds that resolving the "agrarian problem" was of greater importance than limiting executive powers. Therefore, after actively defending its authority over land and water suits throughout the nineteenth and early twentieth centuries, the Supreme Court relinquished to the executive part of its constitutionally sanctioned power. It did so in part because, at the time, restitutions and land grants were not intended to be the basis of a long-term program for the redistribution of landed property; rather, they were based on the fundamental ideas that usurped pueblo lands had to be restored by the executive and that impoverished pueblos had to receive enough land to fulfill their basic subsistence needs.

Chapter 6 returns to Morelos to show how the Zapatista and the National Agrarian Commission's reform programs were reconciled in the early 1920s. After Carranza was deposed and murdered in 1920, President Álvaro Obregón (1920–24) allowed the Zapatistas to govern Morelos and implement land reform on the condition that it be done according to the 6 January 1915 law, now incorporated into article 27 of the 1917 Constitution. From 1920 to 1924, Morelos became the laboratory for the Constitutionalist land reform, with agrarian officials granting lands to 114 of the state's then 150 pueblos in only three years. And yet, among all these land grants, officials approved only two restitutions, prompting scholars to claim that villagers had been betrayed by the more urban, professional cadre of Zapatistas. Chapter 6 challenges this interpretation by demonstrating that the National Agrarian Commission (now staffed with high-ranking Zapatistas), together with interim governor José G. Parres (Zapata's former medic), the Morelos Agrarian Commission (run by sympathetic surveyors), and the Supreme Court (in its most supportive mode), were united in their commitment to ensuring that agrarian reform in Morelos was implemented as swiftly as possible. In fact, archival sources clearly indicate that Parres used his position to overcome two of the greatest limitations of the Constitutionalist reform: the inability of many settlements to petition for a dotación because they lacked legal standing, and the extensive delays that villagers experienced in obtaining land.

There were several reasons why Parres could not grant more restitutions based on the Carranza law during his short tenure. First, most Morelos villages either did not have deeds with discernible land boundaries, could not prove the time and form of an illegal land seizure, or had their lands dispossessed by haciendas before the Lerdo law of 25 June 1856, the Constitutionalists' strict watershed for granting restitutions.⁶¹ Second, agrarian officials wanted to distribute as much land as possible during Obregón's administration, and therefore privileged the more expeditious dotaciones. And third, dotaciones were the only available vehicle for managing complex regional (as opposed to single-village) land matters, including intervillage conflicts and the regional management of vital water resources. As chapter 6 explores in detail, it was in this context that agrarian officials in Morelos—like the courts before them—denied Zapata's hometown of Anenecuilco a restitution and instead granted it a dotación.

The book concludes with a comparison between the Zapatista and Constitutionalist land reforms. Even though postrevolutionary agrarian reform did not "incorporate" Zapatista ideals, as the PRI's propaganda later claimed, the two land reform programs shared several key elements based on the idea of restituting lands by executive fiat, and they both proposed granting expropriated hacienda lands to impoverished villages.⁶² Both revolutionary factions ran into problems restituting usurped pueblo lands and thus ended up privileging equality over colonial land rights. This meant that woodlands and water resources would be communally owned and publicly managed under national laws, and arable land would be distributed in soon-to-be-titled individual parcels to heads of family—albeit with protections to avoid their immediate sale. Furthermore, in both revolutionary camps villagers complained about favoritism, corruption, and abuse of power in the management and distribution of restituted and granted lands. In response, the Zapatista leadership created special authorities to manage "temporary repartos." Similarly, Constitutionalists created temporary forms of local administration responsible for managing restitution or dotación lands for as long as they remained unprivatized. Their accidental permanence was the origin of what today we call the twentieth-century ejido.

The greatest difference between these land reform projects was their intended scope. The Zapatista Plan de Ayala sought to restructure landed property nationally. Although many scholars (contrary to Womack) interpret the Zapatista movement as the revival of Indian communal landholding practices, Samuel Brunk correctly views Zapata as a small farmer who "did not conceive of his rebellion as an attack on property rights, but as a defense of those rights against the voracious hacendados. He was not rebelling against capitalism in general, then, but against a change in the nature and degree of intrusion of capital that threatened the survival of village life in Morelos in a way that it had never been threatened before. Zapata and [the Plan de Ayala's coauthor Otilio] Montaño explicitly rejected monopoly, not private enterprise."[63] And so Zapata and Montaño proposed to reduce the monopolization of arable lands, woodlands, and water resources nationally by at least a third—a radical and ambitious plan for its time.[64]

In contrast, the Constitutionalists' 6 January 1915 law was purposely limited to the restitution of illegally seized pueblo lands and to the granting of enough land to villages for subsistence agriculture. Broader redistributive policies would require different legislation. For instance, the 1916–17 Constitutional Convention delegates proposed reducing land concentration by granting Congress and state legislatures the authority to determine the maximum land extension an individual or corporation could own, and by requiring landowners to break up their holdings and sell any excess.[65] However, this proposal was separate from what agrarian officials could do when implementing the 6 January 1915 law. Scholars who evaluate Carranza's and Obregón's land reforms in terms of the total hectares of land granted misunderstand this key point, and they project onto the past conceptions from the 1930s and 1940s regarding what Mexico's revolutionary agrarian reform was about and should have achieved.

1

The Inherent Difficulties of Winning Pueblo Land and Water Suits in Nineteenth-Century Mexico

> At the end of the day, the law did not concern itself with rightness or wrongness at this level. It sought only to determine who had the strongest claim in any particular case.
> —Brian P. Owensby, *Empire of Law*

Two of the many legends about the Porfiriato are seemingly contradictory: some critics of the regime decried that pueblo representatives lost their ability to take their land and water claims to court, while others argued that pueblos that took their claims to court usually lost because judges were corrupt and biased in favor of landowners. This chapter shows that although many pueblos (as civil corporations) did lose their right to own land with the Liberal reforms of the 1850s and the Constitution of 1857, and, on this basis, judges sometimes denied pueblos juridical standing (the right to take their claims to court), nevertheless archival records show that many village representatives continued to sue outlying haciendas, unscrupulous local authorities, or neighboring pueblos. They sometimes lost their lawsuits because of corrupt judges who sided with landowners or were biased toward the defendant village. Often, however, judges ruled with a degree of fairness, and when village authorities lost their lawsuits, it was frequently because they failed to meet the plaintiff's burden of proof in a country where legal and illegal practices blended throughout the decades and centuries. One common response was for village representatives to try to sidestep the judiciary by sending their petitions to the executive branch. In response, political chiefs and state governments attempted to resolve these matters through arbitration or by setting up special courts. Yet over the course of the nineteenth century, both judges and Supreme Court justices successfully defended the judiciary's purview over contentious land matters. This constant interplay between village petitions for the executive to intervene in village land matters, and the judiciary's defense of its authority over contentious property matters, was a long and important historical precedent that would shape revolutionary agrarian reforms in important ways.

Balance of Power between the Judiciary and the Executive regarding Restitutions

In colonial Mexico the Spanish crown granted Indian pueblos the right to receive inalienable land and water rights sufficient for sustenance and reproduction. The crown also gave pueblos the right to seek recourse in the Indian courts when Spaniards or neighboring villagers invaded these lands.[1] At these courts, Woodrow Borah explains, Indians had special legal protection, and procedures were concise, quick, and inexpensive.[2] With independence, however, the new Mexican state formally eliminated a separate Indian Republic and shut down the Indian courts.[3]

At first, provincial deputations (governing councils that bridged the transition from the Spanish colonial regime to the independent federal states of Mexico) were responsible for channeling pueblo land and water conflicts to the various courts of first instance.[4] Members of the Ocuituco ayuntamiento, for example, complained to the Mexico Provincial Deputation that the surrounding haciendas had taken all their lands, bit by bit. Past governments, they added, had not addressed their complaints and had "only supported the powerful." But, in their words, "now that we have lost their chains that oppressed them for so long," they planned to create a fund to cover the cost of taking their claims to court in order to recover their seized lands. In this case the Mexico Provincial Deputation instructed the *juez de partido* to handle the matter.[5]

When the 1824 Federal Constitution of the United Mexican States made the new nation a federal republic with three branches of government (the legislature, executive, and judiciary), lawmakers debated whether pueblo land and water claims were administrative or judicial matters. For instance, at the Constitutional Congress of the State of Mexico (which, at that time, also included Morelos, Hidalgo, and Guerrero), Deputy José María Jáuregui pointed out that before independence the viceroys had both administrative and judicial responsibilities; now, however, it was necessary to give the legislature exclusive responsibility for issuing laws on land matters and to give the judiciary authority over all pueblo land conflicts.[6] Most other states followed suit. Early Jalisco laws clearly show that by 1825 all land restitution claims were to be heard at the justice tribunals.[7] Thus, when the San Gabriel Indians brought to the Jalisco Senate a suit against the owner of the Guadalupe hacienda for allegedly seizing their *fundo legal*, the senators decided they could not consider the case because it fell under the purview of the courts of justice.[8] In Guerrero in 1826, when Huixtac residents encroached on neighboring pueblo lands, the Taxco *juez de letras* marked the boundaries between Tecalpulco, Taxco el Viejo, and Huixtac, restituting lands usurped from Taxco el Viejo and Tecalpulco.[9] Similarly, after the fall of the Centralist Republic (a unitary political regime that governed from 1835 to 1846), Jalisco's state council informed the governor that the Indians of the Jalisco pueblo were complaining about having been despoiled of their property by the *alcalde* (municipal magistrate) and thus were petitioning for the restitution of their land. The council decided that it was the judicial branch's authority to resolve this matter, and that the complainants could claim their rights there.[10]

And yet there were so many land suits involving village lands and water resources that state governments attempted in several ways to limit them. For instance, in 1838 and again in 1841, authorities in the state of Puebla tried to curtail village land suits by revoking Indian pueblos' right to appear in court, maintaining that court cases "only foment animosities and disturbances."[11] Likewise, in Mexico State an 1850 law required that pueblo representatives obtain permission to litigate from prefects or governors, and before permission was granted, the representatives had to fulfill certain requirements, such as having exhausted arbitration procedures.[12]

Some state governments sought to resolve intervillage boundary conflicts by turning to arbitration. In Veracruz, for example, Governor Ignacio de la Llave issued an April 1856 law justifying privatization by claiming that communal lands created an inordinate number of lawsuits, thus "greatly harming not only plaintiffs but also adjacent property owners." According to this law, it was necessary to end these claims, many of which had remained unresolved for years, "because each one of these lawsuits is a fertile source of frauds, brawls, and assassinations." Article 3 of the law stipulated that all pending lawsuits between indigenous communities would be handled by arbitrators. Villagers had to renounce their right to sue or appeal the arbitrator's resolution, and destroying the arbitrator's boundary markers became a criminal offense.[13] In Oaxaca the 1862 privatization law granted political chiefs authority over intervillage disputes. Historian Jennie Purnell reports that political chiefs "were to convene meetings of all parties to any given dispute, collect evidence as to which party was in possession of the land on a stipulated day, draw up maps, mark boundaries, and distribute private titles, all within a matter of months." Because the task was so complicated and the losing party often challenged arbitrators' decisions, many political chiefs chose to ignore the law.[14]

Other governors created new courts exclusively to handle land matters. For example, in Jalisco, Governor Anastasio Parrodi added a court to the state's existing *juzgados de letras* solely to resolve contentious matters involving Indian lands. His 1857 decree explained that an earlier law assigning a special attorney "for the defense of Indian rights" did not sufficiently protect Indians or prevent them from taking justice into their own hands. Indians could decide if they wanted to proceed with pending suits (or begin new ones) at the courts of first instance or at this special tribunal. All new lawsuits involving pueblo lands would be expeditiously ruled on in this new court, where the judge would first try to arbitrate between the parties. The goal was to promote conciliation. If the parties involved could not reach a settlement, then special tribunal judges had to rule on the case in half the ordinary time.[15]

Governor Epitacio Huerta created a similar arrangement in Michoacán. His 1859 law "to end Indian land matters" stated that his office would name a juez de letras in each department to focus exclusively on resolving all pending land conflicts. The government would also appoint an attorney in each department to represent the Indians in the first instance. Contentious matters would be resolved in a verbal suit with a quick ruling, and the dissatisfied party would have recourse to Michoacán's Supreme Tribunal of Justice.[16]

The short-lived Second Empire (the regime lasting from 1864 to 1867 under the French occupation, with Archduke Maximilian of Austria on the Mexican throne) was noteworthy for its efforts to resolve pueblo land and water lawsuits expeditiously without involving the slow-moving courts. Maximilian's Junta Protectora de las Clases Menesterosas (Council for the Protection of the Impoverished) made department prefectures responsible in the first instance for handling suits filed by pueblos against each other or against private landholders. In cases where two pueblos were involved in a boundary suit, the prefect would decide which of them had more rights, and the losing party had no recourse in the courts. In the case of a pueblo representative suing a private landowner, the prefect would issue (or decline to issue) a license allowing the representative to take the case to court.[17]

Maximilian's proposal to resolve contentious matters between pueblos outside the court system received widespread popular support. In Morelos, for example, Tepoztlán residents "rejoiced in having a sovereign whose governing dictum is equity in justice—in other words, one who defends the judicial culture of the old regime, where the government could arbitrate between corporations, implementing justice outside the courts—since in this way we have no inconveniences or the inflated costs of a trial."[18] This rearrangement of administrative and judicial power in settling village land suits apparently had its complications; less than a year later, Maximilian restored the court's jurisdiction over all contentious land matters. Noting that prefects often had ties with landowners, the agrarian law of September 1866 stated that lawsuits over land and water rights filed by villages against each other or against private landholders would henceforth be handled once again by ordinary judges and courts.[19]

After Maximilian's assassination, the Restored Republic (from 1867 to 1876, under the presidencies of Benito Juárez and Sebastián Lerdo de Tejada) reestablished republican powers and reinstated the 1857 Constitution, which put the judiciary in charge of all contentious land matters.[20] Nevertheless, state governors still sought to limit pueblo land and water suits. In Mexico State, for example, an 1868 law gave political chiefs the authority to grant or deny license to municipal authorities or pueblos to sue.[21] In Puebla, the state congress issued a decree in 1869 by which villages "were obliged to resolve their differences over lands by naming *árbitros amigables componedores*, or individuals with a reputation for honesty and rationality, who would oversee a process of arbitration between two parties."[22] When it came to suits against landowners, the executive would do everything possible to persuade the owner to settle the lawsuit through arbitration.[23] And in Hidalgo, a state law adopted in 1869 decreed that village representatives who wanted to file a suit required the permission of political chiefs.[24]

When the executive overstepped its jurisdiction, however, the judiciary always maintained the upper hand. Under the 1857 Constitution, James explains, "As a general rule, all contentious questions of rights were to be referred to the judicial branch. They could not be decided by the executive branch of government, and when the administration acted in these cases without first waiting for a judicial decision to resolve the contentious matter this was a violation of article 16's competency clause, actionable through amparo."[25] Moreover, "on those occasions when the executive branch of government did overstep these limits as established by this jurisprudence, the assertiveness of the Court seems to be unequivocal."[26] This was especially so with boundary conflicts. For example, when in 1872 the governor of Oaxaca ordered the district prefect to draw a borderline between two indigenous communities, the Supreme Court granted amparo protection to one of the villages, ruling that the executive had no right to draw boundaries because this was the role of the judicial branch.[27] A year later, in an amparo suit against the Oaxaca governor's marking of boundaries between San Miguel Tequixtepec and Tepelmeme, the Supreme Court again ruled that defining property and use rights between two pueblos was a judicial matter; the governor could not even temporarily define boundary lines because judges had to decide in court (*en un juicio*) which titles were valid.[28] When that same year the municipal syndic of Tejúpam petitioned for amparo protection against the Teposcolula district prefect, who had ruled in favor of neighboring Tamazulapan in a boundary dispute, the syndic told the Oaxaca district judge that article 16 of the Constitution stated that in the Mexican Republic no one could be judged by special courts, and the district prefect had acted as a special tribunal. The district judge subsequently denied amparo protection on the grounds that Tejúpam did not have juridical standing. In 1874, however, the Supreme Court reversed the district court's decision and granted amparo protection to the syndic of Tejúpam, confirming that it was the judiciary's exclusive right to judge land-related matters.[29]

The Pueblos' Uncertain Juridical Standing

During the period known as "La Reforma" (from 1855 to 1861, when Liberals issued laws designed to modernize the economy, expand rail, road, and telegraph networks, and secularize education), the national disentailment law of 25 June 1856 (known as the Lerdo law) prohibited civil corporations from owning or administering real estate.[30] Moreover, article 27 of the 1857 Constitution stated, "No civil or ecclesiastical corporation . . . has the legal capacity to acquire or manage real estate, except buildings directly destined for the service or purpose of the institution." Many landowners, judges, and justices interpreted these provisions as pueblos' loss of juridical standing to pursue litigation over communal lands. And yet in Porfirian Mexico we find many lawyers and government authorities complaining about Indians incessantly taking their suits to court. In 1892, for example, well-known Mexico City lawyer Prisciliano María Díaz González lamented that "the greatest sore of our property system are the pueblos' lawsuits." Pueblos, according to Díaz González, "are never in agreement with the judges' verdicts [thus] reducing courts' rulings to nothing more than historical documents."[31]

Until recently, few scholars other than Robert Knowlton had studied these court records. Now, however, historians can shed some empirical light on the question of pueblos' juridical standing. There is no doubt that Liberal laws made the representation of corporate rights in court more difficult—and, in some places and at some times, impossible. Nonetheless, it is also true that pueblo representatives never stopped litigating. Most village attorneys found some legal loophole that permitted them to do so, and many judges and justices either openly challenged the idea that pueblos had lost their juridical standing or found ways of sidestepping the question altogether. For example, Daniela Marino notes that the amparo suit became a resource that allowed pueblo representatives to take their matters to court "regardless of the dogmatic opinions of some justices."[32] Even though articles 101 and 102 of the Constitution and the amparo regulations of 20 January 1869 gave amparo protection only to individuals, the Supreme Court granted what legal scholar Lucio Cabrera Acevedo calls a "communal amparo"—a tacit acknowledgment that pueblo representatives could file an amparo suit even though they represented a collectivity. Indeed, in the first decade that the 1869 amparo law was in effect, when the Supreme Court denied villagers the right to seek amparo protection, it was usually not because they lacked juridical standing.[33] For example, when in 1871 the municipal council of San Bernabé Temoxtitla (Puebla) sued the governor for granting part of their fundo legal to the Santa Marta barrio, the district judge allowed the amparo claim to proceed, arguing that "individual rights are not affected when individuals collectively seek recourse."[34]

Beginning in 1879, however, several landmark Supreme Court cases clearly denied villagers the right to litigate. In Mexico State, for example, Cahuacán pueblo residents filed a survey suit (*juicio de apeo y deslinde*) at the Tlalnepantla court to regain lands allegedly seized by the neighboring hacienda. Displeased with the survey, landowner María de la Luz Servín de Capetillo petitioned for and received amparo protection on the legal grounds that the villagers had no right to litigate collectively.[35] Several similar rulings followed. In Michoacán in 1880, the owner of the Coapa hacienda, backed by the Pátzcuaro prefect, erected fences that allegedly infringed upon Tiripetío pueblo lands. In response, villagers sought the protection of the district court to defend their ancestral right to collect wood and use pastureland, and the judge awarded them amparo protection against the prefect. But when the hacienda owner filed an amparo suit with the Supreme Court questioning why the villagers had been granted amparo protection "given that they were members of a community that legally did not exist," Ignacio L. Vallarta (president of the Supreme Court between 1877 and 1882) denied the villagers the right to represent themselves in court on matters related to communal lands.[36] Similarly, in Veracruz the Chicontepec Indians sued the district prefect for ordering the sale of a communal parcel to pay for the division and distribution (reparto) of privatized communal lands—a sale that, they claimed, in the end only benefited the surveyor and a local land dealer. In October 1881 the Veracruz district judge granted the Indians amparo protection, but when the case reached the Supreme Court in 1882, Vallarta forcefully argued against the villagers' collective juridical standing to defend their communal lands.[37] And in Oaxaca, when Santiago Mitlatongo spokespersons petitioned the district judge for amparo protection against neighboring Nochixtlán residents who, in subdividing and privatizing their communal landholdings, had encroached upon the properties of several Santiago Mitlatongo residents, the Supreme Court pondered whether the "extinguished indigenous communities" could litigate. Vallarta argued against the idea that Indians could litigate as a corporation, and he ruled that municipal governments could not take matters to court in the name of pueblos prior to their privatization, as some states had allowed.[38]

Justice Vallarta continued to deny villagers the right to litigate collectively until his resignation at the end of 1882.[39] According to Cabrera

Acevedo, between 1881 and 1882 Vallarta denied the collective rights of pueblo legal representatives enough times for the decisions to become *jurisprudencia* (a Mexican variant of U.S. judicial precedent).[40] And yet, even after Vallarta's decisions, in some cases the Supreme Court did not question villagers' rights to appear in court. In one 1888 case in Chiapas, for example, villagers petitioned for amparo protection against the San Fernando ayuntamiento for selling the pueblo's ejido lands to a third party. The Supreme Court ruled that these were not valid grounds for an amparo suit; it was a contentious matter that had to be resolved in the lower courts. The justices did not, however, question the petitioners' juridical standing.[41] In Durango, when in 1899 the Cuencamé political chief redrew the boundaries between the Santiago and San Pedro de Ocuila Indian pueblos and the El Sombreretillo hacienda, villagers petitioned successfully and the Supreme Court awarded them amparo protection against the district political authorities.[42]

One way of sidestepping the question of pueblos' legal standing was to make a list of all the male and, in some cases, female heads of household who agreed to act as plaintiffs and present themselves as "the sum of individuals." In Yucatán, for instance, Ticul villagers petitioned for amparo protection against the municipal government, which had sold at public auction a land parcel that belonged to the pueblo's ejidos and that residents relied on for firewood and other household uses. In 1892 the Supreme Court granted amparo protection to Ticul's representative "and the rest of the pueblo's residents."[43] Five years later in Mexico State, when Atarasquillo pueblo residents sued the Huixquilucan pueblo, the Supreme Court accepted the amparo petition by the town's attorney and a list of 101 male names.[44]

According to Marino, if Vallarta was known as the Supreme Court president who denied villagers the right to litigate over communal resources, in 1900 President Silvestre Moreno Cora became the symbol of compromise.[45] In a landmark case in Mexico State, Moreno Cora directly challenged Vallarta's rigid denial of villagers' juridical standing. This case involved the Federal District's San Lorenzo, San Francisco, and Santa Cruz Ayotuxco pueblos. In 1887 the Tlalnepantla judge of first instance had ruled in favor of San Lorenzo, granting the pueblo restitution of some lands. In response, the Huixquilucan municipal syndic representing 432 individuals filed for amparo protection. The district judge denied them juridical standing on three grounds: communal rights were illegal; constitutional rights protected only individuals; and villagers had not proven they owned property individually. President Moreno Cora, however, granted them an exception because the pueblos had been involved in a land suit prior to the 1857 constitutional loss of juridical standing, and lands in litigation could not be privatized until all conflicts were resolved.[46]

During the first decade of the twentieth century, judges and justices continued to show some flexibility in granting pueblo representatives the right to appear in court. In Mexico State, for instance, representatives of three pueblos (Amecameca, San Juan Tehuixtitlán, and Atlautla) filed a suit against the landowning Solórzano family, which had claimed untitled lands on the Guadalupe and San Pedro Mártir haciendas in Puebla and the Gachopinco ranch in Mexico State. In the process, the Solórzano family had invaded what these pueblos considered their lands. Although the Mexico State district judge rejected the pueblos' amparo suit on the grounds that the plaintiffs lacked juridical standing, pueblo representatives petitioned for amparo protection, and the Supreme Court decided that "from the moment that the plaintiffs did not present themselves as *comuneros* (communal landholders) but in their own right, it is irrelevant whether the titles they presented to justify their property were communal and not individual."[47] A similar ruling came in Michoacán. When the lawyer for "the Indians of the extinguished community of Tingambato" petitioned for amparo protection against the municipal president for having sold their communal lands to several individuals, the Supreme Court unanimously decreed the following: "Since it is not the jurisdiction of the administrative authority to order or give possession of an immovable property, because this is the jurisdiction of judicial authorities, it is indisputable that the municipal president has violated the plaintiffs' guarantees of article 16 of the Constitution [which upheld the division of powers

Nineteenth-Century Suits 35

among the executive, judicial, and legislative branches of government] and the amparo must be granted.... The Union's Justice grants amparo protection to the Tingambato Indians, represented by Licenciado Arcadio Marín."[48]

According to Cabrera Acevedo, by 1911 the Porfirian justices had fully rejected Vallarta's jurisprudence.[49]

Judges' Honesty on Trial

If pueblo representatives frequently did manage to take their claims to court despite what many judges and justices considered a lack of juridical standing, why were they largely unable to win their restitution and boundary suits? Traditional histories of the Díaz regime characterize the judiciary as inherently corrupt, with judges inevitably ruling in favor of the powerful. For example, according to Luis González y González, "judges applied the civil code to the rich and the penal code to the poor."[50]

There is no doubt that this characterization was broadly accurate, and many observers at the time would have agreed. In San Luis Potosí, for instance, Juan Santiago, the leader of an Indian uprising in 1875, wrote Porfirio Díaz years later that "things have calmed down (*se han calmado los ánimos*), but what remains unresolved is the matter of rights with regard to municipal lands, because despite the fact that I have the primordial titles that were so dear to get, I have not been able, or wanted, to go to the courts because those in charge of these courts are the people who belong to the haciendas that I would be suing."[51] Similarly, in his 1906 pamphlet regarding a Tetelpa pueblo suit seeking to establish water rights against neighboring hacienda owners, lawyer Luis G. Otero explained why the pueblo had lost suits at the Morelos district court as well as at the state's Superior Tribunal: "We live in times when rich people have much influence in society. Their influence on the [Morelos] government is considerable, and from there it passes on to the tribunals. This one can see in many states of the Republic, where hacienda owners become the governors' friends and any lawsuit against them is impossible."[52] Equally damning was local judge and notary Andrés Molina Enríquez's 1909 condemnation of hacienda owners' "insatiable greed." He cited a manifesto by General Juan Álvarez, a military hero who defeated Antonio López de Santa Anna and briefly became president in 1855, explaining that pueblos sought justice because landowners gradually encroached on private as well as communal lands and subsequently claimed property rights without being able to produce a single title. When pueblos sought justice, Molina claimed, "the courts respond with disdain, persecution, and imprisonment."[53]

The tragic story of Jovito Serrano would become emblematic of the injustices taking place in Morelos at the hands of hacienda owners and their political allies, which included court officials. At the turn of the century, the owner of the Atlihuayán hacienda erected a fence that, according to neighboring Yautepec villagers, encroached on the pueblo's communal lands. The owner then confiscated over four hundred head of cattle that had continued to cross into the now enclosed pasturelands because, he claimed, they were grazing on hacienda lands, destroying fences, and trampling on farmland. The cattle owners elected Jovito Serrano, Miguel Urbina, Ambrosio Castillo, and several other respected villagers to handle the matter. A commission of sixty villagers took their case directly to Porfirio Díaz, who recommended they hire an attorney and deal with the matter in court. For three years, Yautepec representatives pursued this course of action, but to no avail. The judge of first instance failed to conduct the required investigation, and the Yautepec judge ruled against them. When the villagers appealed to the Cuernavaca district court, the judge not only ruled against them but also fined them. Moreover, when Serrano, representing himself and forty-seven men, petitioned the Supreme Court for amparo protection against the judge of first instance and the Yautepec district prefect for violating constitutional articles 14 and 16, the Supreme Court denied him judicial protection—partly on the technicality that only eleven of the thirty-seven cattle owners involved in the lawsuit had signed Serrano's power of attorney. Finally, while dealing with legal matters in Mexico City, Serrano and Castillo were apprehended and deported to a labor camp in Quintana Roo, where Serrano died in November 1905.⁵⁴

Yet despite abundant examples of outright corruption and favoritism by court officials before and during the Porfiriato, scholars have found empirical evidence that casts doubt on any blanket generalizations about a corrupt judiciary. In a detailed study of the Porfirian justice system based on archival evidence, Timo Schaefer concludes that even though "the repressive character of the Porfiriato still [tells] us more about the Díaz regime than those attempting to read a concern with legality, let alone legal equality, into the regime's policies and aspirations," his own evidence challenges "the claim—made by Díaz opponents at the time and informing a significant part of the subsequent historiography—that the legal culture of the Díaz regime was uniformly illiberal and repressive."⁵⁵

With specific regard to pueblo land suits, several scholars have questioned the accepted history of the Porfiriato. Robert J. Knowlton showed that district judges and Supreme Court justices sometimes ruled in favor of granting pueblo residents amparo protection against the abuse of local and state authorities; Justus Fenner Bieling consulted the Chiapas District Court records and found that when surveying companies had conflicts with indigenous communities, judges exhibited surprising "social responsibility," mostly ruling in favor of the villages; Fernando Sierra Zavala concluded that successive Michoacán district courts acted with fairness; and Felipe Ávila Espinosa examined several Supreme Court amparos petitions filed between 1898 and 1914 and concluded that not all court resolutions on amparos favored the rich and powerful. In fact, who the parties were mattered less than who had the stronger evidence.⁵⁶

One characteristic of the Porfirian justice system was the large number of contradictory judgments.⁵⁷ In some cases, pueblo representatives won a lawsuit, only to lose another one years later. In Durango, for example, when the Cuencamé political chief drew boundaries favoring the Sombreretillo hacienda, the Santiago and San Pedro de Ocuila pueblos took their case to court. They proved their rights to continuous possession on the contested lands by presenting an 1877 order from the political chief to clean up the Cuencamé River, which was obstructed by the pueblos' irrigation works. In 1900 the Supreme Court ruled in their favor, owing to their peaceful and continuous possession of the disputed lands for over thirty years. In 1909, however, they lost the case at another court, for which the Supreme Court denied them amparo protection.[58]

Sometimes district courts ruled in favor of pueblo representatives, only to be overruled by a higher court. In Oaxaca, for instance, when the San Miguel el Grande legal representative petitioned for amparo protection against the political chief's boundary marking with neighboring Chalcatongo, the district judge granted them amparo protection but the Supreme Court overturned the verdict, stating that "the pueblo has no legal existence because constitutional article 27 does not recognize it."[59] And in Tlaxcala, when villagers denounced neighboring ranch owners for having illegally acquired pueblo lands and water resources, the district judge ruled in 1900 that the ranch should be restituted to the Calpulalpan pueblo. Two years later, however, the Tlaxcala Supreme Court revoked the ruling, stating that the pueblo had not been able to prove the date of the land seizure, whereas the ranch owners had proven that the property had been legally purchased in 1792.[60]

At other times, however, Supreme Court justices were more sympathetic to pueblo rights than were lower court judges. Marino finds that pueblos in Mexico State perceived the Supreme Court as being more impartial than the local and state courts.[61] Similarly in one intravillage conflict, when the Guerrero District Court granted one Chilapa resident the rights to disputed lands, attorney Cleofas Peralta and fifty-two other residents took the matter to the district judge, who promptly dismissed their case, claiming they lacked juridical standing. Peralta then sought recourse at the Supreme Court, arguing that villagers had for a long time cultivated their parcels, maintained homes, and used the woodlands on these lands. In response, the Supreme Court unanimously recognized the pueblo's right to a hearing based on continuous possession rights. The justices found that "no matter under what title the plaintiffs possess the lands in question, the fact is that some of these individuals have lived on these lands, cultivated them, and cut firewood. Given this, if they are dispossessed of these lands without a hearing, then article 16 of the Constitution, which gives them the right to amparo protection, would be violated."[62]

In Michoacán, when neighboring Tiripetío residents continued to gather wood in what they considered their *montes*, the owner of the Coapa hacienda asked the Pátzcuaro prefect to forbid this practice unless the pueblo residents first obtained his permission. Tiripetío representatives took their complaint to the district judge, who decided that the monte was the Indians' immemorial possession and granted them amparo protection against the prefect. In response, the owner then took the case to the Supreme Court, complaining that the district judge "always favored the Indians," only to find that the justices also ruled in favor of Tiripetío.[63] Even in Morelos, a state infamous for government abuses during the Porfiriato, the Supreme Court defended the rights of a group of Santa María Ahuacatitlán residents against Governor Manuel Alarcón, the Cuernavaca political chief, and the municipal auxiliary. Probably prompted by neighboring hacienda owners' increasing demands for forest and lumber products, Alarcón forbade residents of Santa María Ahuacatitlán from using the pueblo's woodlands for charcoal production, arguing that he had to fulfill his executive responsibilities to preserve woodlands (*conservación de montes*). The Morelos District Court agreed that it was the governor's obligation to protect woodlands and argued further that the plaintiffs had no legal standing. The Supreme Court justices, however, decided that the question of juridical standing had to be determined in a separate suit and, in the meantime, granted the aggrieved party amparo protection from the governor's orders.[64]

Problems Intrinsic to Restitution Claims

Even when judges and justices were favorably inclined toward pueblos, nineteenth-century restitution and boundary suits were difficult to win for a variety of reasons. First, village attorneys suing neighboring property owners over alleged land seizures had to produce substantiating evidence that would shift proof of ownership away from the default position, according to which the defendant was the legal owner. It was the plaintiff's responsibility to substantiate property-rights claims with legal titles based on reliable surveys and perfectly matched boundary lines. Starting in 1825, a Oaxaca law required plaintiffs in restitution suits "to establish (1) what had been dispossessed, including, in the case of land conflicts, the location and boundaries of the lands in question; (2) when and by whom the dispossession had been carried out; and (3) how long the plaintiff had enjoyed usufruct of the disputed good before the act of dispossession."[65] Similarly, in an 1849 Mexico State ruling on a suit brought by the San Vicente Chimalhuacán Chalco representative against the Santiago Mamalhuazuca pueblo and an adjacent *rancho* owner, the Chalco civil judge explained that for real-estate dispossession suits, "It is not sufficient to prove that the seized lands were in the despoiler's possession; it is also necessary for the plaintiff to prove previous possession with legal title and in good faith, as well as the dates of ownership."[66]

Placing the onus on the plaintiff was widely considered unjust. In fact, when in 1854 President Santa Anna desperately tried to gain popular support before being deposed, he proposed reversing the burden of proof in village land restitution claims. Santa Anna had traveled to the region that is now Morelos and Guerrero and, upon his return to the capital, issued a decree acknowledging the widespread and pervasive loss of pueblo lands and water resources. In addition, he made governors and district prefects responsible for identifying communal property seized from all cities, villages, and pueblos, and he reversed the long-standing burden of proof in land-dispute cases. Whereas pueblo representatives had always had to prove their rights to land when making claims, Santa Anna's decree "in defense of the Indians" made property owners responsible for presenting titles proving their ownership. The decree authorized municipal authorities and sub-prefects to demand titles from anyone suspected of having seized communal lands. Those refusing to present their titles would be fined. Individuals without titles had four months to provide a written declaration of any communal or municipal lands they owned, including information regarding the dates of appropriation and their size, location, and boundaries.[67] Although canceled only a month later, the law clearly spoke to the prevailing feeling of unfairness regarding the plaintiff's burden of proof.[68]

Legal proof had to be in the form of titles. Nineteenth-century judges and justices recognized pueblos' colonial titles in the form of *mercedes* (royal land grants) or *composiciones de tierras* (recognition of legal title of de facto ownership). In many cases, however, pueblos did not have titles. Many were founded on private property, on Indian cacique lands, or as settlements on Spanish properties that grew into villages. In the northern states, population centers were often founded by missionaries, conquerors, or miners, and for that reason they never had colonial titles.[69] Nevertheless, many pueblos did have well-established use rights to woodlands (*bosques* and *montes*), where pueblo residents "gathered wood to sell, or for firewood, beams, logs, and charcoal, as well as for lighting, to heat their houses, and to warm their ovens to produce tiles, bricks, and pottery"; to pasturelands, "where residents had access to grass for animal feed, not only for large animals but small ones such as turkeys and chickens"; and to sources of water, "where they could hunt ducks and other birds, fish, and collect clay, *tequesquite* (mineral salt), and limestone," among other uses.[70]

Colonial water titles were valid in the late nineteenth century, but the right to access water resources also depended on later agreements, especially in regions where private owners used waterways for industrial purposes such as paper factories or sugar mills.[71] In one case from Aguascalientes, members of the Indian irrigation council of Jesús María filed for amparo protection in 1902 to defend their rights to a

---

Fig. 1. (*opposite top*) Map of eight Sierra de Juárez pueblos (Oaxaca), 1840. Archivo General de la Nación, Colección Mapas, Planos e Ilustraciones, no. 2365.

Fig. 2. (*opposite bottom*) Map of Santa María del Monte, Tehuacán (Puebla), 1873. Archivo General de la Nación, Colección Mapas, Planos e Ilustraciones, no. 4645.

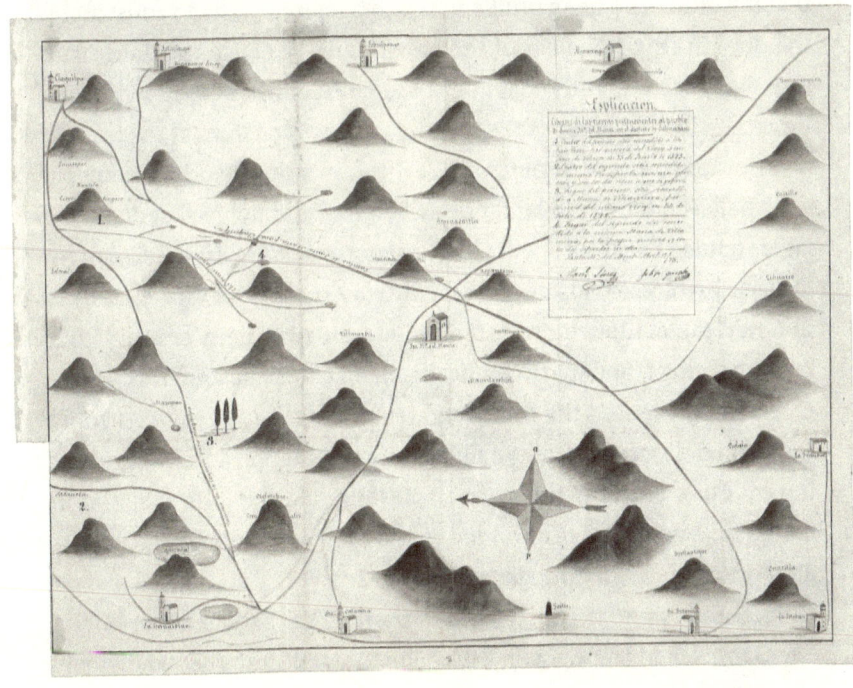

dam built on a river that ran across the pueblo's fundo legal and irrigated most of their communal lands. In 1813 the Jesús María alcalde had, in exchange for some land, granted the owner of the neighboring San José las Trojes hacienda permission to construct an aqueduct on pueblo lands leading to the hacienda. The agreement did not specify the amount of water each party could access, but the Indians understood they could "use irrigation waters on their lands in whatever way and amount they could." Access to this water source created unending conflicts. As time passed and residents had privatized their land parcels de facto, they formed an irrigation association. In 1890 a new hacienda owner claimed property rights to the dam on pueblo lands, and he sued association member Paulín de Luna for having released water from the dam to protect his lands from flooding. De Luna sought amparo protection at the district court, using a combination of colonial laws, the history of the pueblo based on its primordial titles, and Liberal laws governing property rights to water resources. In this particular case, pueblo residents won the suit. The judge ruled in their favor, finding that it would have been unlikely for the hacienda to have constructed the dam in 1813 (the year of the agreement) because the dam structure was very old and most likely had been constructed in viceregal times, "using the labor of these Indians, as was custom at the time."[72]

Another common problem in restitution suits was that many pue-blos believed they held land titles when they did not in fact do so. Villagers tended to call all documents "primordial titles." In the case of two Oaxaca pueblos, for instance, Luis Alberto Arrioja Díaz Viruell analyzes in detail the evidence mustered in an early twentieth-century court case involving a boundary conflict between Guelache and Teococuilco. Guelache presented the following documents: a 1740 *nota geográfica* (a detailed description of the village, its commerce, and its surrounding environment); the titles of a 1748–51 composición for neighboring San Juan; a copy of a note added to the 1526 San Juan Guelache map; a report of the 1786 boundary markings between San Miguel and San Gabriel Etla; an 1852 copy of a land transaction between San Miguel, San Gabriel, and San Agustín Etla; and some 1862 and 1880 agreements between Guelache and Teococuilco. For its part, Teococuilco representatives presented the 1580 titles of the foundation of the pueblo, according to the 1885 testimony of the head of the National Archives; records of the 1853 "dispossession trial" against San Juan Guelache (which they most likely won); an 1880 map; and the 1903 inspection records by the *jefe político* of Ixtlán. In this case, based on the available evidence, Teococuilco won the land suit. Despite presenting all documents as primordial titles, Guelache spokespersons lacked proof of ownership; most of their documents pertained to other pueblos, and several seemed to have been tampered with.[73]

Often cabeceras, sujetos, and barrios claimed the same colonial titles.[74] At least half of all land disputes were between pueblos, or between the municipal cabecera and sujeto villages. Romana Falcón, for example, shows that in 1871 there were twenty-four active land suits in Mexico State. Of these, eleven were against a hacienda or an individual landowner, and thirteen were between pueblos or between pueblos and the cabecera.[75] In another study of Mexico State, Marino notes that all the cases the Huixquilucan pueblo took to the higher courts involved boundary suits with pueblos in neighboring municipalities.[76] And in nineteenth-century Oaxaca, pueblo land conflicts were mostly "from neighboring indigenous towns and not from Spanish settlers."[77] Purnell explains, "Many such disputes were decades if not centuries old, involved three or more parties, and had left in their wake any number of contradictory court decisions and administrative orders as well as histories of violence."[78]

When pueblo representatives could not locate their old titles in municipal records or at the National Archives, some hired forgers. This was nothing new. According to Owensby, by 1600, documentation became so important that "indigenous litigants commonly resorted to unscrupulous tactics in their efforts to prevail in Court. Parties might submit forged titles for judicial review, or a challenger might attempt to swing things in her favor by stealing or forcibly taking *títulos* on which another party planned to rely in seeking an amparo."[79] María de los Ángeles Romero Frizzi, writing about present-day agrarian tribunal cases that still rely on colonial and nineteenth-century documents, observes that paleographers continually find various anomalies, including land parcels with different names (often because of differences between Spanish- and indigenous-language pronunciations), titles that are not originals but certified copies issued by the ayuntamientos (often copied with errors), and forged documents—faked not recently but in the nineteenth century, with some dating as far back as colonial times.[80]

Perhaps the most serious problem in restitution suits was that legal and illegal transactions blended throughout the decades and even centuries. Since colonial times, Owensby concludes, "Legitimate transactions, such as mercedes, sales, donations, rental agreements, and testaments, blended, at time imperceptibly, with usurpations, squatting, fraud, unfair dealings, and outright violence as methods for acquiring property."[81] One Mexico State case is exemplary in this regard. In the early 1840s, the story goes, Calpulalpan residents fled a devastating epidemic, leaving their 1,553 hectares of pueblo lands in the safekeeping of the local priest. When they returned, the priest refused to return their lands and instead created the La Cofradía del Santísimo hacienda (later known as Calpulalpan hacienda). Around 1860, with the nationalization of the Church's landed wealth, one individual bought the hacienda and later bequeathed the property to his grandsons. They, in turn, sold the property to neighboring hacienda owner José Escandón, whose cattle enterprise greatly expanded during the Porfiriato. Thus, when the Calpulalpan residents tried to recover their long-lost property, they found that not only had there been several "legal" transactions since the priest had illegitimately appropriated their lands, but because of the hacienda's expansion, the neighboring San Miguel and San Martín pueblos were also claiming the same lands.[82]

Liberal Laws as Means for Restitution Suits

In a study of nineteenth-century pueblo petitions, Romana Falcón shows that the poor practiced "the art of the petition," that is, they were able to challenge the rich and powerful with their wide-ranging knowledge of the Constitution, the laws, the courts, and the amparo recourse.[83] Interestingly, many of the laws employed by the rich to recover or expand their properties were often turned around and used against them. For example, pueblo attorneys frequently employed the Liberal laws intended to privatize corporate property and federal public lands laws in defense of their communal land and water rights. Land privatization or *terrenos baldíos* (public lands) surveys (which included ejidos) could not occur without first defining the old colonial perimeter through boundary surveys, in which judges (titles and maps in hand), accompanied by pueblo representatives, municipal officials, and district prefects or political chiefs (and, where relevant, lawyers representing neighboring pueblos and landowners), walked the boundary lines, identifying old markers and putting new ones in place. Many pueblo representatives petitioned for access to these surveys in the hope of confirming or expanding their boundaries with neighboring haciendas. In Veracruz, for example, Chiltoyac residents had for decades been in a boundary dispute with the neighboring Paso de San Juan hacienda. In 1877 they successfully "used the land division as a means to win back their usurped lands by notifying the governor that they could not divide their communal lands until the portion usurped by the hacienda had been returned to them."[84]

But it was not only against the rich and powerful that pueblos employed their highly tuned legal skills; they also used them against municipal governments and each other. In Yucatán, for instance, a group of Tekit residents denounced the municipal authorities for allocating pueblo land resources with favoritism, and they petitioned for the privatization of ejido lands as a legal mechanism to acquire land parcels.[85] In Mexico State, San Bartolomé Capulhuac used the Liberal privatization laws to claim lands in dispute with neighboring San Pedro Tlaltizapan. In response, Tlaltizapan's attorney sued Capulhuac for trying to privatize lands to which they claimed to hold colonial title.[86] And in Oaxaca "in 1893, the municipal authorities of Suchiquiltongo requested that the political chief carry out the privatization of its communal lands, in accordance with the provisions of the state law of

1890. As the first step in the process, the political chief was to survey the lands claimed by the village and establish provisional boundary lines with its neighbours."[87]

Ironically, pueblo representatives not only employed the Liberal disentailment laws in their favor when it was to their advantage but also questioned, when useful, their own right to be heard in court. In a boundary conflict between two Mexico State pueblos, Capulhuac's *síndico* (attorney general) argued that according to article 27 of the 1857 Constitution, neither he nor the Tlaltizapan representative had juridical standing—and the lawsuit had to be dismissed on those grounds. In response, both the Tenango first-instance judge and the Mexico State Supreme Tribunal rejected Calpulhuac's claims, maintaining that the interpretation that corporations could not administer land did not mean they could not defend their rights in court. In fact, as long as their communal lands had not been privatized, these corporations had to continue to exist and defend themselves in court.[88]

Pueblos also made use of the federal public lands laws of 20 July 1863 and 15 December 1883, which allowed them to "draw boundary lines in accordance with the old title deeds; any territory not covered in these titles would have to be registered as *excedencias*" (untitled lands). "By law, individuals working such lands could—under certain circumstances—file a claim of ownership (*denuncio*), conduct a survey, and obtain a property title."[89] Kourí, in his work on disentailment in Papantla, Veracruz, documents how one village faction hoped "a public lands law that had often been applied in detriment of the pueblos would now serve to empower them instead." In the case of Papantla, the federal public lands laws were a potential tool in an intravillage conflict between a coalition of mestizo merchants and prosperous Totonac farmers against more impoverished Totonac residents.[90]

In many other cases, village representatives used the federal public lands laws against haciendas and neighboring pueblos. In fact there were so many of these cases that in 1892 lawyer Prisciliano María Díaz González complained that "another of the immense ills that the baldíos claims have brought is to inspire pueblos to sue hacienda owners and other pueblos, in order to win . . . what they were unable to attain in a legal and forthright lawsuit at the state's tribunals."[91] In Yucatán, for example, Dzitbalché municipal authorities petitioned for the survey of the ejido perimeter according to the 1844 Yucatán decree, promising that after the fundo legal was delineated for public use, they would distribute the ejidos among the impoverished heads of family.[92] In Mexico State, after decades of conflicts with the neighboring Amecameca pueblo, the San Juan de Guadalupe hacienda began proceedings to survey the disputed lands according to the federal public lands law. Amecameca representatives complained to President Díaz, who ordered the hacienda owners to suspend proceedings. Organized as an agricultural society, in 1890 Amecamecans "would try to beat the hacienda at its own game."[93] They hired an agronomist to survey their lands based on their colonial titles and following federal public lands laws. In this case, a district judge ruled against them, but in 1901 the Supreme Court granted them amparo protection.[94]

Of course, not all efforts by villagers to use federal public lands laws were successful. In Puebla, Tlancualpican residents in 1895 accused the Jaltepec, Atencingo, Tenango, and Santa Ana haciendas of reducing the pueblo to its urban core (*casco*) and forcing residents to become renters of their own lands. They sought to recover their lands by petitioning for the survey of the pueblo's old ejido perimeters, but they were instead apprehended and tortured by the Jaltepec hacienda manager.[95]

Playing the Judiciary and the Executive against Each Other

Archival documents show that villagers often played the judiciary and the executive against each other in land and water restitution cases. In the last decades of the nineteenth century and the first decade of the twentieth century, dozens of pueblo authorities filed for amparo protection at the district-court level and at the Supreme Court. Amparos were, by definition, the contestation of a law, a court decision, or a government policy. If won, amparos reversed the court's decision or the executive's action "to its original state." In this way, the federal judiciary created important checks and balances, not only on the state

Nineteenth-Century Suits 49

courts and tribunals but also on the executive at both state and federal levels.

There are many examples of this type of amparo reversal in archival holdings. In the Federal District, for instance, the San Andrés Mixquic representative and thirty signatories complained about "looting by the municipal syndic who, taking judicial attributions, conducted a boundary survey" in which he invaded their legally possessed lands. In this case, the district judge granted Mixquic residents amparo protection, arguing, "Whatever reason the municipal government had to intervene in the survey, it will always be true that it took on faculties reserved for the judicial branch."[96] In Tabasco the district court and the Supreme Court granted amparo protection to Huimanguillo residents when, during the privatization of their communal lands, the governor invaded their property. Here the Supreme Court ruled, "The plaintiffs were in possession of the usurped lands and houses without having been heard in a civil court by the appropriate authority, and [since] this usurpation was executed by an administrative order... the procedure lacks legal cause or motive."[97] In Oaxaca the state government and the federal judiciary wrestled over who had authority over pueblo boundary marking. Whereas the Oaxaca law of 14 December 1891 granted extraordinary powers to state officials (including the governor, political chiefs, and municipal authorities) to define pueblos' boundaries as part of the privatization of communal lands, the Supreme Court considered this law unconstitutional.[98] And in Veracruz, when Altotonga pueblo representatives sued municipal authorities for having sold at public auction lands that belonged to them, the Supreme Court unanimously decreed that "whether the possession is backed by a legitimate title or is illegitimate, whether the lands are Altotonga's communal property or not, the municipal corporation has proceeded outside its legitimate powers by exercising authority that corresponds exclusively to the judiciary."[99]

It was not only judges and justices who upheld their authority over contentious property matters; pueblo representatives, too, were adept at hailing the Constitutional separation of powers between the judiciary and the executive—when it served their purposes. For example, in 1871 when Oaxaca governor Félix Díaz ordered the political chief to draw boundary lines between two pueblos in the Coixtlahuaca District, Tequixtepec residents argued, "According to the laws, drawing boundary lines ... is the judiciary's jurisdiction." A year later, the Supreme Court granted them amparo protection on these grounds.[100] Also in Oaxaca, when the Tejúpam municipal syndic sued the Teposcolula District political authorities for having interfered in Tejúpam's land suit against the Tamazulapan pueblo, the syndic argued, "Constitutional article 50 is very clear on the matter and states the following: The supreme power of the Federation is divided in its exercise between legislative, executive, and judicial branches. Two or more of these powers shall never be united in one single person or office. Moreover, article 13 of the same fundamental law states: In the Mexican Republic 'no one may be tried by private laws or special tribunals.'"[101]

Alternatively, when pueblo representatives could not resolve their boundary conflicts in court, or when they knew it would be a costly and delayed uphill battle, they frequently tried to circumvent the judiciary by asking the executive branch of government (municipal officials, district political chiefs, governors, officials from the ministries of Fomento, the Treasury, and Justice, and even the president) to resolve their land conflicts administratively.[102] Executive branch officials responded by trying at various times and in diverse ways to resolve these ongoing and often violent land conflicts outside the justice system, but as soon as defendants demanded the right to be heard in court, the matter had to be resolved by the judiciary. In the Federal District, for instance, leaders from eleven pueblos sent a petition to the Ministry of the Interior asking for permission to recover "with the sole intervention of the local government" some lands that had been taken from them. They explained, "Even though it is true that there are tribunals created exclusively to rule on these contentious matters, we inform you that even though the pueblos have at different times taken their suits to these tribunals and made great efforts to validate their violated rights, these suits have been futile. We have never had favorable results, as one can see in our archive's voluminous files."[103] Similarly in Michoacán, more than one hundred signatories from Tanaco asked the governor to resolve the boundary disputes between four neighboring villages (Urén, Cherán Atzicuirín, Ahuirán, and Urapicho). They had taken their dispute to court but had to abandon the lawsuit because the proceedings were endless, and they lacked funds to cover the related expenses. Exasperated, they asked, "If in our Republic a single man has been able to instill peace among the inhabitants, and we have now been enjoying this peace for about twenty-seven years, why can no one resolve the pueblos' boundary disputes in a tiny fraction of the Republic? Why does the state governor not dictate his wise and prudent government resolutions to fix each pueblo's boundaries and resolve the uncertainty that drives us to armed conflict?"[104]

Despite the judges' frequent refusal to grant pueblo representatives juridical standing, and notwithstanding corrupt and biased judges, on the eve of the revolution hundreds of pueblo representatives were engaged in old and new land suits against other pueblos, municipal governments, local caciques, and landowners. They employed all available laws, including Liberal disentailment and federal public lands laws, in their efforts to regain or expand their lands. They also strategically pitted one branch of government against another. At the outbreak of the Madero revolution, this broad and profoundly litigious rural sector would play a key role alongside those who rose up in arms—many of whom had also experienced decades of litigation.

2

Pueblo Land and Water Claims during the Madero Administration, 1911–1913

> El pueblo oprimido pide respetuosamente al Ciudadano Presidente de la República ... su valiosa intervención a fin de que se nombre un comisionado a costa de los interesados, para que inspeccione los terrenos litigiosos. [The oppressed people respectfully request of the Citizen President of the Republic ... his valuable intervention in appointing a commissioner at the expense of those concerned, to inspect the litigious lands.]
>
> —Representatives of San Juan Atzingo, Puebla, to President Francisco León de la Barra, 1911

On 20 November 1910, Francisco Madero publicly circulated his Plan de San Luis Potosí, a document condemning Porfirio Díaz's fraudulent reelection and calling for the violent overthrow of his dictatorship.[1] This famous proclamation not only ushered in the collapse of the Díaz regime and the outbreak of the Mexican Revolution, but it also set off—during both the interim presidency of Francisco León de la Barra y Quijano (25 May to 6 November 1911) and the democratically elected but short-lived government of Madero (6 November 1911 to 19 February 1913)—a flood of village petitions to settle conflicts over land and water rights outside the judiciary. At the same time, village leaders in several states began taking over hacienda lands, expecting approval if not support from the de la Barra and Madero administrations. But neither of these governments condoned such takeovers, and revolutionary leaders like Emiliano Zapata felt betrayed by Madero's lack of commitment to resolving land and water claims. As a result, in November 1911 Zapata and schoolteacher Otilio Montaño issued the

53

famous Plan de Ayala, a document that disavowed the federal government, reversed the burden of proof for plaintiffs seeking restitution of land and water resources, and allowed pueblos with titles to take back their lands, "arms in hand."

In response to both the flood of nonviolent petitions and armed hacienda takeovers, in early 1912 Madero's Ministry of Development, Colonization, and Industry (Secretaría de Fomento, Colonización e Industria) issued two circulars promoting the survey of the pueblos' ejidos (following Porfirian federal public lands laws) as one legal way for the executive to settle land and water disputes by arbitration. What this chapter shows is that alongside armed uprisings in many states, pueblo leaders continued to challenge landowners, local elites, municipal cabeceras, and neighboring villages by employing all available state laws and procedures, including the two Madero circulars. Ultimately the surveys promoted by the circulars failed when landowners demanded due process, and the Supreme Court upheld constitutional protections of private property as well as the separation of powers between the branches of government. It was in this context that radical legislators debated how the executive could resolve "the agrarian question" outside the court system.

Village Petitions at the Outbreak of the Revolution

To "control the disorders inherent in a revolutionary movement," Madero's Plan de San Luis upheld nearly all Porfirian laws until a new administration could review them. The lone exception was the federal public lands law. Article 3 of the plan justified its annulment because it claimed that Fomento or the judiciary, or both, had abused the laws and, as a result, had dispossessed small landholders—most of them Indians. "Given that it is a matter of justice to *restitute* to the former owners the lands they were dispossessed of in such arbitrary manner," article 3 continued, "such rulings and sentences are declared subject to revision, and those who acquired them in such an immoral manner or their heirs should *restitute* the lands to their original owners, to whom they shall also pay compensation for the damages they suffered."[2] In response, thousands of villagers throughout the country sent commissions and petitions to the office of the president and the Ministries of Fomento, Justice, and the Treasury (Hacienda) in hopes of settling their land and water claims by administrative means.

An analysis of approximately a hundred village petitions unleashed by Madero's Plan de San Luis during the de la Barra and Madero presidencies shows that they originated in nearly every state in the country and from a variety of signatories, including municipal officials and pueblo representatives or Indian authorities (at the submunicipal level), and spokespersons for village factions. Those accused of wrongdoing included not only hacienda owners, political chiefs, and judges (the well-known culprits) but also local leaders, caciques, and local elites who profited from real-estate transactions. The alleged offenders also included neighboring villages engaged in long-simmering boundary disputes. Claims involved both communal lands (entailed as well as privatized—but often without proper titles) in addition to private property owned collectively or individually. Most claimants had already dealt with at least one court (including courts of first instance, district courts, and the Supreme Court) and thus had good reason not to pursue the matter judicially—because the town had lost a land suit in the past, because old suits had never been adjudicated, or because they feared that the defendants had undue influence over judges.

The specific content of these petitions was varied. Some villagers did complain, as the Plan de San Luis suggested, about land dispossessions resulting from terrenos baldíos claims. In Guerrero, for example, Ajuchitlán villagers complained that the laws allowed a few influential residents to acquire village lands. They asked Madero to order that "our lands be restituted and that those who took them pay us indemnity for the twenty-two years we have been without lands, as the Plan de San Luis instructs."[3] And in Jalisco, eighty Santa Cruz de la Soledad Indians cited article 3 of the plan in their petition for the return of lands "taken by a few outsiders without even paying for them, and leaving us without even enough pasturelands for our cattle."[4]

Numerous other signatories petitioned de la Barra and Madero for the restitution of lands lost not through the implementation of the federal public lands laws but due to the expansion of neighboring properties onto village lands. In Durango, Pasaje residents explained to Madero that in 1898 the Santa Catalina Alamo hacienda had taken their lands "like a river in flood," and Peñón Blanco authorities declared, "The final section of article 3 of the Plan de San Luis Potosí led us to join the revolutionists, in the hope that upon the victory of the revolution we would take possession of the twenty-five *sitios* of land of which we had been despoiled."[5]

Some villagers made land restitution claims to the executive and presented their claims with titles in hand. In Zacatecas, for instance, Susticacán pueblo natives told Madero that "since we believe the hour of justice and the promises of the triumphant revolution have arrived, we do not hesitate to petition the nation's president that we may be given possession of these lands, for which we have recovered our titles that safeguard us."[6] Countless other villages, however, petitioned for the restitution of lands and water resources for which they had long-standing use rights but no property titles. In San Luis Potosí, for example, Huasteco Indians from the Concepción hamlet (*ranchería*) claimed to have "hereditary de facto rights" to the lands on which they had built their houses and cultivated sugar cane, bananas, beans, and white maize. The "capitalists of the region," they claimed, were not respecting these use rights.[7]

More than a few village authorities saw the Plan de San Luis as an invitation to denounce land-grabbing caciques. In the Tepic Territory, Juana Ortiz and thirteen other Indian women from Mexcaltitán asked Madero to control the local cacique; otherwise, they said furiously, "Even though we are women, we will kick him out."[8] Similarly, the Tepic Territory lawyer representing the Santa Cruz de Camotlán Indians wrote the following to President Madero: "I am representing one of these typical cases of persecution and land seizure, the consequence of *caciquismo*, which at these moments could stir up agitation and cause great disruption to public order." According to this lawyer, the community had colonial titles proving ownership of some ten thousand hectares divided between Ahuacatlán in Tepic and Mascota in Jalisco (the property having been split up when the Tepic territory seceded from the State of Jalisco). For over a year, the Ahuacatlán cacique (who was also the Tepic Supreme Tribunal magistrate) had threatened to assign (*adjudicar*) to a third party lands the villagers considered theirs. Villagers had petitioned for amparo protection against the land seizure, which they won at both the district court and the Supreme Court. Yet despite the rulings, those who resisted the cacique had their crops stolen, were forced into the army, or had their lives threatened.[9]

Caciques often exerted their power through the ayuntamiento. In Puebla, San Jerónimo Caleras residents complained to Madero that Crescencio Rodríguez Aguilar and his family had dominated the municipal government for many years. Rodríguez justified his position by saying that "just as General Díaz had made himself necessary as President of the Republic, he had made himself necessary in the presidency of their pueblo." The letter's signatories explained that when some years earlier the pueblo won a land suit against the Santo Domingo hacienda, Rodríguez had kept the best lands for himself and his inner circle, thereby proving the wisdom of the popular saying, "The person in charge of dividing and distributing something always keeps the best share" (*el que parte y reparte se queda con la mejor parte*).[10]

Town leaders also wrote to, or sent commissions to meet with, de la Barra and Madero to complain about neighboring pueblos. In one case from Mexico State, the attorney for San Simón de la Laguna asked the president to act as judge in a land conflict with neighboring San Miguel. Calling San Miguel residents "obstinate and foolish Indians," he complained that in a boundary dispute the municipal president of Malacatepec had ruled in San Miguel's favor, even though their titles were pre-Columbian and only titles issued by the Spanish crown had probative value in the courts.[11] Likewise in Sinaloa, the Indians of Guasave complained that their own neighbors usurped their lands. They had petitioned for a land survey, but while it was delayed, their neighbors continued to possess and sell off Guasave lands.[12]

Claims during the Madero Years 57

As many had done in the nineteenth century, village authorities sometimes petitioned for the privatization of communal village properties as a strategy to recover pueblo lands and water resources. In Chiapas, Soyatitán villagers, whose forefathers had received a colonial grant for two thousand hectares but possessed no titles, asked this of Madero: "By your grace and special favor and for the good of the children of the pueblo [we ask you] to resolve what is just with respect to these lands and agree to their division and reparto among the sons of the pueblo."[13] Fifty signatories in Oaxaca also petitioned for the reparto of their communal lands, explaining that although each resident had an individual plot, they did not have the titles with which they could fight off the ayuntamiento's abuses. Stating that they were "convinced that the present government is concerned about the betterment of the proletarian class," they asked for the reparto of their lands according to the terms of the disentailment law of 25 June 1856.[14]

Village leaders interpreted article 3 of the Plan de San Luis as proof that Madero was willing to sort out long-standing appeals outside the court system. Villagers from Mexico State, for instance, wrote to Madero: "From the confines of this pueblo, lost in the mountains of the Jilotepec district, we dare make our voice heard in the hope that the echoes of our misfortune reach you." For years, they claimed, they had been victims of powerful hacienda owners, who not only seized their lands but also invaded local and national roads. Their efforts to reclaim these lands had been futile, they added, because they could not afford attorneys. Their case seemed to be pending at the district court, but they said they had more faith in the federal government to resolve the matter quickly and "with less influence exerted by wealthy locals."[15] And in Sinaloa, the Ocoroni pueblo representative, citing the Plan de San Luis, requested Fomento's intervention in an unresolved 1880 court proceeding against several individuals who had made terrenos baldíos claims on what they considered to be pueblo lands.[16]

Madero, however, was not going to settle land conflicts outside court. He later clarified that the intention of the Plan de San Luis had been "to determine in what cases small landowners, especially Indians, had been improperly despoiled of their lands, in order to restitute these in kind or to force the responsible party to pay indemnification by judicial review procedures [*mediante procedimientos jurídicos*]."[17] Under de la Barra and Madero, then, the executive branch forwarded most land claims to the courts.[18] For example, when Valparaíso (Zacatecas) residents asked the Ministry of Justice for the restitution of lands seized by a neighboring hacienda because they could not afford to take the matter to court, ministry officials replied that such matters were outside their jurisdiction.[19] In like manner, a petition with over eight hundred signatories, from more than a dozen villages in the Tehuacán area in Puebla, requested the return of lands seized by General Juan Hernández, who had acted "with the dictator's support," a reference to Díaz. In response, the governor of Puebla instructed the Tehuacán district prefect to tell villagers that whatever they had paid to process their petitions had been a waste, because the only way to address these land claims was through the judicial authority, "which these days provides assurances."[20]

The old judiciary did, at times, provide assurances to pueblos during the early revolutionary years. In Hidalgo, for example, La Vega de Metztitlán residents petitioned the district court for amparo protection against the governor after he issued decrees allowing a third party to conduct waterworks affecting their lands. They argued they had "just title for the use of the water resources, as well as ownership of lands that derive from the ancient rights of the members of the former Metztitlán community." These rights included "the use of water through dams and canals constructed since time immemorial to channel water and benefit the lands." The district judge refused to grant the petitioners court protection, but the Supreme Court reversed the ruling and granted the residents of Metztitlán an amparo against both the Hidalgo governor and the state legislature. In his individual vote, Justice Manuel Olvera Toro recognized "the clear right of the Indians not to have their land and water possessions altered."[21]

Assurances of this kind, however, would not be enough.

Claims during the Madero Years

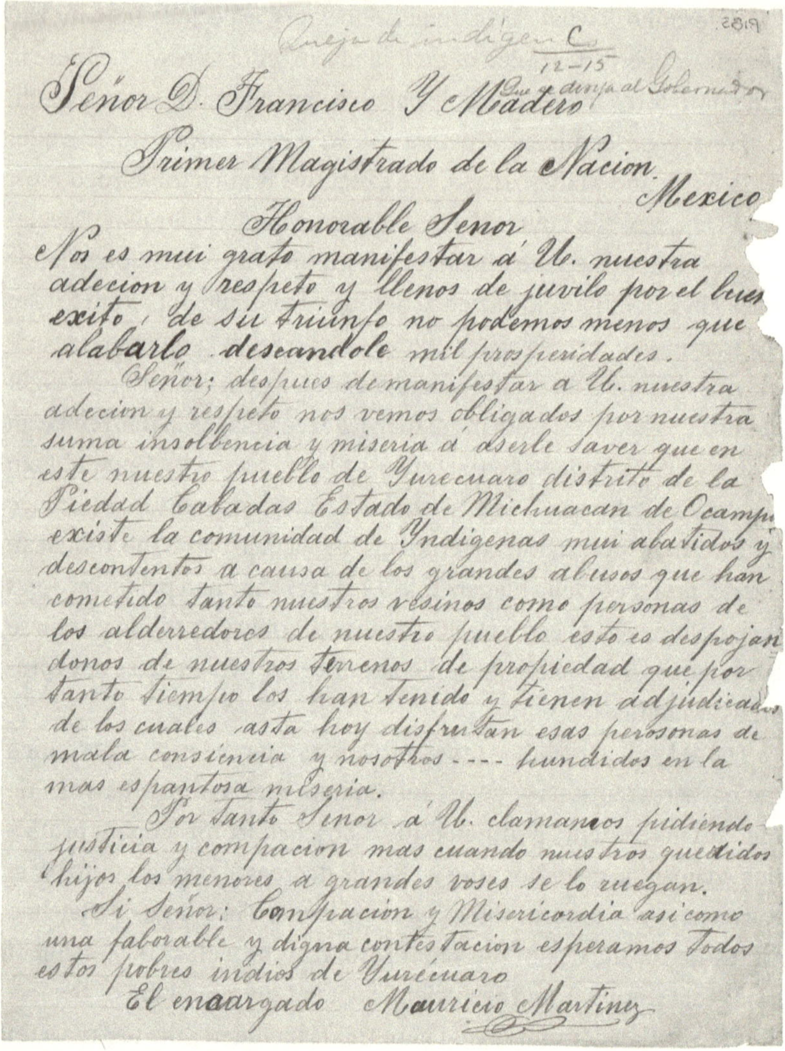

2819

Señor D. Francisco Y. Madero
Primer Magistrado de la Nacion.
Mexico
Honorable Señor
Nos es mui grato manifestar á U. nuestra adecion y respeto y llenos de juvilo por el buen exito, de su triunfo no podemos menos que alabarlo deseandole mil prosperidades.
Señor; despues de manifestar a U. nuestra adecion y respeto nos vemos obligados por nuestra suma insolbencia y miseria á aserle saver que en este nuestro pueblo de Yurecuaro distrito de la Piedad Cabadas Estado de Michuacan de Ocampo existe la comunidad de Yndigenas mui abatidos y descontentos a causa de los grandes abusos que han cometido tanto nuestros vesinos como personas de los alderredores de nuestro pueblo esto es despojandonos de nuestros terrenos de propiedad que por tanto tiempo los han tenido y tienen adjudicados de los cuales asta hoy disfrutan esas personas de mala consiencia y nosotros --- hundidos en la mas espantosa miseria.
Por tanto Señor á U. clamamos pidiendo justicia y compacion mas cuando nuestros queridos hijos los menores a grandes voses se lo ruegan.
Si Señor: Compacion y Misericordia asi como una faborable y digna contestacion esperamos todos estos pobres indios de Yurécuaro
El encargado Mauricio Martinez

Fig. 3. Yurécuaro (Michoacán) petition to Madero, late 1911. Archivo General de la Nación, Fondo Francisco I. Madero, caja 64, exp. 2819.

The Madero-Zapata Fallout: Reversing the Burden of Proof

In December 1910, after Zapata had already become a regional authority in Morelos, he distributed individual parcels on disputed hacienda lands to villagers from Villa de Ayala, Moyotepec, and Anenecuilco.[22] Other such redistributions followed in Morelos. In fact, many of the state's rural dwellers were so convinced that Madero's Plan de San Luis promised the restitution of seized lands and water rights that some of them sought government validation of their takeovers. For example, in the summer of 1911, Cuauchichinola residents were already distributing San Gabriel and Cuauchichinola hacienda lands when they wrote to Madero, telling him that their pueblo was one of the most ancient pueblos founded by the Mexica (and later recognized by the viceregal government) and asking him to fulfill "the just promises of the Plan de San Luis."[23] Similarly, in the fall of 1911 residents of Amacuzac explained that in "revolutionary times" they had repossessed their lands and were now cultivating them to feed their families. These lands, they claimed, had originally been *tierras de común repartimiento*, and they had the titles to prove it. They asked the Madero administration for justice and protection against potential hacienda reprisals.[24]

It was not only in Morelos that town leaders took matters into their own hands, expecting support from the Madero government. In Michoacán, for example, Miguel de la F. Regalado of Atacheo wrote to Madero to say that his pueblo had given him power of attorney for matters related to the restitution of their ancestral lands. Given the promises "Madero the Liberator" had made to the nation, Regalado reported, "Today my pueblo and I take possession of what we own."[25]

Whereas elites and much of the Mexico City press characterized land takeovers as pillage, villagers considered these actions legally justifiable. The case of Jiutepec (Morelos), which was aired in the press, is a good example of how these views differed. In a letter to the director of the newspaper *El País*, Antonio Barrios, attorney for Isabel Sánchez de Corona, the owner of the San Vicente and San Gaspar haciendas, accused villagers of invading de Corona's property. According to Barrios, she had inherited the haciendas from her parents, who had purchased them long ago.[26] In response, Fermín Serna, representative of the Jiutepec villagers, also wrote to the newspaper director, arguing, "Neither Señora de Corona nor her parents have purchased these lands, because no one in Jiutepec has ever had any knowledge of such a sale. If the owner happens to have titles, they are illegal, and we reject them because this pueblo did not give permission for any sale. And if this Señora does have any proof, then it is probably because in the past administration it was customary for hacendados to strip the poor of their properties." Not only did Serna believe that Jiutepec had legitimate rights to these lands, but he also hoped to obtain support from interim president de la Barra, adding that "now that we have an honest government we are ready to challenge Sr. Barrios with regard to this sale because, if there had been one, it was a sham devised to seize the patrimony of the entire pueblo."[27]

De la Barra, however, sided with the elites. In November 1911 he informed the federal Chamber of Deputies that Zapata's movement had made itself popular among the "uncultured classes" of Morelos by offering land distribution (*repartición de tierras*) without respecting property rights.[28] Many landowners in Morelos "held legal title, or at least legal color of title, however unethically obtained." The return of such lands to villagers, according to Peter V. N. Henderson, "would require, at least in the eyes of civilian Maderistas, some sort of legal due process with evidentiary hearing and judicial review." Henderson explains: "This basic disagreement would contribute to the division between Zapata on the one hand and de la Barra and the civilian Maderistas on the other."[29]

To avoid appearing to be common bandits—a stigma Zapata feared deeply—legend has it that, fleeing a military ambush in Villa de Ayala, Zapata and a few trusted men rode through the mountainous terrain of Morelos toward San Marcos Ayoxuxtla in southeastern Puebla, where Zapata summoned all allied revolutionary chiefs to a meeting. In late November 1911, sitting at a rustic wooden table placed in the middle of a humble plaza filled with men wearing crossed cartridge belts and holding carbines, schoolteacher Otilio Montaño read a handwritten manifesto titled the "Plan de Ayala."[30] A formal declaration of rebellion, the document denounced President Francisco I. Madero for having betrayed the revolution (especially when it came to pueblo land restitution) and outlined a land reform program. The fifty-plus revolutionary generals and lesser officials present all signed the document, which ended with "Justice and Law."[31]

For Zapata and Montaño, "justice and law" meant restituting usurped pueblo lands on the basis of evidence presented in the form of land titles.[32] Article 6 of the Plan de Ayala allowed pueblos and citizens with titles to fields, woodlands, and water resources unjustly appropriated by landlords, científicos, or caciques to reclaim their property immediately and defend it, arms in hand. Not all villagers—only those who held titles to the disputed lands—could take over neighboring haciendas. In the eyes of Zapata, Montaño, and the urban professionals who later joined the movement, there was no doubt that pueblos had titles to lands they had lost as a result of illegal transactions. As Manuel Palafox, who would later become the architect of the Zapatista agrarian reform, stated in 1914, "I have studied the agrarian question and the real causes of the Social Revolution in great depth. I can assure you that, of the pueblos in the southern states, 80 percent have titles to prove ownership of their property and have been unjustly dispossessed. I have held in my hands innumerable pueblo titles, and I have clearly felt the theft that the majority of pueblos in this country have been victims of."[33] Similarly, Gonzalo Isunza, one of the first engineers Palafox hired in late 1914 to survey pueblo lands, saw his task as "the return to their legitimate owners of the seized lands which correspond to pueblo ejidos, according to their primordial titles."[34]

Responding to accusations that he and his soldiers were bandits, Zapata stated in a December 1911 manifesto "to all pueblos" that "one cannot call a person a bandit who, weak and helpless, was despoiled of his property by someone strong and powerful, and now that this person cannot tolerate more, he makes a superhuman effort to regain control over that which used to pertain to him. The despoiler is the bandit, not the despoiled!"[35] On the assumption that the despoiler was the bandit, the novel feature of the Plan de Ayala was to reverse the burden of proof. As Santa Anna had proposed half a century earlier (see chapter 1), the Plan de Ayala allowed pueblos with titles immediately to recover their usurped lands, leaving estate owners to make their claims in court. Though Zapata had declared war on the existing government, including the federal judiciary, the Plan de Ayala suspended but did not cancel the defendants' right to be heard in court. They would have to wait to take their claims to "the special tribunals that are created upon the triumph of the Revolution."[36]

Madero's Liberal Laws in Times of Revolutionary Upheaval

Because villagers in Morelos and other states were acting on their own to take back hacienda lands, Madero's Fomento was compelled to respond in one way or another. Heading the ministry, though, was lawyer Rafael Hernández—Madero's cousin—who had strong ties to the Porfiriato.[37] He therefore proposed several measures that did not require legal reforms, including the sale of national lands and the purchase of private property that would be fractioned and sold to villagers on favorable terms. He also responded to pueblos' petitions for the executive to resolve old and new land and water conflicts by issuing two circulars in January and February of 1912, promoting the survey and privatization of communal lands following existing federal public lands laws.[38] Minister Hernández later explained the rationale behind the circulars: there were two or three thousand pueblos throughout Mexico that, for one reason or another, had lost their ejidos, but without precise facts (in the form of deed titles), these cases were difficult to resolve. According to Hernández, the cases could be grouped into three categories: pueblos that still had—to some extent or another—ejidos that had not been privatized; pueblos that had lost their ejidos either because landowners had invaded them or because land speculators had taken advantage of pueblos during land privatization; and pueblos that no longer had ejidos because villagers had sold their parcels. Fomento's circulars would address the first situation: pueblos with ejidos that had not been privatized.[39]

The privatization of the ejidos, a federal matter since the 1880s, required measuring and marking boundaries before distributing them as private parcels.[40] Fomento would hire engineers to survey and privatize pueblos' existing ejidos in the hope that this would allow them to resolve some of their boundary conflicts. Hernández thus advised state governments to hire surveyors "to determine the ejidos of the pueblos, based on their titles," leaving until later their division and distribution into parcels and lots for resident heads of family.[41]

In a revolutionary crisis, Fomento's circulars seem almost irrelevant, and they probably would have been if it had not been for pueblo representatives who, once again, took advantage of all available laws to fight their neighbors over their ancestral land and water resources. If village authorities interpreted article 3 of the Plan de San Luis as a promise by the executive to take over from the judiciary all kinds of land and water claims, then the two circulars issued by Hernández almost certainly raised expectations even further. Even the newspaper *La Patria* incorrectly described the circulars as Fomento's efforts to "distribute lands [el reparto] to the Republic's poor classes."[42] The result was that in only a few months, Fomento claimed to have received petitions for ejido surveys "from a multitude of pueblos," including sixty from Puebla and fifty from Mexico State.[43]

As with the Plan de San Luis, villagers used the circulars to try to settle property conflicts outside the judiciary. Some village authorities solicited a survey to restitute pueblo lands that allegedly had been invaded by neighboring haciendas. In Mexico State, for example, San Antonio Pachuquilla residents claimed to have a 1584 title to one *sitio de ganado mayor* (or 1,755.61 hectares). "Now that the new regime is granting so many guarantees to all inhabitants in general," they wrote, they asked Fomento to send them a surveyor "to have our lands delineated, based on our titles." Their goal was to recover the property that had been seized by the Jaltepec hacienda.[44] Also in Mexico State, a Jocotitlán commission petitioned Madero for the return of their lands, asking for the survey of the pueblo's boundaries with the Tiacaque hacienda. They claimed that owner María del Valle Mier y Terán had encroached on their lands for the past ten years. Seven years earlier, town authorities had taken their complaint to court, but to no avail. They therefore felt "it was necessary that [we], the owners of the pueblo lands in question, came to see the president of the republic to resolve the matter faster."[45]

Villagers also used Madero's circulars to petition for the restitution of water resources. In Puebla, for example, the San Nicolás Tetitzintla municipal auxiliary asked Fomento to name a disentailment commission (*comisión deslindadora*) to conduct a survey of and to divide and distribute their ejidos "to stop the innumerable abuses committed by the hacienda servants who are in possession of the pueblo's ejidos." Some decades earlier, they explained, an individual from Tehuacán had purchased pueblo lands to build an aqueduct and subterranean canals to irrigate his lands. He then sold the ranch to another individual who extended the underground works and harmed the pueblo's irrigation canals, thus breaching the agreement reached with the first owner not to harm the pueblo's water resources. When they took their matter to Fomento, officials determined that the case involved "local waters" that fell under local agreements or the management of municipal, district, and state governments, not federal waters under Fomento's federal jurisdiction.[46]

Villagers also employed the ministry's circulars to revisit earlier communal land privatizations. In Guerrero, for instance, seventy Malinaltepec residents accused several villagers of seizing their privatized land parcels in 1878 (with the backing of the political chief and the judge of first instance). These residents asked Madero "to grant them possession once again or to ratify the boundaries marked in their title and map."[47] Similarly, residents of San José de Gracia, Aguascalientes, reminded Madero that they were "sympathizers of the glorious revolution," and they asked for his help ("within the administrative sphere") in conducting a survey of ejidos in accord with Fomento's circular 2 in order to review a reparto done twenty years earlier.[48] And, in Veracruz, members of the San Andrés Tuxtla distribution commission maintained that officials had conducted a fraudulent and unfair reparto of municipal lands in 1886, which they now wanted corrected.[49]

In some cases, municipal authorities actively employed what they saw as a legal tool for challenging the boundaries of neighboring haciendas. Circular 1 granted ayuntamientos juridical standing to delineate and mark boundaries and to fraction and distribute a pueblo's ejidos (*deslinde, amojonamiento, fraccionamiento y reparto*), and many municipal officials took advantage of this right.[50] In San Luis Potosí, for instance, the municipal president of Villa de Reyes petitioned for the demarcation, boundary marking, fractioning, and distribution of the pueblo's ejidos. However, the neighboring hacienda's owners rejected the survey, claiming that the pueblo had never had ejidos and that their primordial titles were fake. The director of the National Archives certified that three of the four titles presented by the municipal president were indeed fake ("written with the same hand as others that have been presented for study at this office").[51] Romualdo Pérez, the municipal *síndico* (attorney general), either as a lawyer himself or with the assistance of one, wrote a long text in which he explained that the hacienda had encroached on pueblo lands in such a way that it now reached "in all directions of the municipality up to the doors of the town's last dwelling," so extensively that "taking only one step outside the last house, one is already on hacienda lands." The hacienda owner had also tried to fence off the village so that residents could not access the montes to extract wood. Moreover, in 1892 the hacienda owner had attempted to pile rocks to plug up the villagers' water outlets along the river—the very river whose water the residents had used since ancient times to irrigate their orchards on both sides of the communally operated watercourse. When *rivereños* (those with lands along the riverbanks) complained to the municipal and district authorities at the time, they were accused of "disturbing the public peace." One resident was even sent to jail.[52]

In the second part of the text, Pérez analyzed all titles and showed that the pueblo had been founded in 1562, eighty-one years before the hacienda's predecessor was created. Moreover, he used Madero's circular 2 to challenge the landowner's attempt to block the survey. Circular 2 made state governors responsible for hiring surveyors "to determine the ejidos of the pueblos, based on their titles." If during the demarcation of a pueblo's boundaries "neighboring owners who have invaded ejido lands believe they have better rights," circular 2 added, "there will be an opportunity to examine their claims in

Claims during the Madero Years

light of their justificatory documents and for this Ministry to resolve any differences administratively."⁵³ Interpreting this document literally, Pérez accused Fomento of inverting the circular's instructions (that is, that the survey should come before the evaluation of documents).⁵⁴

It seems that not all municipal officials were so proactive. In one interesting case, Atacheo representative Miguel Regalado—speaking for twenty-one other Michoacán pueblos, ten from Mexico State, and one each from Guerrero, Puebla, and Veracruz—petitioned the minister of the interior to cancel Fomento's circular 1. "The pueblos' ayuntamientos are made up of persons who served in the times of General Díaz," he explained. "How are they supposed to achieve justice and attend to the needs of the Indians when it was their members who despoiled them?" Regalado went on to explain that the authorities of Ecuandureo, Tlazazalca, Zacapu (all in Michoacán), and San Francisco Chejé (Mexico State) had already asked their ayuntamientos to conduct a survey of their ejidos, but the authorities found pretexts not to do so. Ironically, Regalado reminded Madero that the 1857 Constitution had stripped ayuntamientos of their right to administer the pueblos' ejidos and requested that only Fomento have the authority to conduct the surveys and act as the arbitrator, "accompanied by a general representative or delegate named by us, who, titles in hand, shows an interest for the pueblos."⁵⁵

If nothing else, Madero's circulars fueled what in many regions was an ongoing, low-intensity conflict between pueblo authorities and hacienda owners. In Mexico State, a commission from Jocotitlán met with President Madero to request a boundary survey of their lands bordering the Tiacaque hacienda. The Jocotitlán officials claimed the matter had languished in court for seven years without a verdict. The newspaper *El País* covered this case and sided with the petitioners. It reported that the villagers, "the owners of the pueblo lands," had been forced to ask Madero to speed up Fomento's survey, and it added that the commission had issued a warning that if the court did not issue a ruling, the villagers would take up arms against the hacienda.⁵⁶

The Limits to Fomento's Circulars: The Constitutional Right to Be Heard in Court

In a memoir of his activities as head of Fomento, Hernández claimed that the survey of the pueblos' ejidos had been successful because the ministry managed to resolve contentious matters through arbitration boards.[57] What he did not explain, however, was that given the constitutional separation of powers between the executive and the judiciary, those who disagreed with the ministry's resolution did retain the right to take their claims to the appropriate courts.[58] And this, in fact, became the program's main limitation.

The case of Hampolol shows how landowners, with the support of the judiciary, managed repeatedly to block implementation of Hernández's circulars. By the late nineteenth century, Hampolol (described in archaeological literature as one of the oldest pueblos in the Yucatán peninsula) had either lost or sold all its pueblo lands. In 1899 village authorities petitioned the courts to redraw their old ejido boundaries, but village authorities lost the survey suit because they could not find the pueblo's titles. In 1906 Hampolol's attorney once again took the matter to court, but the judge had not ruled on the matter by the time Fomento issued its 1912 circulars. Therefore, in 1912 municipal officials (of both the Campeche ayuntamiento and the Hampolol municipal agency), describing the circulars as "the distribution of ejidos—a program christened by the generous blood of our brothers," petitioned Governor Manuel Castilla Brito for another boundary survey. Brito, who had supported Madero against Díaz and became governor under him, was inclined to support the new government's programs. As a result, citing Fomento's circulars 1 and 2, the Campeche district political chief authorized the ejido boundary survey for 30 September, and municipal officials notified the district court and neighboring landowners so that their lawyers could be present.[59]

For nine days, surveyor Francisco Campos Mena and the survey party—composed of villagers, a court official, and several municipal officials—surveyed "an ejido measuring one square league," as established by the 1844 Yucatán law.⁶⁰ They began measuring from the church northward. At a distance of about five hundred meters, they arrived at the boundary line with Eligio Guerrero's hacienda. There, Guerrero and his lawyer showed Campos Mena a long, complicated purchase deed, which the surveyor promptly disqualified on the grounds that Guerrero possessed more land than his maps and titles justified. Campos Mena added that every time successive hacienda owners had conducted a new survey during the Díaz regime, they ended up with an even larger property—without Hampolol's attorney receiving a fair hearing. On this basis, Campos Mena proceeded to measure northward for a total of 2,095 meters. In the days that followed, the surveyor did the same in the remaining three cardinal directions.

Guerrero took the matter to court on two legal grounds. First, he claimed the survey was illegal because the matter had been in the courts since 1906 and public discussion of it elsewhere was therefore prohibited (according to the legal concept of sub judice). Second, the 1912 survey did not respect the 1844 Yucatán privatization law, the 1894 federal public lands law, or Fomento's two 1912 circulars, all of which required surveys to be based on the pueblo's titles. On these grounds, Guerrero demanded that Campos Mena suspend the survey until Fomento officials and the appropriate court could hear his claims.⁶¹

Campos Mena, however, did not postpone the survey. In response, in early October, Guerrero filed for amparo protection at the district court against the Campeche ayuntamiento. The judge refused to grant him an amparo on the technicality that the ayuntamiento had not been the responsible authority—rather, it had been Fomento. A day later, ministry officials asked the judge for the 1899 survey documents so they could "proceed to resolve this matter administratively as instructed in the circulars of 8 January and 17 February." But ministry officials were not able to resolve the matter, and Guerrero filed for amparo protection with the Supreme Court. Two years later, the justices overturned the district court's ruling and granted Guerrero amparo protection, arguing that both the 1894 baldío law and the ministry's circulars stated that the survey had to be based on the pueblo's colonial land titles—which the Hampolol attorney did not possess.⁶² In this and similar cases, by upholding constitutional protections of private property, the judiciary became the main obstacle to the Madero administration's ejido surveys.⁶³

As in the nineteenth century, however, even on these matters the courts were sometimes divided. In Michoacán, for example, San Miguel Guarachita representative Filiberto Ruiz wrote to the Ministry of the Interior to declare that Fomento officials had authorized his pueblo's petition for a boundary survey, and the pueblo wanted to hire a surveyor to measure the fundo legal and the old ejido boundaries based on its titles. But because the neighboring hacienda's owner opposed the survey and the villagers feared being attacked by hacienda employees, Ruiz asked the Ministry of the Interior to send armed forces for the pueblo's protection. With or without that protection, it appears the surveyor began his work because, a month later, Ruiz reported that hacienda landowner Diego Moreno had taken the case to the district judge, who granted him amparo protection and ordered the suspension of the survey. In response, Ruiz took the pueblo's case to the Supreme Court. There the justices revoked the landowner's amparo on the technicality that the district judge could not suspend something that had not yet been ruled on by the Jiquilpan court.⁶⁴

Yet enough judges ruled against the ministry's redrawing of old ejido boundaries that they rendered the circulars ineffective as alternatives for land and water restitutions. The case of San Blas in the Tepic Territory is exemplary. In March 1912 the San Blas municipal president received a telegram from Fomento authorizing him to proceed with the survey, division, and distribution of ejidos in accordance with circulars 1 and 2. In response, the municipal syndic made a list of all resident heads of family, and the municipal president held a town meeting to decide which surveyor to hire (they chose an agrarian engineer from Fomento) and to collect contributions to cover his salary. Municipal officials notified the Tepic District judge, the state's minister of the treasury representative, and the political chief. They also informed neighboring property owners, as required, so that their lawyers could be present during the survey.

Three days after the survey, however, landowner Leonor Mercado viuda de Romano y Leopoldo petitioned the Tepic District Court for amparo protection against the San Blas ayuntamiento for violating her rights under Constitutional article 16 (which upheld the division of powers among the executive, judicial, and legislative branches of government). Municipal officials had, her lawyer claimed, surveyed part of the defendant's properties without her consent. The Tepic District judge agreed, pinpointing the weakness of Hernández's circulars: once owners opposed the survey, San Blas ayuntamiento officials could not legally proceed with the marking of the old ejido boundaries. In April 1912 the Supreme Court justices unanimously upheld the district court's ruling and granted Romano amparo protection against the new boundary survey.[65]

What Was to Be Done about the Judiciary?

In the end, it did not matter how many pueblo representatives flocked to Fomento to petition for the survey of their old pueblo boundaries to resolve a variety of land and water conflicts. With hacienda owners claiming their constitutional right to be heard in court, Fomento's surveys were not going to resolve the numerous existing conflicts. Indeed, in February 1912, the newspaper *El Imparcial* argued that one of the main reasons for spreading rural revolts was that the government had not fulfilled its promises. This, it claimed, was the "official cause of the recent uprisings in Chihuahua, Coahuila, San Luis Potosí, Durango, Zacatecas, Michoacán, Morelos, Puebla, Guerrero, Sonora, and Oaxaca."[66]

In this situation, several urban intellectuals—all no doubt aware of Zapata and Montaño's proposal to create special tribunals "at the triumph of the Revolution"—presented their own proposals to address the problem. For instance, at the Liberal Party convention in April 1912, Eduardo Fuentes proposed creating an "equity tribunal" (*tribunal de equidad*) to resolve land restitutions; its decisions would be definitive and not subject to appeal.[67] Then, in October 1912, Congressman Juan Sarabia of the Twenty-Sixth Legislature coauthored a proposal with

Fuentes and Antonio Díaz Soto y Gama, all members of the Agrarian Commission of the "Extreme Left" of the Liberal Party. The bill maintained that many illegal land transactions had the trappings of legality, particularly cases in which villagers had sold their communal lands. The bill's authors suggested setting aside whether such sales had been legal, saying, "If each one of the dispossessed makes a claim at the federal and state courts, then there would be never-ending lawsuits." Recognizing that the federal government did not have jurisdiction over these matters, the bill would reform the Constitution to establish federal equity courts (*tribunales federales de equidad*).

In many ways, this proposal was a more sophisticated version of the Plan de Ayala. Amending Constitutional article 13 (which stated that in Mexico, except for military courts, no one could be judged by special tribunals) would empower these federal equity courts to resolve without delay—based only on proof of possession and of seizure—the restitution of landholdings, water resources, or woodlands to pueblos, Indian groups, or small-property owners who had been despoiled of their properties by means of physical or moral violence, including baldío claims that had not respected continuous possession rights. The new courts would have the right to pay compensation to third parties who possessed these lands in good faith, as in cases where lands were purchased from someone who had claimed them illegally.

The reasons for the need to circumvent the existing judiciary were, in the words of Sarabia, Fuentes, and Díaz Soto y Gama, a "lack of faith in judges and because those in charge of agrarian justice, rather than following formulaic and lengthy procedures, should be obliged to make a quick examination of the evidence and arguments of both parties in the courts." The new tribunals were needed because state and first-instance courts (the latter, in these congressmen's view, dominated by political chiefs) offered only a fictitious form of justice. "What if," they asked, "someone illegally appropriated land but then sold it to a third person?" The third person would become a possessor in good faith. To resolve this contradiction, the tribunals could condemn the seizure but grant the third-party compensation. "This way," they concluded, "there will be justice for all." Responding to potential accusations that the tribunals would be inherently biased against landowners, Sarabia and his coauthors argued that from the moment all tribunal rulings had to be reviewed by the Supreme Court, fairness would be guaranteed.[68]

Had Sarabia and his coauthors' ideas on agrarian tribunals been influential in the future Constitutionalist movement, perhaps the 1917 Constitution would have allowed the federal executive to establish special agrarian tribunals (anticipating the 1992 reforms by eight decades)—in the same way that article 123 created federal labor conciliation and arbitration boards.[69] But it would be another congressman from the same Twenty-Sixth Legislature who, a few years later, would play a more prominent role in the Constitutionalist ranks. That congressman was Luis Cabrera.[70]

In December 1912, two months after the legislative intervention by Sarabia and his colleagues, Cabrera criticized Fomento's circulars in a famous speech to Congress on the reconstruction of the pueblos' ejidos. He asked, "What would be more natural than that, after the triumph of the [Madero] revolution that promised justice, one would implement the revindication of usurped lands? Fomento accepted the revindication system. It invited all population centers with revindication claims to state approximately what extent of territory they had in earlier time periods and to identify these lands in order to see if it was possible to make a revindication effort." This, however, had not been possible because, according to Cabrera, "in 90 percent of the cases, [hacienda] lands had titles that appeared to be legitimate even when they were not, and therefore villagers could not entrust their restitution to luck or to the uncertainty of judicial procedures." Not even the expedited judicial procedures proposed by Sarabia and his coauthors could resolve the problem. For these reasons, Cabrera proposed not the restitution of pueblo lands but their "reconstitution," giving Fomento the right to expropriate, for public utility (*utilidad pública*), the landholdings needed to reconstruct the ejidos of pueblos that had lost them and to grant ejidos to those pueblos in need of them, or to augment the extent of the existing ones.[71]

Cabrera cautioned against confusing these expropriations with land restitution suits (what he called *reivindicación*). "The agrarian question," he argued, "is beyond the justice that consists of claims and judicial inquiries into the causes of dispossessions committed against the pueblos. The proletarian classes cannot wait for the completion of the extensive judicial procedures involved in inquiries regarding land seizures and dispossessions." If these matters *were* to be resolved, then the way in which they were handled would have to skirt the existing judicial system. In fact, he added, "There comes a point when historic injustices must be remedied outside the justice system."[72]

Interestingly, when former Fomento Minister Hernández was questioned about his opinion of Cabrera's speech, he responded, "In principle, I believe the initiative regarding the reconstitution and restitution of the pueblos' ejidos is good . . . and if it manages to authorize the executive to undertake this reconstitution and restitution, I think it will yield good results."[73]

While the federal judiciary, following the 1857 Constitution, blocked villagers' efforts to restitute pueblo lands according to Fomento's 1912 circulars, Zapatistas sidestepped the judiciary in the regions they controlled, and several radical legislators debated how the executive could resolve "the agrarian question" outside the court system. These radical proposals could hardly have prospered in a country with a judiciary that had for a century protected its jurisdiction over contentious land matters. But when a high-ranking military officer, General Victoriano Huerta, assassinated Madero on 22 February 1913 and the serving justices of the Supreme Court did not step down after the coup, the judiciary lost all credibility and Carranza shut it down in August 1914.[74] The discredit into which the judicial branch fell left a huge vacuum that the Zapatistas, and later the Constitutionalists, promised to fill by restituting pueblo lands by executive fiat.

3

The Zapatista Land Reform, 1911–1916

> These dimensions of agrarian conflict received less attention in an older agrarian history mainly interested in hacienda-peasant relations, and before we set agrarian history completely aside, the new political and social history will need to take this localized and internal conflict more fully into account.
> —William Roseberry, "El estricto apego a la ley"

As thousands of villagers throughout Mexico were taking advantage of the fall of the Díaz regime to file land claims with the de la Barra and Madero governments, in Morelos a revolutionary movement under Emiliano Zapata's leadership allowed pueblo representatives with colonial land and water titles to take back their usurped lands immediately. In the early years, military chiefs acting as first-instance judges provisionally restituted pueblo lands. Later, in response to complaints about favoritism and abuse of power, the General Headquarters of the Liberating Army of the South and Center (henceforth General Headquarters) became the highest judicial authority ruling on restitution suits. As problems and challenges continued to mount, a newly created Ministry of Agriculture and Colonization began to play an increasing role in land reform. With its agrarian commissions led by *ingenieros agrónomos* (agronomists, or engineers with surveying skills) charged with measuring and drawing pueblos' boundaries based on their colonial titles, the ministry assumed the role of second-instance court—and issued final verdicts. Landowners would have to file any subsequent claims with "the special tribunals established after the revolution's triumph."[1]

Supplanting the judiciary with the Ministry of Agriculture and Colonization, however, turned out to be more complicated than expected, because the revolutionaries soon ran into the same obstacles that nineteenth-century judges had encountered. If the Zapatista leadership believed that granting restitutions would be as easy as marking the boundaries found in pueblos' old titles and maps, they soon found that many village representatives did not have titles—or, when they did, the title's boundaries were often vague and imprecise, frequently overlapping with those of neighboring pueblos and thus triggering or reviving intervillage feuds. To overcome such problems, the Zapatistas would grant temporary repartos (managed by elected village caretakers) and leave final resolutions for after "the triumph of the Revolution."[2] Temporary repartos privileged the idea of equality over colonial rights by distributing all arable land in soon-to-be-titled parcels for heads of family (following nineteenth-century disentailment and federal public lands laws), while leaving common-use pasturelands under the administration of pueblo representatives or municipal officials, and placing woodlands and water resources largely under the authority of the Ministry of Agriculture and Colonization.

Early Zapatista Restitutions and Grants

In San Miguel Anenecuilco, Zapata's birthplace, pueblo representatives had been embroiled in a legal dispute with the neighboring El Hospital hacienda since the middle of the nineteenth century.[3] The dispute was about not only land rights but also use rights and respect for colonial agreements between the pueblo and neighboring haciendas.[4] As in so many other cases, in the early part of the nineteenth century Anenecuilco villagers had signed powers of attorney authorizing village leaders to represent the pueblo in all judicial matters. These leaders collected money to send commissions to the National Archives in Mexico City to seek copies of their land titles and to hire lawyers, and they presented their clams to the courts, prefects, governors, and President Porfirio Díaz himself. When village elders elected Zapata as Anenecuilco's council president in September 1909, legend has it that he and council secretary Francisco Franco spent eight days cloistered in the village church reading the pueblo's titles, even commissioning a Náhuatl speaker to translate some of the old documents.⁵ During this time, Zapata became convinced that the documents they possessed substantiated Anenecuilco's land claims. Moreover, on one of the journeys that village representatives made to Mexico City, lawyer Francisco Serralde reviewed their documents and allegedly concluded that their land titles not only upheld the six hundred varas granted to Anenecuilco during colonial times but also gave the village rights to some of the disputed lands under the laws of continuous possession.⁶ With these legal assurances, Anenecuilco representatives asked the governor to allow them to cultivate lands still in dispute with the El Hospital hacienda, now that the rainy season was upon them, with the promise that they would respect the rights of whoever turned out to be the legitimate owner. Around mid-1910, after all attempts at negotiations with hacienda owners had failed, Zapata and eighty armed men rode to the Llano del Huajar fields, where several villagers from Villa de Ayala were farming on plots they rented from the hacienda. The armed party chased the renters off the land, and Zapata distributed the parcels among his men.⁷

At the end of 1910, when he was already a regional authority in Morelos, Zapata distributed individual parcels of disputed lands to villagers from Villa de Ayala, Moyotepec, and Anenecuilco. "In each disputed area," Womack writes, "Zapata had the hacienda fences taken down, conferred with the local farmers, and assigned lots."⁸ In March 1911, when Francisco I. Madero called for an armed revolt to overthrow President Díaz, regional leaders in Morelos, including Zapata, joined the rebellion under the leadership of Pablo Torres Burgos.⁹ Later that same year, after government troops killed Torres Burgos, Zapata was named general and became commander of the Maderista movement in Morelos.¹⁰ Under his leadership, "armed groups of sharecroppers and poor farmers began invading fields in the central and eastern districts of the state."¹¹ And by the summer, "land was indeed being taken, as the campesinos of many villages, presumably with Zapata's at least tacit approval, occupied territory they claimed, just as Zapata had done before the rebellion."¹²

When Zapata broke with Madero in November 1911, he began to lead his own revolution—and for this he needed his own agrarian program.[13] He and Otilio Montaño summoned all the allied revolutionary chiefs to Puebla to sign the Plan de Ayala (see chapter 2), which allowed those pueblos and citizens with titles to fields, woodlands, and water resources that had been unjustly appropriated by landowners to sidestep the judiciary, immediately reclaim their property, and defend it—arms in hand.[14] As Zapata's sphere of influence spread during 1912 from Morelos and southwestern Puebla to the Federal District (Distrito Federal), Mexico State, Guerrero, and, to a lesser extent, Hidalgo and Oaxaca, villagers pledged allegiance to his movement and attempted to settle their long-standing land conflicts outside the court system. In Mexico State, for example, San Martín Malinalco residents wrote to General Genovevo de la O to inform him that the Jalmolonga hacienda had long ago invaded their lands, and that their forefathers had spent a great deal of money trying to defend their titles in the courts. They held a viceregal title that allowed them to demonstrate the precise areas the hacienda had invaded, and on that basis they petitioned de la O for the right to farm these lands. In exchange, they promised to fight the government when necessary.[15]

In addition to waging bloody battles that would determine the balance of power between the Zapatista Liberating Army and the armed forces of Madero (and, later, of Huerta and Carranza), military chiefs took on the role of first-instance judges. They had to interpret—regardless of their own degree of literacy—pueblo titles and maps and determine the rightful owners.[16] In Morelos, for example, Zapata allowed General de la O to take possession of lands that belonged to Santa María Ahuacatitlán "in accordance with the pueblo's titles and maps." If interim governor General Francisco Leyva disagreed with the hacienda takeover, Zapata instructed, then de la O was to "resolve the matter with arms in hand."[17] When Amayuca pueblo leaders claimed that the Tizantes and Chiltepec haciendas had seized lands for which they held primordial titles, Zapata ordered de la O to resolve the matter "following the Plan de Ayala, which gives revolutionary chiefs the authorization to grant pueblos the possession of the lands that were their property."[18] Likewise, in Mexico State, San Martín Malinalco residents asked General de la O to grant them permission to cultivate the pueblo lands invaded by the Jalmolonga hacienda. They explained that first their fathers, and then they themselves, had spent much money in the courts trying to prove—with documents in hand—that they were the rightful owners of several areas invaded by the hacienda.[19]

Early on, the Revolutionary Junta of the State of Morelos (headed by Emiliano and his brother Eufemio Zapata, Montaño, and other chiefs) became the highest judicial authority handling pueblo land restitutions. In April 1912 the Revolutionary Junta conducted a ceremony celebrating the restitution of Ixcamilpa's (Puebla) lands. In what is now considered the first Zapatista land restitution, we know that although the Plan de Ayala allowed pueblos and citizens with titles to recover their usurped lands immediately, villagers nevertheless had to present a formal petition to the Revolutionary Junta for the restitution of their lands, display their titles, and prove that the current landowners had seized them illegally. The junta, rather than the established courts, would issue a verdict and, if favorable, grant villagers permission to "enter into possession of the lands, montes, and water resources that belong to them and have belonged to them since colonial times, upheld by the legitimate colonial titles of New Spain, today Mexico." Villagers could then draw boundaries in accordance with their maps.[20]

In the spring of 1913 Zapata "reorganized the rebel high command as the Revolutionary Junta of the Center and South of the Republic." A few months later he issued instructions for military chiefs and officials, including directives regarding land reform.[21] One set of instructions stated: "The pueblos in general should take possession of their lands as long as they have their corresponding titles and as indicated by the Plan de Ayala; and chiefs and officials will grant the pueblos their moral and material support in order to fulfil the dispositions of the Plan de Ayala, if and when the pueblos solicit such help."[22]

Regarding these instructions, Womack notes, "Most remarkable was the decentralization of authority to carry out the agrarian reform prescribed in article 6 of the Ayala plan. Before, it seems that only the Morelos junta could review villagers' titles and restore their lands; and only in one case, in Ixcamilpa, Puebla, had the junta formally done so. But now officers in the field were to lend their 'moral and material support' to villages presenting titles and filing reclamations."[23] In practice, however, these instructions were less about decentralizing authority than they were about imposing order and hierarchy. They were a directive to military chiefs to lend their armed assistance when they were asked to do so, but not to meddle in pueblo affairs unless requested.[24] Moreover, the instructions did not cancel the underlying premise that a higher authority had to ratify the restitution. This becomes clear in a later communication, when Zapata authorized San Antonio Acahualco (Mexico State) villagers to "immediately take possession of their usurped lands, but only if it is your legitimate property. If to repossess these lands you require the help of the armed forces, then go to the nearest chief of the Liberating Army, showing him this letter, so that he provides the necessary assistance. Opportunely, the Minister of Agriculture will legalize the possession."[25]

Almost inevitably, Zapatista military chiefs ran into unanticipated problems as they acted to restore pueblo lands. For instance, hacienda land takeovers frequently triggered or revived intervillage boundary disputes.[26] As villagers invaded hacienda lands, they often trespassed on what neighboring pueblos considered their ancestral lands and water resources. In one early example from 1911, the Cuautla municipal president informed Zapata of the conflicts that had been sparked when residents from one pueblo invaded the lands and water resources of another. He reported that he had "tried to resolve the difficulties that, on account of the triumph of the cause, have arisen between some pueblos, because residents from one pueblo, claiming to have better rights, have seized the lands of others, and it is therefore a complete disorder."[27] In Mexico State, San Juan Xochiaca authorities complained to General de la O that San Simón el Alto residents had invaded their farmlands, pasturelands, and woodlands. They claimed that this invasion reversed an 1872 court decree "that protected their fundo legal

Zapatista Land Reform 81

and additional lands."[28] Also in Mexico State, Acatzingo representatives complained to de la O that neighboring villagers had occupied their lands. For years, they said, they had defended their lands against the potentially encroaching Tenería hacienda, which had been unable "to take away the rights of this oppressed pueblo." Now, however, they confronted an invasion from neighboring villagers.[29]

Revolutionary chiefs also had to resolve complaints by small landowners whose parcels fell within pueblos' old boundaries. In Morelos, for instance, twenty Atlacholoaya residents complained that Colonel Modesto Rangel had distributed irrigated fields to which they held property titles.[30] And in Guerrero, Olinalá resident Valentino Hernández complained to Zapata that he and his five sons had long worked a land parcel that General Remigio Cortés wanted to seize.[31] In fact, these problems were so widespread in Guerrero that Lieutenant Colonel José L. Tapia, following the Plan de Ayala, instructed Ahuatepec representatives to "proceed to take possession of the aforementioned lands," but cautioning them "not to overstep the title limits [and] always respect the properties that sympathetic villagers had legally acquired."[32]

Furthermore, pueblo land restitution procedures created conflicts between villagers and former hacienda renters and sharecroppers. In the famous mid-1910 takeover of the El Hospital hacienda lands, for example, Zapata and his men chased off neighboring Villa de Ayala residents who had been renting from the hacienda.[33] Also in Morelos, Ocuituco residents, who claimed to have titles and a map for several fields seized by the Santa Clara hacienda, fought with neighboring Metepec villagers who had been renting these pasturelands from the hacienda for many years. Metepec representatives protested that if the lands were taken from them, they would lose their entire livelihood.[34] And in Mexico State, Pachuquilla residents took possession of Jaltepec hacienda lands that Almoloya residents had been renting.[35]

Some matters were simply too complicated for military chiefs to resolve, and, following the Plan de Ayala, they counted on a future justice system that would serve as a second-instance court. In Guerrero, land restoration was particularly complex because villagers often petitioned for the restoration of lands that had been disentailed and then legally sold. In one such case, Coachimalco village leaders petitioned General Otilio Montaño for the return of lands "adjudicated" by the residents of neighboring pueblos.[36] In these situations, determining which land sales had been illegal was a difficult matter. For example, when Colonel Trinidad A. Paniagua, military chief of the Zaragoza district, measured the Totolapan pueblo boundaries based on their colonial titles, he took land from José Sánchez, who held one of these "adjudication" titles. Paniagua claimed Sánchez had acted in bad faith because one could not adjudicate pueblo lands. He also declared, however, that the boundary measurements were merely provisional, and that Sánchez could claim his right to compensation at the special tribunals established after "the triumph of the Revolution." Paniagua reminded those present at the boundary survey that soon "the matter would be placed on the scales of justice."[37]

In late 1913 or early 1914 the Revolutionary Junta became General Headquarters, a military authority that also took charge of political, economic, and social affairs.[38] As much as Zapata might have wanted pueblos to manage land restitutions autonomously, General Headquarters became deeply involved in these matters as it responded to hundreds of complaints about military chiefs' widespread corruption and favoritism. Many chiefs abused their power, taking the best lands for themselves and their closest allies. In Morelos, Coatetelco residents reported to Zapata that military chief Florencio Ponciano had assassinated a village representative in charge of land distribution and threatened to do the same to others.[39] Residents also complained about being excluded from Colonel Modesto Rangel's distribution of farming rights to the El Puente hacienda.[40] Two months later General Headquarters ordered Rangel not to get involved in the distribution of Chiconcuac hacienda lands, calling him "a man without conscience who only tries to profit and never acts with justice."[41] And in Mexico State, ninety Zumpahuacán villagers protested they did not want Colonel Castañeda intervening in land distribution because "he is a traitor."[42]

Hacienda Land Confiscations

Land restitution was the Zapatista movement's central goal, but it was not the only one. The Plan de Ayala had promised villagers whose pueblos had not lost land to neighboring estates but which were nonetheless landless—described in article 7 of the Plan as "the immense majority of Mexican pueblos and citizens who are owners of no more than the land they walk on"—that they, too, would receive land from expropriated haciendas.[43] In expropriating private property, Zapata and Montaño followed nineteenth-century legal precedent. The 1857 Constitution allowed state legislatures to expropriate land for public utility (mainly for the construction of roads and railways) so long as they offered prior compensation; and the Plan de Ayala proposed to seize, with prior compensation, a third of the lands belonging to powerful landowners who monopolized agricultural resources. Just as the program of the Mexican Liberal Party (founded in 1906 by Ricardo Flores Magón and others in opposition to Porfirio Díaz) had expanded the concept of public utility to include the broader concept of "benefits for all and not only a few," the Plan de Ayala broadened the right of expropriation for public utility to include "prosperity and well-being."[44]

The Plan de Ayala also allowed Zapatistas to nationalize the properties of the "enemies of the Revolution," whom they defined as "landlords, científicos [the label attached to Díaz's senior advisers], or caciques who opposed the present plan directly or indirectly."[45] This would be done to pay for war indemnifications and pensions for the widows and orphans of those who died fighting for the Plan de Ayala.[46] To justify land nationalization without compensation, Montaño, a great admirer of the nineteenth-century Reforma heroes, especially President Benito Juárez, explained that Zapatistas would follow the Liberal privatization laws regarding ecclesiastical property decreed by "the immortal Juárez"—a reference to the federal law of 12 July 1859 (and its regulatory law of 13 July 1859) nationalizing church property.[47] This radical law argued that because ecclesiastical property had always belonged to "the Nation," once sold, the church would not receive compensatory payment and all profits would go to the state treasury.⁴⁸ Moreover, the 1859 law gave the executive the right to expropriate land without judicial involvement. Following this precedent Manuel Palafox Ibarrola, the person most responsible for the reorganization and centralization of General Headquarters, later stated, "For the nationalization of the properties of the enemies of the Revolution, there will be no special tribunals . . . not now and not after the triumph of the cause because, as the Plan de Ayala states, special tribunals will only be established for land restitution cases."⁴⁹

Exactly when the Zapatistas started expropriating hacienda lands is unclear. The February 1914 instructions to distribute the lands belonging to enemies of the revolution mention an October 1913 law that no one has yet located. Brunk argues that the existence of this law meant that Zapata authorized the seizure of enemy property "earlier than Womack . . . recognizes." Moreover, there is a difference between the takeover of haciendas' sugarcane mills by the revolutionary chiefs (a topic not addressed in this book) and the distribution of hacienda lands as parcels to landless villagers.⁵⁰ In fact, the Zapatista leadership might have authorized the first hacienda land takeovers when it became clear that the land received by the pueblos as restitutions was insufficient to grant plots to all residents needing land. In November 1912, for example, Tecomatlán (Puebla) representatives informed General de la O that "the 600 varas of fundo legal that the Spaniards granted the pueblo are not sufficient for the sustenance of resident families." They therefore asked him to distribute to them enough hacienda lands to meet their needs.⁵¹

Regardless of the timing, hacienda land takeovers were plagued by favoritism and attempts at personal gain. In Puebla, for instance, Texcalapa hacienda residents, sharecroppers, and renters informed Zapata they had had good relations with the hacienda's owners for the past seventy-five years. They had paid good salaries, had not charged them rent on their homes, had allowed them to gather wood on the montes, and in general had treated them with consideration. In 1914, however, Zapata had given two Texcalapa sharecroppers, Felipe Sosa and Delfino Velasco, permission to manage the hacienda lands. Citing the Plan de Ayala, Sosa and Velasco made all villagers sign a document pledging their allegiance to the Zapatista cause, but they then brought in outsiders, some from as far away as Oaxaca, who took their lands. These strangers, the villagers complained to Zapata, seemed intent on "despoiling us of our rights, our labor, and our crops, and even charging rent on our lands." As many as 142 men and 22 widows signed a letter in which they appealed for Zapata's protection and threatened to take up arms against the two men (Sosa and Velasco) they called caciques. The chief of the Reyes Márquez brigade forwarded the letter to Zapata with a note saying he was concerned about a potential uprising. In response, General Headquarters sent the following instructions: "The Texcalapa neighbors should take possession of the irrigated and rainfed lands and cultivate them without having to pay any contribution to Felipe Sosa or Delfino Velasco, who, like all other neighbors, will each obtain one parcel of land to farm on."[52]

One of the first questions that arose about expropriating hacienda lands was whether to seize all lands or only those that had been illegally appropriated. For example, Brigadier General Crispín Galeana, Zapatista military chief of the Morelos region of Guerrero, differentiated between confiscating legally and illegally acquired lands. His circular no. 5 of 19 May 1914 ordered all municipal presidents and district authorities in the area he controlled to "ignore all dispositions not dictated by this office or from the Chief of Arms, on the grounds that several revolutionary chiefs have incorrectly interpreted the Plan de Ayala because the lands that can be distributed according to this plan must either be vacant lands or *illegally* acquired lands. For now, this should be respected, and order should be kept. The reparto referred to here will be verified at the triumph of the Revolution." Galeana added that those who did not obey this disposition "would be severely punished."[53]

Much abuse of power occurred when dealing with small- and medium-sized properties.[54] The Plan de Ayala authorized the nationalization of properties held by "enemies of the Revolution," among which were caciques—a malleable term often used derogatorily in factional and intravillage conflicts. For instance, in Guerrero, Lieutenant Colonel José L. Tapia accused a man of being a cacique—and, thus, an enemy of the Revolution—and took his land. The municipal president, however, vouched for the fellow, saying that not only was he *not* a cacique but he also had receipts proving the man had made payments to the revolutionary forces.[55] Similarly in Puebla, Zapata instructed Celso Ramos, the municipal president of Xicotlán, to distribute "enemy property" in parcels to sixty-two individuals. Ramos later informed Zapata that he had conducted the distribution (*repartición*) of lands to all the sons of the pueblo—not just to heads of family but also to orphans and widows. He justified taking these fields by saying that the owners sided with the enemy government and their sons had volunteered in the federal army. Ramos explained that they were "not hacendados or científicos, but they have been caciques." In an unanticipated turn of events, the so-called caciques, backed by Zapatista Colonel Rosalino Mendoza, then challenged the reparto. It became so unclear who "the enemy" was that the new municipal president, Ezequiel Herrera, had to ask Zapata to judge which of the two factions was in the right.[56]

Revolutionary Engineers and the Professionalization of the Zapatista Agrarian Reform

With hundreds of villagers complaining to Zapata about abuse of power and corruption in the restitution and granting of land, the urban professionals who joined the Zapatista movement "engineered an official agrarian reform."[57] And they did so much earlier than it has been previously assumed.[58] The main architect of this reform was Manuel Palafox, a former engineering student from Puebla who traveled "as a salesman and accountant for companies in various parts of the Republic, from Oaxaca to Sinaloa." In October 1911 Palafox, representing the owner of the Tenango hacienda, met with Zapata to try to bribe him.[59] Although it is unclear to historians precisely why he stayed and began to assist the movement, Palafox came to be, according to Womack, the most important Zapatista secretary.⁶⁰ He served as secretary of the Revolutionary Junta of the South and Center of the Republic in the spring of 1913, secretary of General Headquarters in late 1913 or early 1914, Zapatista minister of agriculture and colonization in the fall of 1914, and minister of agriculture and colonization of the Aguascalientes Convention government in 1915.⁶¹ "As he coordinated plans and dispatched instructions," Womack explains, "rebel operations went on in clearer patterns."⁶²

According to Womack, Palafox probably began authoring Zapatista decrees as early as the summer of 1913. But the main features of his program began to appear most clearly in February 1914—namely, his efforts to bring order and fairness to a process that was riddled with abuse of power, corruption, and favoritism. He did so by adopting the procedures found in Liberal laws for the boundary measurement and privatization of communal lands, very likely suggested to him by one or more agronomists.⁶³ For instance, Palafox's February 1914 "Instructions for the Distribution of Lands Owned by Enemies of the Revolution" began by explaining the difference between pueblo land restitutions and grants from nationalized properties.⁶⁴ They stipulated that "the lands will be returned to the villages and citizens who have the corresponding titles to their properties, as indicated by the Plan de Ayala, and the rest—the lands that are not the legitimate property of the enemies of the Revolution—will be subdivided and distributed in parcels to the pueblos who need them."

Expropriated lands were to be distributed on the basis of equality and need. Echoing almost to the letter nineteenth-century Liberal privatization guidelines or the more recent federal public lands laws found in Madero's 1912 circulars, the instructions specified that parcels had to be of equal value (accounting for both size and quality) to achieve fair distribution.⁶⁵ To avoid favoritism, the distribution of parcels (reparto) was to be conducted by raffle.⁶⁶ Those in charge of land distribution had to prepare a map of the allotted parcels, with the names of the beneficiaries, so that General Headquarters could review and authorize them.⁶⁷ No one could acquire more than one parcel for the sustenance of a nuclear family.[68] Once Headquarters approved the map and declared the distribution had been conducted justly and without favoritism, Zapatista officials would give each beneficiary a title.[69] Moreover, the revolutionary repartos in Zapatista regions contained safeguards for villagers: land granted to villages or individuals could not be sold, and all future sale contracts would be void.[70] Palafox could have adopted these safeguards from the nineteenth-century Liberal reparto laws that contained temporary protections for Indians and the poor, or perhaps from Constitutionalist chief Lucio Blanco's expropriation of the Los Borregos hacienda in Matamoros, Tamaulipas, which forbade the transfer of properties to third parties for a determined period (see chapter 4).[71] According to Womack, Blanco had "recently earned a reputation for agrarian sympathies by expropriating a local hacienda and dividing it among its peons."[72]

Heading the program of land distribution would be Palafox's Ministry of Agriculture. In September 1914 Palafox issued two new directives: a decree on the nationalization of properties belonging to enemies of the Revolution, and instructions to the Morelos Agrarian Commissions.[73] Together these laws sought to create an orderly land distribution that began with restoring pueblo lands based on primordial titles, followed by Ministry of Agriculture officials deciding which of the remaining lands would be confiscated and granted to landless villagers (as well as to the orphans and widows of those who had died in combat). When it came to land restitution, Palafox instructed the agrarian commissions to summon all campesinos immediately so they could present their land claims and agronomists could restore lands to pueblos and individuals according to pueblos' land titles. In cases where villagers did not have titles, ministry officials would assume judicial functions and decide which party was the rightful owner. Agrarian commissions were to resolve all conflicts, thus replacing military chiefs in this role.[74] In fact, Palafox's September 1914 regulations clearly stated that "lawsuit cases between pueblos or between individuals are to be submitted to the Ministry of Agriculture for their study and ruling."[75]

When it came to land restitution, Palafox initially suggested in September 1914 that land titles would be considered valid if they had been issued before 1856. This was the first time a Zapatista document made restitution time-conditional. Palafox or the agronomists advising him might have been inspired by ideas circulating in revolutionary circles that originated in Andrés Molina Enríquez's *Los grandes problemas nacionales* (1909), which blamed the loss of pueblo lands on the implementation of the 1856 Lerdo law.[76] Albeit unknown to Palafox, enforcement of this suggestion would probably have invalidated most of the pueblos' land restitution claims in Morelos.

Zapatistas at the time (and most historians until the late 1980s) believed that hacienda encroachment on pueblo lands was a relatively recent occurrence. In 1988, however, Horacio Crespo made a crucial discovery: the territorial boundaries of most haciendas in the Morelos sugar-producing region had already been drawn by the end of the seventeenth century. This expansion coincided with a century-long demographic catastrophe that severely depopulated Indian pueblos. Thus, when the pueblos' populations gradually recovered in the following century, haciendas and pueblos clashed over the control of land and water resources in what Crespo describes as "conflicts that continued with increasing virulence throughout the nineteenth century."[77] Whereas many Morelos pueblos did have colonial titles to land, numerous individuals had legalized sales and purchases in the following centuries by registering their lands, paying taxes, and often selling parts of them to third parties. Consequently, by the end of the nineteenth century and the beginning of the twentieth, under civil code rules, these properties had become legitimately private.

So how does Crespo explain the late nineteenth- and early twentieth-century pueblo land and water losses in the sugar-producing regions of Morelos? Haciendas commonly controlled lands of three different types: high-quality irrigated lands for commercial crops and, to a lesser extent, private consumption; low-quality rain-fed lands that were leased out to landless villagers, thereby ensuring that hacienda owners would have access to enough labor to cultivate their commercial crops; and a reserve space.[78] At the end of the Porfiriato, with the growth of the national market and the opening of world markets for the sale of products like sugar, hacienda owners extended irrigation systems for commercial agriculture onto rain-fed rental lands. This shift coincided with the growth of the cattle industry both on haciendas and in villages. Moreover, starting in 1900 with the fall of sugar prices, hacienda owners sought to increase productivity and lower their costs by continuing to expand irrigation systems and commercial agriculture onto rental lands, thus displacing thousands of tenants who were not fully absorbed into the expanding hacienda economy.[79] According to Crespo, the crisis of the Porfirian political system at the end of 1910 and the beginning of 1911 coincided with the loss of rain-fed lands for thousands of poor renters (*temporaleros*), lands that many of them had been cultivating for generations.[80]

That 1856 would not serve as a reliable marker for the restitution of pueblo lands was, however, only one of many problems that Palafox would try to sidestep.

The Aguascalientes Convention's Land Reform under Palafox

As allies with the Villistas in the Aguascalientes Convention government (December 1914 to the summer of 1915), and with Eulalio Gutiérrez, Roque González Garza, and Francisco Lagos Cházaro as successive Convention presidents, Zapata governed Morelos and implemented his agrarian reform there and in neighboring states.[81] To pursue their land reform projects, the Conventionist forces adopted Palafox's idea of hiring agronomy students and graduates of the National School of Agriculture in Mexico City. Most of these agronomists had been supporters of Madero's efforts to oust Díaz, and they now joined the revolutionary armies to offer their technical know-how.[82] In Chihuahua, Minister of Agriculture Manuel Bonilla believed that pueblo land restitution should be handled by the judiciary. He recruited twelve agronomists to aid with technical matters (such as the study of the state's soil and water resources) and gather information that would benefit his agricultural development programs.[83] In Morelos, Palafox set up

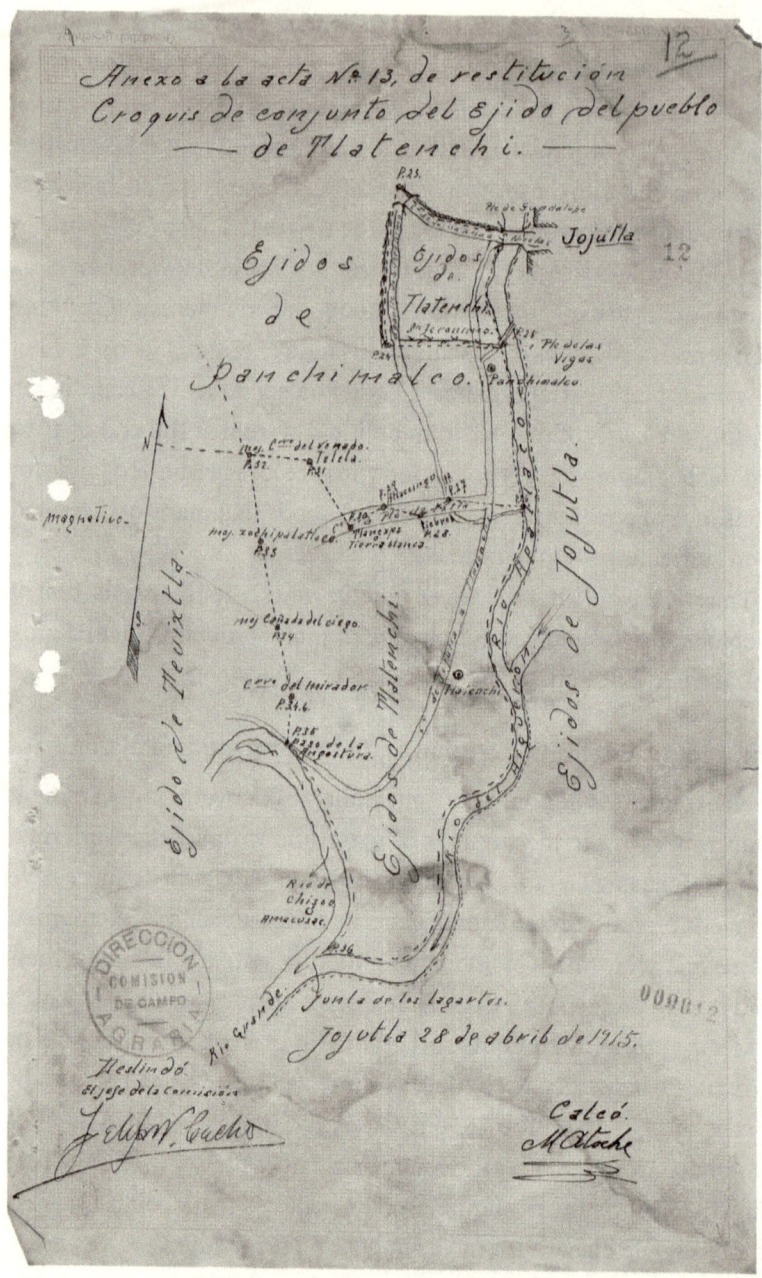

Fig. 4. Zapatista restitution map, 28 April 1915. Archivo General Agrario, Acervo Histórico, exp. 23/3052, leg. 1, plano único, San Miguel Huajintla, Amacuzac, Morelos.

agrarian commissions in the districts of Cuernavaca, Cuautla, Jojutla, Jonacatepec, Yautepec, and Tetecala.[84] Archival documents show that Palafox managed to create agrarian commissions for the Federal District, Guerrero, Mexico State, and Puebla, and that he was planning on creating commissions for Hidalgo and Oaxaca.[85]

Intervillage Conflicts Resolved with Temporary Repartos

The agrarian commissions' greatest challenges were intervillage conflicts. Almost all population centers in the Zapatista multistate region had some type of border dispute with their neighbors—some of them going back decades or even centuries.[86] Land distribution often revived these disputes when revolutionary chiefs or agrarian commissions distributed hacienda lands that two or more population centers claimed as their own.[87] In Mexico State, for example, Acatzingo representatives explained to General de la O that they had successfully defended their lands against the potentially encroaching Tenería hacienda, only to have them invaded by neighboring villagers after the former hacienda owners had fled.[88] And in Puebla, Tzicatlán residents complained to Zapata that after having won a suit against the Tenango hacienda (across the state border in Morelos), they now were being dispossessed by neighboring Axochiapan villagers.[89]

The greatest challenge for Zapatista leaders was ruling on the basis of colonial land titles. In nineteenth-century intervillage boundary disputes, plaintiffs and defendants had the same burden of proof, and the party with the stronger evidence in the form of land titles would in principle prevail. The Zapatista leadership followed this precedent, relying on evidence in the form of colonial titles. In many instances, however, there was simply no way to determine which party had the stronger case for land ownership because of diverse and overlapping land possession, use, and ownership rights (described in chapter 1).[90] For example, both Amilcingo and neighboring Huazulco had land titles, but Huazulco's did not define boundaries, whereas Amilcingo's did.[91] San Andrés Hueyapan had titles demarcating boundary lines "as legally required," but Tlacotepec's titles did not.[92] And when the Yautepec

Agrarian Commission was unable to draw boundary lines between Atlatlahucan and Oaxtepec, Chief Surveyor Rubio commented, "These problems continually surface, given the differences in boundaries that the primordial titles indicate."[93] Similarly in the Federal District, General Fortino Ayaquica reported to Zapata that he and his chiefs were having too many difficulties with the Xochimilco repartos and asked him to send an agrarian commission because, he wrote, "you well know we cannot do more than what is within our capacity, for if we set about recognizing the maps or documents from viceregal times for each village we would have to eliminate modern pueblos that now exist."[94]

Agronomist Marte R. Gómez came to the same conclusion. He observed that even though Tlacotepec (Morelos) villagers had primordial titles granting the pueblo one thousand varas from the church in the four cardinal directions, if the surveyors had followed these measurements, they would have had to include in their restitution half the plaza of the neighboring pueblo, Zacualpan de Amilpas. "Marking boundaries that corresponded with present-day reality was a triumph," Gómez declared retrospectively, and surveyors did so by "reducing the lands of Tlacotepec, so that Zacualpan was not left without anything."[95] What Gómez did not say was that the other village affected by the Tlacotepec titles was San Felipe Cuapexco, across the border in Puebla, where residents complained that the map the surveyors were using to demarcate Tlacotepec's property invaded their lands, for which they also had titles. In response, General Headquarters ordered the agrarian commission to demarcate Tlacotepec's boundaries only in Morelos, not in Puebla.[96]

Because of the extraordinary difficulties that Zapatista leaders encountered in their attempts to resolve boundary disputes, they agreed that they would postpone final resolution of these matters until after "the triumph of the Revolution."[97] In the meantime, they proposed temporary arrangements. In Morelos, when the Yautepec Agrarian Commission failed to draw boundary lines between Atlatlahucan and Oaxtepec, the Ministry of Agriculture and Colonization ordered villagers temporarily to cultivate land parcels on a first-come, first-served basis.⁹⁸ One surveyor reported that he had settled the conflicts between Tlacotepec and San Andrés Hueyapan and between San Bartolo and Temoac by negotiating agreements between them, "in the understanding that these are only for this present year and that next year they will recognize the boundaries drawn by this commission, in accordance with the titles and needs of each pueblo."⁹⁹ And General Brigadier Marcelino Rodríguez reported from his Zacualpan de Amilpas revolutionary camp that "when the agrarian commission drew the [Morelos] pueblos' boundaries, they had to augment or subtract part of their lands, whereas pueblos from neighboring Puebla did not get any lands and will be unable to farm. Therefore ... so as not to worsen the existing maize shortage, I have ordered that to avoid difficulties all pueblos should continue cultivating on the lands they farmed last year and, when the land division (fraccionamiento) is completed and the distributed plot titles are issued, this temporary provision will cease to have effect."¹⁰⁰

Privileging Equity over Colonial Property Rights

Zapatistas never gave up on the idea of restituting usurped pueblo lands. A letter from October 1914 signed by Zapata (but probably authored by Palafox) states that "most pueblos in the southern region have primordial titles that grant them rights to possess the lands that have been seized from them, even when these seizures are ages-old, and I understand that it is the same in the entire country. I tell you this because I have seen innumerable ancient pueblo titles."¹⁰¹ In practice, however, land restitutions and grants were difficult to differentiate and became conflated in the term "reparto." In Puebla, for example, Colonel Dolores Damián distributed lands on the Boquería hacienda. Here, even though it was a restitution, land distribution (repartos) had to be "provisional, equitable, and for the benefit of the poor."¹⁰² Also in Puebla, workers on the Texcalapa hacienda in Santiago Petlalcingo identified themselves as "heirs to these lands," but because they had no titles, Zapatista chiefs distributed land according to the hacienda's property perimeter rather than according to the pueblos' old boundaries—leaving it

Fig. 5. Minutes from the Tlatenchi (Morelos) Zapatista restitution, 11 April 1915. Archivo General Agrario, Acervo Histórico, exp. 23/3084, leg. 1, f. 5.

Torres, Juan Aviles, Apolonio Barron y José
Vergara

Con [ello] se termino el acta dándose lectura
a la [...] presencia de todos y firmaron de
conformidad.

Reforma, Libertad, Justicia y Ley

Enci[...]

No firmaron por no saber:
José Vergara
Eucario Velazquez
José Ruiz
Fran.co Beltran
Felinior de la Rosa
Modesto Franco
Cresto Vidal
Esteval Leon
Antonio Reyes
Juan Hernandez
Ramon Barrios
Fran.co Ortiz
Nilerio Sandoval
[Ti]mogdes Diaz
Nicolas Garcia
Gerardo Cardeños
Andres Torres
Fran.co Dimas
Fredencio Hernandez
Prosspero Peña
Julio Romero
Franquilino Iturbide
Angel Velazquez
Roman de la Rosa
Manuel Reyes

Por no saber firmar el Ayudante
J. Diaz

Pueblo [...]
Román Diaz

Miguel Torres

Juan B. Aviles

Apolo[nio] [...]
Remig[io] Cristoval [...]

Ger[...] Remijio Diaz

J[...] Crescenciano Diaz

Y[...] Yncente Gonzales

Silverio [...]

Eustaquio Cervantes
Felix [...]
[...] Machado
[...] Vazquez
[...] Melesio Marquez
Baile[...] Abascen
[...]arro Macario [...]
Gonzales Prefecto Rodriguez
[...]Rosa Fran.co Vidal Ricardo Diaz
Anto[nio] An[...]

unclear whether this had been a division of expropriated property into individual plots or the restitution of usurped pueblo lands that could be managed in whatever way the petitioners chose.[103]

Village representatives and military chiefs also suggested combining restitutions with land grants. For instance, when General Paniagua called for neighboring pueblos in Guerrero to present their land titles at his military camp, the Tlaquiltepec *comisario* (submunicipal official) and *principales* (village elders) argued that neighboring Huamuxtitlán had surplus lands that could be granted to them.[104] Similarly, after the agrarian commission in Mexico State had measured Tepexoyuca's old pueblo boundaries and while the villagers were waiting for Zapata to place boundary markers and issue "their communal title," they asked him for permission to harvest some small wheat fields on the Texcalco ranch, which was situated outside their property's boundaries.[105] And when granting the San Lucas del Pulque pueblo provisional possession of the lands, woodlands, and water resources that had been seized from the villagers by the San Lucas hacienda, General de la O added that because the hacienda owner had joined the Constitutionalists, he was also expropriating the entire property.[106]

So how did the Zapatistas manage situations in which pueblo land restitutions and grants from expropriated properties overlapped? Brunk makes a very important point when he notes that in July 1917 the Zapatista leadership drafted an agrarian law that gave "the goal of a rough equity among villages clear priority over any particular villager's titles to land."[107] Privileging equity over colonial rights to land had become their practice much earlier, especially when it came to arable land.

Arable Land

During the height of the Zapatista land reform effort (and not unlike the Liberal privatization of pueblo communal lands or the federal public lands laws), Zapatista leaders distributed arable land—both rain-fed and irrigated—in soon-to-be-titled individual parcels to heads of nuclear families (*jefes o cabezas de familia*). Surveyor Alfonso Cruz claimed to have authored the first regulations for agrarian commissions, including instructions on how to distribute land according to "the needs of the average campesino family, composed of six members." The "family parcel," he explained, should be large enough "for the sustenance of a campesino family, considering food, clothes, medical attention, modest periodic diversions, and a little savings."[108] To distribute family parcels with equity, villagers had to conduct a census. In one early example, the Agriculture Office of Mexico State's interim governor General Gustavo Baz stated that pueblos seeking land had to fulfill certain requirements: petitions had to be signed by three village elders, the municipal president, and the síndico; appeals had to include land titles and all available evidence regarding the claimed property; and villagers had to conduct a population census so that restituted lands could be divided into equal plots for all heads of family.[109]

Palafox probably intended that these parcels for heads of family would become private property. In January 1915 Palafox asked Zapata to order his military chiefs to provide assistance to surveyors so they could distribute land as soon as possible, according to the bylaws of his ministry and "in conformity with the wishes of the majority of the pueblo residents." His goal, he explained to Zapata, was to conduct the repartos of farmlands, woodlands, and water resources "with complete justice" so that entire pueblos could receive arable land without excluding anyone (taking into account absentee fighters so that they, too, could receive parcels), "until the Ministry of Agriculture has placed in the hands of each one of these new landowners the title to their corresponding parcel."[110]

Palafox's intentions as to whether cultivatable plots would become private property are less clear in his October 1915 law. Here Palafox explained that "the Nation" recognized the right of every Mexican to possess and cultivate a land parcel whose products would be enough to cover the needs of a (nuclear) family. Expropriated lands had to be divided into parcels and distributed—preferably to campesinos, renters, and sharecroppers. Municipal governments were obliged to carry out the law's dispositions, immediately giving pueblos and individuals possession of lands that belonged to them according to the law—with agrarian commissions correcting errors that might occur during the distribution. The Ministry of Agriculture and Colonization would send survey teams to measure these parcels properly, respecting pueblo lands and land exempted from expropriation. Land granted to villages or individuals could not, though, be sold or alienated in any way; property rights over land parcels granted by the General Headquarters could be bequeathed only to a family member, and land had to be cultivated or the beneficiaries would forfeit the parcel.[111] Given the similarities between Porfirian federal public lands laws, nineteenth-century state disentailment laws, and this October 1915 law, however, it is highly probable that Palafox ultimately planned to distribute arable lands as small private parcels for heads of family.[112]

In practice, and throughout 1915, the Zapatista land reform consisted of the distribution of arable land in parcels to the heads of family listed in a pueblo census. In Puebla, when Brigadier General F. Sabino Díaz distributed land in Tlalancaleca, he also sent the minister of agriculture and colonization a census of those who had rights to reparto lands, as well as the survey conducted by the agrarian commission. Only then could he ask the ministry's Sección de Fraccionamiento (Land Subdivision and Distribution Office) for authorization to distribute lands.[113] In Mexico State, Baz's Office of Agriculture had a very active Sección de Fraccionamiento. In its communication number 872, it instructed the Joquicingo municipal president: "If when marking boundary lines of the lands belonging to the pueblo it turns out that they are insufficient for the needs of the pueblo, this should be justified with a population census by family [and] they will receive what is missing by taking nationalized lands nearest to the pueblo."[114] In Morelos, Palafox directed municipal authorities to conduct a census of all residents (using the Ministry of Agriculture's blueprint) to distribute land "according to the needs of the pueblo." In Metepec, for instance, Palafox ordered Eusebio Salazar, chief of the Cuautla District agrarian commission, to "distribute enough lands for the needs of the residents, forming their ejido in such a way that each resident has his [or her] corresponding parcel."[115]

It is quite remarkable that later Zapatista laws, which were usually influenced by more radical urban advisers who opposed the idea of private property, continued to uphold Palafox's central tenets. For instance, the January 1917 instructions on the boundary marking, division, and distribution of ejidos continued to conflate restitutions and grants and to privilege equity over colonial land rights. Municipal representatives had to call a meeting with neighboring pueblo representatives and, according to the titles and testimonies, they had to draw boundaries between them and survey their ejidos (which in this case meant all former pueblo lands included in the primordial title). If all neighbors agreed with the boundaries, then they could be drawn. But if disputes arose, municipal representatives were to place temporary boundary markers, which would be settled later by an agrarian commission.

The next step was to conduct a census of a pueblo's families. The census questions included the names of all family members; whether the head of family was an agriculturalist or intended to be one; whether the family held properties, and if so, their extent and how they had been acquired; and whether any family member was an enemy of the Revolution. Census takers also had to identify widows and soldiers. On the basis of this survey, the nationalization and distribution of property could proceed. Lands belonging to the pueblos or those that they possessed would also be divided among impoverished *labradores* (agricultural laborers) and those who wished to dedicate themselves to agriculture. All arable lands, whether restituted, possessed by the pueblos, or confiscated, had to be divided into plots of equal size for all farmers.[116]

Common, Urban, and Public Property

Even as military chiefs and municipal officials distributed all agricultural lands as individual (and soon-to-be-titled) parcels, they left pasturelands for common use, created urban areas under municipal authority, and left montes and water resources for common and public use.

In Morelos, Ahuacatitlán hacienda peons received rain-fed land as individual parcels, while pasturelands were held in common "to avoid difficulties."[117] In Guerrero, Colonel José L. Tapia restored the Tlalixtaquilla pueblo lands "based on their primordial titles," distributed irrigated fields as individual parcels, and preserved pasturelands for common use.[118] And in Mexico State, General de la O's division engineers (Gonzalo Isunza, José Cervantes, and José J. Serrano) directed all procedures related to land restitution for San Antonio la Isla. Municipal officials presented to the surveyors their titles, several agreements signed by neighboring pueblos, and the minutes of the election held so that pueblo residents could choose their representatives from among the eldest and most knowledgeable members of the community. The municipal officials did so, they informed General Zapata, "following your recommendation to avoid all possible conflicts with neighboring villages, without invading their jurisdiction, always respecting their rights, as proven in the minutes and the map created by the ingenieros." Restituted lands included cultivated areas that they planned to distribute as individual parcels to the most impoverished residents. They would divide the rest of the lands into parcels for resident heads of household that still granted services to the Liberating Army, as well as to widows who had to support families with minor children. Finally, they would distribute parcels for all single adult men, "granting them economic independence and the ability to sustain their new families." While they waited for the titles "that the government of the Republic" would issue, the ayuntamiento would dispense temporary titles that prohibited the sale or taxation of the parcels. Before the reparto, however, they would set aside one portion for common pasturelands. Pueblo residents who had enough land to make a living would only have access to these common pasturelands.[119]

Zapatista leaders also planned to renew or create urban areas under municipal authority where needed. In Guerrero, for example, Colonel José L. Tapia traced the outline of the pueblo's fundo legal (urban site) measuring eight hundred meters square, sketching out where to place public buildings and then tracing the streets.[120] And in Mexico State, in the case of San Antonio la Isla mentioned earlier, the survey engineers decided, given that "many residents do not have roofs over their heads, something inhumane and incompatible with the triumph of the

Revolution," they had to create a new urban center (*colonia*) for one hundred homeless residents, all of whom would receive an urban lot by raffle. The surveyors had selected the most convenient and hygienic area, which, unfortunately, was on cultivated fields—meaning they would have to wait with the planning until after the harvest. The new urban site would be named "Colonia General Emiliano Zapata," and its streets would carry the names of generals, such as Genovevo de la O.[121]

Many villages in the Zapatista regions had for centuries to some extent preserved woodlands, which they held in common in one form or another and defended from neighboring villages, haciendas, and paper mills.[122] Residents depended on these lands to provide both firewood and wood used for other household needs. In pueblos such as Santa María Ahuacatitlán (Morelos), many residents made a living as charcoal merchants. When it came to village woodlands, Zapata was adamant about granting municipal authorities total autonomy. For example, in early February 1915 he reproached General de la O for having meddled in the management of woodlands: "Under no circumstance should you prohibit the Ocotepec [Morelos] pueblo and its surroundings to cut wood to sell to the railroad, because the objective of the Revolution is precisely to give possession to the pueblos of the lands, woodlands, and water resources they were despoiled of, and if you now forbid them to make whatever use of these resources that behooves them—not allowing them to cut wood and use its product for the sustenance for their families—that is equal to betraying the Revolution by overstepping its ideals."[123] And when Morelos chiefs forbade villagers from using lumber for building and manufacturing, General Headquarters issued a circular allowing these acts as a way "to help the people who are in such bad condition on account of the Revolution's consequences."[124]

Palafox, on the other hand, wanted the Ministry of Agriculture and Colonization to control excessive tilling and to preserve woodlands for future generations. In one instance, in response to news that in many pueblos villagers had destroyed the montes, he instructed Metepec's (Morelos) municipal authorities to inform villagers they could utilize

Zapatista Land Reform 103

the montes "with moderation, meaning that those engaged in felling should only cut mature and well-developed trees, protecting younger ones, and replanting new ones so that the monte is not destroyed."[125] Moreover, the 26 October 1915 agrarian law declared montes national property, "of which the Ministry of Agriculture will be in charge of inspection in the form it determines and which will be exploited in communal form by the pueblos to whose jurisdiction they belong."[126]

When it came to water resources, Alejandro Tortolero Villaseñor argues that it was "landowners' monopolisation of the state's abundant water resources [that] helped to make Morelos a focal point of the revolutionary upheaval."[127] By the end of the nineteenth century, haciendas in Morelos had control over most water resources. The federal government had granted hacendados numerous water concessions, and they had invested in technologically sophisticated hydraulic systems (including large canals, siphon aqueducts, and electric pumps) with which they could irrigate rain-fed lands they had previously rented out to (or that belonged to) neighboring villagers.[128] For instance, villagers from San Miguel Tlaltetelco claimed they had legitimate rights to land and water from the nearby volcano, but the Díaz government had granted concessions to these resources to powerful men such as Ángel Noriega Sánchez and later his son Francisco, owners of the Tamacoco mill, who then took control of the pueblo's water resources.[129] Huazulco residents complained to Zapata that when the Santa Clara hacienda owners rebuilt their *caja de agua* (small deposits that help regulate the flow of a river or canal), they reduced the pueblo's access to water, leaving them without enough to irrigate their parcels. Citing the Plan de Ayala, they petitioned Zapata for license to expand their water usage.[130] Five days later Zapata not only granted them permission to destroy the caja de agua the Santa Clara hacienda had built but also ordered the villagers to divide access to the water into equal parts with neighboring Temoac.[131]

At first, it was military chiefs and municipal officials who oversaw the administration of water resources. The task was complicated because municipal officials had to share water resources not just with all population centers within their territorial jurisdiction with some degree of equity, but also with the confiscated hacienda sugar mills and other factories operated by Zapatista military chiefs. In Morelos, when General de la O gave the Miacatlán municipal president access to water "for all villagers," the local official had to manage three different water resources—*and* he had to share them with the Miacatlán hacienda.[132] And in Puebla, San Miguel and San Antonio Cuautla residents complained to Zapata that General Fortino Ayaquica, the chief in charge of the San Bernardo hacienda, had deprived them of the potable water they had enjoyed before the revolution. In response, General Headquarters ordered the chief to divide the water into three equal parts for San Miguel, San Antonio Cuautla, and the hacienda.[133]

Oftentimes, military chiefs in charge of managing confiscated hacienda factories did not behave much better than had the former owners. As the following examples from Morelos show, there were constant complaints about hacienda managers not sharing water resources with neighboring villages. San Miguel and San Antonio Cuautla residents complained that Lieutenant Colonel Silvestre Pinzón did not share the water he controlled. General Headquarters had to instruct the chief's superior, General Saavedra, to make sure that the water was distributed in equal parts between the hacienda and the two pueblos.[134] Xoxocotla residents told General Headquarters that General Pedro Saavedra did not grant them enough water. Saavedra responded by saying that when he asked the villagers to clean the canal (*apantle*) that carried water from the hacienda to the pueblo, they did not cooperate—and furthermore, all they did was waste the water.[135]

Intervillage conflicts over water resources also abounded. In Morelos, for example, Ticumán residents complained that neighboring Atlihuayán villagers were not allowing them access to their ancient water resources.[136] In Puebla, Huilango villagers reported to Zapata that neighboring San Lucas Tulcingo residents not only had received a restitution of land and water resources large enough to irrigate their crops but also were trying to take water resources that had belonged to Huilango since antiquity.[137] Moreover, ayuntamiento officials often favored the head townships. When the Cuentepec (Morelos) municipal auxiliary petitioned the Miacatlán municipal president to grant them land, the latter replied that it would not be possible to do so because he had already distributed most of the lands to the cabecera and there was not enough water to irrigate more land parcels. If he were to distribute more lands, he would have to take water from the Miacatlán cabecera, leaving most residents there without enough water to irrigate their reparto lands.[138]

The equitable distribution of water was difficult even for trained engineers. When the agrarian commission distributed water from the Popocatepetl volcano's ice thaw to several pueblos in Morelos, they sidestepped Nepantla and Atlatlahucan villagers, who then complained to Palafox. A few months later, General Headquarters instructed the nearby Tamacoco paper mill to help. The mill needed to find a way to grant the villagers in Nepantla and Atlatlahucan enough water to satisfy their personal needs and those of their animals. To make this possible, the course of the river had to be diverted through a canyon.[139]

As problems with water resources mounted in the Zapatista region, the Ministry of Agriculture and Colonization tried to centralize its management of them.[140] The agrarian law of 26 October 1915 stated, "All water resources, regardless of their use, are declared national property, even those considered to come under the states' jurisdiction, without the need for any kind of compensation. In all use of water resources, agricultural needs will always have precedence, and only when these needs are satisfied will water be used for generating power and other uses. It is the exclusive jurisdiction of the Ministry of Agriculture and Colonization to issue bylaws regarding water."[141]

The Zapatistas never managed to fully implement their land reform. The Constitutionalists defeated the Villista allies in the north and confined the Zapatista movement to Morelos, a war-devastated state with many displaced, hungry, and impoverished residents. Most repartos remained temporary, and the Ministry of Agriculture and Colonization was not able to resolve many intervillage conflicts or grant permanent titles to arable land parcels. The Zapatistas were also unable to create the "special tribunals [to be] established after the triumph of the Revolution," where landowners could be heard and where intervillage conflicts might possibly be settled.

In the meantime, the Constitutionalists had begun their own land reform program. They, too, granted the executive jurisdiction over land restitutions and expropriations for land grants, and they made all beneficiaries of Zapatista repartos outside Morelos renew the process of applying for restitutions and grants, thus sending them back to the drawing board—but this time through the Constitutionalists' agrarian administration.

4

The Constitutionalist Land Reform in the Absence of the Judiciary, 1914–1917

> Varias ejecutorias insistieron que el procedimiento de dotación y restitución de ejidos era administrativo ... aunque en su esencia tenía carácter judicial o hacía las veces de un proceso judicial. [Several rulings insisted that the ejido grant and restitution procedure was administrative ... although in its essence it had a judicial nature or served as a judicial process.]
> —Lucio Cabrera Acevedo, *La Suprema Corte de Justicia durante los años constitucionalistas (1917–1920)*, vol. 1

With the Zapatistas conducting repartos in Morelos and in parts of neighboring states, and with several Constitutionalist generals and governors implementing their own reforms, Venustiano Carranza was compelled by circumstances to come up with his own land reform program. A landowner himself, Carranza rejected far-reaching redistributive initiatives based on the expropriation of large landed properties (*latifundios*). Instead, in early 1915 Carranza signed Finance Minister Luis Cabrera's law, which focused more narrowly on pueblo land and water restitutions and grants for subsistence agriculture. Despite Cabrera's earlier insistence on avoiding the revindication of usurped pueblo lands, the 6 January 1915 law granted Carranza's executive branch judicial authority over pueblo land restitutions. This was possible in part because, after the Constitutionalist army deposed Huerta and made its triumphant entrance into Mexico City in August 1914, Carranza— self-proclaimed "First Chief" of the Constitutionalist forces—shut down the Supreme Court and all district courts.[1]

Not only was the Carrancista land reform not negligible, as most scholars have claimed, but during Carranza's regime the main procedures for Mexico's twentieth-century land reform were accidentally set—with the help of litigious rural dwellers. Village representatives, accustomed to taking advantage of all available laws, and to siding with the executive against the judiciary, quickly adopted the language of Carranza's law to submit their petitions. In fact, the massive participation of rural dwellers and each villages' particularities would shape the central characteristics of the Constitutionalists' restitutions and grants. What "restitutions and grants" meant in each case would be shaped by negotiations among village authorities and National Agrarian Commission (Comisión Nacional Agraria, or CNA) surveyors and delegates. Moreover, as agrarian officials began to outline the features of the Constitutionalists' restitutions and grants, CNA delegates also managed to make all regional land reforms conform to what were now federal rules and regulations.

Types of Land Reform Adopted by Constitutionalist Forces

Early on, many military chiefs and state governors affiliated with Carranza's Constitutionalist movement designed (and a few managed to implement) some variant of land reform in the regions or states under their control. They did so mainly by expanding the state's right to expropriate private property. The 1857 Constitution had allowed federal, state, and municipal governments to expropriate private property for public utility, including the draining of marshlands, the construction of roads, the building of railroads, and so forth. In fact, early in Madero's presidency, the Supreme Court had explained that the word *property* in article 27 of the 1857 Constitution was not an absolute right but rather one with limitations. One of those limitations was the state's authority to expropriate private property with prior compensation when the public interest demanded it.[2] During the Revolution, a motley crew of revolutionaries expanded the state's limited right to expropriate private property to redistribute land.[3]

For example, Lucio Blanco, Constitutionalist chief of military operations in Tamaulipas and Nuevo León, created an agrarian commission to expropriate the enemy's haciendas, mainly targeting former Díaz supporters. In what is often hailed as the first Constitutionalist land grant, in August 1913 Blanco expropriated the large Los Borregos hacienda on the banks of the Río Grande, which had formerly belonged to Félix Díaz (Porfirio Díaz's nephew and a general who had fought against Madero). An unknown number of Blanco's soldiers and eleven sharecroppers, tenant farmers, and peons received plots in proportion to the size of their families. In one case, a peon with a wife and four children who had lived on the hacienda for sixteen years received a fifty-five-hectare plot and a provisional property title. Probably influenced by the U.S. Homestead Act, the 1862 law that encouraged westward migration by granting public lands to settlers who agreed to work on and improve their properties over a five-year period, the Los Borregos beneficiaries had to agree to several conditions when they received title to their land, including the obligation to cultivate the parcel for a specified time and under the conditions stipulated in the forthcoming regulations issued by "the government that emanated from the Revolution." Like the U.S. Homestead Act exemptions (which included provisions to protect the family from "pauperization"), third parties could not embargo or tax the land, and beneficiaries could not sell or transfer their parcel to a third party—except to heirs. Fulfilling these clauses guaranteed the beneficiary's property rights; failing to do so resulted in the loss of the beneficiary's rights, with the parcel reverting back to national property.[4]

Sharing a similar philosophy regarding the need for small private property, Pastor Rouaix Méndez, Constitutionalist governor of Durango and a former land surveyor under Díaz, authored the state's agrarian law of October 1913.[5] He believed that lack of access to small private property condemned the rural working class to peonage, and he suggested purchasing hacienda lands and distributing them to residents of neighboring towns in the form of individual private plots. If haciendas refused to sell, the government would expropriate their lands and sell them to landless villagers. Influenced by the colonization laws that were important in Mexico's northern states, the law promoted the creation of new towns, each of which would receive a two-thousand-hectare land grant. In a few instances, Rouaix managed to implement his law. For example, in November 1913 he founded Villa Madero on lands expropriated from the San Gabriel and Tapona haciendas, and in August 1914 he granted expropriated lands from the San José Buenavista hacienda to Bermejillo residents in the form of a fundo legal and ejidos.[6]

Farther south, Constitutionalists combined expropriation policies with the restitution of pueblo lands by executive means. In March 1913, for example, General Alberto Carrera Torres, chief of the Constitutionalist military in Ciudad del Maíz (San Luis Potosí), issued an "executive law for the distribution of land" that ordered the confiscation of all estates belonging to Díaz and Huerta supporters. An agrarian junta would grant farmers and soldiers provisional but inalienable titles to ten-hectare plots; the titles would later be formalized by the federal executive. All villages, large and small, had the right to name a chief and begin conducting these repartos. Chiefs had to send the agrarian junta an inventory of the distributed plots and a census of beneficiaries and their family members. Beneficiaries included married men aged eighteen and older, single men twenty-one and older, and widows in charge of minors. Interestingly, Carrera's executive law for the distribution of land also intended to resolve restitution claims outside the court system. Article 20 stated, "All lands that have been arbitrarily seized from the Indians of the Republic by Porfirian, Felicista, and other bandits will be immediately returned once the Constitutionalist chiefs have control over them, distributing them among the Indians in accordance with this law's dispositions."[7]

In Veracruz, Governor Cándido Aguilar's agrarian policies also combined the breakup of large estates with pueblo land restitutions. In 1914 Aguilar created the Veracruz Agrarian Commission to "delimit, subdivide, [and] adjudicate in favor of landless individuals ... all lands that the government has obtained and will obtain by purchase, inspections of land titles, expropriation, or other just measures." Aguilar's measure leveled the burden of proof by requiring landowners to present their titles and maps to agrarian officers in order to justify their property claims, and the agrarian commission would restitute illegally appropriated pueblo lands that neighboring landowners could not validate.[8] It did not take long for villagers to send their claims to Aguilar's agrarian commission. For instance, residents of Santa María Magdalena de Xico conducted a census "of the Indian descendants of the first settlers who were interested in recovering the lands belonging to the pueblo" and petitioned for the restitution of San Marcos de León hacienda lands.[9]

With military chiefs and governors designing or implementing their own versions of land reform in the regions or states under their control, Carranza needed to issue a unifying agrarian law for his Constitutionalist movement. "The supreme task for Carranza, or any would-be national authority," Knight explains, "was the integration, by force or cajolery, of these scattered leaders and movements into a sound, legitimate, national regime."[10] Little did anyone suspect at the time that the law Carranza signed to establish his national authority would create the framework for a singular agrarian reform that endured for the next seventy-seven years.

The Constitutionalists' Agrarian Law

On 15 December 1914 Pastor Rouaix, then in charge of Carranza's Office of Fomento, and José I. Novelo, a former congressman under Madero, coauthored an "agrarian law project."[11] As in other land reform plans at the time, they proposed to expropriate private property "when the public interest demanded it." Rouaix and Novelo defined "public interest" to include the following: creating pueblos in regions dominated by latifundios, as Rouaix had already done in Durango; establishing agricultural colonies in fertile lands where the government could build irrigation works; and expropriating uncultivated private properties over five thousand hectares. Remarkably, the authors suggested expropriating land for public utility to restitute lands to pueblos that depended on agriculture, when restitutions did not require any type of expropriation, given that they were judicial procedures that determined who the legal owner of a property was. One reason why Rouaix and Novelo may have made restitutions subject to expropriations, and thus technically a grant, was to allow Fomento officials to dispense with such complicated judicial matters as the burden of proof.

The 1914 agrarian law project also granted to residents of pueblos (and other types of population centers) whose primary activity was agriculture and to groups of agricultural workers ownership of enough land *para las necesidades de su población*, meaning a parcel large enough for the fulfillment of a family's basic needs and adequate water resources to care for their crops. Individuals who received rights to a parcel (Mexican citizens and landless farmers who had less than one thousand pesos in capital) would have to sign a contract with Fomento in which they promised to pay for the land in annual installments, cultivate it within two years, not sell or mortgage it, and transmit it only to their legitimate heirs. The same requirements applied to heirs for a thirty-year period.[12]

Carranza, himself owner of considerable amounts of land, differed from many of his revolutionary chiefs and civilian advisers in that he was opposed to breaking up large estates for fear of destroying commercial agriculture.[13] In comparing the attitude of revolutionary Pancho Villa toward haciendas with that of Carranza, Friedrich Katz notes that "Carranza had objected to their confiscation in the first place. When he could not prevent his generals from occupying haciendas, he was successful in preventing any kind of link between confiscation of these estates and promises of later land division."[14] This is probably why Carranza rejected Rouaix and Novelo's 1914 agrarian law project for widespread land redistribution. Instead he signed a much more limited law primarily designed for the restitution of illegally seized pueblo lands and for expropriations that would be limited to granting enough land to villages for subsistence agriculture. In fact, in what became the famous 6 January 1915 law, Cabrera explained that it did not address larger redistributive policies because they would constitute "another aspect of the agrarian problem over which the executive has not yet legislated."[15]

Fig. 6. Representatives of Cuecillos Ranch in charge of the Constitutionalist land restitution (1914). Archivo General Agrario, Acervo Histórico, exp. 24/4974, leg. 7, f. 29, San Antonio Calpulalpan, Calpulalpan, Tlaxcala.

As Tannenbaum explained, in the 6 January 1915 agrarian law, "restitution occupied the most prominent place both in the law and in the reasons given for the legislation."[16] The irony is that Cabrera had strongly argued against any type of pueblo land restitution (revindicación) in his famous speech to Congress in December of 1912, calling such actions "naïve solutions." In fact, he had said that "the agrarian question is so important that I consider it to be above the justice system (*la alta justicia*), above the system of restitutions (reivindicaciones)."[17] But Constitutionalists had to respond to village petitions for land and water restitutions, provide an alternative to the Zapatista land reform, and bring under control Carrancistas implementing their own restitutions. For this, the 6 January 1915 law created within Fomento a hierarchical agrarian bureaucracy as a substitute for judges and courts to rule on land restitutions. This bureaucracy was composed of a CNA, "local" agrarian commissions in each federal state or territory, and as many "executive committees" as necessary in each state to identify, measure, and provisionally distribute lands. In this quasi-court system,

114 *Constitutionalist Land Reform*

governors became judges of first instance, and the federal executive became "the highest judge who would dictate the definitive agrarian resolution in the hearings that culminated the agrarian procedures."[18]

Although Cabrera had warned in 1912 that "the proletarian classes could not wait for the extensive judicial procedures involved in inquiries regarding land seizures and dispossessions," his law upheld the plaintiff's old burden of proof by requiring village representatives to prove ownership of pueblo lands (they had to possess titles that indicated clearly defined boundaries) and to demonstrate when and how their lands had been illegally appropriated (*fecha y circunstancia del despojo*). Given that Cabrera's ideological justification for the law was to reverse illegal practices carried out in the name of the Lerdo law during the Díaz regime, the 1915 law added a third condition not previously required by the courts: pueblo land loss had to have occurred after the Lerdo law was adopted on 25 June 1856.[19] If, as Cabrera had warned in 1912, few pueblos would be able to meet the strict requirements of legal processes, then the provisions of the 6 January 1915 law would make it even more difficult for them to do so.

Why would Cabrera have upheld (and even augmented) the judicial requirements for pueblo land and water restitutions? One possible reason is that he saw restitutions as secondary to allowing landless pueblos to petition for expropriated lands in the form of a dotación. In fact, anticipating most restitutions to fail, Cabrera had included in the law article 3, which stated: "The pueblos that need ejidos [here, communal lands] but lack them, or that could not win a restitution suit because they lacked titles, were unable to identify [the boundaries], or because the lands were sold legally, could obtain enough land to reconstitute the ejidos, according to the needs of their population, by expropriating the necessary lands from adjoining properties, with compensation from the federal government."[20]

What Cabrera could not have foreseen was that within less than a year after the publication of the 6 January 1915 law, village representatives sent Carranza's Ministry of Development (Fomento) almost one thousand land petitions of various kinds.[21] Fomento's officials and later CNA delegates would then shape the 6 January 1915 law as they ruled on these petitions.

Implementing Land Restitutions

In response to the wave of petitions, from 31 October 1916 (the day of the first presidential ruling, called "resolution") until the end of 1917, the CNA—under the directorship of Pastor Rouaix and in collaboration with several prominent delegates who favored land reform (including Andrés Molina Enríquez)—ruled on thirty-nine restitution claims. This was no small number, considering the relatively short period and the lengthy nature of these quasi-court proceedings. Nor was it surprising that CNA delegates granted only six restitutions (discussed below), given that the only way to win a restitution claim was for pueblo representatives to provide the strict corroborating evidence required by the Constitutionalists' law. A close analysis of these positive "presidential resolutions" shows how agrarian officials followed quasi-judicial procedures and acted like judges when weighing the evidence presented by the parties involved. It also shows how agrarian procedures became "executive jurisprudence," meaning that they set legal precedent in the same way that a court would have.

Carranza issued his first presidential restitution to Iztapalapa, a Federal District pueblo of largely Zapatista affiliation. Residents had begun petitioning for land only six days after Carranza signed his agrarian law. In response, in July 1915, the Federal District governor granted Iztapalapa a provisional restitution, and the local agrarian commission examined the pueblo's titles when the commission became operational in early 1916. No doubt there were political motives for restituting the lands of a pueblo with Zapatista sympathies, but this was also a relatively straightforward case: in 1862 the minister of finance had sold pueblo lands to third parties, claiming they were terrenos baldíos, and so the CNA resolved that the hacienda's land purchases had been made in violation of the Lerdo law.

In the Iztapalapa ruling, CNA delegates clearly articulated the government's justification for taking over land restitution suits that had until then been under court jurisdiction. First, the ruling justified Carranza's wartime authority over the legislative and judicial branches by citing "the ample and extraordinary faculties with which [he was] invested." It went on to argue that the executive was able to restitute Iztapalapa's seized lands "legally because these dispositions and the law [of 6 January 1915] from which they originate are administrative matters, and their aim was to allow 'the Public Powers' to resolve claims quickly and efficiently—as had been the widespread practice in similar cases since colonial law."[22] This ruling set a legal precedent for the federal executive to arrogate court functions at a time when the Supreme Court could not protect its jurisdiction—as it had in the nineteenth and early twentieth centuries.

San Cosme Xaloztoc (Tlaxcala), Carranza's second restitution case in a state with complicated allegiances to the Constitutionalists, was also relatively straightforward when it came to the burden of proof.[23] Although pueblo representatives could muster an authentic title (*escritura de adjudicación*) issued by the federal government in July 1876 to the municipal syndic, landowner Elena Sesma viuda de Ruiz had purchased the lands in question from fellow hacienda owner Luis García Teruel, who did not have legal title to the lands he had sold. The villagers won their claim because, as agrarian officials argued (adopting the legal terminology used in court rulings), "no one could transfer a greater right than he or she had."[24] This ruling also produced binding executive jurisprudence, as became evident in the CNA's third successful restitution case.

In this third case, Arocutín (Michoacán) representatives won their claim because they possessed titles, issued in 1599 by Viceroy Gaspar de Zúñiga y Acevedo, with clearly demarcated boundaries. These titles had been ratified by Mexico's Real Audiencia in 1785 during the pueblo's successful lawsuit against a neighboring landowner. Pueblo representatives could also prove that one resident had illegally sold village lands to a third party in 1898 and subsequently notarized the sales deed. CNA delegates declared the sale illegal, "following not only civil precedent but also agrarian jurisprudence [*jurisprudencia agraria*], as in the case of San Cosme Xaloztoc."[25]

The fourth successful restitution involved San Juan Ixtayopan (Federal District). In this case, CNA delegates clearly went to great lengths to justify a restitution, even though the landowner had fled and pueblo residents had already taken over the disputed lands. This case is interesting because the presidential resolution clarified that restituted lands were not limited to former ejidos but could include any type of illegally seized communal property—including montes and water resources. The San Juan Ixtayopan ruling became not merely executive jurisprudence but "executive legislation," given the quasi-legislative way in which the CNA issued rulings regarding the nature and distribution of property.[26] Its decision became the CNA's circular 8, which stated that villagers could petition for the restitution of ejidos, tierras de común repartimiento, and any other type of common lands that had been seized.[27]

La Purísima Concepción Catorce (San Luis Potosí) was the focus of the fifth successful restitution. Residents won their claim because it involved an illegal land seizure by one of Díaz's infamous survey companies. Whereas some companies had taken advantage of the many gray areas concerning pueblo land rights, the Rafael García Martínez Company had blatantly violated existing laws by surveying and selling pueblo lands. Catorce pueblo representatives not only possessed colonial titles but also had company records showing very clearly how, when, and for how much they had illegally sold these pueblo lands.[28]

The sixth of the CNA's 1916–17 favorable restitution cases shows that agrarian officials stretched the law's strict legal requirements to grant as many restitutions as possible. In Tlaxcala, San Lorenzo Axocomanitla residents won their restitution claim to the El Potrero fields, even though the titles they presented had ostensibly been forged. In this case, CNA delegates decided that "even though the paleographic expert concludes that the title is fake ... we cannot ignore that the Indians of our pueblos in general, and San Lorenzo in particular, are incapable of judging the authenticity and legitimacy of their titles." They then proceeded to disregard the evidence that the titles had been falsified, ruling that the disputed El Potrero fields were not clearly delineated in the landowners' titles.[29]

If the available archival evidence shows that agrarian officials were favorably inclined toward restitution petitions, why did the CNA reject the remaining thirty-three petitions it reviewed between October 1916 and December 1917? By far the most common reason was that the pueblos' titles were faulty. As discussed in chapter 1, titles could, in fact, have a variety of defects. Colonial grants were often imprecise and overlapped with neighboring properties or pueblos.[30] Many pueblos had access to lands for which only the ayuntamiento held titles. In states such as Oaxaca, many pueblos had no titles because they were founded on *cacicazgo* lands.[31] Many other villages possessed old documents that were not proper titles; often they were simply purchase deeds unrelated to the pueblo lands in question, or even court rulings that did not prove land ownership.[32] And pueblos often presented falsified titles. Historian Laura Gómez Santana found at least eighteen pueblos with fake titles in Jalisco in 1915.[33] In one of these instances, the Jamay Indian commission sent the governor of Jalisco a restitution claim (which the claimants had previously lost in court) involving lands allegedly seized by neighboring haciendas during the Díaz dictatorship. The commission presented the pueblo's "colonial" titles, and on that basis the governor authorized a provisional restitution of twelve hundred hectares from the San Agustín hacienda. The hacienda owner questioned the validity of the titles, however, pointing out that the pueblo could not have been founded by Hernán Cortés because the Spanish conqueror had never been in that region.[34] In contrast to the San Lorenzo Axocomanitla (Tlaxcala) case discussed earlier, the lands in question were clearly identified in the landowner's titles, so agrarian officials could not rule in favor of the pueblo.

Apart from pueblo representatives being unable to fulfill the strict legal requirements of the 6 January 1915 law, there were two main reasons why restitutions failed. The first was that many villagers petitioned to have private properties restituted, and agrarian officials rejected these claims because the law exclusively addressed communal lands. For example, the Federal District Agrarian Commission rejected a petition from San Juan Xochimilco because it concerned private property rather than "lands belonging to a pueblo." The residents were told to take their case to the appropriate judicial authorities.[35] CNA delegates made the same argument when ninety-six villagers from the Tlaxcalan pueblos of San Lorenzo Axocomanitla, Zacatelco, Teacalco, La Concordia, and San Jerónimo Zacualpan petitioned for the restitution of lands they had purchased from the Santa Ana Portales hacienda in 1883, but had then lost to the Zacatelco tax collector when they were unable to pay what they owed. Town leaders took the matter to the Zacatelco court of first instance, where they lost the suit. Subsequently, they appealed for and won amparo protection from the district court, only to have it repealed by the Supreme Court. Then, in October 1915 (citing the 6 January 1915 law), they took their case to the governor of Tlaxcala. A month later, both the Tlaxcala Agrarian Commission and the governor ruled in their favor. Ultimately, however, CNA delegates rejected the restitution claim, arguing that the petitioners were individuals who had purchased private property, not pueblos that had lost their communal lands.[36]

The denial of restitution on the grounds that the 6 January 1915 law addressed only communal lands also extended to legally disentailed pueblo lands. In the case of Xaltocan (Mexico State), for instance, pueblo representatives petitioned for the restitution of lands allegedly encroached upon by the Santa Lucía and El Tular haciendas. Government surveyors found that the pueblo had received several colonial grants totaling 1,460 hectares but that these lands had not been illegally appropriated by private landowners.[37] Rather, they had been subdivided and privatized in 11.5-hectare lots, which residents subsequently sold.[38] In this and related cases, CNA delegates could not reverse sales of legally disentailed pueblo lands.

The second main reason the CNA denied restitution petitions was that in many cases both the plaintiffs and defendants were pueblos. In other words, CNA delegates were willing to serve as judges in land suits involving haciendas but not in cases involving intervillage boundary conflicts. For instance, when in January 1916 Pamatácuaro (Michoacán) representatives accused three neighboring pueblos of invading their lands, the state agrarian commission set up an arbitration meeting (*junta de avenencia*) at which plaintiffs and defendants presented their land titles. As in nineteenth-century boundary suits, agrarian officials surveyed and marked the agreed-upon boundaries between these four pueblos. Among other agreements, Pamatácuaro and Sicuicho residents agreed to respect an 1837 boundary survey that had been canceled in 1906 by a former Pamatácuaro representative who had later been accused of fraud. Agrarian officials allowed the pueblos to temporarily use the lands within their new boundaries, until the CNA issued its final resolution. When the matter reached the CNA, however, the delegates flatly determined that intervillage boundary conflicts did not fall within the purview of the 6 January 1915 law.[39]

In a similar case, San Miguel Chapultepec (Mexico State) residents had, during the Conventionist government, received a provisional restitution from the Atenco hacienda that neighboring Mexicaltepec residents also claimed as theirs. To settle the matter once and for all, in 1916 San Miguel residents tried to legalize their Zapatista restitution at the newly established Carrancista agrarian commission. Because both pueblos shared the same colonial title but the joint title did not define what each village owned, CNA delegates concluded that "it is undeniable that the clarification of these intervillage conflicts [*contiendas de pueblo a pueblo*] should be of the exclusive jurisdiction of judicial authorities and not of agrarian authorities."[40] And in 1917, CNA delegates denied three restitution petitions from Tlaxcala on the grounds that they were intervillage boundary conflicts. In the case of La Trinidad Chimalpa, for example, residents accused neighboring Quiahuixtlán of seizing their lands. Agrarian officials declared, "Given that it is a dispute between two pueblos . . . the matter was not under its jurisdiction." They therefore directed the villagers to "the competent authorities."[41]

The Dotación

As early as February 1915, villagers began to petition for a land grant.[42] Furthermore, between October 1916 and December 1917, twenty-three of the thirty-three pueblos whose restitution petitions were rejected received a dotación instead. Examining the available archival materials, one can identify three different types of dotaciones. First and foremost, dotaciones compensated for failed restitutions. Second, villages with landless farmers either obtained land equal to a sitio de ganado mayor (a unit of land area used in making colonial land grants, measuring 1,755.61 hectares) or enough land to satisfy the exact number of landless heads of family residing in the beneficiary population center. And third—unintentionally—dotaciones legalized existing communal lands that had not been privatized during the nineteenth century or the early twentieth.

Compensations for Failed Restitutions

Above all, the dotación was a way of sidestepping the restitution's strict burden of proof requirements. This measure allowed the CNA to take action when village representatives did not have titles, their titles failed to delimit clear boundaries, they could not prove when or which lands had been illegally seized, or pueblo residents had legally sold their lands but a younger generation wanted those sales nullified.[43]

Village leaders petitioning for land restitutions but lacking titles because they had lost them, could not find them at the National Archives, or had never possessed them at all could cite article 3 of the 6 January 1915 law and petition for a dotación instead. In Hidalgo, La Estanzuela residents, who had recently repossessed former pueblo lands allegedly seized by the La Concepción hacienda, petitioned for restitution to legitimize their control of the recovered lands. The paleographer who examined the pueblo's documents, however, declared that they were not land titles. As a result, the governor rejected the restitution claim, but he granted the villagers 890 hectares of expropriated hacienda lands instead.[44]

When pueblo representatives could not unambiguously demarcate the old pueblo boundaries, article 3 allowed the agrarian administration to grant a dotación instead. In Tabasco, for example, a Fomento surveyor filed the following report on his visit to Villa de Tacotalpa: "I went to this village, where they had forgotten the lands of their forefathers, and I could not reconstruct the boundaries. However, fortunately, the law states that those who need ejidos but cannot identify them because they were legally sold can instead receive an ejido grant from expropriated lands paid for by the federal government."[45] Similarly, when the surveyor could not identify the San Juan Tilcuautla (Hidalgo) pueblo boundaries, he decided that villagers would receive instead a 1,495-hectare dotación, while retaining the right to petition for restitution when they were able to better substantiate their claim.[46] Also in Hidalgo, when Tlanalapa representatives presented titles with only generic boundary markings (mentioning *nopales*, palm trees, hills, and other commonplace landmarks) corresponding to an area that differed greatly in size from that calculated by the surveyors, CNA delegates granted them 1,756 hectares of land instead.[47]

Finally, pueblo residents whose forefathers had legally sold their privatized plots and could therefore not win a restitution claim could petition for a dotación instead. In Colima, for instance, Suchitlán representatives explained that their precolonial lands had been disentailed in 1863, and that residents had then sold all their plots at low prices to the neighboring Nogueras and San Antonio haciendas, on which they then had to work as peons. Because these sales had been legal, they petitioned for a dotación instead. As a result, in April 1916 the CNA granted them enough land "to reconstruct the pueblos' ejidos."[48] Similarly in Veracruz, when Acula residents filed for the restitution of their lands, they were unable to provide the evidence necessary to substantiate their claim because, first in 1890 and then again in 1905, villagers had divided, distributed, privatized, and legally sold their land plots. They therefore decided to petition for a dotación instead.[49]

Reconstituting Ejidos according to Need

The 6 January 1915 law also promised that the federal executive would grant enough land to villages to reconstitute their ejidos according to the population's needs. How much land to grant, which type of property these lands would be (national, private, or communal), and who the beneficiaries would be were not clearly defined at the outset. Consequently, state agrarian commissions immediately sought clarification from federal authorities. CNA circular 1, for example, responded to a query from the Zacatecas Agrarian Commission regarding the extension of the lands they were to restitute or grant. CNA delegates decided that if pueblos had titles to their lands, the boundaries specified in the titles should be respected—no matter how much land was involved. If pueblos did not have titles, agrarian surveyors and officials were to follow state laws issued before 1857. But if the state in question had no legislation determining the size of ejidos, then it was to follow colonial laws on the matter—which determined that ejido boundaries should measure 2,095 meters, beginning at the center of town and stretching outward in the four cardinal directions (or, where this was not possible, a square with sides measuring 4,190 meters).[50]

A month later, however, the head of the Michoacán Agrarian Commission met with CNA delegates in Mexico City and informed them of a pueblo that had received a twenty-five-thousand-hectare colonial land grant (*merced*), proving that colonial grants could in fact be much larger than those proposed by CNA delegates. José I. Novelo, then head of the CNA's legal office, argued that the Michoacán case was exceptional, given that most colonial laws granted pueblos only a square league (about 1,755 hectares). Gustavo Durán, chief of the CNA's agrarian office, however, recalled that colonial laws granted a square league not only for fundos legales but also for agricultural lands (*terrenos de común repartimiento*). The officials then reread several colonial laws and concluded that the CNA would have to include *all* pueblo lands in any grant they made, "taking the word ejido in a broad sense." Rouaix confirmed that where ejido grants to pueblos were concerned, these could not be limited to what the colonial legislation defined as ejidos; instead, the word "ejido" had to be taken in a generic sense.[51]

During the first few years of the Constitutionalist land reform, an ejido "in a broad sense" meant one of two things. On the one hand, surveyors, state agrarian commissions, governors, and CNA delegates often granted dotaciones according to the extent of the sitio de ganado mayor (1,755.61 hectares). They sometimes granted two sitios, or even just half a sitio—but frequently the sitio was the unit of measurement that determined the size of the CNA's "reconstituted ejidos," regardless of the town's population, the quality of available lands, or any other consideration in determining how much land each village needed for its "well-being and development."⁵² In his 1929 Autonomous National University law thesis on agrarian presidential resolutions, Ángel Carvajal maintained that "during the initial phase of the agrarian reform, population centers [*núcleos peticionarios*] received a sitio de ganado mayor because [officials] confused the nature of the ejido with that of the colonial ejido." He goes on to identify twenty-one presidential resolutions between 1917 and 1919 that granted beneficiaries one sitio de ganado mayor.⁵³

Ejido "in a generic sense" also meant the area required to grant enough land for the subsistence of resident heads of family engaged in agriculture. In Puebla in 1915, for example, surveyors studied pueblo maps and titles and granted three-hectare plots to each resident head of family. But agrarian officials considered this size too little for family subsistence, and in January 1916 the Puebla Agrarian Commission issued bylaws that ended the three-hectare policy. Instead, surveyors were to conduct censuses of resident heads of family and collect the following information: name, number of family members, whether they were landless (and, if not, how much land they possessed), civil status, age, gender, and literacy. This information would be used to determine the amount of land to be allotted.⁵⁴

In some cases, the goal of providing subsistence plots for heads of family coincided with sitio de ganado mayor measurements. In Michoacán, for example, Teremendo representatives petitioned for a dotación, claiming "the pueblo [had] 442 families and 1,500 inhabitants of whom only 35 [had] land [and therefore] this collectivity lack[ed] the necessary lands for its subsistence." But instead of granting the necessary plots to all resident heads of family, CNA delegates granted the village 1,755 hectares (one sitio de ganado mayor). In this case, a sitio de ganado mayor was roughly equivalent to four hectares per head of

Constitutionalist Land Reform 125

family—a parcel size surveyors generally considered large enough for subsistence farming on arable lands.[55] In many other cases, however, providing subsistence plots for heads of family reliant on agriculture meant granting less than a sitio de ganado mayor. In Santiago Tlajomulco, for instance, the Hidalgo Agrarian Commission suggested granting one sitio de ganado mayor, but CNA delegates awarded the village the equivalent of four-hectare plots for one hundred heads of families, thus greatly reducing the size of the dotación from 1,755.61 to 400 hectares.[56] Similarly in Medellín, the Veracruz Agrarian Commission first granted a dotación measuring 1,755.61 hectares, but a year later CNA delegates reduced it to five hectares each for 109 heads of family "given that the quality of the land was very high."[57]

Confirming Existing Pueblo Lands

Quite accidentally, dotaciones became a vehicle for legalizing existing communal pueblo lands. Surveyors soon discovered that despite nineteenth-century disentailment laws, many pueblos owned communal lands, especially in the form of woodlands and pasturelands. Among the seventy-one villages that received a presidential resolution between 1916 and 1917, twenty-three, or about one-third, possessed communal lands. Whereas officials from state-level agrarian commissions readily supported legalizing existing pueblo lands, CNA delegates decided that the titling of communal lands was beyond the purview of Fomento. This became clear in the Arocutín (Michoacán) presidential resolution.

In 1915 Arocutín representatives took their restitution claim to the governor. Two years later the Michoacán Agrarian Commission returned to Arocutín the lands they had claimed from the Porumbo hacienda. It turned out, however, that the villagers possessed communal lands that were not included in their titles. On the basis of surveyor Luis Breña's report, the commission delegates agreed to confirm "the possession and ownership of the remaining lands that the pueblo presently possesses." Yet three months later, CNA delegates decided to restitute only those lands within the pueblo's boundaries as specified by titles, concluding,

"The confirmation of existing pueblo possession and ownership rights is not within the purview of the agrarian law ... and therefore [the CNA] cannot deal with it without surpassing the limits of article 6 of the law, which restricts the agrarian reform to restitutions and dotaciones."[58]

And yet on the same day that Rouaix rejected titling Arocutín's communal lands as part of a land restitution, CNA delegates included them in a grant to the Atasta (Campeche) pueblo. In this case, representatives made a claim in August 1916 for the restitution of their ejidos, which had allegedly been seized by the Cerrillos hacienda. The Campeche Agrarian Commission suggested restituting these lands, but the CNA delegates argued that the pueblo representatives had neither titles nor proof of dispossession. But because officials could authorize a dotación when restitution failed, the CNA delegates concluded, "Given that the Atasta pueblo needs ejido lands and possesses only a small area of 40 hectares, which is insufficient for the needs of the pueblo, it is just to grant the pueblo under consideration 800 hectares ... *including the 40 hectares it already possesses.*"[59]

This resolution set the precedent for allowing pueblo representatives and agrarian officials to include existing communal lands in dotación procedures, even when this was not within the CNA's jurisdiction. For instance, when San Antonio Sahcabchén (Campeche) representatives petitioned for the restitution of their lands, the state agrarian commission concluded that they could not legally justify their claim, but they instead granted the village a dotación of 2,673 hectares of farmlands, "including the lands that the pueblo currently possesses." In effect, officials validated 1,795 hectares of communal lands—more than twice the amount of new land granted by dotación.[60] From then on, agrarian officials used existing communal lands to complete a sitio de ganado mayor. To list but a few examples, Tolcayuca (Hidalgo) legalized 711 hectares of communal lands; Coquimatlán (Colima), 880 hectares; Santa María Coatepec (Puebla), 1,148 hectares; Santiago Tequixquiac (Mexico State), almost 1,500 hectares; Erongarícuaro (Michoacán), 2,640 hectares; and San Ildefonso Tultepec (Querétaro), 6,383 hectares.[61]

As the CNA delegates defined the rules for restitutions and dotaciones in response to individual village circumstances, they also centralized all other land reform efforts (except for the Zapatista repartos).

Consolidating Constitutionalist Land Reform

By the end of 1916, state governors had set up twenty-two agrarian commissions to supplant all other revolutionary offices engaged in land reform. Together with the CNA in Mexico City, they reviewed all previous land reform actions that did not conform to the 6 January 1915 law.[62] In Puebla, for example, San Andrés Payuca representatives had in October 1914 petitioned Constitutionalist general Antonio Medina for the restitution of their ejidos, which had been granted by King Phillip III of Spain but then allegedly seized by neighboring haciendas. Medina's Junta Agraria de Teziutlán immediately surveyed the Santa Lugarda and La Concepción hacienda lands in preparation for restituting former pueblo communal lands. In 1916, however, CNA officers instructed Payuca representatives to take their case to the recently established Puebla Agrarian Commission for review.[63] In a similar case, in 1915 the Constitutionalist governor of Chiapas, Jesús Agustín Castro, ordered hacienda owners to grant land to their peons; he also nullified all ejido land sales and instructed municipal presidents to divide communal lands into five-hectare plots to be distributed among the poor, leaving the landowner with only one plot. Given that some state courts continued to function, several landowners appealed to the local judge, who ruled against Castro. In this case Fomento officials agreed with the judge, deeming the reparto illegal because it was contrary to the 6 January 1915 law.[64] And in Veracruz, Governor Cándido Aguilar's agrarian commission continued to be operational throughout most of 1915—perhaps owing to the belief that states would retain some autonomy over their land reforms. In one case, Aguilar issued a "manifesto" intended to resolve the long-standing conflict between the Ayahualulco and Ixhuacán de los Reyes pueblos and the Tenextepec hacienda. Claiming that past governments had allowed haci-

Fig. 7. Venustiano Carranza and the Puebla Agrarian Commission overseeing a land grant. Secretaria de Cultura, Fototeca Nacional del Instituto Nacional de Antropología e Historia, no. 39935. Reproduction authorized by the Instituto Nacional de Antropología e Historia.

enda owners to act with impunity, and noting that the hacienda had never proven ownership of the lands bordering Ayahualulco, Aguilar nullified all government resolutions since 1876 and allowed villagers to take control over all pueblo lands covered by their titles. Pueblo residents had use rights to individual plots until officials could conduct a formal survey and the federal executive could issue titles.[65] Aguilar's restitution, although similar in some ways to those conducted under the 6 January 1915 law, nonetheless remained outside Fomento's hierarchical agrarian administration. Thus even in Veracruz, where the governor was Carranza's son-in-law, the CNA rejected all land reform projects that did not conform to the 1915 law. Indeed, in November 1916 Carranza himself sent telegrams to all municipal presidents in Veracruz cautioning civil authorities not to infringe on the jurisdiction of the newly created local agrarian commission.[66]

Constitutionalist Land Reform 129

Village Agency

As the CNA reined in all independent Constitutionalist land reform actions, village representatives contributed to this centralizing process by readily adopting the 6 January 1915 law and by sending their claims first to Fomento and then, starting in January 1916, to the CNA. They did so for many reasons, including to revisit old land claims, because the state court system was in disarray, to reverse earlier court rulings, because pueblo representatives could not execute favorable court rulings, to legalize revolutionary land takeovers, or to revisit earlier Constitutionalist repartos.

Many pueblo spokespersons had been waiting for an opportunity to revisit old claims not resolved by the courts. In Hidalgo, for example, it took the Tepenene representative and more than one hundred signatories only five days to petition for a restitution, citing Carranza's new law.[67] Historian Jennie Purnell observes that in Michoacán, the Constitutionalist agrarian reform provided Naranja chief Joaquín de la Cruz "with a new vehicle through which to pursue the community's land claims, an effort in which he had been engaged since the 1890s as the communities' legal representative in matters dealing with the Liberal reparto."[68] And Alberto Mendiola Bringas, who had for many years represented a dozen or so pueblos in the Texcoco (Mexico State) district in their land suits, also quickly took advantage of Carranza's law to petition for restitutions.[69]

Rural dwellers flocked to the Constitutionalist agrarian commissions because the state court system was in disarray and the federal courts were closed. Carranza's agrarian administration became the only available channel for villagers' longstanding claims over lands they disputed with haciendas and neighboring pueblos. In Veracruz, for instance, the Acula municipal president had sued a neighboring landowner in 1912 for allegedly appropriating a large tract of pueblo lands. When the courts ceased to function "due to the revolutionary disturbances," village leaders took their restitution claim to the agrarian authorities.[70] And in Mexico State in September 1914, sixty-five San

Lucas Totolmaloya residents issued a formal complaint to the Aculco ayuntamiento against the La Estancia hacienda for allegedly seizing pueblo lands. The municipal official had told them that "given that the matter in question is a judicial matter, you must go to the judicial authority to demand justice." But when the president of the newly established Mexico State Agrarian Commission found records of this 1914 claim, he suggested that Totolmaloya leaders instead begin restitution proceedings following the 6 January 1915 law.[71]

Many pueblo representatives petitioned for restitutions to reverse earlier court rulings. In Mexico State, for instance, Mayorazgo de la Concepción de León representatives petitioned for a land restitution after losing an amparo suit in 1912; in Hidalgo, Tlanalapa residents did so after losing a court case between 1868 and 1873.[72] In Tlaxcala, San Lorenzo Axocomanitla leaders lost their claims to the El Potrero fields in the courts; they took the matter to the Tlaxcala Agrarian Commission instead.[73] In fact, some court rulings were decades—if not centuries—old. In the case of San Juan de las Manzanas (Mexico State), representatives petitioned the agrarian administration to resolve a matter that had not been taken to the courts since before Independence.[74]

Sometimes villagers took their claims to the agrarian administration because they could not execute earlier favorable court rulings. In Guanajuato, for example, the representative of the San Bartolomé Aguascalientes "Indian natives" appealed for restitution of the El Hervidero spring, which had allegedly been seized six years earlier by the owner of the San Antonio Calichar hacienda. The representative accused the landowner of being affiliated with the científicos, of being a perpetual senator under Díaz, and of having too much power in the region due to his family ties to former governors. Villagers, their representative explained, had won amparo protection at the district court, but they had not been able to enforce the court ruling. For that reason, in early 1916 the pueblo representative sent the agrarian commission a petition seeking restitution of the water source, explaining: "I have faith in the Revolution as the redeemer of my race, and in order to achieve

Constitutionalist Land Reform 131

this redemption the doors of justice, which have until now been shut to us, must be opened."⁷⁵

Villagers who had received land from revolutionary chiefs readily adopted the 6 January 1915 procedures because they wanted their gains legalized by the victorious revolutionary faction. In Tlaxcala, for instance, Domingo Arenas was first allied with Zapata for two years and then implemented his reforms autonomously.⁷⁶ After Arenas signed a unification pact with Carranza in December 1916, representatives from approximately sixty villages petitioned the Tlaxcala Agrarian Commission to legalize the hacienda lands they then had in their possession.⁷⁷ Similarly, across the former Zapatista regions, many villagers used the Constitutionalist law to legalize existing land takeovers. Whereas most Morelos residents remained staunch Zapatistas, in other states Zapatismo was often only one of several possible political affiliations.

In fact, villagers who initially petitioned Zapatista chiefs for land restitutions readily changed sides when the Constitutionalists gained national status. In Hidalgo, for example, representatives from the Tetepango and Ajacuba pueblos first sent Conventionist officers a petition requesting the return of their fundo legal and ejidos (allegedly seized by several neighboring haciendas), citing the Plan de Ayala. Then, "once the constitutional order was reestablished," they petitioned Carrancista officials for a land restitution—citing the 6 January 1915 law and denying that they had received possession of their lands from Zapatista General Arturo del Castillo or that they had ever been allied with the Zapatistas (*jamás ha sido grato el zapatismo*).⁷⁸ Also in Hidalgo, Huitexcalco chiefs first conducted a reparto during the Conventionist government in early 1915, but in mid-1916 they asked the Carranza administration to sanction their land distribution.⁷⁹ Likewise in Mexico State, forty-six Muitejé residents first petitioned Zapatista Governor Baz for restitution of their lands. But after the Constitutionalists issued a 29 September 1915 decree that nullified "all acts and procedures dictated by the so-called Ministry of Agriculture and Development or any other office not part of the Constitutionalist government," they instead petitioned for a restitution based on the 6 January 1915 law.⁸⁰

Pueblo representatives also employed the 6 January 1915 law to revisit earlier Constitutionalist repartos. In Puebla, Santa María Ixtiyucan representatives petitioned General Francisco Coss for the restitution of their pueblo lands in February 1915. But as the provisional governor of Puebla, Morelos, and Tlaxcala, Coss had issued a manifesto on 2 February 1915 allowing commissions made up of municipal officials and pueblo representatives to review land titles and decide on alleged pueblo land seizures.[81] All enemy haciendas and Church lands could be surveyed and distributed among the landless inhabitants of neighboring pueblos—giving preference to the widows and orphans of revolutionaries.[82] In Ixtiyucan, Coss authorized a commission to redraw the old pueblo boundaries, taking land from five neighboring haciendas. After the Puebla Agrarian Commission was established, however, residents argued that the "early reparto" had not followed the 6 January 1915 law. They also complained that the lands restituted by the Coss commission were too far away from the urban center; they petitioned instead for lands from immediately adjoining haciendas.[83]

Not only did villagers readily adopt Carrancista laws, but they also often assumed quite pragmatic positions on the issue of restitutions versus dotaciones, carefully considering the relative merits of these two procedures. In Michoacán, for example, villagers from the Purhépecha region of La Ciénega lodged thirteen petitions between 1915 and 1916—but only after holding general assemblies to discuss whether they would have better chances of success with a restitution or a dotación. In one case, villagers decided they would gain more land by seeking a dotación rather than a restitution.[84] Similarly in Zacatecas, when the Santo Tomás representative could not find the documents necessary to prove that the town had won an 1848–50 lawsuit against the Griegos hacienda, he immediately petitioned for a dotación.[85] Three pueblos on the outskirts of Oaxaca City had a similar experience. In Nazareno Etla, residents petitioned for restitution, only to realize a month later that they lacked the necessary titles and proof of having lost their lands after 1856. They subsequently petitioned for a dotación.[86] Farther south, San Lorenzo Cacaotepec villagers petitioned for a restitution,

Constitutionalist Land Reform 133

but upon realizing that their land titles showed they were already in possession of the communal lands they held title to, they also sought a dotación.[87] Finally, farther east, Santa María del Tule representatives petitioned for a land restitution, but they informed the governor that if the restitution petition failed "for whatever reason," they would petition for a land grant.[88]

A law that was meant to sidestep far-reaching redistributive initiatives based on the expropriation of large landed properties, compete with Zapatista land reform, and control independent Carrancista rural programs attracted thousands of petition signatories across the country. In response to these petitions the CNA began to define a much more complex reform that ended up shifting power from the courts to agrarian commissions in state capitals and from the Supreme Court to the CNA in Mexico City at a time when the federal judiciary had been shut down by the Constitutionalists. What happened starting in 1917, when Congress reinstated the Supreme Court?

5

The Return of the Judiciary in Uncertain Times, 1917–1924

> Esta ley imperfecta, inadecuada para resolver la situación agraria en todas las regiones del país, vino a ser ya ... la base de las demás disposiciones que se vienen dictando para satisfacer las demandas imperiosas de nuestra deficiente organización agrícola. [This imperfect law, inadequate to resolve the agrarian situation in all regions of the country, has become ... the basis of further rulings issued to fulfill the imperative demands of our deficient agricultural system.]
> —Antonio Villarreal Muñoz, *Restitución y dotación de ejidos*

At the Constitutional Convention called by Carranza in Querétaro (20 November 1916 to 31 January 1917), the delegates in charge of writing article 27 of the 1917 Constitution incorporated the 6 January 1915 law into its provisions. Therefore, when Congress elected a new Supreme Court in 1917, thereby reopening amparo proceedings nationwide, the CNA (now under the Secretaría de Agricultura y Fomento, or Ministry of Agriculture and Development) had already assumed authority over restitution claims and land expropriations for dotaciones. Despite having for many decades protected their authority over contentious property matters, the justices of the reinstated Supreme Court fully supported the executive's extended jurisdiction over land reform procedures—even though such authority overstepped the separation of powers guaranteed by the new constitution.[1] In fact, from Carranza's presidency (which lasted from 1 May 1917 until his assassination on 21 May 1920) until the end of Álvaro Obregón's administration (1920–24), the Supreme Court's amparo rulings legitimated the executive's wartime takeover of judicial authority.² In the process, landowners *and* villagers lost their rights to due process before a state (as opposed to a federal) court.

Perhaps the Supreme Court justices backed this state of exception because the goal of the 6 January 1915 law was to resolve quickly an urgent problem, not to create population centers with their own patrimony, juridical standing, and administrative and representative organs under the tutelage of the federal executive, operating parallel to the autonomous municipal governments. In fact CNA delegates did not consider restituted or granted properties to be an indivisible whole. Instead they created distinct regulations for different resources: urban plots, woodlands, water resources, and arable land. Lands restituted or granted for the creation or expansion of urban areas would be dedicated to public services under municipal authority, with the rest divided into private plots for houses and gardens. Restituted and granted woodlands and water resources would be owned communally and—at least initially—managed by municipal authorities under federal legislation. And restituted or granted arable lands would be distributed in parcels to heads of family and held in common—but only until future laws privatized them, albeit under state regulations designed to stop beneficiaries from selling or losing them.

Neither the Carranza nor the Obregón administration issued laws that would permanently define restituted or granted property, and the resulting legal limbo created, in the words of one government official, "uncertainty in the pueblos as to the person or persons who should provisionally administer ejidos and the other lands that belong to them—uncertainty that results in many parcels not being cultivated in a timely fashion."³ In response, CNA delegates created in 1917 the *comité particular administrativo* (local administrative committee, CPA) as a temporary form of local governance and justice parallel to municipal authorities. This parallel form of authority, created for both restitution and dotación beneficiaries, would establish the basis for what would become the twentieth-century "ejido" as most scholars know it.

The Supreme Court's Role in Revolutionary Agrarian Reform

Constitutional Convention delegates proposed two different types of land reform.[4] First, they incorporated some of the Constitutionalists' redistributive programs that were set aside when the 6 January 1915 law limited the scope of land reform to restitutions and dotaciones.[5] These initiatives included creating new agricultural centers (a type of colonization project under the Ministry of Agriculture and Development) and reducing land concentration by giving Congress and state legislators the right to subdivide large landholdings to promote small- and medium-size agricultural units. Each state or territory would have the right to determine the maximum land extension an individual or corporation could own, and landowners would be required to break up their holdings and sell any excess. If they refused to do so, state governments had the authority to expropriate land in exchange for state government bonds. Landowners' claims would be a judicial matter, resolved by the courts within a period of one month. This was a radical proposal that allowed state governments to redistribute large landholdings.[6]

The second type of land reform was to incorporate the January 1915 law into the Constitution. But the same delegates who gave the judiciary a key role in the redistributive land expropriations mentioned above did not address the judiciary's role in the restitution of communal lands or expropriations for dotaciones. Instead the delegates upheld the executive's extended authority over these land reform procedures—originally claimed by Carranza in a time of civil war. How did the Supreme Court justices reconcile restitution and dotación proceedings when the 1917 Constitution upheld the separation of powers between the executive and the judiciary? The answer to this question is key to understanding Mexico's revolutionary land reform.

Validating Executive Judicial Authority

The Supreme Court played a central role in the early agrarian reform, because landowners whose property was affected immediately sought

Fig. 8. Justices of the First Revolutionary Supreme Court, 1917. Secretaria de Cultura, Fototeca Nacional del Instituto Nacional de Antropología e Historia, no. 40202. Reproduction authorized by the Instituto Nacional de Antropología e Historia.

amparo protection against the executive in the federal courts. In one early case, Elena Sesma viuda de Ruiz sought amparo protection against the governor of Tlaxcala and the state agrarian commission for violating her rights under Constitutional articles 14 and 16 after they had restituted hacienda lands to San Cosme Xaloztoc. Article 14 stated that "no person shall be deprived of life, liberty, property, possessions, or rights without a trial by a duly created court," and Sesma de Ruiz's lawyer argued that neither the Tlaxcala Agrarian Commission nor the governor could be considered duly created courts. Moreover, article 16 specified that "no one shall be molested in his person, family, domicile, papers, or possessions except by virtue of an order in writing from the competent authority," and the plaintiff's lawyer argued that neither the Tlaxcala Agrarian Commission nor the CNA were competent authorities to decide land rights.[7] Because of these two constitutional provisions, Sesma de Ruiz won an amparo suit at the district court.[8] Yet, in what was an earthshaking decision for all landowners in Mexico, the first reinstated Supreme Court (1 June 1917 to 31 May 1919) unanimously overturned the district court's ruling. All eleven justices agreed that "the 6 January 1915 law was a matter of general interest and public order because it aimed at resolving one of the most transcendental problems facing the country: the agrarian problem."[9] At a time when the Zapatistas in Morelos continued to threaten the new establishment, the Supreme Court justices allowed the executive to resolve contentious land matters—even though it violated constitutional articles 14 and 16—on the grounds that resolving the "agrarian problem" was more important than limiting executive powers.

The same happened with amparos filed against dotaciones. For example, when Tlaxcala landowner Ricardo Carvajal filed for amparo protection against the dotación to the Panotla pueblo, claiming that only the judiciary had the power to expropriate land, the Supreme Court clarified that "the 6 January 1915 law and [Constitutional] article 27 stipulate that it is the administrative and not the judicial authorities who have jurisdiction over agrarian matters."[10] Similarly, Concepción Petriciolli viuda de Kennedy sought amparo recourse against the expropriation of part of her hacienda lands for the Santa Inés Tecuexcomac (Tlaxcala) dotación, claiming she could not be dispossessed of her property except in court. The Supreme Court ruled, however, that "the dotación, conducted according to the 6 January 1915 law, does not have to be decided by trial but can be implemented by following legal procedures."[11] Finally, in Mexico State, when José Ignacio Villamil petitioned the district court to suspend a dotación from his property to the Tequixquiac pueblo, the Supreme Court unanimously agreed that "land dotación to the pueblos is the exclusive competence of the administrative authority."[12]

The second reinstated Supreme Court (1 June 1919 to 1 June 1923) not only upheld this violation of the provisions of article 14 but also acknowledged that the federal executive had become a new court (violating constitutional article 13, which stated that no one could be judged by special tribunals, except for military courts). The justices articulated this position in a case that involved not landowners but land beneficiaries. When Xochimilco representative Facundo Olivares appealed for amparo protection against a presidential resolution that had revoked the Federal District Agrarian Commission's restitution, the Supreme Court ruled that presidential resolutions on restitutions and dotaciones were not a matter of charity (*donaciones graciosas*) but were judicial resolutions. It held that the initial village petition to the Federal District governor was a real lawsuit (*demanda*); the procedures following the 6 January 1915 law constituted a real trial (*juicio*); and the presidential resolution was a real ruling (*cosa juzgada*) that could not be modified.[13]

Creating New Social Rights

In ruling on the amparos brought to the Supreme Court in response to the implementation of the 6 January 1915 law, the justices transformed the dotación into a distinct form of land expropriation. There were essentially three ways that dotación expropriation differed from all other expropriations sanctioned by the 1917 Constitution, which (like the 1857 Constitution) allowed for the occupation of private property for public utility and with prior compensation. First, the executive could expropriate land for dotaciones without court involvement—the requirement for all other forms of expropriation, including the one specified in article 27 for the breakup of large estates to promote small- and medium-size agricultural holdings. In Rafael de Salcedo y Echave's amparo suit against the expropriation of his lands for the San Pedro Totoltepec (Mexico State) dotación, the Supreme Court differentiated between these two types of expropriation, ruling that "land dotaciones have not been instituted with the goal of breaking up large landed properties, but rather for the goal of satisfying the urgent need for land for the development and well-being of the pueblos." Therefore expropriations for dotaciones could be conducted independently of the judiciary.[14]

Second, the Supreme Court redefined the concept of public utility as outlined in article 27. As Carlos R. Herrera-Martin explains for expropriations in general, the Supreme Court imposed strict limits on the executive by making sure that the public utility requirement was properly justified. One requisite, for example, was that the executive had to transfer expropriated property to a public body, such as the ayuntamiento or the state government.[15] In dotación expropriations, however, agrarian officials did not have to transfer property to a public body; instead, they could transfer it to landless village residents as a collectivity. To this end, the justices employed language that transformed the notion of public utility into the concept of social rights.

This transformation began with a 1917 amparo suit from Oaxaca. When the landowning Sada family filed suit over the expropriation of their hacienda lands for a dotación to the Nazareno Etla pueblo, claiming that the action violated federal civil procedures (*código de procedimientos civiles*), both the Oaxaca District Court and the Supreme Court denied the Sadas amparo protection. The justices argued that the 6 January 1915 law was a constitutional law issued to satisfy public needs, and they defined these public needs as "common prosperity and well-being." Moreover, they also claimed that "if the execution of the dispositions intended to satisfy public needs were suspended, the State would suffer grave damages, and the dominant spirit of the 1917 Constitution would be violated."[16]

This definition of social rights was employed from then onward.[17] By December 1918 the Supreme Court's role in protecting the abstract concept of society became legal precedent. For instance, when Genaro G. García requested amparo protection against the governor of Zacatecas for expropriating two dams and sixteen thousand hectares of his property, the court denied his request, claiming that suspending the dotación would cause "damage to society." The justices noted that the court had already "established jurisprudence," considering that "society was directly affected by the suspension of the [agrarian] precepts adopted by the Constitution, which are aimed at the political, social, and economic reorganization of the country." According to the justices, society was directly affected when the state failed to distribute lands among people who otherwise had no means of subsistence.[18]

The third way in which the Supreme Court made dotaciones different from all other forms of expropriation had to do with the compensation requirement. The first and second reinstated Supreme Courts remained exacting with regard to nonagrarian expropriations. In one early case, both the district court and the Supreme Court granted Manuel Pineda amparo protection against the Puebla ayuntamiento for expropriating part of his property to build a road. The Supreme Court argued that expropriation could not proceed unless it was for public utility and with prior compensation, and in this case the ayuntamiento had failed to compensate Pineda.[19] Instead, according to Marte R. Gómez, the dotación was an expropriation with conditional compensation after the fact.[20] Landowners could access the judiciary only *after* a presidential resolution—and then only to claim compensation.[21]

Landowners' Rights to Be Heard in Court

Essentially, during the first two revolutionary Supreme Courts, landowners lost their right to be heard before or during restitution and dotación procedures. Nowhere was this clearer than in the amparo suit filed by landowner Manuel Baigts. Asserting his right to a court hearing under the terms of constitutional article 14, Baigts petitioned the Oaxaca District Court for amparo protection against the state's agrarian commission for expropriating his hacienda lands for the Nazareno Etla dotación. His lawyer wanted to appeal the Oaxaca Agrarian Commission's ruling because these lands did not directly border the pueblo (a requisite for dotaciones). In similar cases, the lawyer argued, the Oaxaca Agrarian Commission had heard all parties; in his case, however, it did not. Baigts's lawyer no longer claimed that agrarian officials had no judicial rights. In fact he accepted that the executive could now fulfill "court formalities." But he did argue that in his case, these formalities had not been observed because he had not been heard by the Oaxaca Agrarian Commission.

In response to the Baigts amparo, the district judge bluntly informed the plaintiff that he would not be heard at court "because the law did not require it." When the case reached the Supreme Court, the justices reiterated that "article 27 limits the rights guaranteed in Articles 14 and 16 and, therefore, these cannot be considered as violated when property is expropriated for public utility unless, while doing it, [the state] infringes on article 27." Further, the justices argued that "the 6 January 1915 law, which is integral to Constitutional article 27, establishes the procedures for implementing expropriations to grant lands to the pueblos, and does not require that in these cases the owners of the expropriated lands be previously heard in court."[22]

In the Baigts amparo, justices were interpreting article 10 of the 6 January 1915 law, which allowed landowners to access the judiciary only *after* the presidential resolution had been issued—and, then, only to claim compensation.[23] At that time, Cabrera Acevedo explains, "no one really understood with certainty the nature of the court case referred to by the 6 January 1915 law."[24] And so, citing article 10 became a common way to indefinitely postpone the right of a landowner to be heard in court. For example, when an official from the Mexico State Agrarian Commission asked landowner Dolores Quintanilla viuda de Orvañanos to present her land titles, she refused, claiming that the official had no authority over the matter. Just as the Zapatistas had done earlier, she complained, the agrarian commission was violating her rights under constitutional article 16. In response, the agrarian official clarified that "the commission under my charge ... has its origins in the special 6 January 1915 law, essentially a revolutionary law whose objective has been to vindicate the rights of the pueblos against the irregularities suffered under previous governments.... Subjecting the commission's procedures to the slow and intricate judicial transactions of the courts would be to distort the objective and the essence of the law." The official then informed Quintanilla that he would offer no further explanation, and if she thought that her rights had been infringed, she could take her claims to court *after* the land restitution, when she would have the right to request compensation.[25]

Villagers' Due Process

It was not only landowners who lost their right to due process. With article 27 the pueblos regained their juridical standing, but villagers lost their right to take their grievances to the state courts if they so preferred. Civil courts remained in charge of private property disputes, but the agrarian administration took over all matters related to the restitution of former communal lands. In Hidalgo, for example, when El Puente residents petitioned for the restitution of the Cerro de Arévalo fields, agrarian commission officials noted that the claim concerned a specific property rather than the reclamation of former communal lands. The officials deliberated over the difference between a private property dispute—which, they agreed, continued to be a court matter—and a restitution claim. After a long investigation the officials concluded that the Cerro de Arévalo fields had in fact been part of the pueblo's [colonial] ejido (adjudicated in 1901 by the local political chief in favor of a third party, thus violating the law of 25 June 1856) and thus an agrarian rather than a civil matter.[26]

Some village representatives immediately began using the federal executive's new authority to their advantage. In Mexico State, for instance, when Almoloya del Río villagers petitioned for the restitution of the pueblo's communal lands, landowner Santiago Castro sued the local agrarian commission in the court of first instance. The judge ruled in Castro's favor and ordered the municipal president to respect his property. In response, village representative Felipe Luna requested that the agrarian commission order the judge to "mind his own business," given that this was an agrarian matter. The infuriated judge could not challenge agrarian law, so he ordered Luna's arrest for "insolent behavior toward a judge."[27] Similarly, when San Francisco del Malpaís representatives petitioned the governor of Durango for the restitution of their lands, the owner of the Casa Blanca hacienda responded by filing a "land recovery suit" in the court of first instance. In response, the Malpaís representatives argued that "since many of these lands are part of what we have claimed for restitution, it is neither legal nor rational that the same matter be discussed by two different authorities, particularly when article 27 and the 6 January 1915 law are clear as to the procedures in such cases."[28]

Pueblo representatives generally had an easier time taking their claims to the agrarian administration than to the courts, given that agrarian officials and staff (engineers, surveyors, and inspectors) were hired to implement land reforms successfully and tended to favor villagers over landowners. Moreover, under President Álvaro Obregón the CNA established the office of pueblo attorney general (*procurador de pueblos*) in each state to assist village representatives with their restitution and dotación petitions free of charge. The decree of 22 November 1921 created this office to help communities with the bureaucratic procedures required for restitutions or grants, to represent the community in the case of an amparo suit, and to mediate disputes between or within villages.[29] There is evidence of *procuradores* assisting villagers in Campeche, Chihuahua, Mexico State, Guerrero, Hidalgo, Nuevo León, Oaxaca, Sonora, and Veracruz in the 1920s.[30]

The greatest support that village representatives received with procedural requisites had already become the hallmark of revolutionary agrarian reform: those who could not substantiate their restitution claims could appeal for a dotación as part of the same case file.[31] This procedural simplification became precedent in 1918 when Mexico State landowner Rafael G. de Salceda y Echave appealed for amparo protection against the San Pedro Totoltepec dotación, claiming that "the case file, having been opened as a land restitution, should not have been completed as a dotación case file." In response, the Supreme Court ruled that "it is not against the law to decree the ejido dotación in the same case file as the one for a land restitution, when the latter has been denied."[32] In this way, between 1915 and 1924, hundreds of appeals nationwide began as restitutions and ended up as dotaciones within the same case file, although not all dotaciones received favorable resolutions, and many dotaciones amounted to fewer hectares than villagers had claimed for restitution.

Village authorities did retain their collective right to amparo protection in the district courts and the Supreme Court. In April 1918, for example, the Tlalixtac de Cabrera representative sued the Oaxaca Agrarian Commission, which had taken six hundred hectares of the pueblo's lands and granted them to neighboring Santa María del Tule. The Supreme Court awarded the Tlalixtac villagers amparo protection, ruling that "even though the reparto or dotación of ejidos to the pueblos is of public utility, so is the preservation of the ejidos of those pueblos that already have them." In this case, the justices considered that the damages suffered by Tlalixtac would be greater than those suffered by Santa María del Tule if the latter were denied the land grant.[33]

In a few other cases, villagers were able to obtain amparo protection in the district courts and the Supreme Court when the agrarian administration violated procedural laws. In the case of Xochimilco, for example, Carranza had initially granted the Ciénega Chica and part of the Ciénega Grande lands to the residents, but he later recanted under pressure from the Federal District governor. In response, representative Facundo Olivares petitioned the federal courts for amparo protection, which the Supreme Court granted on the grounds that presidential resolutions were irrevocable, even by the president himself.[34]

Given the nature of the amparo, however, this was not always the best recourse for villagers dealing with agrarian matters. In the case of land restitutions, village representatives could file for amparo protection against a presidential resolution that denied restoration of their lands, but they still needed additional corroborating evidence to win the claim. In Hidalgo, for example, Atotonilco residents solicited amparo protection against a presidential resolution that rejected their 1916 restitution appeal and granted a dotación instead. But the amparo petition fell through for the same reason the original restitution petition had failed: the villagers did not have land titles, and they could not prove when or how their lands had been seized from them.[35]

In the case of dotaciones, villagers could file an amparo suit against a presidential resolution denying them enough land for family subsistence. These suits were largely in vain, however, because the essence of the amparo was to *overturn* an unfair law or abuse of power—not to encourage state action. In Mexico State, for example, when Agostadero representatives appealed for a dotación after a failed restitution, the president rejected it, claiming they did not lack ejidos because they already possessed 2,873 hectares for 222 heads of family. Representative Zeferino González filed for amparo protection against the presidential resolution in the district court, but he lost the suit because, according to the judge, "agrarian authorities have the power to estimate not only the need for land dotaciones but also whether they are appropriate. Because these are subjective factors . . . they cannot be the basis for an amparo suit by a pueblo that did not receive lands via dotación. [The denial of dotación] does not imply a violation of guarantees because the amparo is nothing other than the return of that which had belonged to the aggrieved before the claim."[36]

The Provisional Ejido

Reasons why the Supreme Court may have allowed numerous challenges to the 1917 Constitution created by the 6 January 1915 law include not only that Carranza and his advisers did not intend for land restitutions and grants to become the basis of long-lasting, nationwide land redistribution but also that CNA delegates did not intend for restituted and granted resources to become an indivisible whole. In fact, between 1917 and 1924 federal agrarian officials and Supreme Court justices began to confer different types of resources—urban plots, woodlands, water resources, and agricultural parcels—with distinctive forms of administration and property rights.

Urban Lots

Restituted or granted fundos legales, or town sites, would be used for streets, plazas, public establishments, and other services, and the remainder of the land had to be subdivided and distributed among pueblo residents in the form of urban lots.[37] Residents acquired full ownership of the plots on which they could build their homes; they had to pay taxes, and, in exchange, they received public services, including police services, from a popularly elected municipal council.[38] Fundos legales were matters of state and municipal, not federal, law, and at that level the CNA did not want to overstep its authority. Therefore, when villagers petitioned for the restitution or the granting of fundos legales, CNA delegates concealed grants for urban sites in ejido grants. For example, when the Coahuila Agrarian Commission granted Villa de Castaños one-quarter of a sitio de ganado mayor for its fundo legal and one-half and three-quarters sitios for ejidos, CNA delegates decided they did not have the authority to grant land for the fundo legal "unless it was part of the ejidos in general." As a result, they granted three sitios for "ejidos *and* fundo legal."[39] And when the governor of Puebla granted land to a ranchería within a hacienda, specifying that 736 hectares were for agriculture and 99 hectares were to complete the fundo legal, the CNA corrected his ruling by granting the same total amount of land but stating that "completing the fundo legal" was not the CNA's competence.[40]

Woodlands

Many villagers petitioned directly for woodlands (or restitutions and grants of lands that included woodlands) because of the important resources these lands provided. Early agrarian regulations first considered restituted or granted woodlands (sometimes called bosques, *terrenos forestales*, or montes) to be under the authority of the municipal government, albeit under federal regulations for their use and conservation.[41] In Puebla, for instance, CNA delegates placed San Lorenzo Teotipilco's granted woodlands under municipal authority and made "its exploitation subject to the future rules issued for their conservation."[42] Starting in 1921, local administrative committees (comités particulares administrativos, CPAs) were to manage the common use of pasture lands and woodlands, also following federal regulations for their conservation. Soon, all presidential resolutions included a paragraph stating that beneficiaries had to preserve and reforest granted woodlands.[43] For example, when Tetepango (Hidalgo) residents received a land grant, CNA delegates added that climatological and meteorological conditions depended on the conservation of woodlands, making them "natural resources for public prosperity." For this reason, "residents of Tetepango are obliged to maintain, conserve, and foment the existing forest vegetation on granted lands and use them in common, with all proceeds going to public services."[44] Supreme Court justices agreed. They declared that "society and the State" would be harmed by the destruction of woodlands because deforestation affected rainfall and because trees were part of public wealth (*riqueza pública*).[45]

Water Resources

In some ways, the restitution and granting of water resources was like that of land. During the Porfiriato, when pueblos petitioned for the restoration of their colonial rights to water, they had to take their claims to court.[46] After 1915 agrarian officials restituted water resources to pueblos whose representatives could prove their property rights, the usurpation of their sources of water, and the loss of access to them after 1856.[47] When pueblos could not prove their colonial or nineteenth-century rights to water resources but clearly needed them, CNA delegates could grant water dotaciones. As Michael D. Wolfe explains, article 27 made access to water (like land) a social right.[48] Supreme Court justices then made the restitution and granting of water resources a state imperative. For example, when CNA delegates granted Tlaxcoapan (Hidalgo) residents access to the Tepeji River by reducing the amount of water that the San Miguel Chingú hacienda could access, the justices rejected the landowners' amparo petition on the grounds that "the general interest concerns not only the ejido land grant but also access to water resources for the grant beneficiaries. Therefore, society and the State will incur damages if the amparo is granted."[49]

In other ways, however, water restitutions and grants were quite different from those for land because pueblo rights (in case of restitutions) and village needs (in case of dotaciones) were conditioned on regional considerations regarding the equitable distribution of water resources. The CNA's Department of Land, Water, and Colonization (Departamento de Tierras, Aguas y Colonización) had to consider the needs of all the parties using the same water source—be they land reform beneficiaries, private property owners, water associations, or neighboring villages.[50] For instance, when San Juan Tezontla (Mexico State) villagers petitioned for the restitution of their water resources, representatives of neighboring villages complained that the river waters served seven pueblos in addition to the petitioners' village. In this and many other cases, the CNA had to consider the needs of all pueblos in the region.[51] Moreover, villages often required access to water for both urban and rural uses.[52] Most important, access to water often required the construction, restoration, or adaptation of hydraulic infrastructure, and these works would be directed by the CNA's Department of Land, Water, and Colonization.[53]

Agricultural Lands

The 6 January 1915 law explicitly stated that it did not intend to "revive the old [Indian] communities or create similar ones." For the time being, however, restituted and granted lands were to be held in common—until future regulations determined "the [legal] condition of the restituted or granted lands and the manner and timing of their division among residents, who in the meantime will have common use rights." Arable lands would at some future time be distributed as individual private parcels (*pleno dominio*), with the necessary limitations to prevent land hoarding by speculators.[54] Constitutional article 27 further specified that pueblos (and other recognized corporations, such as *condueñazgos*, *rancherías*, *congregaciones*, and *tribus*) that had communal lands or those receiving restitutions could hold lands, woodlands, and water resources in common—but only until a future law determined how to divide and distribute (agricultural) lands ("hacer el repartimiento únicamente de las tierras"). Whereas woodlands and water resources would remain communal property, arable lands would be inalienable before and after being privatized.[55] Similarly, the Supreme Court interpreted the 6 January 1915 law as one that restituted and granted "lands whose property will not belong to the pueblo in common but will be divided into private property."[56] The justices also clarified that "the objectives of the laws on the granting of lands to pueblos is not to revive the old colonial ejidos.... Their objective is to provide pueblos with the basic elements they lack and grant them economic independence, however limited."[57] As Kourí notes, article 27 "contained an (unresolved) tension between the recognition of the legality of communal property and the expectation that, sooner or later, [communal property] would be converted into individual private property farms."[58]

Arable land would at some point be privatized, but individual parcels would remain inalienable so that recipients would not sell or lose them. Cabrera's ideas about protecting future private property came from Andrés Molina Enríquez, who believed that only time and experience would teach land beneficiaries the benefits of individual private property.[59] Moreover, at the time many Mexicans had been impressed by the U.S. and Canadian homestead acts, which protected a nuclear family by freeing small-size property from taxes and embargos but also made the property inalienable and nontransferrable except by inheritance. As explained in chapter 4, many revolutionaries (mainly from northern states) had already adopted what in Mexico became known as family patrimony to protect land reform beneficiaries from land-grabbers and "powerful monopolizers."[60] Even Pancho Villa's May 1915 agrarian law regarding the breaking up of large landholdings via expropriation and the creation of small private farms made governors responsible for issuing laws for the creation and protection of "family patrimony," which would make land parcels up to twenty-four hectares inalienable and not subject to taxation or embargo.[61] Similarly, some Constitutional delegates in 1916-17 promoted the concept of family patrimony in both articles 27 and 123.[62] In its protections for workers, article 123 (which had been debated first) stated that civil laws in each state would determine the types of property (*bienes*) that could constitute family patrimony, which would be inalienable and not subject to embargo or taxation and could be transmitted only by inheritance. Similarly, article 27 (in a section unrelated to the restitution or granting of village lands) decreed that the states' civil laws "will organize family patrimony, determining the properties that would constitute it, on the basis that they would be inalienable and not subject to embargo or taxation."63 Yet despite these constitutional provisions, the idea of inalienable private property remained undefined in agrarian law during this time period.

Who Would the Agrarian Reform Beneficiaries Be?

Despite the legal limbo surrounding arable parcels, government officials responsible for implementing agrarian reform defined who in each beneficiary village would receive a private urban plot, a parcel of arable land (that would be privatized in some near future but would remain inalienable), and use rights to woodlands and water resources. To determine grant beneficiaries, a census commission would conduct a population census and an "agrarian census" in each petitioning village.64 Census commissions comprised three representatives: one from the state agrarian commission, one from the ayuntamiento, and one village representative elected by a simple majority.65 In theory, restitution procedures did not require censuses. But because many restitutions ultimately became dotaciones, most agrarian commission officials began their fieldwork by conducting censuses in all villages. Village leaders did the same. In Guerrero, for example, Tepetlacingo representatives informed the agrarian commission that "if, despite the legitimacy of our [restitution] petition, the documents we have supplied ... are insufficient for a favorable resolution, we enclose the general and agrarian censuses so that we can receive a dotación large enough to meet our needs and guarantee our economic independence."66

Agrarian censuses were modeled on nineteenth-century privatization tallies. Potential parcel beneficiaries were heads of nuclear families. "Family" was defined as nuclear rather than extended (one that included parents, children, and perhaps a dependent—often an elderly person). This was the conjugal unit favored by the Catholic Church, as well as by government officials for taxation purposes. The census listed resident heads of family (*jefe o cabeza de familia*), followed by the head's spouse and offspring, and it also recorded age, sex, and civil status, which together created a complex gendered hierarchy of potential rights-bearing individuals. Potential beneficiaries included married heads of family, who were obliged to provide for their spouse and offspring, as well as adult single males, who would have to provide for their *future* spouse and offspring. The census also granted rights to widows with children and single mothers.

As Heidi Tinsman has suggested in the Chilean context, Mexico's revolutionary agrarian reform arguably strengthened notions of the male provider and of male leadership in the family, given that only women lacking a male head of family could acquire parcel rights.[67] Like the Liberal privatization laws before them, however, revolutionary agrarian laws protected a small but important percentage of women whose legal status changed throughout their life cycle and was often negotiable. In both San Juan Quetzalcoapan (Tlaxcala) and San Juan (Chihuahua), for instance, around 30 percent of potential beneficiaries were women.[68] In Tuliman (Guerrero), 28 percent were women.[69] On average, roughly 15 to 20 percent of the heads of family listed in a typical agrarian census were women. This percentage, however small, was significant because it meant that women could transcend traditional gender roles. If a woman's civil status changed (and many women were abandoned or became widowed during the revolutionary fighting), then she could theoretically negotiate her right to a parcel as head of family—something women often did. In some villages, a dotación often increased the percentage of women with use rights to land parcels. In Hidalgo, for example, San Agustín Tlaxiaca officials conducted two censuses. One listed the number of individuals already in possession of small parcels of land, and another listed landless heads of nuclear families. Whereas 17 percent of women had access to land before the dotación, 32 percent were listed as heads of family.[70] In San Jerónimo (Hidalgo), 10 percent of women owned small urban lots or agricultural parcels, while 30 percent of women were listed on the agrarian census as heads of family.[71]

As in nineteenth-century privatization censuses, civil marriage was not a requirement for parcel rights.[72] For example, the San Agustín Tlaxiaca (Hidalgo) census listed all female heads of family as single.

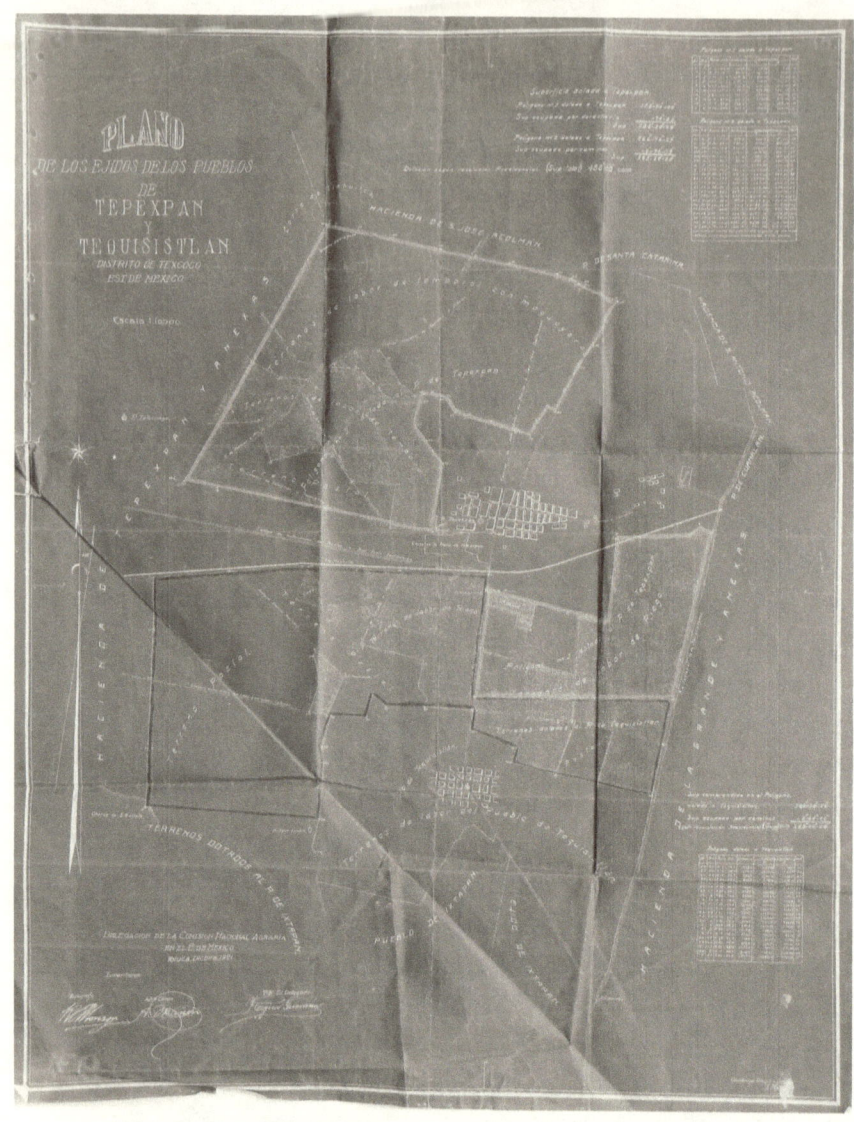

Fig. 9. Land grant map of Tepexpan and Tequisistlán (Mexico State) by the National Agrarian Commission, December 1921. Archivo Histórico y Biblioteca Central del Agua, CONAGUA-AHA, Fondo Aguas Nacionales, caja 5, exp. 72, f. 14.

The Xpechil (Yucatán) census listed eleven female heads of family as living in a conjugal unit (*vive maritalmente*). In Cucurpe (Sonora), where women comprised 21 percent of all heads of family, civil statuses included single, married, widowed, and even *puta* (a derogatory term for a female sex worker); none of these categories appears to have influenced officials' decisions regarding the right to serve as head of family.[73]

The census category that affected women the most was profession, because agrarian rights beneficiaries had to be farmers—and, at the time, agriculture was considered a male occupation. Heather Fowler-Salamini has shown how municipal census takers during the Díaz regime equated *jefes de familia* with male heads of household by allowing women only one occupational category: *doméstica* (housewife/homemaker).[74] Agrarian censuses also tended to categorize women's labor as household work. In the Federal District, all eighty women in the Santa María Aztahuacan census were listed as engaged in domestic activities, as were all the women in Santa Clara (San Luis Potosí).[75] In Tabasco the agrarian census for Villa de Tacotalpa listed every woman's occupation as that "of her sex."[76] Categorizations of this kind had important practical implications. Landowners had ten days in which to review the census, and they often tried to reduce the number of potential parcel beneficiaries so as to minimize the amount of land that would be expropriated.[77] For instance, when the administrator of the agricultural company El Encero (Veracruz) reviewed the El Chico census and found sixteen housewives (*dedicadas a quehaceres domésticos*), he argued that they could not be considered heads of family engaged in agriculture. Owing to this census category, agrarian officials excluded three of these women.[78]

There were, however, important exceptions elsewhere in the country. In Tuliman (Guerrero) the census classified a few women as labrador (farmer).[79] In San Luis Potosí several female residents of Jesús María were listed as *agricultor* (agriculturalist).[80] In Veracruz the Santa Cruz census categories included women as labrador and agricultor.[81] In the Federal District, women's professions in San Juanico Nextipac included

Return of the Judiciary 155

de campo (farmer) and *jornalero* (day laborer).⁸² In Oaxaca, the census of Santo Domingo Jalieza listed all adult women as *molenderas* (corn grinders), while that of Santa María Huatulco included molenderas, seamstresses, and cooks.⁸³

The Carranza-era agrarian census also included two categories that had not appeared in nineteenth-century privatization censuses: profession and relative poverty (amount of land and/or other property owned, such as capital or livestock). Potential parcel beneficiaries were adult farmers who did not have enough land to earn twice the average daily wage (*jornal*) characteristic of the region. In San Luis Potosí, for example, the Tanque Colorado census representative was instructed not to include professionals, individuals registered in the census as owning land parcels equal to or larger than those intended for dotación beneficiaries, or anyone possessing agricultural capital of more than one thousand pesos.⁸⁴ In Tuzantán (Chiapas), agrarian officials excluded several men because they had more than one thousand pesos in capital and were merchants.⁸⁵

Parallel Forms of Local Government

As agrarian officials proceeded to determine who in every restituted or granted village could become a beneficiary, villagers often complained to state agrarian commissions and the CNA about local abuses of power and unequal access to restituted and granted land and water resources. In response, the CNA created new forms of administration parallel to municipal authorities. In every village that received land in the form of a restitution or a dotación, heads of family (including women) had to elect by simple majority at least three representatives to form a local administrative committee (comité particular administrativo, or CPA) responsible for overseeing "the lands communally owned by the pueblos" and their gratis use.⁸⁶ Once the state government had provisionally granted or restituted land, CPAs had "the broadest faculties" to administer, preserve, and make productive the lands possessed communally by pueblos, including their provisional subdivision among residents.⁸⁷ In San Pedro Totoltepec (Mexico State), for example, Toluca municipal officials, the governor, and the president of the state agrarian commission conducted a ceremony in which CPA members promised "with all loyalty and patriotism to fulfill their legal obligations during their tenure ... until the lands are subdivided." Officials also noted that if the agrarian laws did not subdivide the parcels within a year, CPA members would have to surrender their posts to a new, democratically elected committee.[88]

In the absence of clear rules concerning the property rights of those who received restituted and granted lands, agrarian laws continued to increase CPAs' authority as instruments of governance and administration that operated independently of municipal and state governments. Circular 48 of 1921, for example, allowed CPAs not only to divide farmlands seasonally into parcels for heads of family but also to manage the common use of woodlands and pasturelands and name a commissioner for the management of water resources.[89] In addition, CPAs were supposed to collect taxes on parcels and communal lands (10 percent for the federal government, 15 percent for state governments, and 5 percent for ayuntamientos—with the remaining 70 percent for pueblo public services under CPA administration). These public services often included managing sources of water for domestic use, repairing infrastructure, and setting up schools—all of which were officially ayuntamiento responsibilities.[90] In Puebla, for example, the Zoyapetlayoca CPA managed the village's water resources both for cropland irrigation and domestic use, and it planned to reopen a school that had been closed for three years "now that the ejidatarios have agreed to contribute 15 percent of their future crops."[91] Similarly in Mexico State, San Pedro Totoltepec CPA members wrote a report explaining how they had repaired rural roads, constructed bridges, distributed parcels among heads of family, and reserved some land for an experimental agricultural farm "for the practical agricultural education of the sons and daughters of the pueblo."[92]

The CPAs' authority over village resources independently of municipal governments was problematic in two ways. First, many revolutionary factions agreed on the need for autonomous municipalities, and

Return of the Judiciary 157

they included calls for the "free municipality" (*municipio libre*) in their legal proclamations. Carranza's 26 December 1914 decree, for example, demanded the dissolution of political chiefs and the emancipation of municipalities.[93] In 1917 these demands were incorporated into article 115 of the Constitution, and the municipality became the political and territorial basis of all states, forbidding intermediary governments or territorial divisions between municipalities and states.

Second, the CPAs' independent authority over local land and water management created problems because in practice, CPA members tended to engage in widespread corruption, favoritism, and abuse of power.[94] Often they only represented the interests of the few. In an example from Guerrero, forty-one Chontalcoatlán residents signed a letter addressed to the CNA president in which they complained about the CPA's abuse of power:

> Since the so-called Agricultural Committee was formed, we have always condemned the conduct of its members on account of their strange and harmful actions toward the residents of this humble pueblo. The president and the committee continuously insult and threaten us, only because we do not approve of their projects and their ideas related to agrarianism. We are not in agreement with their doctrines, nor are we in agreement with how they molest nonviolent, hardworking, and honest pueblo men. We know that most social classes are not in agreement with the unjust and undoubtedly illegal proceedings of the so-called Agricultural Committee.[95]

Villagers frequently accused CPA members of corrupt practices in the management of parcel rights.[96] In Hidalgo, for example, Tlanalapa resident Aurelia Islas viuda de Ramírez protested to a CNA inspector that the police commander had seized her parcel and then granted it to a resident without parcel rights. Because the CPA refused to hear her complaint, she asked the inspector to grant her justice. In fact there were so many complaints of this kind from Tlanalapa residents that a Hidalgo agrarian official reported that the village had suffered eight years of "corrupt repartos." The official said that although a few residents had parcels of eighteen to twenty-one hectares each, "the poorest, who really needed the benefits of ejido lands, had none." In response to the widespread complaints, agrarian officials instructed the CPA president to conduct a new reparto that would benefit the needy.[97] And in Oaxaca, municipal officials and several villagers from Nazareno Etla complained to the CNA about the CPA (at the time called *junta de aprovechamiento de ejidos*). They argued that "from the first moment that the [members of the] junta began their tasks, they attracted the antipathy of all residents—or of the great majority of them—because of their acts of oppression, reprisal, and vengeance, threatening to take away the parcels residents had received or charging arbitrary and exaggerated quotas for the payment of contributions to the state treasury, even while they exempted themselves and their families or their favorites from paying what they owed."[98]

Despite complaints about corruption and favoritism, all subsequent laws strengthened this new form of local authority. For instance, Obregón's circular 48 (1921) canceled the rule that members of CPAs had to be renewed every year by majority vote, allowing them to remain in power until 20 percent of all agriculturalists with voting rights manifested nonconformity.[99] The following year, circular 51—famous as the antecedent to the cooperative forms of organization established for agrarian reform beneficiaries in the 1930s—ratified the CPAs' increased authority by stating that as long there were no implementing regulations for article 27, CPAs would remain in charge of villagers' "collective well-being." It justified the increase in CPA authority on the grounds that elected individuals with technical skills to run cooperatives required some stability in their positions.[100] Ironically, when President Plutarco Elías Calles (1924–28) tried to privatize restituted and granted arable land (but not woodlands or water resources), he preserved these local forms of government that operated parallel to municipal authorities. In fact, when Calles's 1925 law on ejido parcel patrimony sought to create family patrimony laws for restituted and granted arable land, he turned CPAs into "ejido commissars" (*comisarios ejidales*).¹⁰¹ Congressman Manuel Aguayo pinpointed the problem of combining family patrimony with the creation of parallel forms of local government. What agrarian officials under Calles called "ejido parcel patrimony," Aguayo said, was family patrimony, as authorized by the 1917 Constitution. The problem with the Calles law was that it placed family patrimony parcels under the authority of commissars who could adjudicate, distribute, and administer land, whereas the family patrimony authorized by articles 27 and 123 did not require oversight. Therefore, he argued, commissar boards should not exist.¹⁰²

And yet, as problematic as these local authorities often were, they became the building blocks of what we know as the twentieth-century ejido—namely, population centers that became corporate owners of restituted and granted lands with their own local authorities parallel to those of municipalities.

In just a few years, the Supreme Court's amparo rulings helped formalize two types of legal procedures that were without precedent: restitution suits judged by the executive and land expropriations without prior compensation and not for public utility but, rather, for the subsistence needs of impoverished villages. In the process, the justices also redefined the landowners' and the beneficiaries' rights to be heard in court.

By contrast, the CNA delegates failed to define the nature of restituted and granted lands, with important future consequences. Restituted or granted properties were not intended to be an indivisible whole, as they would become after 1934; CNA delegates created distinct regulations for different resources (urban plots, woodlands, water resources, and arable land) but famously failed to define property rights over arable parcels. Because property rights over restituted and granted lands remained in limbo, especially when it came to arable parcels, CNA delegates allowed local agrarian authorities (later called *comisariados ejidales* for dotaciones and *comisariados de bienes comunales* for both land restitutions and legalized preexisting communal lands) gradually to mushroom across the countryside and become forms of local authority parallel to municipal governments, setting the stage for the post-1934 ejidos.[103]

Perhaps the repercussions of these voids were difficult to see at the time because most states were implementing land reform piecemeal. Paradoxically, it would be in Morelos, after Zapata's death, where the Carranza-Obregón agrarian reform would be fully implemented.

6

The Morelos Laboratory, 1920–1924

> Lo justo y moral es conciliar los intereses de todos los habitantes de la región, a fin de distribuir la tierra proporcionalmente al número de pueblos y haciendas afectables. [The just and moral is to reconcile the interests of all the inhabitants of the region in order to distribute available hacienda lands proportionally to the pueblos.]
> —CNA delegates, 2 June 1922 session

After Emiliano Zapata's assassination in April 1919, the Zapatista leadership joined supporters of General Álvaro Obregón in signing the April 1920 Plan de Agua Prieta, which repudiated the Carranza administration. In exchange, Obregón allowed Zapatistas to govern Morelos and implement land reform—albeit on the condition that they distribute lands according to the 6 January 1915 law. The Zapatista interim governor (with support from the CNA and the Supreme Court) pushed Carrancista land reform procedures to their limits, especially when it came to granting political status to settlements on hacienda lands and giving provisional land possessions to villages.[1] In this way Morelos became a laboratory for the Constitutionalist land reform, with the National Agrarian Commission granting provisional land grants to as many as 114 of the 150 existing population centers by the end of 1925.[2]

John Womack Jr. views the 1920s reparto in Morelos as a triumph for Zapatismo, a process that turned the state into "a place where villagers could remain villagers, endowed decently and by right, economically enfranchised."[3] Arturo Warman, on the other hand, claims that Obregón's reparto wiped the slate clean—ignoring the Zapatista land reform, making peasants dependent on state institutions, and allowing rich, abusive leaders to take advantage of poor, honest folk.[4] Guillermo de la Peña is less ideological in his study of the Morelos highlands. He points out that the average time it took villagers to receive land, from their initial petition to the presidential resolution, was a long six years. In addition, the reality was that the amount of arable land per head of family was very small, and water-supply problems remained largely unresolved.[5]

These limitations were, however, inherent in the implementation of the 6 January 1915 law in all states. In fact the Morelos land reform was as good as it got—given the strict limitations of Carranza's law.[6] Moreover, the Morelos reform was unprecedented in that the state agrarian commission, the governor, the CNA, the Supreme Court, and the president of the Republic were all united in their commitment to seeing the law implemented as quickly as possible.[7] If there were to be a state in which the 6 January 1915 law was fully implemented (despite the red tape, delayed procedures, and small land grants), it would be Morelos. Nowhere else in Mexico did agrarian officials grant land to so many villages in such a short time. Yet among all these land grants, officials managed to rule favorably on only two restitution claims (as opposed to dotaciones). One of the villages denied a restitution was, ironically, Zapata's hometown of Anenecuilco. Based on an extensive review of archival records, this chapter will explain why.

The early efforts at land reform in Morelos made two things clear. First, the village-by-village restitution and grant procedures embodied in Carranza's 6 January 1915 law were never intended to be a tool for regional land and water reform. But between restitutions and grants, the latter were more expedient when agrarian surveyors and officials were confronted with intervillage boundary conflicts, or when they had to distribute hacienda lands and water resources among many adjoining villages. Second, even the more effective dotaciones were insufficiently flexible when it came to regional planning, a fact most obvious when it came to hydrologic planning, which was regional by nature.

The Morelos Laboratory 163

The Parres Reforms in Morelos

"At home in 1920," Womack concludes, "the Zapatistas had emerged in almost absolute control." Their leaders were General Genovevo de la O as state military commander; Dr. José G. Parres (the leading medic in the Liberation Army of the South) as provisional governor between June 1920 and December 1923; engineer Carlos M. Peralta (alias "Atl," the former head Zapatista spy in Mexico City in 1917) as the Morelos secretary of state; and Jenaro Amezcua (a high-ranking Zapatista officer who represented the movement in the Convention government) as the Secretaría de Fomento's top-ranking representative in Morelos.[8] At the CNA, Zapatista sympathizer General Antonio I. Villarreal González served as secretary general between July 1920 and December 1921.[9] In fact several top Zapatistas became CNA council members, including Miguel Mendoza López Schwerdtfeger (the Zapatista headquarters secretary and minister of justice) and the famous Zapatista general Gildardo Magaña.[10] In addition, during this period CNA delegates opened doors to many of the surveyors who, like Marte R. Gómez, had been part of the 1915 agrarian commissions.[11]

With so many high-ranking Zapatistas in power, optimism soared. In July 1920 Brigadier General Serafín M. Robles, a Zapatista who had participated in the negotiations with Obregón, triumphantly informed other revolutionaries that "the pueblo land reparto is going to be conducted immediately and according to the Plan de Ayala."[12] Agrarian reform would, in fact, be conducted right away—but not according to the Plan de Ayala. However much the surveyors tried to respect the old Zapatista repartos (and they often did), the reform would be conducted according to the 6 January 1915 law. In signing the Agua Prieta plan, the Zapatistas had accepted agrarian reform based on article 27 of the Constitution.[13]

Governor Parres accepted the conditions integral to the Constitutionalist law. He hailed the Plan de Ayala and all Zapatista land reform efforts conducted during the revolutionary years, but he also accepted established dotación and restitution procedures, stating that they would be only the beginning of land reform: "The 6 January 1915 law, incorporated into article 27, has been accepted by us as part of the revolutionary unification of the Republic, [and] it resolves one phase of the agrarian problem, favoring with its principles pueblo and village residents, leaving for the near future the breakup of large landholdings, as Zapata promised."[14] The response of many villagers was enthusiastic.[15] Tetelcingo residents, for instance, praised "the active efforts of our current governor . . . in fulfilling the promises made by the Revolution headed by Señor General Emiliano Zapata."[16] Several pueblo representatives immediately sought contact with the new Morelos Agrarian Commission (under Alfredo C. Ortega) to resolve the numerous land issues that remained pending after the 1914–15 Zapatista repartos. Some village leaders had tried earlier to resolve their land conflicts through the Carrancista agrarian commission in Cuautla, where Pablo González (a brutal general sent to pacify Morelos) had his headquarters, but most petitions apparently went unanswered. Now they hoped the new commission would resolve their problems.[17]

In some cases, villagers went to the agrarian commission to revisit the Zapatista repartos. Tecajec delegates, for example, explained how the village had lost access to its water resources: "The Tecajec lands are cross-cut by an irrigation canal belonging to the Santa Clara hacienda, and this canal has not supplied us with water since the revolution, when the residents of Ocuituco took it all to irrigate their lands, leaving us not even enough water for domestic use and forcing Tecajec residents to fetch water from the bottom of the Iluca gorge."[18] In Atlatlahucan the 1921 census revealed that the Zapatista reparto had been highly unequal, with a few people holding parcels fifty hectares and larger while 365 heads of family did not have enough land to earn a living.[19]

Other Morelos residents complained about the return of several landowners (or their managers or tenants) who began charging rent on occupied hacienda lands. In Amacuzac, for example, villagers had occupied the lands of the San Gabriel hacienda in 1910, but by December 1919 the San Gabriel manager (backed by the Tetecala municipal authorities installed by General González) tried to force them to pay back rent after their harvest. Having been ignored by the Cuautla Agrarian Commission in 1919, the Amacuzac representatives took their claims to the Ministry of Agriculture and later to Parres's new agrarian commission.[20] In fact enough landowners had returned to Morelos during the winter of 1919–20 that in October 1920, Villarreal issued an accord authored by CNA council member (and Zapatista) Ángel Barrios that allowed villagers to keep control of reparto lands until the Morelos Agrarian Commission could legalize them. The accord stated: "Given that the Morelos hacienda owners threaten to appropriate the lands that are already being cultivated by the pueblos of this state, in order to avoid the grave damage that pueblos would suffer from these seizures while their petitions for land are being definitively resolved, the National Agrarian Commission urges the governor of Morelos and the municipal authorities of the state to allow these pueblos to preserve the land they were cultivating ... within the boundaries designated by the state agrarian commissions in 1915."[21]

As the agrarian commission began work in Morelos, Governor Parres used his position to overcome two of the greatest limitations of the Carrancista reform: first, the inability of many settlements to petition for a dotación because they lacked official political status; and second, the prolonged delays villagers faced in obtaining land parcels through a complicated, multilayered land reform program prone to bureaucratic rigidity, personnel shortages, and defiance from landowners. Parres addressed these challenges by issuing decree no. 5 on 4 September 1920. It promised both to deal expeditiously with land requests and to issue certificates of political status to settlements that had no legal recognition, given that "the political category of a pueblo is second to the economic needs of its residents."[22] In fact, between July 1920 and the end of his term in December 1923, Governor Parres awarded political status to fifty-three settlements (mostly on hacienda lands) and accelerated the restitution and dotación process by granting more than one hundred provisional possessions—and he did this in record time.[23]

Granting political status to population centers so that they could petition for a dotación was a contentious issue. In 1917 the CNA's circular 27 had restricted the collective right to seek a dotación to population centers with a recognized political status (*categoría política*) and an independent existence (*vida independiente*), specifically excluding settlements on factory and hacienda lands and mining camps. The circular did not, however, forbid population centers from applying for political recognition.[24] In fact state legislatures were able to grant political status to such irregular settlements as hacienda peons and displaced villagers. In 1918, for example, the Durango legislature gave workers, sharecroppers, and renters living on three Durango haciendas the political status required to petition for and obtain fundos legales.[25] Villarreal later issued a circular instructing governors to encourage state legislatures to grant political recognition to settlements of workers and their families living on large estates so that state agrarian commissions and the CNA could process dotación petitions.[26]

Many landowners challenged the political-status certificates Parres granted to settlements within hacienda boundaries. Eva Escobar viuda de Alarcón, for example, claimed that the Temilpa dotación was illegal because the petitioners were *acasillados* (hacienda peons living on hacienda lands) who had been living on the hacienda as sugar refinery workers.[27] The Vidal family, owners of the San José Vista Hermosa hacienda, also argued that granting political recognition to hacienda settlements was illegal:

> On this hacienda, as on all other Morelos haciendas, next to the *casco* [main residential buildings] there are houses and other structures built by the hacienda owners to house the estate's workers. These buildings are together called the hacienda's *real*. In the political-municipal order, population centers have been called haciendas, and the government has intervened in matters concerning them, such as naming authorities or providing schooling and other services—even though most of these services have been financed by the haciendas. [These *reales*] have never had their own existence as pueblos, given that only hacienda workers—never outsiders—have been allowed to live there, as opposed to other population centers with their own

The Morelos Laboratory 167

status, where anyone can go and live on the condition that the person construct his or her home on lands previously purchased or rented.[28]

Luis García Pimentel denounced the Ixtlilco petitioners for being "owners only of the *jacales* [huts] they inhabited," whereas they had always recognized that the hacienda was his property.[29] And when Parres granted the San Ignacio housing settlement a political-status certificate, García Pimentel filed an amparo suit and instructed the state agrarian commission to halt all dotación procedures on the Tenango hacienda until the Supreme Court ruled on the matter. The agrarian commission responded that there was no law permitting the suspension of a dotación on those grounds. Not only did agrarian officials ignore the amparo suit, but Parres also continued to grant political status to other settlements within other García Pimentel haciendas.[30]

Provisional possession had been a contentious matter during the Carranza regime, and it remained so during the Parres reforms. Early on, Carranza passed a decree reforming articles 7, 8, and 9 of the 6 January 1915 law. Known as the 19 September 1916 decree, it forbade governors from granting a village provisional possession before the CNA had a chance to study the case file, make a recommendation, and forward it to the president for his resolution.[31] After 1917, CNA proponents of provisional possession claimed that when members of the Constitutional Convention (1916-17) incorporated the 6 January 1915 law into article 27, they had automatically canceled the 19 September 1916 decree.[32] Under Villarreal's presidency the CNA allowed governors to grant provisional possessions under special circumstances, such as not leaving lands fallow in times of food shortages.[33] For instance, Villarreal supported interim Durango governor General Enrique Nájera's decision to grant provisional possessions to thirteen villages on the grounds that taking advantage of the agricultural cycle was an urgent public health matter. The same decree that authorized the Durango provisional restitutions also encouraged all other governors to follow Nájera's example.[34]

One of the proactive governors was Parres, who granted more than one hundred provisional possessions during his three and a half years as interim governor. On average, Morelos Agrarian Commission officials granted provisional possessions within a month of Parres's resolution, making it the fastest reform process in the country. Most important, the CNA later ratified provisional possessions in Morelos in nearly every case, most often without later reducing the amount of land or water resources provisionally granted (as often happened elsewhere). In fact in some instances CNA delegates even expanded the size of a land grant, especially when the population had grown while agrarian officials were processing the case file.[35]

It is not surprising that landowners often challenged Parres's granting of provisional possessions. Hacienda owner Luis García Pimentel, for example, repeatedly argued that there was no proof that the members of the Constitutional Convention had failed to incorporate the 6 January 1915 law into article 27 *with* its 19 September 1916 reforms. Furthermore, he pointed out that the CNA was not a legislative body that could issue opinions on this matter. Isabel S. de Corona similarly appealed the provisional possession granted to the San Francisco Zacualpan pueblo by citing the 19 September 1916 decree.[36] In fact all landowners who filed amparo suits against provisional possessions cited this law. According to Marte R. Gómez, if a landowner discovered that the state agrarian commission was about to grant a provisional possession that affected his or her property, the landowner would immediately file for amparo protection. To avoid this, explains Gómez, the Morelos Agrarian Commission implemented the "early bird" tactic (*madruguete*): by the time landowners petitioned for amparo protection, agrarian officials had already granted the provisional possession.[37]

The Role of the Judiciary in the Morelos Land Reform

In his retrospective chronicle of CNA politics in the 1920s, Marte R. Gómez observes that the Supreme Court had posed an obstacle to the Morelos reforms.[38] Indeed scholars often blame the judiciary for obstructing justice in these matters.[39] Yet hacienda owners were so

The Morelos Laboratory 169

desperate that sixteen of them wrote a public letter to the governor, begging him to order the CNA and the Morelos Agrarian Commission to suspend the processing of any grant petition that might affect the sugar-producing estates and to return to their legitimate owners the lands they had been despoiled of.[40] In fact, archival records for the 1920-24 period show that however much they might have delayed procedures, Morelos district court judges granted protection to landowners in only a very few cases—and the Supreme Court reversed all of them.[41]

One reason why the Supreme Court denied so many of these amparos was that by the time Morelos landowners began filing suits, the justices had already set precedents regarding several agrarian matters that made it almost impossible for landowners to win amparo suits against any aspect of the 6 January 1915 law (see chapter 5).

An effective way for the Supreme Court to strike down landowners' amparo petitions was for justices to invoke the court's role as the guardian of the interests of "society and the state." In one Morelos case, the representative of the Pérez Cortina family (owners of the Santa Cruz Vista Alegre hacienda) sent the court eight typed pages pinpointing the legal inconsistencies in Obregón's 28 December 1920 ejido law. (In fact, Obregón canceled it less than a year later, precisely because of its internal contradictions.)[42] The landowners claimed that the agrarian administration had violated their right to be notified; they had been informed of the opening of dotación proceedings, but the 1920 ejido law stipulated that owners had to be notified of the closing of such proceedings as well. The justices with one stroke disqualified all possible plaintiff claims by concluding that legal dispositions related to resolving the agrarian problem were of public interest and that an amparo could not be justified because it would cause damage to society and the state.[43] In a similar case landowner Manuel Araoz petitioned the Morelos district court for amparo protection against a dotación to the Atlacholoaya pueblo. When the district judge denied the petition, the lawyer for the plaintiff demonstrated in detail the judge's manifold legal errors and inaccuracies. Yet when the case reached the Supreme Court, the justices struck it down with a single sentence: fulfillment of the dotación was in the interests of society and the state.⁴⁴

Another basis on which the Supreme Court rejected landowners' amparo petitions in Morelos was to uphold article 10 of the 6 January 1915 law, which allowed landowners to seek redress before the judiciary only *after* a presidential resolution had been issued—and then only to claim compensation. In the case of Tetelilla, for example, Parres granted the village an 840-hectare dotación, but two years later the presidential resolution extended it to 1,176 hectares. This extension included a water source that the García Pimentel family did not want to lose, and they filed for amparo protection against the presidential resolution at the district court. The district judge granted the amparo because, in his opinion, given the number of beneficiaries, the additional three-hundred-hectare dotación had been excessive. The Supreme Court revoked the district judge's amparo, however, because article 10 of the 6 January 1915 law—which was "now constitutional law"—stated that the injured party first had, within a year, to take the claim to the tribunals (ostensibly the states' civil courts) and, as long as this *juicio* (suit) was not concluded, the injured party could not petition for amparo protection.⁴⁵

Supreme Court Justice Guzmán Vaca wrote a dissenting opinion in this case in which he addressed the paradox of article 10. A juicio meant that landowners had the right to be heard in court before a presidential resolution was issued, but landowners only had the right to claim amparo protection at the district court and the Supreme Court after the fact. Moreover, a juicio meant that landowners had a fair chance of winning the suit (thereby revoking the presidential resolution and reclaiming their lands), but agrarian law made it impossible for the landowner to reverse a presidential resolution and have his or her lands returned because the owner could only claim compensation. What Guzmán Vaca described as the fallacies of article 10 were in fact clear to all, but the justices nevertheless employed article 10 repeatedly to deny landowners the right to challenge presidential resolutions on agrarian matters, in Morelos and other states.⁴⁶

In Morelos, where Parres granted more than one hundred provisional possessions during his short tenure, Supreme Court justices cited article 10 of the 6 January 1915 law as a means of sidestepping debates regarding the 19 September 1916 decree (that is, debates over whether governors had the right to grant villages' provisional lands before the CNA had the chance to study the case file and make a recommendation). When landowners in Morelos sought amparo protection against provisional possessions granted by Parres, they found that the court had altogether sidestepped the question of the validity of the 19 September 1916 circular. Instead the justices ruled on procedural grounds—that is, when landowners made an amparo claim against a provisional possession, they ruled against them on the grounds that the legal process had not been exhausted. For instance, when María Portillo de Diez de Sollano petitioned for suspension of the provisional possession granted to the Xochitepec pueblo (arguing that the 19 September 1916 decree was still valid), the court denied her petition on the grounds that article 10 of the 6 January 1915 law made the governor's resolution (a first-instance ruling) dependent on the CNA's recommendations and the final presidential resolution (a second-instance ruling). To be valid, an amparo claim had to be filed *after* the second-instance ruling.[47]

Morelos and the Problem with Restitutions

Interim governor Parres and CNA president Villarreal, with the full support of the Supreme Court, distributed as much land to Morelos villagers as the 6 January 1915 law would allow. Yet of the hundred-plus resolutions, Parres (and his successors) managed to rule positively on only two restitution claims. But they did not (as Warman asserts) privilege dotaciones to make land beneficiaries "dependent on government largesse rather than on their own ancient claims to land."[48] Instead Parres and his administration wanted to distribute land expeditiously, and restitution claims—whether filed in the courts before the 1910 Revolution or in the agrarian offices thereafter—involved drawn-out judicial procedures with stringent proof requirements that Morelos town leaders could not easily meet. Parres sought to complete land distribution during his interim governorship, and it was only through dotaciones that Morelos officials would be able to grant land to so many population centers in such a brief time. If between 1920 and 1924 they had not favored the dotación as the legal vehicle for land distribution, it is likely that they would have managed to distribute land to only half as many villages as they did, given that approximately fifty of the hundred-plus land petitions were for restitutions.[49] In fact Parres did not even remain in power long enough to see through the only two successful restitution claims made in all of Morelos during his tenure. An analysis of these two successful cases shows why restitutions were such long, complex matters, and why dotaciones were a much more expedient alternative to restitutions.

San Francisco Ocoxaltepec, the first successful restitution case, was completed in December 1924, a year after Parres was replaced as governor. Like many other restitution claims, this one involved the loss of more than one set of lands, each under different circumstances. The first property was the 183-hectare Jalatlaco rancho, which had been purchased by the pueblo's ancestors in 1875. At that time, it was illegal for villages (as corporations) to purchase land, so pueblo representative Miguel Díaz bought the lands in his own name and then bequeathed them to pueblo residents on his death. The problem was that under the laws forbidding communal land ownership, Miguel Díaz's will was not legally binding, and in 1902 the San Rafael paper factory, with the Ministry of the Treasury's consent, claimed these lands as untitled. In 1922 the Morelos agrarian administration decided that Miguel Díaz's will had in fact been illegal. But because the villagers could prove that they had possessed the lands for twenty-seven years (and thus had acquisitive prescription rights, which they acquired through peaceful possession over a period of time) *and* possessed documents proving the 1902 land loss to the paper company, the CNA declared that the acquisition by the Ministry of the Treasury had been an illegal land seizure.

The second Ocoxaltepec property was the 159-hectare Zacamilpa rancho, for which the residents had colonial titles. Sometime late in the nineteenth century, village elders had rented the land to one

Agustín Yáñez, who then illegally bequeathed it to his offspring. Here too Ocoxaltepec representatives were able to prove both original ownership and illegal seizure after 1856. (They also held a document issued by the Conventionist government on 19 August 1915 that granted them restitution of both ranchos.) In December 1924 Governor Ismael Velasco, Parres's successor, restituted both ranchos. Two years passed, however, before the CNA finished reviewing the documentation and survey results and then ratified the restitution.[50]

Ahuacatitlán, the second successful restitution case, took even longer to complete. In December 1921 village representatives petitioned for the return of pueblo lands seized by the Temixco hacienda. They explained that around 1870, when the villagers had failed to pay taxes, the Morelos government under General Francisco Leyva embargoed 5,271 hectares of their land and sold it to the Temixco hacienda. The six villagers who challenged the hacienda's right to pueblo lands were banished to Quintana Roo and never seen again. The village fought four separate legal battles with the hacienda between 1889 and 1905, but they had no success.

At first, Ahuacatitlán representatives had difficulty providing the proof required to substantiate the restitution claim, and the agrarian officials recommended that they petition for a dotación instead. The Ahuacatitlán executive committee complained that the officials were trying to grant them a dotación of lands they probably already possessed, warning that "the residents will not accept a reduction of their lands with a dotación." One way to break the impasse was for the CNA to appoint a procurador de pueblos to counsel the Ahuacatitlán representatives on how to prove that their lands had been seized after 1856 in violation of article 1 of the 6 January 1915 law. Six years later, in 1929, after overcoming some doubts about whether their old titles were authentic, the Ahuacatitlán representatives managed to win their claim and recover the entire 5,271 hectares.[51]

It took several years and much effort on the part of many individuals to win favorable rulings on Ocoxaltepec's and Ahuacatitlán's restitution claims—and these were pueblos that managed to present titles with clear boundaries and had proof of illegal land seizures after 1856. As in other states at the time, however, many town leaders in Morelos lacked authentic land titles with discernible boundaries. In describing the factors that delayed the Parres reform, de la Peña notes that restitutions "demanded the presentation of documents which were both authentic and clear. The authenticity could not always be proved.... It was difficult to mark precise boundaries based on colonial documents. References to 'a big tree,' 'a stone in the shape of a cow' ... were difficult to locate after 400 years."[52] Moreover, some pueblos (such as Huejotengo) had authentic documents but not deeds.[53] Other pueblo representatives, knowingly or naively, presented fake titles.[54] Many others did not understand the complicated agrarian laws and procedures. Some representatives claimed restitutions even when their settlements had never had political status.[55] Furthermore, if we accept Horacio Crespo's thesis that most pueblo lands in the sugar-producing region had already been seized by the end of the seventeenth century, then the claims from this part of Morelos would automatically fall outside the 6 January 1915 requirement that the pueblo land loss had to have occurred after the Lerdo law was adopted on 25 June 1856.[56] Besides, many pueblo land sales had been legal transactions. Ethical or not, they had been legitimate sales under the laws that existed at the time and could not be disputed as an agrarian restitution claim. One clear example was Ocuituco. In the 1860s Ocuituco representatives sold the fields known as "Cuatzin de San Antonio" to the Santa Clara hacienda for two thousand pesos. Claiming that the pueblo's nineteenth-century representatives had not acted in good faith, in December 1919 Ocuituco petitioned the CNA for restitution of the San Antonio Cuautzingo pasturelands and their water source. In 1922, however, the Morelos Agrarian Commission declared that the sale had been legal and was therefore not protected under article 1 of the 6 January 1915 law.[57]

Because representatives of approximately fifty Morelos villages petitioned for restitutions and many of them were doomed from the start, Governor Parres and his advisers saw the dotación as the only way to sidestep the legal morass in which these claims could become mired.

Apart from Ocoxaltepec and Ahuacatitlán, Parres and his successors processed all other restitution petitions as dotaciones—with the proviso that the pueblos reserved their right to claim restitution at some point in the future when they had more or better substantiating evidence.

The Anenecuilco Question

One of the great mysteries of the Parres land reform in Morelos is why officials did not grant Zapata's hometown of Anenecuilco the land restitution its residents fought so hard to acquire. The case is important not only because legend has it that Zapata decided to organize the Revolution of the South after studying the pueblo's titles and deciding he had solid proof to support their long-ignored court claims, but also because many academics have extrapolated from this particular case to draw conclusions about what they believe was the nature of postrevolutionary peasant-state relations. A close examination of the extensive documentation on Anenecuilco at the Archivo General Agrario reveals a more complicated story.

Governor Parres and Morelos Agrarian Commission president Alfredo C. Ortega planned to make both Anenecuilco and neighboring Villa de Ayala showcases of their land reform program. A few months after Parres became interim governor, agrarian commission officials asked the pueblos' leaders to sign a blueprint for a land petition. On 26 September 1920 Francisco Franco Salazar ("the man Zapata had appointed to protect the documents that supported Anenecuilco's land claims") and fifteen other men, including José Robles (another trusted ally and Anenecuilco representative during the Zapatistas' 2 July 1915 boundary marking), signed the petition.[58] A day later Villa de Ayala representatives signed a petition as well.[59]

Two days after receiving the Anenecuilco and Villa de Ayala petitions, Ortega declared the Morelos Agrarian Commission "in permanent session until they resolved the Anenecuilco and Villa de Ayala petitions." Villa de Ayala petitioned for a dotación, which the commission immediately approved. Anenecuilco petitioned for a restitución, but commission officials concluded that the file did not contain enough evidence to justify restoration of the claimed lands. Immediately, therefore, officials granted the pueblo a dotación instead. On this matter, the Morelos Agrarian Commission's minutes book stated the following: "Regarding the restitution demanded by the Anenecuilco pueblo... the petition is denied on the grounds that even though it is true that it justifies the need for ejido lands, it is also true that it does not provide all evidentiary proof to justify the right it claims to have over the areas of land solicited for restitution."[60]

Only six days later (on 2 October 1920), and for the entire world to see, Governor Parres formally granted provisional land possession to Anenecuilco and Villa de Ayala. Present at the ceremony were Zapatista generals Genovevo de la O, Rafael Castillo C., Carlos Víctor Ariza, Luis Sánchez Galán, and Serafín Robles (a man so trusted by Zapata that he became part of his escort and his private secretary).[61] The grant provided Anenecuilco villagers enough land from the Tenextepango, Cuahuixtla, and El Hospital haciendas "to satisfy the needs of all heads of family," leaving them with the right to claim a restitution when they had more substantiating evidence.[62]

There are three possible ways of interpreting the problem of missing evidentiary proof, and they are not mutually exclusive. One possibility is that because the Anenecuilco case was so closely associated with General Zapata and his Plan de Ayala, it was symbolically important for the village to be the first recipient of a provisional land possession under Parres's decree number 5. A dotación greatly sped up this temporary land award.[63] Agrarian officials probably knew that if they waited for Franco to present Anenecuilco's documents, Parres would not have managed to grant Anenecuilco provisional possession two days later. As agrarian officials were aware, pueblo "titles" usually comprised a large number of colonial documents and maps, as well as nineteenth-century land transactions and court documents, that took a team of paleographers and surveyors many months to examine and survey. Therefore, the only way to grant provisional possession swiftly (in a form that had any chance of being ratified later) was through a dotación.

Fig. 10. Merced of San Miguel Anenecuilco, Morelos, 1853 (copy of 1614 original). Archivo General de la Nación Colección Mapas, Planos e Ilustraciones, no. 206.

Several documents substantiate this first explanation. On 28 October 1920, CNA delegate Regino Guzmán complained that he had not been informed of the provisional land distribution, in the process of which the Morelos Agrarian Commission had made several procedural mistakes. In Guzmán's opinion, officials were "privileging the political over the juridical ... making pomp with the Plan de Ayala, which is not a law, and this is why landowners are on guard, waiting for officials to infringe upon legal procedures in order to sue for amparo protection." He further commented, "The governor of the state is a very good person, very correct, very thoughtful, and of irreproachable conduct.... His wish is that the agrarian matter progresses more and more, [and he is] always in favor of the pueblos of the state.... And this is why he bends the rules [*se sale del camino legal*], opening the way to amparo suits." In fact, a few days later, the district court informed the governor and the agrarian commission that they had three days in which to provide information on the provisional possession because landowner Manuel Araoz had filed an amparo suit and the hearing was to be held on 12 November.⁶⁴

Two additional documents—both from CNA delegates—appear to substantiate the interpretation that Anenecuilco had received a dotación (as opposed to initiating a restitution suit) because government officials wanted Anenecuilco to serve as the flagship of the Parres reforms. The first was authored by Marte R. Gómez (CNA associate director at the time), who wrote in his 1922 "complementary report on the processing of the San Miguel Anenecuilco file" that it was "clear that the [agrarian commission] ruling did not give the pueblo enough time to prove their rights."⁶⁵ The second supporting document is a report by the CNA delegate who reviewed the matter two years later; he speculated that the Morelos Agrarian Commission granted both Anenecuilco and Villa de Ayala a dotación "so as to accelerate the process."⁶⁶

Womack also subscribes to this version of events. From what Franco later told historian Jesús Sotelo Inclán, Womack concludes as follows: "The governor's response was a fast shuffle, a favor instead of justice. Since the agronomists in the National Agrarian Commission and the

Department of Agriculture had decided that reform deriving from old, often faulty titles would only confuse the issue, the land Parrés [*sic*] provided the Anenecuilcans was not a restitution but a grant—over twelve hundred acres, about what they had asked him to recognize as their own. The Anenecuilcans had little choice but to accept."[67] Thus, given the evidence, it is quite possible that Zapata's hometown was denied a restitution of its original lands simply because CNA members realized a dotación was the more expedient and irrevocable solution.

A second explanation for Anenecuilco's failure to receive restitution is that pueblo messengers Franco and Robles did not fully understand at what point they should deliver the documents in their custody. The blueprint they signed was primarily a petition for provisional land possession—Parres's central strategy for expediting land distribution—and only subsequently a request for restitution. (If a restitution petition failed, it made way for a dotación.) The blueprint's language was confusing with regard to when to present substantiating evidence if making a restitution claim: "[We ask] that until we present supporting evidence and our case is conclusively studied, we be given provisional possession of the lands found within the area that we claim for restitution.... In time, we will present the agrarian authorities with evidence of the property rights that our pueblo has or has had in the past, or, in lieu of this, we will provide the [survey] commissions with the information needed to justify a grant."[68] Moreover, the documents Franco and Robles signed stated that pueblo representatives were "responsible for traveling to the National Archives in search of the documents that accredit the rights to the lands that the pueblo has or had, and exhibiting them to the agrarian authorities to make a restitution claim."[69] Although Franco and Robles already had possession of Anenecuilco's titles, this language implied that they would have at least the time needed to travel to the National Archives in Mexico City and back before they were required to submit them.

A third possible explanation for the restitution failure is that proposed by historian René Sánchez Beltrán, who speculates that the Anenecuilco representatives did not submit their titles for fear of losing them.⁷⁰ Given the symbolic significance of the Anenecuilco documents for the Zapatista Revolution, it is possible that Franco and Robles did not fully trust the Parres administration with the pueblo's documents. After all, legend has it that Zapata, who at different times entrusted the pueblo's documents to Robles and Franco, on one occasion told Robles, "If you lose them, compadre, you will dry hung from a tree."⁷¹ When Zapata took the papers from Robles and entrusted them to Franco, he forbade him from participating in combat because, from then on, "his sole mission was to save these documents." On another occasion, when Michoacán representatives visited him in Morelos, Zapata asked Franco to show the documents to the visitors and said "por esto peleo"—translated by Womack as "this . . . I am fighting for."⁷² According to Sotelo, Zapata often said, "I'm bound to die someday, but my pueblo's papers stand to get guaranteed."⁷³ Comments along these lines might possibly explain why the Anenecuilco representatives did not surrender the crucial documents in time to have petitioned for the desired restitution.⁷⁴

Whatever the reason Franco and Robles might have had for not delivering the pueblo documents in their custody, in the meantime agrarian officials proceeded expeditiously. In October 1921, CNA council member General Ángel Barrios (an old Zapatista who in 1913 had overseen the Mexico State forces and had also granted lands) went to the Morelos Agrarian Commission to collect all completed case files (including Anenecuilco's incomplete file) to process them "as quickly as possible."⁷⁵ Only later, in early November 1921, did Franco and Robles finally take the Anenecuilco documents to the Morelos Agrarian Commission. There they met with Ortega and undersecretary Ricardo Sarmiento. According to Franco, "after taking note of some of the facts of how we were stripped by the landowners, [Ortega] said that the Anenecuilco pueblo was going to be provisionally granted a dotación of five hundred hectares—four hundred irrigated hectares and one hundred hectares of hill [*cerril*] lands. He told us to take our titles with us, and he said that at the time of the restitution he would call us with our documents so that the delegate could present them to the National Commission in Mexico for the return of the lands, water resources, and woodlands."⁷⁶ But what Ortega apparently did not explain—or what Franco and Robles did not understand—was that with the Anenecuilco case file already under review at the CNA, they would have to wait until after the presidential resolution before they could file for a new restitution.⁷⁷

At several CNA sessions in June and November 1922, Marte R. Gómez ruled positively on twelve Morelos dotaciones: Anenecuilco, Villa de Ayala, Amacuzac, Huazulco, Tecajec, Atlacholoaya, Popotlán, Tepatitlán, San Gabriel, Tenextepango, Cocoyoc, and Cuautlixco. He later explained how important this had been for him: "I could now have a clear conscience that I had not defrauded the trust of the Morelos campesinos."⁷⁸ On 30 November 1922 the presidential resolution denied Anenecuilco's restitution "for lack of substantiating proof" (*por falta de pruebas que la justificara*) and granted a dotación instead. Perhaps one reason Gómez believed he could have a clear conscience was that he had expanded the five-hundred-hectare dotación to seven hundred hectares, including 381 hectares of irrigated lands from the Coahuixtla hacienda, 319 hectares of monte lands from the El Hospital hacienda, and several sources of water.⁷⁹

Gómez was not the only one who felt this had been a good deal for Anenecuilco. Although he characterizes the dotación as a "fast shuffle," Womack views the presidential resolution in a positive light. Listing all the influential Zapatistas in government at the time, he explains that "from these connections Anenecuilco benefitted greatly. In November 1922, the President expanded its provisional grant to nearly 1,700 acres [688 ha], with over 900 acres [364 ha] taken from Manuel Araoz's Coahuixtla hacienda and over 750 [304 ha] from the Alonso heirs' El Hospital."⁸⁰

Franco and Robles, however, were not content. Two months after Anenecuilco's presidential resolution of January 1923, they returned to the Morelos Agrarian Commission. Ortega had passed away, and Sarmiento had succeeded him as president of the commission. In reporting their meeting to CNA delegates, Franco and Robles claimed that Sarmiento had deceived them: "Even though [Morelos Agrarian Commission] president Ricardo Sarmiento had our titles in his hands [in November 1921], today he claims that the representatives Francisco Franco and José Robles did not present their titles, nor did they provide any proof of having been despoiled by the landowners, and for that reason there is no restitution. We inform this tribunal [the CNA] that he [Sarmiento] has acted deceitfully. We inform this tribunal under your charge that the Anenecuilco pueblo is the cradle of the Revolution, the principal basis for pueblo restitutions and dotaciones."[81]

At some point, Franco and Robles must have understood that any possibility of petitioning for restitution under the terms of the 6 January 1915 law and its regulations would have to occur after completing the dotación case file. This understanding seems clear in a letter they addressed to President Obregón on 28 February 1923. In it, Franco and Robles expressed their dissatisfaction with the presidential resolution, as well as the reasons and conditions for ultimately accepting it:

> Having seen the presidential resolution for the ... 26 September 1920 petition, we are not in agreement with this resolution. We ask you to open a new case file for restitution, given that we have the primordial titles that protect the lands we claim, as well as proof of the land seizure of which we were victims.... We want it to be on record that we will abide by the terms of the presidential resolution [for the dotación] in order to cultivate these lands, with the understanding that if we have the necessary proof of the land seizure, after the dotación we receive restitution.[82]

When in April 1923 Franco and Robles (then members of the administrative committee in charge of the dotación lands) signed the definitive possession act, they added a clause stating that the villagers "possess property titles to their old ejidos, which are more extensive than what is now granted."[83]

In 1927 Franco and Robles once again petitioned for a restitution, and archival evidence shows why they steadfastly pursued the matter. It was not so much because a restitution symbolized some form of abstract justice or independence from the state (as Warman argues) but because of a very concrete matter: the dotación did not include the irrigated Llano del Huajar fields that Zapata had seized from the El Hospital hacienda in 1910 and then formally restored to a number of Anenecuilco residents on 23 June 1915.[84]

The restitution case took six years from start to finish. Franco surrendered copies of the titles that Zapata had entrusted to him, and a second round of investigations and surveys began. In 1927 CNA delegates and surveyors produced a forty-five-page typewritten report explaining that the lands covered by the titles had already been included in the original dotación (although, as noted, it did not include the irrigated Llano del Huajar fields). As a result, on 7 November 1929 interim President Emilio Portes Gil (1928–30) denied Anenecuilco's restitution petition for a second time.[85]

On 7 March 1935 Franco and Robles wrote directly to President Lázaro Cárdenas, who was already famous for his progressive stance on peasant land rights. That same year, Cárdenas personally visited the region and offered Anenecuilco residents the El Zacoaco gorge, which included over 4,000 hectares of monte lands, approximately 250 hectares of rain-fed lands, and 380 irrigated hectares of the Llano del Huajar fields. This offer was not in the form of a restitution but rather as an "automatic extension" with lands purchased from a group of military officials who had recently acquired them from the El Hospital hacienda owners. Cárdenas justified the grant as "a historic moment, given that these fields were the source of General Zapata's ideals and the lands that Zapata had distributed on 23 June 1915, according to the records on file."[86]

In 1935 Cárdenas proceeded to grant Anenecuilco 4,105 hectares of monte and rain-fed lands, but only 244 of the 380 irrigated hectares promised from the Llano del Huajar fields. A year later, surveyors tried to add the missing 136 hectares, but the presidential resolution of 1938 again excluded these irrigated fields because, it turned out, the state agrarian commission under Parres had granted them to Villa de Ayala in 1922. But the Anenecuilcans, who during Zapatista rule had been in possession of the contested 136 hectares of irrigated fields, had not surrendered them to Villa de Ayala representatives in 1922. In fact it was not until 1943 that Villa de Ayala residents, with "arms in hand," took possession of them.[87]

Did Anenecuilco have titles to prove that the El Hospital hacienda had illegally usurped the Llano del Huajar fields? Probably so, but short of re-creating the 1927 survey in situ (with the same old boundary markers), it is impossible to know definitively why the forty-five-page CNA report claimed otherwise. There is, however, one possible explanation. According to Alicia Hernández Chávez, after the population of Anenecuilco had decreased considerably in 1607, Viceroy Luis de Velasco granted the Convalescent Hospital in Mexico City a land concession from Anenecuilco's old merced. This concession clearly stated that the villagers could annul it if they ever needed these lands for subsistence.[88] Were the Llano del Huajar fields part of these lands? Most likely they were. Villagers knew the terrain well, and a property four hundred hectares in size was hard to miss even in vague colonial titles. Therefore, following the Plan de Ayala, Zapata probably did have the right to restore these fields to Anenecuilco. But under the terms of the 6 January 1915 law, he did not. If the Llano del Huajar fields had been part of the lands (temporarily) ceded to El Hospital but were then not returned, then the land seizure would have occurred long *before* 1856, thereby failing to fulfil one of the three requirements for a Constitutionalist restitution—namely, to demonstrate that pueblo land loss occurred *after* the Lerdo law of 25 June 1856.

In this regard, Warman was correct in stating that Anenecuilco's land grant had not been an act of justice. But what in retrospect was a tangle of hurried decisions, errors, oversights, and possibly a cover-up does not amount to saying that Anenecuilco's dotación was "a unilateral concession of the State, like a favor from a powerful figure who retains for himself the right to watch over the fulfillment of his supreme edict and to intervene overtly in its administration to create a political clientele."[89] Land reform in revolutionary Mexico was far more complex than what the dominant narrative suggests.

The Regional Challenges of the Village-Focused Carrancista Agrarian Reform

Agrarian surveyors and officials worried less about granting restitutions (as opposed to dotaciones) than about how to deal with the limitations of a land reform law based on the rights or needs of individual villages. One of the most pressing problems they faced, which the Zapatistas had also failed to resolve, was intervillage conflict. As de la Peña explains, "Things were complicated by the fact that, under Zapata's regime in 1914–1915, plots had been occupied by people of one village which were now claimed by people from another village." In the Los Altos de Morelos region alone, residents from Tetelcingo, Nepantla, and Yecapixtla had invaded Atlatlahucan, and Atlatlahucan villagers had invaded Oaxtepec, Yecapixtla, Pazulco, Tepalcingo, and Nepantla.[90] Other conflicts involved old boundary disputes. In the Jonacatepec region, agrarian surveyors invested much time and effort in marking the pueblos' boundaries required for restitutions and land grants and ameliorating "the conflicts stemming from the beliefs that some pueblos have about others invading their ejidos." After the survey of eight pueblos, Governor Parres held a meeting with their representatives; some agreed with the boundary markings, but others did not.[91]

Another problem with restitution and grant procedures was that agrarian officials had to carve up expropriated haciendas in such a way that all petitioning villages received enough land for residents' subsistence. When one village asked for a restitution or a dotación, officials had to consider petitions from neighboring pueblos as well. This was greatly complicated by the fact that village representatives did not all petition for land at the same time. For example, when CNA delegates studied the possibility of granting land to El Puente, they had to consider the provisional possessions already granted to Alpuyeca, Xochitepec, Tetlama, and Atlacholoaya.[92] By the time the El Hospital workers acquired political-status recognition, Anenecuilco, Villa de Ayala, and Coyotepec had already received provisional possessions from the El Hospital hacienda.[93] And when CNA delegates studied

San Martín Temoac's claim to provisional possession of Santa Clara hacienda lands, the Morelos Agrarian Commission had already ruled on the provisional possessions of Popotlán, Huazulco, Tecajec, Zacualpan, and Tlacotepec.[94]

The case of Amacuzac illustrates the limitations of the Carrancista agrarian reform. CNA surveyor D. Manjarrez wrote a seven-thousand-word report on the work he conducted over the course of seven months in the Poniente region of Morelos. In it he explained that Amacuzac's supposed primordial titles were not actually deeds but certificates of eighteenth-century land transactions in which Amacuzac was mentioned only as the neighboring village. Manjarrez met with the villagers to explain that their documents were not deeds, even though he feared doing so would cause disillusionment and generate mistrust toward him. He told them that if they petitioned for a dotación, they could later, with more substantive evidence, petition for a restitution. He carefully studied how much land and water Amacuzac villagers required for their subsistence, and he decided to grant them 7,274 hectares. CNA delegates, however, reduced the grant to 3,400 hectares, explaining that other pueblos needed San Gabriel hacienda lands as well, and that "what is fair and moral is to reconcile the interests of all the inhabitants of the region with the goal of distributing land proportionately among the pueblos from the available hacienda lands."[95]

The limits to the Carrancista village-focused reform were, however, most obvious when dealing with access to water resources.[96] Laura R. Valladares de la Cruz, for example, found that several canals built by the Santa Clara hacienda to irrigate its sugar cane crops had been partially destroyed during the revolutionary fighting. When the Parres administration began to implement land reform, the canal system not only had to be restored but also had to be adapted to provide ten potential land-beneficiary villages with access to water. The struggle over access to these water resources unsettled the region for decades.[97]

Achieving fairness in the distribution of water resources necessarily required going beyond the 6 January 1915 law and CNA circulars. All villages, whether land beneficiaries or not, required access to water—

not only to irrigate all commercial and some subsistence crops but also for urban domestic use. Department of Water engineers had to conduct hydrologic studies that did not differentiate between villages with land restitutions or grants and those without.[98] Furthermore, the Carrancista land reform did not seek to eliminate all private property; haciendas could keep some of their lands—usually their irrigated lands and water resources. In Morelos, haciendas had throughout the centuries invested large sums of money in constructing canals, dams, and other hydrologic infrastructure.[99] During the Zapatista years (1911–19), villagers took over much of the haciendas' water infrastructure.[100] Now engineers had to find "equitable" solutions.

One way of resolving more equitably the general need for access to water resources was for the Ministry of Agriculture to federalize rivers. Indeed, between 1920 and 1922 the Ministry of Agriculture federalized the most important rivers in Morelos, allowing the CNA's Department of Water to process all requests for access to federal water, whether linked to restitution and grant petitions or not.[101] When, for instance, Department of Water officials considered Itzamatitlán's water grant, they had to study all Yautepec River tributaries. Before the Revolution, the owner of the San Carlos hacienda had altered the watercourse to supply the main hacienda buildings, including a cattle trough. During the Revolution, Itzamatitlán residents had redirected the watercourse for irrigation and urban domestic use, leaving the San Carlos hacienda dry. As part of the Itzamatitlán dotación, Department of Water engineers recommended granting the hacienda one-tenth and the pueblo nine-tenths of the water supply. In determining how to allocate the available supply of water, the engineers also decided to protect the Oacalco sugar mill's access to water. Their rationale was that the mill was the only one in operation in Morelos at the time and that it was therefore valuable both to land reform beneficiaries in nine surrounding pueblos and to other sugar cane growers.[102]

Fig. 11. (*opposite*) Land grant map for San Gabriel Amacuzac (Morelos), 23 November 1922. Archivo General Agrario, Planos de Morelos, Plano 651.

PLANO
DEL EJIDO DEFINITIVO DE LA CONGREGACION DE
SAN GABRIEL
MUNICIPIO DE AMACUZAC EX-DISTRITO DE TETECALA
ESTADO DE MORELOS
ESCALA 1:10000

The first state in which the Constitutionalist agrarian reform—with all its limitations—was fully implemented was Zapata's homeland. Keen support from state government and agrarian commission officials, CNA delegates, and Supreme Court justices made the Morelos laboratory the most successful showcase so far. And yet it was during land reform in Morelos that many of the limitations of the 6 January 1915 law became obvious. For example, justice based on colonial property rights in the form of restitutions to pueblos—whether ruled on by the judiciary or the executive—could not be guaranteed in a country where land titles often overlapped and where, for centuries, legal and illegal transactions had become intermingled. Furthermore, piecemeal land and water grants to individual villages, approved at different times, would not guarantee equitable or proportional distribution of resources among villages lying within the same geographic area and depending on the same sources of water.

Despite these limitations, after the Morelos repartos in the early 1920s, challenging the principles of the 6 January 1915 law would become politically impossible. Obregón's embrace of the Zapatistas on the condition that implementation of land reform in Morelos be based on the 6 January 1915 law was perhaps one of the first fruitful examples of what proved to be postrevolutionary state officials' more general effort to reconcile opposing interests. Once Zapatistas in Morelos adopted the 6 January 1915 law, it was hard not to think that the Plan de Ayala (itself gaining stature as one of the founding documents of the new postrevolutionary state) and article 27 of the Constitution were somehow linked, making it difficult for anyone to propose a different kind of reform.[103] The displaced alternatives might have included more democratic forms of local administration, more regionally equitable and ecologically sound forms of land distribution, and the involvement of the judiciary in the settling of intervillage boundary disputes with some measure of fairness.

Epilogue

*Zapatista and Constitutionalist
Agrarian Reforms Compared*

Revolución, revolucionario. Términos que se repiten a lo largo de la obra que carecen totalmente de sentido y significado. (Revolution, revolutionary. Terms that are repeated throughout the work that totally lack sense and meaning.)
—René Avilés Fabila, *El gran solitario del palacio*

After Zapata's assassination in 1919, the Obregón administration tried to unite warring factions by promoting the idea that all sides were fighting for the same agrarian ideals. Other political leaders followed suit. At the first Agrarian Congress in 1923, Antonio Díaz Soto y Gama (the Zapatista delegate to the Aguascalientes Convention) stated that President Obregón was "the executor of the thought of Emiliano Zapata."[1] A year later, at a ceremony held on the fifth anniversary of Zapata's death, "several people spoke, including one who asked those listening to be thankful that they had an honest politician in Calles, who would implement Zapata's program without corruption. The crowd chanted 'vivas' for Calles, who then proclaimed, 'the agrarian program of Zapata is mine.'"[2] From 1929 onward the long-ruling Institutional Revolutionary Party, or PRI, regularly claimed that the 6 January 1915 law and article 27 of the 1917 Constitution incorporated Zapata's principles. For example, when in 1954 Agrarian Department chief Cástulo Villaseñor granted land to the Ixcamilpa pueblo, he said that General Zapata's 1912 restitution was a "response to the legitimate aspirations of the peasantry," and, as such, "a matter with legal consequences (*hecho legal*) that the 6 January 1915 law [and now this grant] sanctioned."[3] Many academics adopted this widespread belief. For example, Ignacio Marván Laborde, in his monumental analysis of the 1916–17 Constitutional Convention, states that regarding agrarian matters article 27 "is a true dialectic synthesis" of five documents, including the Plan de Ayala.[4]

After an in-depth study of Andrés Molina Enríquez's influence on Luis Cabrera, Emilio Kourí concludes that although the Zapatista movement did serve as a political catalyst (without it, Carranza would have faced less pressure to implement his own reforms), Zapatismo was not the ideological inspiration for the Constitutionalist agrarian program; rather, they sprang from different intellectual roots.[5] This book has also shown that these reforms unfolded in parallel, with little or no cross-pollination. And yet there were many important points of similarity between the two agrarian reform programs, mainly because both were products of their times. Both programs responded to widespread village petitions (and rural uprisings); both had to deal with the existing legal framework, even when trying to transform it; both relied on agrarian surveyors using the tools and procedures for land distribution available at the time; and in their implementation both were shaped by unforeseen local abuses of power and intervillage conflicts.

Both the Zapatista and the Constitutionalist movements responded to historic, widespread demands by village leaders to resolve their land claims outside the protracted, expensive, and often-biased court system. Attempting to resolve land conflicts outside the judiciary was not new. Throughout the nineteenth century, federal officials, state governors, and political chiefs tried different ways of resolving them—short of invading judicial authority. But amid revolutionary fighting and civil war, both movements disavowed the existing federal judiciary. Neither Zapata nor Carranza rejected the federal courts specifically in order to implement their land reforms, but once they did, their laws allowed the executive to assume judicial functions for contentious land matters.

As noted above, sidestepping the judiciary was not a completely unusual political move. During the nineteenth century, numerous officials, including President López de Santa Anna and Maximilian of Habsburg, suggested that the executive branch of government take over contentious land matters. Moreover, after the Madero Revolution brought down the regime of Porfirio Díaz, an ongoing debate began over how best to resolve by administrative (rather than judicial) means the profusion of pending village court cases. Madero promoted the privatization of communal lands as a method for resolving pueblo land boundary disputes by arbitration, while still respecting the court jurisdiction over contentious land matters. So, too, did Villista minister of agriculture Manuel Bonilla, who believed that land restoration suits should be resolved by the judiciary. Zapata and Montaño, however, allowed villagers to take back lands to which they had colonial titles, reversing the nineteenth-century burden of proof and allowing the Ministry of Agriculture to act as a court issuing the final verdict. Similarly, the more radical members of Congress proposed sidestepping the 1857 Constitution's separation of powers so as to enable the executive to arrogate court functions.

Both the Zapatista and the Constitutionalist reforms focused first and foremost on the restitution of pueblo communal lands. We know from the hundreds of village appeals to de la Barra and Madero that these petitions raised numerous issues, including the reversal of land dispossessions that resulted from claims (denuncios) to terrenos baldíos by wealthy, land-grabbing locals; the privatization of pueblo communal lands or the review of earlier land privatizations deemed to have been unfairly implemented; the settlement of longstanding boundary disputes with neighboring pueblos; and so forth. And yet for Zapata and his early advisers, restoring usurped pueblo lands was the central goal, followed by the expropriation of hacienda lands for landless villagers. Similarly, Carranza's 6 January 1915 law focused first and foremost on restitutions, offering dotaciones when restitutions failed.

To handle these land restitution suits outside the judicial system, both revolutionary programs created a multitiered quasi-judiciary. In

Zapatista regions, military chiefs acted early on as first-instance judges, evaluating pueblo documents and provisionally restoring seized lands, while General Headquarters (and later the Ministry of Agriculture) became a second-instance court responsible for reviewing the chiefs' decisions. For the rest of the country, Carranza's 1915 law created a hierarchical agrarian bureaucracy within the Ministry of Development to substitute for judges and courts. Governors became judges of first instance and the federal executive "the highest judge, who would dictate the definitive agrarian resolution in the hearings that culminated the agrarian procedures."[6]

Zapatistas and Carrancistas equally required the active participation of a sizable number of villagers in their reform efforts. Much like in the past, when village representatives had to push their cases forward (by acquiring power of attorney, collecting money so they could send commissions to the National Archives to ask for copies of their land titles, hiring lawyers, and taking their clams to the courts), so they now had to follow various procedures. Regardless of whether villagers took up arms and invaded hacienda lands or peacefully petitioned for land grants, they all had to show their titles and solicit a land survey at a quasi-court—whether it was Zapatista chiefs and agrarian commissions or, later, Carrancista state agrarian commissions.

Following the precedent of nineteenth- and early-twentieth-century revindication suits, both revolutionary factions remained committed to ruling on restitutions based on evidence. They differed, however, in how they reinterpreted the plaintiff's burden of proof. In nineteenth-century land suits involving pueblos and neighboring private properties, the burden of proof fell squarely on the plaintiff. Village representatives had to produce substantiating evidence that would shift proof of ownership away from the default position, which recognized the defendant as the legal owner. The Plan de Ayala reversed this default position: pueblos with titles could immediately recover their allegedly usurped lands, leaving the final hearing until "the triumph of the Revolution." In contrast, Cabrera made the burden of proof an even greater obstacle than it had been in nineteenth-century land-revindication suits. The 6 January 1915 law upheld the plaintiff's burden of proof by requiring village authorities to prove their ownership of pueblo lands and demonstrate when and how the lands had been illegally appropriated. It also added a third requirement: proof that the loss had occurred after 25 June 1856. These requirements made pueblo land restitution almost impossible.

In practice, both land reforms found ways to sidestep the plaintiff's burden of proof. Zapatistas simply considered all pueblo documents as proof of ownership until tribunals (to be established after the triumph of the Revolution) could issue a ruling. In the meantime, they proposed temporary arrangements in which they privileged equity among villages over ancient pueblo land rights. Likewise, Constitutionalists found a way to sidestep strict proof requirements when villages came up short for whatever reason (such as not having titles, their titles not delimiting clear boundaries, being unable to prove when or which lands had been seized, or having lost their property before 1856) by allowing landless pueblos to petition for expropriated lands in the form of a dotación.

Neither revolutionary faction required land expropriation for restitutions because land restoration was a judicial decision over which party had a stronger legal position. Land grants, however, did require some form of land expropriation, and both factions adopted existing laws—although they redefined the concept of public utility. Zapata and Montaño broadened the authority to expropriate for public utility to include "prosperity and well-being." Later, article 4 of the 25 October 1915 law stated that a future Zapatista national government would expropriate all large private estates for public utility and with compensation. Here, "public utility" meant that every Mexican had a right to possess and cultivate enough land for family subsistence.[7] The 6 January 1915 law, on the other hand, allowed landless villagers to petition for the expropriation of lands for dotaciones, broadening the concept of public utility to include the following: compensation for failed restitutions, the right of newly established or newly independent pueblos to fundo legal and ejido properties, and the "reconstitution of the ejidos" to satisfy the subsistence needs of impoverished resident farmers. Moreover, starting in 1917, the first two postrevolutionary Supreme Courts redefined public utility as well. Although the justices imposed strict limits on the executive in nonagrarian land expropriations, they eased the rules for what became known as revolutionary social rights.

When it came to defining the agrarian reform's property regime, both the Zapatista and the Constitutionalist programs legalized communal landholdings, thereby reversing the 1857 Constitution's (article 27) prohibition on civil corporations acquiring or administering communal lands. Neither program, however, focused on ethnicity in terms of whether village residents spoke an indigenous language or self-identified as Indians—many of which did. Rather, by privileging restitutions, both the Plan de Ayala and the 6 January 1915 law focused on the return of colonial Indian pueblo lands, regardless of whether residents in the revolutionary present were Indian or mestizo or whether beneficiary villages were multiethnic.

The Zapatista land reform (certainly before 1917) and the early Constitutionalist land reform were more Liberal than cooperativist, communalist, socialist, or anarchist. Although both legalized existing corporate properties, neither the Zapatista nor the Constitutionalist reforms (prior to 1934) advocated communal forms of property for agricultural lands. Zapatistas promised to respect each village's traditions. Palafox famously declared in 1914 that the "repartition of lands will be carried out in conformity with the customs and usages of each pueblo.... That is, if a certain pueblo wants the communal system, so it will be executed, and if another pueblo wants the division of land in order to admit small [individual] property, so it will be done."[8] Yet in practice, Zapatistas gradually issued different rules for distinct types of resources. Woodlands and sources of water would be communally owned and publicly managed under the bylaws of the Ministry of Agriculture. Agricultural lands, however, were a different matter. Not unlike the Liberal privatization of pueblo communal lands or the federal public lands laws, Zapatista leaders distributed arable land in soon-to-be-titled individual parcels to heads of nuclear families. Similarly, Constitutionalists also gradually developed different bylaws for woodlands, water resources, and arable land. Article 27 specified that rural population centers would have communal rights to land, woodlands, and water resources, but only until new regulations determined the subdivision of arable lands.

Both land reforms planned to distribute arable land in private property parcels with safeguards for the nuclear family, thus incorporating existing nineteenth- and early twentieth-century ideas about family patrimony (civil laws that made landed property inalienable, not subject to embargo or taxation, and transmittable only by inheritance). Zapatista reparto regulations insisted that no one could acquire more than one parcel, and this parcel was exclusively for the sustenance of a nuclear family. Once General Headquarters officials approved a map of the allotted parcels with the names of beneficiaries—*and* confirmed that the distribution had been conducted justly and without favoritism— Zapatista officials would grant each beneficiary a title. Land granted to villages or individuals could not be sold or in any way alienated; it could only be bequeathed to spouses or the beneficiary's closest relatives, and the land had to be cultivated or the beneficiary risked forfeiting the parcel. Similarly, Constitutionalist laws determined that arable lands would, at some future time, be distributed in individual private parcels (*pleno dominio*), with the necessary limitations to avoid land hoarding by speculators.

Because neither reform managed to issue private property titles for arable land parcels to heads of family, and because villagers affiliated with both revolutionary factions complained about abuse of power and corruption in the handling of land distribution, both projects required temporary local forms of administration. The similarities between Zapatista village representatives and Constitutionalist local administrative committees, or CPAs, were remarkable. First, local representatives had to be democratically elected to one-year terms. Villagers in Morelos and neighboring Zapatista regions had to elect two or more representatives for land reform through direct elections for one-year terms, while villagers in the Constitutionalist states had to elect by simple majority at least three representatives to serve on the CPA. If parcels were not privatized within a year, CPA members would have to surrender their posts to a new democratically elected committee. Second, these elected representatives would oversee communal or public lands. Zapatista village representatives were to care for pueblo lands, the fundo legal, woodlands, and grasslands, as well as the surplus parcels left over after the reparto, which they could rent out under contracts approved by the residents. In comparison, CPAs had "the broadest faculties" to administer, preserve, and make productive those lands possessed communally by the pueblos, including their provisional subdivision among residents. This included dividing arable lands into parcels for heads of family, managing the common use of woodlands and pasturelands, and naming a commissioner to manage water resources. Third, both forms of local representation overstepped municipal jurisdiction. Zapatista village representatives were instructed to invest income generated by woodlands, grasslands, and leftover parcel rentals in public education. Meanwhile, CPAs collected taxes on parcels and communal lands, keeping 70 percent for the pueblo's public services (managing water resources for domestic use, repairing infrastructure, setting up schools, and so forth).[9]

The central difference between these two revolutionary projects was that the Zapatistas intended land reform to be a national program to restructure property relations more broadly, whereas for the Constitutionalists agrarian reform was a temporary, limited effort to address a specific problem identified as the root cause of the rural revolutionary uprising. This key difference had important implications for the relationship between the executive and the judiciary, the relationship between the federal government and free and sovereign municipalities, and the question of how to deal with intervillage land and water conflicts.

Where the judiciary was concerned, Zapatistas planned either to create or reinstate, in some near future, a higher-level court or tribunal to weigh evidence and rule on land rights in the last instance. In their Plan de Ayala, Zapata and Montaño planned on creating "special tribunals established after the triumph of the Revolution" where landowners could be heard. Perhaps if the Aguascalientes Convention had prevailed over the Constitutionalists, these special tribunals would have been part of a reestablished federal judiciary.[10] By contrast, the Constitutionalists did not require special tribunals because they expected the executive to rule quickly on restitutions and grants, with article 10 of the 6 January 1915 law granting landowners access to the federal judiciary—albeit only after a presidential resolution had been issued and then only to claim compensation.

The Zapatistas relied on municipal authorities who pledged allegiance to the Plan de Ayala, and the Ministry of Agriculture worked with them to distribute land when there were no local conflicts or complaints of abuse of power or corruption. Their plans to restructure property relations had no legal reason to exclude municipal authorities from land reform (even though in practice they did so by creating temporary local forms of administration). In comparison, the Constitutionalist program was an interim federal program that would only temporarily sidestep municipal authorities, without violating the constitutional provision (article 115) that made the municipio libre ("free municipality") the basis of territorial division and political organization of the federal states. In principle, privatized arable land parcels, even with family patrimony-type limitations, did not require local forms of administration and oversight. Moreover, CNA delegates did not intend the CPAs to become permanent forms of administration parallel to the municipal governments. But as successive authorities made the 6 January 1915 law the foundation of a more extensive land reform—while preserving local authorities parallel to municipal governments—they also made permanent this Constitutional contradiction.

The third key difference between these two revolutionary programs was how they handled boundary conflicts between villages, one of the greatest sources of twentieth-century rural violence. During the height of the Zapatista land distribution, dozens of intervillage disputes forced the leadership to hear and resolve boundary conflicts. Military chiefs, state agrarian commissions, General Headquarters (sometimes Zapata personally), and the Ministry of Agriculture unsuccessfully tried to draw boundary lines between two or more neighboring pueblos. In fact settling land disputes between and among villages became the main challenge confronting the Ministry of Agriculture. In turn, when officials from Carranza's state-level agrarian commissions discovered that many villages had boundary disputes not with haciendas but with other population centers, the National Agrarian Commission, under the directorship of Pastor Rouaix, ruled that boundary-conflict resolution between or among villages did not fall under the purview of the Secretaría de Fomento and thus should continue to be a judicial matter.[11]

Ultimately, the major practical difference between the two most important land reform programs in revolutionary Mexico lay in their outcomes. The Zapatista land reform was meant to redistribute land throughout the country, but it remained an unfulfilled utopia. In contrast, the 6 January 1915 law was intended to resolve quickly an urgent problem in a time of war, but it accidentally became the pillar of a program that redistributed about half the national territory to more than thirty thousand population centers, created corporate rights to land and water resources, and established permanent authorities and representative organs parallel to the municipal governments recognized by the Constitution. In doing so, it profoundly transformed the history of twentieth-century Mexico.

GLOSSARY

alcalde   Spanish municipal magistrate, who had both judicial and administrative functions

amparo   a set of federal judicial procedures through which individuals and, after 1917, groups can contest a law or the action of a government agency. District and supreme courts decide whether to grant these individuals and groups "the protection of Federal Justice." A successful amparo suit returns a situation to the *status quo ante*, the way it was before a government action occurred (Zamora, *Mexican Law*, 257–86).

ayuntamiento   elected municipal council in charge of governing and administering a municipality

barrios   cabecera wards or quarters

bosques   woodlands

cabecera   chief town in a municipality

cacicazgo   a term invented by the Spanish "to describe the rights, privileges, and properties of the Indian rulers" (John K. Chance, "Los Villagómez de Suchitepec," 501)

cacique   In colonial Mexico, a cacique, or *cacica*, was an Indian notable (Lockhart, *Nahuas after Conquest*, 133). In the nineteenth century the term acquired the more general meaning of local or regional leader (Lynch, *Caudillos in Spanish America*, 6). In twentieth-century Mexico, a cacique was "a local or regional boss whose eminently personalist domination typically rests on a combination of family- and kinship-based (including ritual kinship, *compadrazgo*) alliances and patron-client networks, control over patronage resources and coercive sanctions—including the threat or actual use of physical violence against rivals" (Middlebrook, "Caciquismo and Democracy," 412).

condueñazgos   private associations of share-holding landowners (Kourí, *Pueblo Divided*, 3) *congregaciones*   In many states, a political category granted to population centers with a smaller population than pueblos

composición or *composiciones de tierras*   recognition of legal title of de facto ownership

comuneros   communal landholders

Constitutionalists   followers of Venustiano Carranza Garza, a Liberal hacienda owner who became governor of Coahuila, first chief of the Constitutionalist army, head of the Preconstitutionalist government, and finally president of Mexico (1917-20)

denuncio   claim to untitled lands

dotación   land expropriated from one or several haciendas and granted to neighboring impoverished villages for subsistence agriculture

ejido/ejidos   In this book, the term "ejido" or "ejidos" can have one of four meanings.

  (1) Colonial ejidos were one of several entailed land components of the Indian pueblos, which were property-holding corporations. In theory, each Indian pueblo had a *fundo legal* (the town site, with houses and garden plots), *ejidos de los pueblos* (nonagricultural lands surrounding the fundo legal, usually used collectively to pasture animals and for the cutting and gathering of wood and wildlife products), *propios* (land held by the ayuntamiento, usually rented out for income), and *tierras de común repartimiento* (agricultural land communally owned by the pueblo and allotted as parcels to heads of families, oftentimes considered and treated as de facto private property) (Kourí, "Interpreting the Expropriation," 79-80, and "Sobre la propiedad comunal," 1939).

  (2) In the nineteenth century, Kourí explains, ejidos were exempted from the Reforma laws, which were intended to disentail propios and tierras de repartimiento. Although the Díaz regime canceled this exception, by the beginning of the twentieth century in central Mexico most remaining entailed lands were primarily ejidos; this is why government authorities and villagers too indiscriminately used the term "ejidos" to refer to the different types of land that had belonged to pueblos (Kourí, "La invención del ejido," 58-59; see also Kourí, "Sobre la propiedad comunal de los pueblos," 1939).

  (3) The early Constitutionalists called all lands granted or restituted "ejidos" (see chapter 4).

  (4) With the agrarian code of 1934, the ejido (singular) became the name for a population center that received a grant or a restitution. The ejido

had its own patrimony, juridical standing, and administrative and representative organs under the tutelage of the federal executive and operating parallel to the autonomous municipal governments. In the 1940s, agrarian laws began to differentiate between the ejido for population centers with granted lands and the comunidad agraria (agrarian community) or simply comunidad (community) for population centers with restituted lands or those with existing communal properties. (Antonio Azuela de la Cueva uses the term "provisional ejido" for the period 1915-34 and "perpetual ejido" for 1934-92 in "La jurisprudencia y la formación del régimen agrario," 351.)

excedencias "untitled—that is, public—lands occupied by individuals who owned or had legal rights to an immediately adjacent territory" (Kourí, Pueblo Divided, 218)

fundo legal generally assumed to be the town site of a pueblo, with houses and garden plots. (For how this complex colonial term changed from being an area of protection for population centers from cattle ranches to a pueblo urban site, see Castro Gutiérrez, "Los ires y devenires del fundo legal de los pueblos de indios.")

jefe político chief political officer at the district level, appointed by the executive

juez de letras a professionally trained judge, as opposed to the *juez de paz*, who could practice on the basis of his honorable reputation rather than professional training (most judges being men in the period this book covers)

juez de primer instancia court of first instance

juicio trial

juicio de apeo y deslinde survey suit

juridical standing the right to take claims to court

jurisprudencia According to José María Serna de la Garza ("The Concept of Jurisprudencia in Mexican Law," 132), "This term refers to constant and unvarying criteria to interpret and apply the Constitution, federal and state statutes and rulings and international treaties, expressed in the decisions of either the Supreme Court of Justice sitting en banc or of one of its Chambers, the collegiate circuit courts, as well as the Federal Electoral Tribunal. After meeting certain conditions and requirements . . . the decisions issued by these courts may acquire binding authority with regard to lower courts. The notion of *Jurisprudencia* has certain similarities with the common law notion of precedent, however . . . there are important differences between the two concepts."

Maderistas   followers of Francisco Ignacio Madero González, the son of a wealthy landowning family from Coahuila, who led an uprising against President Porfirio Díaz, which ignited the Mexican Revolution, usually dated 1910–20. Madero became a democratically elected president of Mexico in November 1911 and was assassinated in February 1913.

merced   colonial land grant

montes   woodlands

Porfiriato   the regime of dictator Porfirio Díaz (1876–80, 1884–1911)

primordial titles, or ***títulos primordiales***   Formally, títulos primordiales are Náhuatl-language land titles. In the nineteenth century, however, villagers and officials used the term for colonial pueblo land and water deeds. Usually, when villagers claimed to have títulos primordiales, they believed they had deeds. Oftentimes, however, they included documents that were not deeds, such as pictorial maps, pueblo boundary agreements, and court records.

procurador de pueblos   pueblo attorney general

propios   land held by the ayuntamiento, usually rented out for income

provincial deputations   governing councils that bridged the transition from the Spanish colonial regime to the independent federal states of Mexico

pueblo   Though this book loosely refers to all rural population centers as villages or towns, the term "pueblo" is employed when it so appears in archival materials or, following Emilio Kourí ("Interpreting the Expropriation," 77–82), as a political status, or *categoría política*, alongside other political categories such as *ciudad*, *villa*, *congregación*, and *ranchería*. Pueblos had a *cabecera*, or head township. They could also have *barrios* and *sujetos* (subordinate population centers). Oftentimes, cabeceras, barrios, and sujetos called themselves pueblos and used the same deeds to claim land (often from each other). For this reason, the term "pueblo" in this book refers somewhat generically to all villages that at some point had, or whose villagers believed they had, colonial rights to corporate lands and water resources.

reparto   land distribution, usually in individual arable land parcels

restitution   restoration of usurped lands and water resources; a judicial procedure in the nineteenth and early twentieth centuries, and an executive matter in revolutionary and postrevolutionary Mexico

síndico   municipal attorney general

sitio de ganado mayor   colonial land measurements for grants equivalent to 1,755.61 hectares *sujetos*   smaller towns within a cabecera's jurisdiction

terrenos baldíos   public lands

tierras de común repartimiento   agricultural land communally owned by a pueblo and allotted as parcels to heads of families, often considered and treated as de facto private property (Kourí, "Sobre la propiedad communal," 1931)

tinterillos   legal agents without formal law accreditation

tribus   tribes. The term was sometimes used as synonymous to "ethnic group." For example, often the Yaquis and Mayos of northern Mexico were called tribes.

vara   Castilian surveying unit; possibly equivalent to 83.80 cm (Cortés I. and Ramírez, "Rescate de antiguas medidas iberoamericanas," np)

Zapatistas   followers of Emiliano Zapata Salazar (1879–1919), a farmer and horse trainer from Morelos who led a revolutionary movement in south-central Mexico

NOTES

Abbreviations

ACSCJN	Archivo Central de la Suprema Corte de Justicia de la Nación	
	FSCJN	Fondo Suprema Corte de Justicia de la Nación
AGA	Archivo General Agrario	
AGEV	Archivo General del Estado de Veracruz	
	ACAM	Archivo de la Comisión Agraria Mixta
	CLDC	Colección de Leyes, Decretos y Circulares
AGN	Archivo General de la Nación	
	FB	Fondo Archivo de Buscas y Traslado de Tierras
	FCR-EZ	Fondo Colección Revolución, Sección Emiliano Zapata
	FCR-RRC	Fondo Colección Revolución, Revolución y Régimen Constitucionalista
	FG Leg	Fondo Gobernación, Legajos
	FGO	Fondo Genovevo de la O
	FGPR	Fondo Gobernación Período Revolucionario
	FG s/s	Fondo Gobernación, sin sección
	FJ	Fondo Justicia
	FJ-JDM	Fondo Justicia Siglo XIX, Juzgado Distrito Morelos
	FJPCM	Fondo Junta Protectora de las Clases Menesterosas
	FLCF	Fondo Leyes y Circulares de Fomento
	FM	Fondo Francisco I. Madero

	FNDB	Fondo Nacionalización y Desamortización de Bienes
	FSAF-CNA	Fondo Secretaría de Agricultura y Fomento, Comisión Nacional Agraria
	FSCR	Fondo Soberana Convención Revolucionaria
	FSJ	Fondo Secretaría de Justicia
AHA	Archivo Histórico del Agua	
	FAN	Fondo Aguas Nacionales
	FAS	Fondo Aprovechamientos Superficiales
AHUNAM	Archivo Histórico de la Universidad Nacional Autónoma de México	
	AGM	Archivo Gildardo y Octavio Magaña Cerda
	FLB	Fondo León de la Barra
CEHM-Carso	Centro de Estudios de Historia de México Carso. Fundación Carlos Slim	
	FJA	Fondo Jenaro Amezcua
DOF	*Diario Oficial de la Federación*	
IEDM	Instituto Estatal de Documentación de Morelos	
	GT	Gobierno Tierras
RAN-Ver	Registro Agrario Nacional-Veracruz	
	ACCA	Archivo del Cuerpo Consultivo Agrario
SJF	*Semanario Judicial de la Federación*	
UIA	Universidad Iberoamericana-Biblioteca Francisco Xavier Clavijero, Acervos Históricos	
	CPD	Colección Porfirio Díaz

Introduction

1. Although revolutionary Pancho Villa also advocated land reform in northern Mexico, "only a limited land distribution was carried out in the Villista-held territories." Katz, "Agrarian Policies and Ideas," 28.
2. For the various definitions of *ejido*, see the glossary.
3. Translation in Womack, *Zapata*, 96.
4. The text of the Plan de Ayala is reproduced in Fabila, *Cinco siglos*, 181-84. The handwritten version of the Plan de Ayala, dated 28 November 1911, is found at the Jenaro Amezcua Archives at the Centro de Estu-

dios de Historia de México. See image at https://www.bibliotecas.tv/zapata/1911/PlandeAyala28nov1911/z28nov11a.html. A (predated) 25 November 1911 version published by the *Diario del Hogar* on 15 December 1911 is translated by Womack in *Zapata*, 400-404. Both Magaña, *Emiliano Zapata y el agrarismo en México*, 2:80-83, and Palacios, *Emiliano Zapata: Datos biográfico-históricos*, 70-73, date the signing of the Plan de Ayala as 28 November 1911.

5. "Ley que declara nulas todas las enajenaciones de tierras, aguas y montes pertenecientes a los pueblos, otorgados en contravención a lo dispuesto en la ley de 25 de junio de 1856" (6 January 1915), henceforth 6 January 1915 law, reproduced in Fabila, *Cinco siglos*, 228-32.

6. Tannenbaum, *Mexican Agrarian Revolution*, 252-53. He refers to changes between the 6 January 1915 law, article 27 of the 1917 Constitution, and the 1927 Law of Grants and Restitutions ("Ley de dotaciones y restituciones"). Tannenbaum's central observation comes from Mexican legal scholar Narciso Bassols's unpublished document "Consideraciones generales," prepared for the National Agrarian Commission and later published as *La Nueva Ley Agraria* in 1927 (Tannenbaum, *Mexican Agrarian Revolution*, 238n4). Fernando Escalante Gonzalbo also points out that between the 6 January 1915 law and article 27 there was a shift from the right of pueblos to recover land granted by the Spanish crown to "rights based on needs." In fact, he sees this change as the basis of "the entire agrarian legislation and a good part of later revolutionary law." See Escalante Gonzalbo, "El lenguaje del Artículo 27 constitucional," 235.

7. Cabrera Acevedo, *La Suprema Corte de Justicia durante los años constitucionalistas (1917-1920)*, 1:42. Most scholars disregard Cabrera Acevedo's work and claim that the Supreme Court mostly favored landowners and purposefully obstructed land reform efforts. For a recent example, see Sánchez, "Entre el caudillo."

8. This argument first appeared in Baitenmann, "Ejerciendo la justicia." The analysis of the first two revolutionary Supreme Courts partially follows James, *Mexico's Supreme Court*.

9. When Womack wrote *Zapata and the Mexican Revolution*, he had access to only the Archivo Gildardo y Octavio Magaña Cerda at the Archivo Histórico de la Universidad Nacional Autónoma de México. Womack's section on land reform (224-35) is based on Gómez's *Las comisiones agrarias del sur*, on an analysis of Minister of Agriculture Manuel Palafox's "A las comisiones agrarias del estado de Morelos"

(10 September 1914), and to a lesser extent on Palafox's agrarian law of 26 October 1915 (both reprinted in Fabela, *Documentos históricos*, 21:118-21 and 246-53). Since then, the following archival collections have become available (1) at the Archivo General de la Nación, the Fondo Colección Cuartel General del Sur, the Fondo Colección Revolución (Sección Emiliano Zapata), the Fondo Emiliano Zapata, the Fondo Genovevo de la O, the Fondo Gobernación Período Revolucionario, and the Fondo Soberana Convención Revolucionaria; and (2) at the Centro de Estudios de Historia de México, Fundación Carlos Slim, the Archivo Jenaro Amezcua.

Of the hundreds of books and articles about Zapata's movement after Womack's *Zapata*, only a few studies include some details on the implementation of land reform based on archival documentation, including Alanís Boyzo, *Historia de la revolución*, 174-85; Anaya Pérez, *Rebelión y revolución en Chalco-Amecameca*, 2:160-63; Ávila Sánchez, *Aspectos históricos*, 81-88; LaFrance, *Revolution in Mexico's Heartland*, 37-39, 65, 69, 137-39, 177-78; Tortolero Villaseñor, *Notarios y Agricultores*, 263-73; and Herrera Sipriano, *La revolución en la montaña de Guerrero*, 179-212. All other publications focus mainly on the military or political side of the movement.

10. Ulloa, *Historia de la Revolución Mexicana*, 6:347-403. Alan Knight, in *Mexican Revolution*, 2:174-76, also disagrees with the assessment that the Constitutionalist revolution was conservative. Scholars who argue that Carranza was reluctant to implement land reform include Cumberland, *Mexican Revolution*, 383; Silva Herzog, *El agrarismo mexicano*, 246-47; Simpson, *Ejido*, 78-81; and Tannenbaum, *Mexican Agrarian Revolution*, 183-84.

11. Village representatives (and they were all men at the time) often had power of attorney to act for the population at large or were elected municipal officials. Town spokespersons could be elected *ayuntamiento* officials at the *cabecera* or head township (*presidente*, *síndico*) or at the sujetos level (*ayudante*, *comisario*), traditional Indian representatives (*principales*, *mayordomos*), or some other form of legitimate authority. At other times, representatives spoke only for village factions or their own interests. In both cases, they often sought to bolster their power by rallying villagers around the idea of recovering their ancestral rights to land and water resources. On pueblo representatives, see Falcón, "El arte de la petición," 477-78, and Kourí, "Sobre la propiedad comunal de los pueblos," 1932.

Some representatives and petitioners self-identified as Indians; others did not. Ethnicity and colonial land titles did not always correspond. Former Indian pueblos could become multiethnic cities and still preserve their Colonial Indian rights to land, water resources, and woodlands. In both Indian and mestizo pueblos, "families or individuals owned and worked most available agricultural land; in both... municipal governments owned—and regulated residents' use of—surrounding grazing, wood, and shrub lands (ejidos); finally, in both mestizo and indigenous towns, municipal governments often owned tracts of agricultural land that was either rented out or—in indigenous towns—worked collectively in order to defray civil and religious expenses." Schaefer, *Liberalism as Utopia*, 134.

12. Galante, "La historiografía reciente," 104–5.
13. Oftentimes villagers relied on lawyers or the so-called *tinterillos* (legal agents without formal law accreditation). See, among others, Lira González, "Abogados, tinterillos y huizacheros."
14. Marino, "Buscando su lugar," 243. See also Camacho Pichardo, "En pro de los privilegios 'sin excepciones'"; Falcón, "El arte de la petición"; and Marino, "La fuerza de la ley," 207–8. See the glossary for the definition of *amparo*.
15. See, for example, Chassen-López, *From Liberal to Revolutionary Oaxaca*, 92, 94; Jacobs, *Ranchero Revolt*, 47–48; Mendoza García, "Desamortización y pequeños propietarios indígenas," 245; Ortiz Yam, "Formación de ejidos," 26–27; and Purnell, "'With All Due Respect,'" 92.
16. Roseberry, "El estricto apego a la ley," 28.
17. I thank Antonio Escobar Ohmstede for pointing this out.
18. See also Brunk, *¡Emiliano Zapata!*, 197.
19. Antonio Azuela de la Cueva uses the term "provisional ejido" for the period 1915–34 and "perpetual ejido" for 1934–92 ("La jurisprudencia," 351). On the relationship between municipal and agrarian local authorities, see Azuela, "Ciudadanía y gestión urbana"; Baitenmann, "Rural Agency and State Formation," chap. 7; and Baitenmann, "Las paradojas."
20. Noteworthy exceptions are Birrichaga Gardida, "¿Ejidatarios o comuneros?"; Santos García, "Élites e indígenas"; and Velasco Toro and García Ruiz, "Restitución de tierras."
21. Unless otherwise noted, all translations from the original Spanish are by the author. González Roa, *Parte general de un informe*, 18–22.

22. Bassols, *La nueva ley agraria*, 72–82, quotation from 82.
23. For a discussion of these founding myths, see Knight, "Land and Society in Revolutionary Mexico," and Kourí, "Interpreting the Expropriation."
24. Preamble of the constitutional reforms to article 27 (23 December 1931) quoted in Archivo Central de la Suprema Corte de Justicia de la Nación (ACSCJN), expediente (exp.) 246.
25. Article 14 states, "No person shall be deprived of life, liberty, property, possessions, or rights without a trial by a duly created court in which the essential formalities of procedure are observed and in accordance with laws issued prior to the act." Translation of the Mexican Constitution by the Organization of American States, accessed 12 June 2019, http://www.oas.org/juridico/mla/en/mex/en_mex-int-text-const.pdf.
26. Mendieta y Núñez, *El problema agrario*, 190.
27. Tannenbaum, *Mexican Agrarian Revolution*, 198, 232–34.
28. Simpson, *Ejido*, 60.
29. Whetten, *Rural Mexico*, 115. See also de la Peña, *Legacy of Promises*, 75.
30. Fix Zamudio, "Lineamientos fundamentales," 894–97.
31. Chávez Padrón, *El proceso social agrario*, 34–35.
32. García Ramírez, in "Establecimiento y horizonte," 35, cites the following congresses where this issue was discussed: the Primer Congreso Revolucionario de Derecho Agrario (Mexico D.F., 1959); the 1961 Congreso Nacional Agrario de Toluca; and the VIII Congreso Mexicano de Derecho Procesal (Xalapa, 1979). Earlier yet, the 1959 Congreso Nacional Agrario de Toluca called for "establishing an ejidal justice system . . . that will allow the *ejidatario* [ejido grant beneficiary] and *colono* [agrarian colony beneficiary] to present his or her complaints about violation of his or her agrarian rights and abuse by the ejido authorities and obtain quick or efficient justice" (40).
33. Armienta Calderón, "Algunos aspectos relevantes," 14.
34. de Ibarrola, *Derecho agrario*, 426.
35. Silva Herzog, *El agrarismo mexicano*, 236–37.
36. de la Peña, *El pueblo y su tierra*, 306.
37. Reyes Osorio et al., *Estructura agraria*.
38. Gilly, *La revolución interrumpida*, 179.
39. Córdova, *La ideología de la Revolución Mexicana*.
40. For the "metaconstitutional faculties" of the executive, see García Ramírez, founding magistrate of the 1992 agrarian tribunals, in "Establecimiento y horizonte," 35.

41. According to President Felipe Calderón Hijojosa's *Tercer Informe de Gobierno* (*Gobierno de los Estados Unidos Mexicanos*, 265), from 1992 to mid-2006 these courts issued 370,000 agrarian resolutions dealing with issues ranging from unresolved inheritance disputes to historic inter- and intravillage land conflicts.
42. For some important exceptions of studies that begin before the 1910 Revolution, see Nugent, *Spent Cartridges of Revolution*; Purnell, *Popular Movements and State Formation*; and Velázquez, *Territorios fragmentados*.

    The classic books on Mexico's land laws did have a *longue durée*, usually starting with precolonial land tenure and ending with revolutionary laws and decrees. But in the absence of access to relevant archival materials, these studies could not address the way in which villagers adopted, used, rejected, or manipulated this legislation in these different historical periods. See, for example, Fabila, *Cinco siglos*; Lemus, *Derecho Agrario Mexicano*; Luna Arroyo and Alcérreca, *Derecho agrario mexicano*; Mendieta y Núñez, *El problema agrario de México*; Rincón Serrano, *El ejido mexicano*; and Silva Herzog, *El agrarismo mexicano*.
43. Warman, "*We Come to Object*," 136. In 1980 Guillermo de la Peña also wrote a history of agrarian reform in Morelos. In his work he explained that villagers could petition for the restitution of their lands as well as for a grant. Although his analysis is by no means uncritical of official land reform—hence his title *A Legacy of Promises*—he goes against the Warman trend by characterizing *dotaciones* as an innovation. Grants "circumvented the numerous difficulties inherent in land restitution: frequently old communal deeds were difficult or impossible to find or boundaries impossible to define, taking as a basis colonial measurements and references. In addition, the dotación procedures implied that large landholdings could be expropriated even if they had not invaded communal land" (English quotation from *Legacy of Promises*, 74-75).
44. Hall, "Álvaro Obregón and the Politics of Mexican Land Reform," 220.
45. Markiewicz, *Mexican Revolution*, 23-24.
46. Sanderson, *Land Reform in Mexico*, 88-90.
47. Purnell, *Popular Movements and State Formation*, 59.
48. Nugent, *Spent Cartridges of Revolution*, 91.
49. Nugent and Alonso, "Multiple Selective Traditions," 212, 229, 244, citing Bartra, *Los herederos de Zapata*, 16-21.

50. Craib, *Cartographic Mexico*, 245.
51. Gledhill, "Introducción," 23.
52. Palacios, "Las restituciones de la Revolución," 127. See also Hernández Hernández, "La querella por la tierra," 79.
53. Azuela, "El problema con las ideas que detrás," 103. Azuela lists several social scientists who make this mistake. For more a recent gaffe, this time by a legal scholar, see Ordóñez Cifuentes, "Antecedentes y naturaleza," 119.
54. It was not until the 1942 Agrarian Code that officials created the *comunidad agraria* (agrarian community) for beneficiaries of restituted lands alongside the "ejido" for dotación beneficiaries—although the 1940 Agrarian Code already differentiated between *comisariados ejidales* (ejido boards) for dotación beneficiaries and *comisariados de bienes comunales* (communal property boards) for beneficiaries of restituted lands. For the 1940 code see Fabila, *Cinco siglos*, 592–660. For the 1942 code see DOF, 27 April 1943, 9–43.
55. In "Between State and Market," Jonathan Fox and Gustavo Gordillo present a more nuanced view, in which the ejido organization (meaning both restitution and dotación beneficiaries) served not only as a form of governmental control but also as a resource for independent campesino organization.
56. For an analysis of the historical interpretation of the Porfiriato embedded in this law, see Kourí "Interpreting the Expropriation."
57. See the glossary for the meaning of *primordial title*.
58. Marino, "La fuerza de la ley," 207–8; Owensby, *Empire of Law*, 100.
59. I thank Emilio Kourí for clarifying the nature of Madero's circulars.
60. Article 6 of the Plan de Ayala, reprinted in Fabila, *Cinco siglos*, 181–84. On the Plan de Ayala's reversal of the burden of proof, see Brunk, *¡Emiliano Zapata!*, 67.
61. "Ley de desamortización de las fincas rústicas y urbanas de las corporaciones civiles y religiosas de México" (25 June 1856), issued by Fomento secretary Miguel Lerdo de Tejada and therefore known as the Lerdo law, reproduced in Fabila, *Cinco siglos*, 91–95.
62. For the idea that Zapatismo was not the ideological inspiration for the Constitutionalist agrarian program, see Kourí, "La invención del ejido," and especially his detailed history of the ideas that influenced the Constitutionalists in "Interpreting the Expropriation." For a history of how Zapatismo was incorporated into the official language of postrevolutionary governments, see Ávila Espinosa, "La

batalla por los símbolos," and Brunk, *Posthumous Career of Emiliano Zapata*, 66.

63. Brunk, *¡Emiliano Zapata!*, 68. There is a long-standing debate as to whether the Zapatista revolutionary movement was Indian (a different question than whether the villagers involved in the movement identified as Indians—and many did). For an explanation of the "scholarly effort to resuscitate Zapata's Indianness in the face of Womack's insistence that he had been a mestizo," see Brunk, *Posthumous Career*, 231. Womack reopens this debate in his 2017 preface to the second edition of his translated book; the preface is titled "Prólogo: historias por estudiar sobre la Revolución del Sur (1911–1920): lo que aún no sabemos, lo que valdría la pena saber," in *Zapata y la Revolución Mexicana*, 21–22.

64. The Plan de Ayala proposed to seize, with prior compensation, a third of the lands belonging to powerful landowners who monopolized agricultural resources (text in Fabila, *Cinco siglos*, 181–84); article 4 of the 25 October 1915 law stated that all Mexicans had the right to own and cultivate enough land to fulfill the needs of a family and to create small private properties (*la pequeña propiedad*); all large private estates above certain sizes (anywhere between one hundred and fifteen hundred hectares, depending on land type and climate) would be expropriated for public utility and with compensation (text in Lemus, *Derecho agrario mexicano*, 227–33).

65. "Durante el próximo periodo constitucional, el Congreso de la Unión y las Legislaturas de los Estados, en sus respectivas jurisdicciones, expedirán leyes para llevar a cabo el fraccionamiento de las grandes propiedades" (text of article 27 of the 1917 Constitution in Fabila, *Cinco siglos*, 261–64). In 1964 Lucio Mendieta y Núñez and Luis G. Alcérreca proposed new agrarian legislation that would address the fact that neither Congress nor the state legislatures had issued laws on the breakup of large estates or *fraccionamiento de latifundios* (*Un anteproyecto de Nuevo Código Agrario*, 140).

1. Nineteenth-Century Suits

1. For the role of the Juzgado General de Indios (1592–1812), see Borah, *Justice by Insurance*, and Owensby, *Empire of Law* and "Comunidades indígenas y gobernanza."

2. Borah, "La justificación del Juzgado General de Indios," 147. There are many examples showing that legal proceedings at the Indian courts

could also be slow. For example, in 1830 San Juan Zacazonapan (Mexico State) had a pending lawsuit against the Santa María Magdalena hacienda that was over sixty years old (AGN, FJ, vol. 126, exp. 13, fs. 298-302v.).

3. Borah, *Justice by Insurance*, 312-13; Lira González, "Extinción del Juzgado de Indios," 299-317; Owensby, "Comunidades indígenas," 103.

4. Noriega Elío, "Estudio introductorio," in *La Diputación Provincial de México*, 2:22, 33, 37. Provincial deputations were short-lived but important administrative entities created before federal states came into being. They were operational in two time periods: 1812-14 and 1820-23 (see Benson, *Provincial Deputation in Mexico*, and Anna, *Forging Mexico*, 55-56, 68). On the continuity of land restitution claims from the colonial era to the nineteenth century and the revolution of 1910, see Karst, "Latin American Land Reform," 331.

5. AGN, FJ, vol. 14, exp. 43, fs. 430-46 (January 1822), and *La Diputación Provincial de México*, 2:266. Many other deputations did the same. The Calimaya ayuntamiento asked for guidance regarding Tepemajalco residents who claimed rights to seized land, and the New Spain Provincial Deputation responded by sending them to the *juez de primera instancia* (*La Diputación Provincial de Nueva España. Actas de sesiones, 1820-1821*, 1:192). Several years later, when the Nexquipayac ayuntamiento solicited "the reintegration of the lands that belonged to them," the deputation ordered the Texcoco *juez de letras* to settle the matter with the neighboring haciendas (*La Diputación Provincial de México*, 2:327).

Because the specific terms used for local judges varied by state, the Spanish-language names employed here are those used in the archival or secondary sources.

6. *Actas del congreso constituyente del estado libre de México*, 102 (1 April 1824), and Birrichaga Gardida, "Administración de tierras," 176-77.

7. See, for example, *Colección de acuerdos, órdenes y decretos*, 1:28 (19 September 1825), 83 (22 January 1849), and passim.

8. *Colección de acuerdos, órdenes y decretos*, 1:28 (19 September 1825).

9. AGA, Reconocimiento y Titulación de Bienes Comunales, exp. 276.1/1985, leg. 11, fs. 33-36, Tecalpulco, Taxco de Alarcón, Guerrero.

10. *Colección de acuerdos, órdenes y decretos*, 1:83 (22 January 1849).

11. AGN, FG s/s, caja 246, exp. 26, fs. 1-3 (1838, 1841).

12. "Reglamento para el gobierno interior del Tribunal Superior de Justicia del Estado Libre y Soberano de México" (27 June 1850), reprinted in Huitrón, *El poder judicial en el Estado de México*, 2:215-27.

13. Neighboring private-property owners could also sidestep the courts (if they informed the district prefect), or they could proceed with a court case. See AGN, FJPCM, vol. 1, exp. 5, fs. 97-99 (7 August 1861).
14. Purnell, "Citizens and Sons of the Pueblo," 222.
15. *Colección de acuerdos, órdenes y decretos*, 3:92-96 (22 October 1857).
16. *Ley expedida por el Gobierno del Estado de Michoacán*, 3-7.
17. "Ley para determinar las diferencias sobre tierras y aguas entre los pueblos" (1 November 1865), reproduced in Fabila, *Cinco siglos*, 126-27.
18. Marino, "Ahora que Dios nos ha dado padre," 1396, citing Granados García, "Comunidad indígena," 63.
19. "Ley agraria del imperio que concede fundo legal y ejido a los pueblos que carecen de él" (16 September 1866), reproduced in Fabila, *Cinco siglos*, 131-32.
20. James, *Mexico's Supreme Court*, 59.
21. Falcón, *El jefe político*, 418; and Marino, "La fuerza de la ley," 223. Romana Falcón notes that starting in 1868 Mexico State laws made prefects and political chiefs responsible for avoiding land suits and providing conciliation and arbitration before granting or denying ayuntamientos, municipios, or pueblos a license to litigate. Arbitrators had to be lawyers, and they were to make conciliation binding. Given that the parties did have the final right to take their claims to court, the laws encouraged jefes políticos not to grant pueblos license to litigate. Falcón, *El jefe político*, 413-16.
22. Gobierno del Estado Libre y Soberano de Puebla, "Decreto No. 122 del 2º Congreso Constitucional, sobre litigios pendientes entre los pueblos del Estado y nombramiento de arbitradores amigables componedores," qtd. in Mallon, *Peasant and Nation*, 121, 386n61.
23. Marino, "'La medida de su existencia,'" 298.
24. "Decreto del Estado de Hidalgo del 21 de abril de 1869," qtd. in Knowlton, "Tribunales federales y terrenos," 84-85.
25. James, *Mexico's Supreme Court*, 59.
26. James, *Mexico's Supreme Court*, 60.
27. Cabrera Acevedo, *La Suprema Corte de Justicia*, 53-54.
28. *SJF*, época 1, tomo 5, pp. 127-31 (24 February 1874).
29. *SJF*, época 1, tomo 5, pp. 605-9 (6 March 1874).
30. Reproduced in Fabila, *Cinco siglos*, 91-95.
31. Díaz González, *Sentencia del Tribunal de Circuito de México*, 4.
32. Marino, *Huixquilucan*, 178.
33. Cabrera Acevedo, *La Suprema Corte de Justicia en La República Restaurada*, 53; Knowlton, "Tribunales federales y terrenos rurales," 72.

34. *SJF*, época 1, tomo 2, pp. 339-43 (1871).
35. Cabrera Acevedo, *La Suprema Corte de Justicia en el primer periodo del porfirismo (1877-1882)*, 269-72, (9 January 1879).
36. Cabrera Acevedo, *La Suprema Corte de Justicia en el primer periodo del porfirismo*, 279-81 (14 January 1880).
37. *SJF*, época 2, tomo 4, pp. 400-431 (9 January 1882); Knowlton, "Tribunales federales," 74-77; Cabrera Acevedo, *La Suprema Corte de Justicia en el primer periodo del porfirismo*, 569-71; González Navarro, "Vallarta, indios y extranjeros," 1075-76; Marino, "Buscando su lugar," 245. For a study of the lack of juridical standing of agricultural societies in three pueblos in Mexico State, see Neri Guarneros, "Sociedades agrícolas en resistencia."
38. For more on Vallarta's sentences, see Cabrera Acevedo, *La Suprema Corte de Justicia en el primer periodo del porfirismo*, 571-79; Cabrera Acevedo, *La Suprema Corte de Justicia a principios del siglo XX*, 22-23; Knowlton, "Tribunales federales," 77-81; and Marino, "Buscando su lugar."
39. See, for example, the case involving San Bartolomé Tepetitlán and San Francisco de Sayula villagers against the Endó hacienda, in *SJF*, época 2, tomo 5, pp. 553-75 (9 November 1882). See also Cabrera Acevedo, *La Suprema Corte de Justicia en el primer periodo del porfirismo*, 579-84; and Knowlton, "Tribunales federales," 82-85.
40. Cabrera Acevedo, *Suprema Corte de Justicia a principios del siglo XX*, 22-23. The 1857 Constitution adopted the 1847 "Otero formula" that "limits the effects of rulings in amparo cases to the litigants" (Zamora et al., *Mexican Law*, 84): "That is, the judicial ruling did not have general applicability, even if the court found a law, widespread policy, or governmental practice unconstitutional" (Suárez-Potts, *Making of Law*, 5-6). And yet, "under the post-1917 governments, as well as intermittently before then, the federal judiciary adhered to a narrow policy of *stare decisis*. In general, five consistent, consecutive rulings by the Supreme Court on a legal point (*tesis*) established a controlling precedent, *jurisprudencia*, on lower federal courts and on its own subsequent decision making" (Suárez-Potts, *Making of Law*, 6).
41. *SJF*, época 2, tomo 15, pp. 494-95 (25 October 1888).
42. AGA, Restitución de tierras, exp. 24/703, leg. 3, fs. 70-74, 127-28, General Severino Ceniceros (Antes Santiago y San Pedro de Ocuila), Cuencamé, Durango. See also AGA, Restitución de tierras, 24/5050, leg. 3, fs. 36-38, Santa Bárbara Acuicuizcatepec, Xaltocan, Tlaxcala;

SJF, época 3, tomo 8, pp. 531-33 (12 September 1893), and "Sentencia del juez segundo de distrito en el Distrito Federal, en un asunto de terrenos baldíos. 13 de mayo de 1893," in Cabrera Acevedo, *La Suprema Corte de Justicia durante el fortalecimiento del porfirismo (1882-1888)*, 355-59.

43. *SJF*, época 3, tomo 6, pp. 1010-11 (29 November 1892).
44. Marino, *Huixquilucan*, 178.
45. Marino, "Buscando su lugar," 243-44; "La fuerza de la ley," 228, and "'La medida de su existencia,'" 301-3.
46. Marino, "La modernidad a juicio," 290-91, 294-96, 312-16. See also Lira, "El amparo," 85-86, and the case of the "extinguished community of Acuitzio," in *SJF*, época 4, tomo 6, pp. 992-1000 (29 December 1900).
47. Paraphrased ruling. *SJF*, época 4, tomo 9, pp. 228-46 (20 November 1901). See also Camacho, "En pro de los privilegios," 258-59, 268, 275.
48. *SJF*, época 4, tomo 36, pp. 509-11 (27 January 1908). Similarly, in 1908 the Supreme Court granted amparo protection to Huixtac and Temaxcalapa against the prefecture of Aldama (Guerrero), who in 1885 had adjudicated their lands to residents from neighboring Teucizapan. *Al público*, printed pamphlet found in AGN, FEZ, caja 18, exp. 4, fs. 3-4. And in Mexico State, the district judge denied Calimaya representatives amparo protection, but the Supreme Court justices reversed the ruling, claiming that the disputed lands were community property for the use of the pueblo residents. *SJF*, época 4, tomo 19, pp. 136-39 (10 May 1904).
49. Cabrera Acevedo, *La Suprema Corte de Justicia a principios del siglo XX*, 22-23. In 1901 the federal government amended the 1857 Constitution to allow Indian villages to own and administer land corporately (*las corporaciones civiles podrán poseer y administrar bienes raíces destinados a su sostenimiento*). Andrés Lira believes this change was mainly meant to benefit private welfare associations. See also Stevens, "Agrarian Policy and Instability," 1982; Schenk, "The *desamortización* in the Sultepec District," 218; and Knowlton, "El ejido mexicano en el siglo XIX," 86.
50. González y González, *Obras completas*, 145.
51. Universidad Iberoamericana (UIA), Colección Porfirio Díaz (CPD), leg. 005, doc. 002872 (date 1880). Santiago ended his letter by adding that he did not believe it was "superfluous to say that five thousand Indians, heads of family, obey me." On this uprising, see, for example, Luz Carregha Lamadrid, "En torno a los levantamientos armados," 169-71.

52. Otero, *Asunto del pueblo de Tetelpa*, 3.
53. Molina Enríquez, *Los grandes problemas nacionales*, 159. On Molina, see Kourí, "Interpreting," 90–104; and Shadle, *Andrés Molina Enríquez*, especially Shadle's bibliography.
54. SJF, época 4, tomo 22, pp. 428–37 (7 March 1905); Sedano, *Revolucionarios surianos y memorias*, 41–49, 81–82; Womack, *Zapata*, 50–51; and Magaña, *Emiliano Zapata y el agrarismo*, 1:84–86.
55. Schaefer, *Liberalism as Utopia*, 203.
56. Knowlton, "Tribunales federales," 72; Fenner Bieling, "La defensa de las tierras colectivas en Chiapa," 885–86, 893; Sierra Zavala, "El juicio de amparo," 427; and Ávila Espinosa, *La justicia durante el porfiriato y la revolución*, 5:12. See also Holden, *Mexico and the Surveys of Public Lands*.
57. See, for example, Knowlton, "Tribunales federales," 92–93, 95–96; Neri Guarneros, "Sociedades agrícolas," 32–33; and Marino, "La medida de su existencia," 302–3.
58. AGA, Restitución de tierras, exp. 24/703, leg. 3, fs. 70–74, 83–89, Santiago y San Pedro de Ocuila, Cuencamé, Durango.
59. ACSCJN, FSCJN, exp. 2398 (1913).
60. AGA, Restitución de tierras, exp. 24/4974, leg. 7, fs. 1–4, 15, 25; leg. 8, fs. 33–37, San Antonio Calpulalpan, San Antonio Calpulalpan, Tlaxcala. (AGA archives are classified by names of town, municipality, and state. Sometimes the name of the town is the same as that of the municipality.)
61. Marino, "La medida de su existencia," 307.
62. This court ruling granted them juridical standing—albeit a decade later. SJF, época 4, tomo 48, pp. 56–59 (8 March 1910). See also the case of the Supreme Court granting amparo protection to Calimaya (Mexico State) in 1904, in Camacho Pichardo, "En pro de los privilegios," 265–69.
63. "Ejecución de las sentencias de amparo por T. Saenz" (14 January 1880), reproduced in Cabrera Acevedo, *La Suprema Corte de Justicia en el primer periodo del porfirismo*, 279–81.
64. AGN, FJ-JDM, caja 100, exp. 516, f. 102 (1905).
65. Schaefer, *Liberalism as Utopia*, 153.
66. AGA, Restitución de tierras, exp. 24/12024, leg 3, f. 155, San Vicente Chimalhuacán, Ozumba, Mexico State. *Rancho*, in this context, refers to a small- or medium-sized private property.
67. AGN, FG, leg. 221, exp. 3, fs. 395–97; Cypher, "Reconstructing Community," 176–77; Díaz Soto y Gama, *Historia del agrarismo en México*, 372–73.

68. Marino, "La fuerza de la ley," 207-8. On ambiguous property rights in colonial times, see Owensby, *Empire of Law*, 90-129. Santa Anna's decree also prompted many village representatives to travel to the National Archives in Mexico City to search for their titles. Teotihuacán residents, for example, used the decree to try to recover their usurped water resources. Their attorney petitioned Fomento to order the judge to conduct an on-site inspection of their springs and to request hacienda owners to present the titles that legitimated the water rights they claimed. Birrichaga Gardida, "Lucha y defensa de los pueblos," 260-61.
69. Fernández de Castro, "Agrarian Reform from Below," 328.
70. Molina Enríquez, *Los grandes problemas nacionales*, 126.
71. Castañeda González, *Las aguas de Atlixco*, 167.
72. Delgado Aguilar, "La comunidad de riego," 211-23.
73. Arrioja Díaz Viruell, "Conflictos por tierras y pesquisas documentales en el Valle de Oaxaca, 1912," 193-94. In 1912, Guelache representatives spent many weeks at the National Archives but did not find their titles. Arrioja believes that the titles were not lost but rather never existed, given that Guelache was probably established on cacique lands (202-3).
74. The author thanks Antonio Escobar Ohmstede for pointing this out.
75. Falcón, *El jefe político*, 446-47.
76. Marino, "Tierras y aguas de Huixquilucan," 284.
77. Schaefer, *Liberalism as Utopia*, 153. See also the archival documents listed in Méndez Martínez, *Límites, mapas y títulos*.
78. Purnell, "Citizens and Sons," 221.
79. Owensby, *Empire of Law*, 100.
80. "Lawyers," she warns, "must understand that titles are not black and white, false or authentic." Romero Frizzi, "Conflictos agrarios," 77-81, quotation from 81. For studies of forged titles, see, for example, Barrera and Barrera, "La falsificación de títulos de tierras a principios del siglo XX"; Camacho Altamirano, "Los derechos de la propiedad de la tierra y del agua," 111-12; Carrillo Cázares, "'Chiquisnaquis' un indio escribano, artífice de títulos primordiales"; Yannakakis, "Witnesses, Spatial Practices"; García Castro and Arzate Becerril, "Ilustración, justicia, y títulos de tierras"; Ruiz Medrano, *Mexico's Indigenous Communities*, 173-79; Wood, "Pedro Villafranca y Juan Gertrudis Navarrete"; and Villa-Flores, "Archivos y falsarios."
81. Owensby, *Empire of Law*, 96.

82. Salinas Sandoval, "Problemas por tierras," 7–8. See also the restitution claims in DOF, 28 June 1927, and DOF, 12 September 1930. On the phenomenon of haciendas' expansion (due to their gradual transformation into agricultural companies) and contraction (due to partial sales or fractioning through inheritance), see Escobar Ohmstede, "Tierra y agua," 95–98.

83. Falcón, "El arte de la petición," 472. See also Mallon, *Peasant and Nation*; Marino, *Huixquilucan*; Guardino, *Peasants, Politics*; Escobar Ohmstede, "Los pueblos indios huastecos"; and the bibliography in Galante, "La historiografía reciente."

84. Craib, *Cartographic Mexico*, 68. See also AGA, Solicitud de los vecinos para que se deslinden las tierras de sus ejidos, 23/140, Villa de Dzitbalché, municipio Calkiní, Campeche, 1873; Chassen-López, *From Liberal to Revolutionary Oaxaca*, 92, 94; Mendoza García, "Desamortización y pequeños propietarios," 245; and Neri Guarneros, "Sociedades agrícolas," 31.

85. Ortiz Yam, "Formación de ejidos," 26–27.

86. García, *Informe a la vista*, 87–96.

87. Purnell, "Citizens and Sons," 227.

88. García, *Informe a la vista*, 87–96. For a similar situation in Ayotuxco (Mexico State), see Marino, "'La medida de su existencia,'" 303–4.

89. Kourí, *Pueblo Divided*, 218. Kourí explains that "excedencias were untitled—that is, public—lands occupied by individuals who owned or had legal rights to an immediately adjoining territory. Demasías, meanwhile, represented the difference between the actual and the legal size of a particular landed property," 218.

90. Kourí, *Pueblo Divided*, 218–21, 257–60, quote from 219.

91. Díaz González, *Sentencia del Tribunal*, 4.

92. The ejido measurement came to a halt, however, when neighboring Calkiní representatives rejected the survey for invading what they considered to be their pueblo lands and water resources and took the matter to court. AGA, Dotación de tierras, exp. 23/140 (histórico), leg. 0, fs. 19, 22–23, Dzitbalché, Calkiní, Campeche.

93. Kourí, *Pueblo Divided*, 221.

94. Aboites Aguilar and Morales Cosme, "Amecameca, 1922," 69–75. The amparo did not stop the landowners from continuing to fell their woodlands.

95. Ávila Espinosa, *Los orígenes del zapatismo*, 260; and AGN, FM, caja 3, exp. 67-2, fs. 2022–23 (15 January 1912).

96. SJF, época 2, tomo 12, pp. 668–70 (17 June 1887).

97. Cited in Knowlton, "Tribunales federales," 93 (27 June 1893).
98. Purnell, "Citizens and Sons," 221-22, 226-27, citing ACSCJN, FSCJN, exp. 2398 (1913).
99. *SJF*, época 3, tomo 8, pp. 531-33 (12 September 1893).
100. Cabrera Acevedo, *La Suprema Corte de Justicia en la República Restaurada, 1867-1876*, 53-54; *SJF*, época 1, tomo 5, pp. 127-31 (24 February 1874).
101. *SJF*, época 1, tomo 5, pp. 605 (6 March 1874). They were citing article 49, not article 50. *SJF*, época 1, tomo 5, pp. 608. English translations of the Constitutional articles can be found in https://www.oas.org/juridico/mla/en/mex/en_mex-int-text-const.pdf. The district judge denied amparo protection, claiming that Tejúpam did not have juridical standing. In 1874, however, the Supreme Court overturned the district court's ruling and granted Tejúpam amparo protection, confirming it was the judiciary's exclusive right to judge land-related matters. *SJF*, época 1, tomo 5, pp. 605-9 (6 March 1874).
102. Fomento, or Development, was called Ministerio de Fomento from 1853 to 1861; Secretaría de Estado y Despacho de Fomento from 1861 to 1917; and Secretaría de Agricultura y Fomento from 1917 to 1946. See, for example, Blanco Martínez and Moncada Maya, "El Ministerio de Fomento," and Zuleta, "La Secretaría de Fomento."
103. AGN, FG s/s, secc. 2a877(8)4, caja 72, exp. 143, fs. 2, 11 (December 1877).
104. Zárate H., "Comunidad, reformas liberales," 37-39 (20 August 1903).

2. Claims during the Madero Years

1. The epigraph is from "Representatives of San Juan Atzingo, Puebla, to President Francisco León de la Barra." AHUNAM, AGM, FLB, caja 29, exp. 160, f. 44 (11 July 1911).
2. All quotes are from the Plan de San Luis Potosí, reproduced in Fabila, *Cinco siglos*, 177-80. Emphasis added.
3. AGN, FM, caja 3, exp. 64-1, fs. 1966-67 (8 January 1912). In Tamaulipas, "the Indians of the extinct San Joaquín del Monte Mission" wrote to de la Barra to condemn the illegal *denuncio* (claim) of terrenos baldíos they had long possessed. AHUNAM, AGM, FLB caja 29, exp. 159, fs. 50-51 (17 July 1911).
4. AHUNAM, AGM, FLB, 33:180 (29 June 1911).
5. For Pasaje, see AGN, FM, caja 64, exps. 2773 and 2774 (6, 16 December 1911). Peñón Blanco's translated quotation is from Fernández de Castro, "Agrarian Reform from Below," 616. On other land petitions during this period in Durango, see 615-29.

6. AGN, FM, caja 64, exp. 2896 (5 July 1912). Similarly, in Guanajuato, the San Miguel Octopan representative informed Madero that even though his pueblo had land titles, its lands had been invaded by haciendas from all directions, in an onrush like that of "the four winds." "Given the promises of the Plan de San Luis," he added, "we, your humble children, will help you until we spill the last drop of our blood." AGN, FM, caja 47, exp. 1289-1, f. 35481 (21 January 1912). In San Luis Potosí, over seventy Indians from San Francisco de la Palma claimed to have been "in quiet and peaceful possession of the lands granted to us by the viceroys, and whose titles are in our possession," but several haciendas, including that of former president Manuel González, had seized some portion of them. AGN, FM, caja 64, exp. 2814 (1 February 1913). See also AGN, FSJ, caja 781, exp. 6077, 6091, 6095, 6105, 6114, 6126, and 6130; AGN, FSJ, caja 782, exp. 6191; and AGN, FM, caja 64, exp. 2883.

7. AGN, FM, caja 64, exp. 2784 (26 January 1912). In Chiapas, Mazatán residents informed Madero that they had lost lands they had held "since time immemorial" and were now left with families to feed but no lands to cultivate. AGN, FM, caja 64, exp. 2889 (27 April 1912). And in Durango, Arenal residents denounced the Navacoyán hacienda owners who, allegedly backed by the governor, had invaded lands the villagers had held "in quiet and peaceful possession," leaving them without pasturelands for their animals or wood with which to cook their food. They had sued the hacienda, but because they did not have titles, the court ruled in favor of the hacienda owner. AHUNAM, AGM, FLB, caja 37, exp. 204, fs. 20-21 (3 August 1911).

8. AGN, FM, caja 64, exp. 2789 (17 July 1912).

9. AGN, FSJ, caja 782, exp. 6200, fs. 1-10 (December 1911). Similarly, in Guerrero around one hundred signatories (including women) from the Malinaltepec, Iliatenco, Tierra Blanca, and Paso Morelos pueblos petitioned for the restitution of the lands that had been seized from them by a rich resident of Puebla. AGN, FM, caja 64, exp. 2894 (30 June 1912). In Puebla, Santo Tomás Otlaltepec natives cited the Plan de San Luis Potosí to petition for the return of pueblo lands held by two caciques who had been "protected by the former regime [and] who took advantage of poor and mostly illiterate farmers." AGN, FSJ, caja 782, exp. 6296, fs. 1-2 (27 August 1911). Also in Puebla, a Santa Catarina Ilamacingo resident petitioned for "the fulfillment of article 3, last section, of the Plan de San Luis," accusing Puebla caciques of

having despoiled them of their lands "even though they were in possession of the pueblos' primordial titles." AHUNAM, AGM, FLB, caja 40, exp. 213, f. 44 (12 September 1911). In Michoacán, over 200 San Juan Parangaricutiro Indians complained that local authorities had, without the villagers' approval, rented their montes out to the Mexican Woodlands Company, leaving them without access to woodland products. AHUNAM, AGM, FLB, caja 60, exp. 320, fs. 21–29 (1 September 1911). And in Mexico State, 650 San Pedro Totoltepec residents asked de la Barra to remove the auxiliary judge for having granted the neighboring hacienda rights to their lands. AHUNAM, AGM, FLB, caja 36, exp. 194, fs. 53–59 (2 August 1911).

10. AGN, FM, caja 64, exp. 2937 (28 January 1913). See also the petitions from Tláhuac (D.F.), AGN, FM, caja 99, exp. 30, f. 12 (no date); Paraíso (Tabasco), AGN, FM, caja 64, exp. 2762 (11 November 1911); Tlancingo (Hidalgo), AGN, FM caja 64, exp. 2763 (13 November 1911); and Ciudad Valles (San Luis Potosí), AGN, FM, caja 64, exp. 2784 (26 January 1912).

11. AGN, FM, caja 64, exp. 2897 (20 July 1912). In a similar case, Chilacachapa residents in Guerrero argued that they had held possession of some lands since time immemorial. However, because they had lost their titles, several neighboring pueblos (including La Estacada, Zoquiapan, El Durazno, and Almolonga) invaded their lands. AHUNAM, AGM, FLB, caja 51, exp. 262, f. 80 (27 September 1911). In Jalisco, San Lucas Evangelista authorities denounced neighboring villagers for having despoiled them of their fundo legal, and they were now being threatened for trying to defend their rights. AGN, FM, caja 76, exp. 21, f. 230 (27 December 1912).

12. AHUNAM, AGM, FLB, caja 63, exp. 337, fs. 32–33 (12 August 1911).

13. AGN, FM, caja 14, exp. 342-2, f. 11068 (12 May 1912). In Sonora approximately one hundred villagers from Natora requested a reparto to recover lands lost to a third party. AGN, FM, caja 64, exp. 2849 (30 November 1911). In Durango, Guarisamey residents petitioned for "the adjudication of property and the reparto of the lands that should be distributed to us." They explained that twelve years before, President Díaz, through Fomento, had ordered a reparto among all residents of the pueblo, "but here in San Dimas they annulled this order." AGN, FM, caja 64, exp. 2891 (19 June 1912). See also the Temalacatzingo (Guerrero) petition to the governor urging "that the lands be distributed with justice and equity," in Herrera Sipriano, *La Revolución en la Montaña de Guerrero*, 208. Similarly, fifty-one Apapantilla

(Puebla) residents sought a boundary survey to recover their lands; AHUNAM, AGM, FLB, caja 61, exp. 325, fs. 9–10 (24 September 1911).

14. AGN, Fondo Gobernación Período Revolucionario (FGPR), caja 66, exp. 10, f. 2 (6 October 1912). In an example from Jalisco, members of the Sayula distribution commission (elected by the Indians to conduct the distribution of formerly communal lands as individual private parcels) complained they had been unable to conduct their survey work because they lacked land titles. "Recognizing [Madero] as the father of our nation," they asked him to "instruct Fomento to send us a copy of the original titles that protect our lands, most of which have been seized, and to restitute the viceregal privileges granted to us." AGN, FM, caja 64, exp. 2786 (23 May 1912).

Village commissions also petitioned the Madero government to revisit corrupt or unfair repartos. In Hidalgo, Tulancingo authorities complained about the unequal distribution of land in the village following the privatization of communal village properties, given that only a dozen or so individuals benefited from land that could otherwise have been divided into more than six thousand parcels. AGN, FM, caja 64, exp. 2763 (13 November 1911). In Michoacán, addressing Madero as "our progressive hero who we know will care for rich and poor alike," more than three hundred Indians from Coalcomán asked for the return of lands lost to caciques, local leaders, and hacienda owners during the 1871 reparto. They did not argue against land privatization per se; rather, they complained about the unfair distribution of privatized communal village lands. AGN, FM, caja 64, exp. 2780 (27 December 1911). Similarly, in Guerrero, Tehuilotepec residents asked Madero to commission a surveyor to conduct a new reparto in order to fairly distribute land among heads of family by raffle. They claimed that local authorities had conducted a reparto in 1888 and decided that the privatized lands should remain undivided and under the administration of a local board. Then, although all villagers had paid twenty-two pesos per share, local authorities appropriated the best lands for themselves. Village authorities had in 1908 petitioned for a new reparto, but the court archives had been burned during the 1910 Revolution. AGN, FM, caja 3, exp. 49-1, fs. 1726–27 (31 December 1911). In Mexico State, San Simón Zozocoltepec Indians asked Madero to reverse the land reparto conducted by the political chief in 1890 because many impoverished Indians had not been able to pay the fees involved in communal village land privatization and had sold their

parcels for unfairly low sums. AGN, FM, caja 3, exp. 70-2, fs. 2092-98 (13 January 1912).
15. AGN, FM, caja 64, exp. 2879 (9 January 1912).
16. AGN, FM, caja 64, exp. 2766 (16 November 1911). See also the correspondence from Amacuzac, AGN, FM, caja 64, exp. 2764 (15 November 1911); Santiago Tuxtla (Veracruz), AGN, FM, caja 64, exp. 2913-14 (12 September 1912); and San Bernabé Amaxac (Tlaxcala), AGN, FM, caja 64, exp. 2926 (25 December 1912).
17. "Primer Informe de Gobierno," (1 April 1912), 437. See also González Navarro, "El maderismo y la revolución agraria," 6 (citing *El Imparcial*, 21 June 1911), and James, *Mexico's Supreme Court*, 34.
18. When a Chapultepec commission met with de la Barra to complain about neighboring haciendas' invasion of their lands and their lack of access to pasturelands, de la Barra forwarded the complaint to the Mexico State governor, who then told the commission that the matter was for the courts to resolve. AHUNAM, AGM, FLB, caja 33, exp. 180, fs. 60-62 (1 September 1911). In the Federal District, Xochimilco residents wrote to the minister of justice, explaining they had been in possession of *chinampas* (floating gardens) bordering San Antonio Coapa hacienda lands since time immemorial. They claimed they had always possessed these chinampas in peace, without being bothered by former governments or even hacienda owners. Three months earlier, however, the neighboring hacienda administrator had threatened to use force and political influence against them. In response to this complaint, Ministry of Justice officials told the villagers to take the matter to the courts. AGN, FSJ, caja 782, exp. 6308, fs. 1-3 (17 March 1911). In Jalisco, when the ayuntamiento of Villa de Zacoalco petitioned Madero for the return of municipal lands, government officials responded that they should hire a lawyer and take the matter to the appropriate judicial authority. AGN, FM, 64: 2887 (2 April 1912). In Tlaxcala, 150 San Pablo Zitlaltepec residents asked Madero to restitute lands they had purchased from the ayuntamiento in 1882, but the government replied that "if they had the titles that accredited the possession of the monte, they should take them to the courts." AGN, FM, caja 64, exp. 2916-17 (24 September 1912). In the Tepic Territory, the Sayamota Indians claimed to have colonial titles for lands seized by private landowners, and they asked for Madero's support. Madero forwarded the petition to the Jefe Político del Territorio de Tepic, who claimed that this was a civil court, rather than an administrative, mat-

ter and that the residents should be "assured that the laws are and should be equal for all." AGN, FM, caja 23, exp. 615, fs. 17835-37 (19 November-30 December 1911). And in Puebla, where residents of Tepexi el Viejo, citing the Plan de San Luis, asked for the restitution of their lands, government officials told them to take the matter to the courts. AGN, FM, caja 64, exp. 2902 (29 July 1912).

19. AGN, FSJ, caja 781, exp. 6114, fs. 1-2 (18 June 1911).
20. AGN, FSJ, caja 749, exp. 884, fs. 1-4 (18 September 1911).
21. SJF, época 4, tomo 41, pp. 579-93 (9 December 1911), quote from 581; Cabrera Acevedo, *La Suprema Corte de Justicia a principios del siglo XX*, 22-23.
22. Womack, *Zapata*, 64-65, and Sotelo Inclán, *Raíz y razón de Zapata*, 188-89.
23. Womack, *Zapata*, 102.
24. AGN, FM, caja 64, exp. 2764 (15 September 1911). Between February and September of 1911, seven Morelos pueblos and three rancherías sent their representatives to the National Archives to solicit official copies of their colonial titles. These rancherías were, in chronological order, the Las Anonas, Xicatlacotla, and Cuaxitlán in the Tlalquiltenango municipality (AGN, FB, vol. 41, exp. 8, f. 88, 25 February 1911); San Marcos Cuauchichinola (AGN, FB, vol. 41, exp. 22, f. 379, 21 July 1911); San Mateo Ixtla (AGN, FB, vol. 41, exp. 23, f. 383, 24 July 1911); Ahuehuetzingo (AGN, FB, vol. 41, exp. 24, f. 387, 25 July 1911); San Pedro and San Pablo Tehuixtla (AGN, FB, vol. 41, exp. 25, f. 391, 4 August 1911); Tetelcingo (AGN, FB, vol. 41, exp. 31, f. 496, 28 August 1911); and San Guillermo Totolapan (AGN, FB, vol. 41 bis, exp. 36, f. 22, 4 September 1911).
25. Ochoa Serrano, *Los agraristas de Atacheo*, 83-84 (August 1911).
26. *El País*, 1 July 1911, 2.
27. *El País*, 5 July 1911, 3, also cited by Womack, *Zapata*, 102, as an example of Morelos villagers "publicizing their insurgency."
28. González Navarro, "Zapata y la revolución agraria mexicana," 9-10, citing *Diario de los Debates de la Cámara de Diputados*, 25th Legislature, vol. 3 (4 November 1911), pp. 2-4.
29. All quotes are from Henderson, *In the Absence of Don Porfirio*, 87-88.
30. On Zapata's fear of being labeled a bandit, see Brunk, *¡Emiliano Zapata!*, 62, and Brunk, "Zapata and the City Boys," 38. See also chapter 3. On the signing of the Plan de Ayala, see Huizer, "Emiliano Zapata and the Peasant Guerrillas in the Mexican Revolution," 382;

Magaña, *Emiliano Zapata y el agrarismo en México*, 2:80-83; Palacios, *El Plan de Ayala*, 43-44, 53-56; Rosoff and Aguilat, *Así firmaron el Plan de Ayala*, 35-40; Sedano P., *Revolucionarios surianos*, 139-42; Womack, *Zapata*, 126.

31. A handwritten version of the Plan de Ayala, dated 28 November 1911, and held in the Jenaro Amezcua Archives at the Centro de Estudios de Historia de México (CEHM-CARSO, FJA), ended with "Justice and Law." In the version predated 25 November 1911 and published by the *Diario del Hogar* on 15 December 1911, the text ends with "Liberty, Justice, and Law." See Womack, *Zapata and the Mexican Revolution*, 400-404. By April 1912 Zapatista declarations ended with "Reform, Liberty, Justice, and Law." See, for example, Ixcamilpa (Puebla) reparto orders by the Revolutionary Junta, reprinted in Palacios, *Emiliano Zapata*, 81-82. See also Baitenmann, "Zapata's Justice."
32. They also justified hacienda expropriations by citing the nineteenth-century laws that nationalized church property; see chapter 3.
33. Letter from Palafox to Atenor Sala (28 September 1914) in Sala, *Emiliano Zapata y el problema agrario*, 63-66. For background on Palafox and other Zapatista urban professionals, see Ávila Espinosa, "El Consejo Ejecutivo de la República y el proyecto de legislación estatal Zapatista," 255-58; Brunk, "Zapata and the City Boys." See also chapter 3.
34. AGN, FEZ, caja 2, exp. 7, f. 20 (26 December 1914).
35. "Manifiesto a todos los pueblos en general" (31 December 1911), text in Fabela, *Documentos históricos*, vol. 6, *Revolución y régimen maderista*, part 2, 483-84. Translation from Brunk, "'The Sad Situation of Civilians and Soldiers,'" 337.
36. The Plan de Ayala is reprinted in Fabila, *Cinco siglos*, 181-84. On the Plan de Ayala reversing the burden of proof, see Brunk, *¡Emiliano Zapata!*, 67.
37. Hernández headed Fomento from July 1911 to November 1912. MacGregor, *La XXVI Legislatura*, 18.
38. Circular 1 (8 January 1912), in DOF, 16 January 1912; and Secretaría de Fomento, *Colección de leyes sobre tierras*, 172-74; circular 2 (17 February 1912), DOF, 26 February 1912; and Secretaría de Fomento, *Colección de leyes sobre tierras*, 174-75. For a summary of Madero's agrarian and agricultural policies, see González Navarro, "El maderismo."
39. *El País*, 5 December 1912, 1.
40. The author thanks Emilio Kourí for this clarification.

41. Circular 2 (17 February 1912), *DOF*, 26 February 1912; and Secretaría de Fomento, *Colección de leyes sobre tierras*, 174-75.
42. *La Patria*, 22 February 1912, 3.
43. One official report cited 187 pueblo petitions, including 60 from Puebla, 50 from Mexico State, and 26 from Michoacán. See *Memoria de la Secretaría de Fomento*, lxxii-lxxv.
44. AGN, FM, caja 64, exp. 2911 (12 September 1912).
45. *El País*, 14 April 1912, 3.
46. AHA, FAS, caja 4574, exp. 60840, fs. 2, 14. Quotation from 17 (7 November 1912). On water rights, see Aboites Aguilar, Birrichaga Gardida, and Garay Trejo, "El manejo de las aguas," 23.
47. AGN, FM, caja 64, exp. 2894 (30 June 1912).
48. AGN, FM, caja 14, exp. 326, fs. 10503-4 (5 April 1912).
49. Fomento forwarded the complaint to the governor, and three months later the district prefect requested a surveyor. AGN, FGPR, caja 230, exp. 106, fs. 1-11 (15 January 1913).
50. Municipal authorities were responsible for informing the political chief, state government, district judge, and the ministries of Fomento and Treasury of their plans so that authorities from each of these offices could be present during the land survey. Furthermore, they were to inform neighboring villages and property owners. After all these parties were informed, and were present when possible, a surveyor could proceed to redraw the old ejido boundaries based on the pueblo's titles. After redrawing the old boundary lines, the surveyor had to demarcate the fundo legal (destined exclusively for urban lots, streets, schools, markets, plazas, postal and telegraph services, and so forth, as well as lands reserved for roads, cemeteries, hospitals, avenues, slaughterhouses, and other public uses). The remainder of the lands would be divided and distributed as equitably as possible among heads of family. Municipal officials had to send to Fomento the list of beneficiaries (with the number and size of each parcel) so that ministry officials could issue titles in accordance with the 18 December 1909 terrenos baldíos law. Circular 1 (8 January 1912), in *DOF*, 16 January 1912; and Secretaría de Fomento, *Colección de leyes sobre tierras*, 172-74.
51. *Cuestión de ejidos y linderos*, quote from archive official, 1.
52. *Cuestión de ejidos y linderos*, 13-40.
53. *Cuestión de ejidos y linderos*, 174-75.
54. *Cuestión de ejidos y linderos*, 19.

55. AGN, FGPR, caja 95, exp. 22, fs. 1–3 (6 January 1913).
56. *El País*, 13 abril 1912, 3. See also AGN, FSJ, caja 756, exp. 1707, fs. 1–4 (11 September 1911).
57. *Memoria de la Secretaría de Fomento*, 72–75.
58. Circular 2 (17 February 1912), *DOF*, 26 February 1912; and Secretaría de Fomento, *Colección de leyes sobre tierras*, 174–75.
59. ACSCJN, FSCJN, exp. 4237, fs. 7–18 (1912).
60. For the 1844 Yucatán law, see de la Torre, *Legislación de Terrenos Baldíos*, 118–20.
61. AGA, Documentos históricos, exp. 23/117, leg. none, fs. 3, 6–10, 11–12, 13–18, 40–46, 64, 89 (September to December 1912), Hampolol, Campeche, Campeche.
62. ACSCJN, FSCJN, exp. 4237, fs. 7–18 (1912).
63. See also the case of Copándaro (Michoacán), where resident Indians petitioned for the survey of their ex-communal lands but the owner of the neighboring property blocked the survey and Fomento officials told them to take the matter to court. AGN, FM, caja 27, exp. 737, fs. 20913–15 (27 July 2012).
64. AGN, FGPR, caja 95, exp. 19, f. 1 (16 October 1912), f. 16 (11 November 1912), f. 23 (23 January 1913). Ruiz then asked the governor and the minister of the interior to replace the district judge because, according to him, it was well known that the judge took bribes from landowners and always ruled in their favor. The documents are not clear regarding the role of the juez de letras and that of the district court. The judge was probably not replaced, but a year and a half later—and under a different regime—Fomento's agrarian section decided to proceed with the boundary survey, division, and distribution of Guarachita's ejidos. AGN, FGPR, caja 96, exp. 99, fs. 1–6 (16 October 1914).
65. ACSCJN, FSCJN, exp. 989 (1912–13).
66. *El Imparcial*, 14 February 1912, 1, 7.
67. González Navarro, "El maderismo," 17–18.
68. "Proyecto de ley sobre adiciones a la Constitución General respecto de la materia agraria," reprinted in Silva Herzog, *La cuestión de la tierra*, 2:219–46.
69. On the history of federal labor conciliation and arbitration boards, see Middlebrook, *Paradox of Revolution*; James, *Mexico's Supreme Court*; and Suárez-Potts, *Making of Law*.
70. Luis Cabrera was "a professor and dean of the national law school who went on to serve as diputado during Madero's presidency and then

became an influential advisor and cabinet minister under Carranza." Kourí, "Interpreting the Expropriation," 104–5. See also Meyer, *Luis Cabrera*.

71. Discurso del Dip. Lic. Luis Cabrera (*Diario de los Debates*, 3 December 1912), reproduced in Fabila, *Cinco siglos*, 184–205. For an in-depth study of what Cabrera's reconstitution meant, see Kourí, "Interpreting the expropriation" and Kourí, "Los pueblos y sus tierras."
72. "La reconstrucción de los ejidos de los pueblos como medio de suprimir la esclavitud del jornalero mexicano," reprinted in Silva Herzog, *La cuestión de la tierra*, 2:277–310.
73. *El País*, 5 December 1912, 1.
74. Suárez-Potts, *Making of Law*, 7.

3. Zapatista Land Reform

1. Plan de Ayala, reproduced in Fabila, *Cinco siglos*, 181–84.
2. See, for example, the boundary dispute between Cacalutla (Guerrero) and Tlaltepexi (Puebla), where representatives signed an agreement not to cultivate disputed lands "until the triumph of the Revolution, [when] the one with the most rights will receive the lands." AGN, FEZ, caja 19, exp. 2, f. 155 (28 May 1915). On boundary disputes, see Baitenmann, "Zapata's Justice."
3. The Zapatista land and water reform took place during three overlapping periods. The first period was from late 1910 until late 1913, when hacienda land takeovers by villagers spread and the military leadership began to define the role it would play in land reform. The second period ran from 1914 to late 1916, when the Zapatistas had consolidated their military power in the region (and nationally as well, by joining the Aguascalientes Convention government). At this point, General Headquarters and later the Ministry of Agriculture and Colonization tried to create a more centralized administration for land and water restitutions and grants. And the third period was from 1915 until Zapata's death in 1919, when urban professionals (many with anarcho-syndicalist ideas) wrote legislation that would remain unimplemented, largely because of Carranza's military incursions into Morelos and the gradual takeover of state governments in what had been the Zapatista multistate region.
4. See, for example, Hernández Chávez, *Anenecuilco*.
5. Zapata's election was made famous in Womack's opening paragraphs in the prologue of *Zapata*, 3–9. See also Brunk, *¡Emiliano Zapata!*, 19, 25–29.
6. Hernández Chávez, *Anenecuilco*, 143–47.

7. Womack, *Zapata*, 64-65; Sotelo Inclán, *Raíz y razón*, 184-85. Sotelo Inclán called the Llano del Huajar fields "El Cuajar."
8. Womack, *Zapata*, 64-65, quotation from 65; Sotelo Inclán, *Raíz y razón*, 188-89.
9. Other reasons regional leaders in Morelos rebelled included taxes, military conscription, the displacement of renters, and repression by the federal military. See Ávila Espinosa, *Los orígenes del zapatismo*.
10. Magaña, *Emiliano Zapata y el agrarismo en México*, 1:99-102.
11. Womack, *Zapata*, 87 (May-August 1911).
12. Brunk, *¡Emiliano Zapata!*, 44.
13. For the reasons behind Zapata's break with Madero and the need for an agrarian program, see Brunk, *¡Emiliano Zapata!*, 62-63.
14. See article 6 of the Plan de Ayala, in Fabila, *Cinco siglos*, 181-84.
15. Brunk, *¡Emiliano Zapata!*, 71; AGN, FGO, caja, 1, exp. 3, f. 27 (20 August 1912), and AGN, FGO, caja 1, exp. 3, f. 95 (18 October 1912). Born in Santa María Ahuacatitlán, coal merchant Genovevo de la O had a long history of protecting his pueblo woodlands from the Temixco hacienda's sawmill operator. He joined the Maderista revolutionary movement as the head of three thousand men and later joined forces with Zapata. In recognition of his many military feats, in April 1912 Zapata named de la O a brigadier general, and in 1917 he became a general of the Liberating Army of the Center and South. See Martha Rodríguez García, "Genovevo de la O."
16. On the military history of Zapatismo, see, among others, Brunk, *¡Emiliano Zapata!*; Pineda Gómez, *La irrupción zapatista*; Pineda Gómez, *La revolución del sur*; Pineda Gómez, *Ejército Libertador*; Pineda Gómez, "La guerra zapatista"; and Womack, *Zapata*.
17. AGN, FGO, caja 11, exp. 10, f. 2 (17 March 1912).
18. Zapata also told de la O that he could delegate this matter to a lower-ranking military chief. AGN, FGO, caja 11, exp. 10, f. 28 (17 January 1913).
19. AGN, FGO, caja 1, exp. 3, f. 95 (18 October 1912).
20. Text reproduced in Palacios, *Emiliano Zapata*, 81-82 (30 April 1912).
21. Womack, *Zapata*, 172-73.
22. "Instrucciones a que deberán sujetarse los jefes y oficiales del Ejército Libertador del Sur y Centro" (28 July 1913): AGN, FGO, caja 19, exp. 7, f. 13; also reproduced in Magaña, *Emiliano Zapata*, 3:267-68.
23. Womack, *Zapata*, 172-73.
24. See, for example, the Spanish wording in the "Instructions to Military Chiefs and Officials" (4 June 1913): "8. Los pueblos reconoce-

rán los terrenos que sean de su legítima propiedad y de acuerdo con lo que dice el Plan de Ayala, en su parte relativa, tomarán posesión de los mismos, haciendo respetar sus derechos por medio de la fuerza de las armas, cuando sea necesario. 9. Los jefes y oficiales del Ejército Libertador apoyarán por medio de la fuerza la posesión de terrenos de los pueblos, siempre y cuando éstos soliciten su intervención o que las circunstancias exijan la mediación directa de los jefes." "Instrucciones a que deberán sujetarse los jefes y oficiales del Ejército Libertador del Sur y Centro de la República" (4 June 1914): AGN, FGO, caja 19, exp. 7, f. 12; also reproduced in Espejel López, Olivera de Bonfil, and Rueda, *Emiliano Zapata. Antología*, 137-38.

25. AGN, FEZ, caja 17, exp. 9, f. 41 (11 December 1914).
26. See also Ávila Espinosa, *Los orígenes del zapatismo*, 280; Ávila Espinosa, "Los conflictos internos," 334; Ávila Sánchez, *Aspectos históricos*, 82; Brunk, *¡Emiliano Zapata!*, 148; and Herrera Sipriano, *La Revolución*, 328-29. The term *zapatistas* (people fighting alongside Zapata), according to Salvador Rueda Smithers, appeared for the first time in the newspaper *El País* on 17 August 1911 to differentiate the Morelos rebels from the rest of the Madero revolutionaries. Rueda Smithers, *El paraíso de la caña*, 206.
27. Barreto Mark, "Entre campesinos, arrendatarios y el Plan de Ayala," 192 (29 May 1911).
28. AGN, FGO, caja 1, exp. 7, f. 49 (2 April 1913), and caja 1, exp. 7, fs. 56-57 (5 April 1913).
29. AGN, FGO, caja 1, exp. 7, f. 62 (17 April 1913). See also the case that residents of San Pablo Tejalpa (Mexico State) filed against the neighboring pueblo in AGN, FGO, caja 1, exp. 7, f. 52 (9 April 1913).
30. AGN, FEZ, caja 17, exp. 8, fs. 29-30 (November 1914).
31. AGN, FEZ, caja 2, exp. 7, f. 26 (27 December 1914). See also AGN, FEZ, caja 17, exp. 5, f. 6 (22 August 1914).
32. AGN, FEZ, caja 2, exp. 4, f. 63 (9 December 1914).
33. Womack, *Zapata*, 64-65, and Sotelo Inclán, *Raíz y razón*, 184-85.
34. AGN, FGO, caja 16, exp. 3, f. 77 (18 August 1914).
35. AGN, FEZ, caja 19, exp. 2, fs. 52-53 (8 June 1915). On land renters, see also AGN, FEZ, caja 17, exp. 6, f. 42 (21 September 1914), Miacatlán (Morelos); AGN, FEZ, caja 18, exp. 2, f. 103 (10 February 1915), Jocotitlán (Guerrero); and AGN, FEZ, caja 6, exp. 1, f. 133 (25 February 1915), Coatzingo (Puebla).

36. AGN, FGO, caja 15, exp. 3, f. 63 (29 July 1914). On the Zapatistas in Guerrero, see Herrera Sipriano, *La revolución en la montaña*, 184.
37. AHUNAM, AGM, FLB, caja 79, exp. 92, f. 396 (2 August 1914). See also the case of Mezquitlán, in which both locals and individuals from neighboring villages had illegally purchased pueblo lands based on adjudication laws. AGN, FGO, caja 15, exp. 1, f. 43 (20 July 1914).
38. See, for example, Espejel, "La organización del movimiento Zapatista," 35; and Ávila Espinosa, *Las corrientes revolucionarias*, 188.
39. AGN, FGO, caja 1, exp. 8, fs. 14-15 (22 May 1913).
40. AGN, FEZ, caja 17, exp. 7, f. 105 (28 October 1914).
41. AGN, FEZ, caja 17, exp. 9, f. 58-60 (29 December 1914).
42. AGN, FEZ, caja 17, exp. 7, f. 105 (28 October 1914).
43. Article 7 of the Plan de Ayala, reproduced in Fabila, *Cinco siglos*, 181-84.
44. For the Flores Magón program, see "Manifiesto," *Regeneración*, 23 September 1911. Montaño did not use the words "public utility" in the Plan de Ayala, but Zapata or one of his advisers did so in later writings. See, for example, Zapata's 4 September 1914 letter to Atenor Sala in Magaña, *Emiliano Zapata*, 4:308-10.
45. The Plan de Ayala used the term "nationalization" for the expropriation with indemnification of one-third of all lands belonging to large landholders ("monopolizers") and for the expropriation of two-thirds of the properties of "the enemies of the revolution." Later laws talk about confiscating enemy properties, and these are mostly businesses and urban estates. This book, when possible, adopts the usage found in the laws or archival documents; otherwise it uses the term "expropriation."
46. Translations by Womack, *Zapata*, 400-404. Womack writes that the special disposition on behalf of widows and orphans in the Plan de Ayala was without precedent in revolutionary plans (*Zapata*, 398). It was, however, common military policy. See, for example, the *pensión federal vitalicia* (life-long federal pension) for the family members of deceased soldiers in ACSCJN, Asuntos Económicos, exp. 51096 (1901).
47. On Montaño's admiration for Juárez, see Ávila Espinosa, "El Consejo Ejecutivo," 256. As Timo Schaefer explains, "historians of Mexico have used the term 'popular liberalism' to denote popular actors' participation on the Liberal side of the country's political conflicts as well as their appropriation, for purposes often at odds with those of elite liberals, of a rights-based and anti-colonial political idiom" (*Liberalism as Utopia*, 6). For the case of Morelos, see Mallon, *Peasant and Nation*.

48. Fabila, *Cinco siglos*, 104-12; Knowlton, *Church Property and the Mexican Reform*, 73-77; Muñoz Bravo, "Los promotores de la desamortización," 30.
49. Letter from Palafox to Atenor Sala (28 September 1914) in Sala, *Emiliano Zapata*, 63-66.
50. "Instrucciones para establecer la repartición de terrenos pertenecientes a los enemigos de la revolución" (11 February 1914), reproduced in Espejel López, Olivera de Bonfil, and Rueda, *Emiliano Zapata. Antología*, 181-82, and Brunk, *¡Emiliano Zapata!*, 149-50, 298n17. The takeover of the hacienda sugar industry is a separate and little-studied topic. See, for example, Womack, "Los estudios del zapatismo," 28.
51. AGN, FGO, caja 1, exp. 3, f. 120 (21 November 1912).
52. AGN, FEZ, caja 9, exp. 2, fs. 43-44 (18 July 1915).
53. Circular 5 (19 May 1914), reproduced in Herrera Sipriano, *La Revolución en la montaña*, 184. Italics mine.
54. Zapatista files at the AGN contain many nineteenth- and early twentieth-century sales deeds submitted by owners who wanted Zapata to protect their small properties. See, for example, AGN, FCR-EZ, caja 3, exp. 16, fs. 1-14, and AGN, FEZ, caja 6, exp. 1, f. 126, for nineteenth-century adjudication titles and sales deeds, as well as AGN, FEZ, caja 1, exp. 4, fs. 1, 3-5; AGN, FEZ, caja 1, exp. 1, fs. 1-2, for early twentieth-century purchase and sales deeds.
55. AGN, FEZ, caja 2, exp. 7, f. 25 (27 December 1914).
56. AGN, FEZ, caja 18, exp. 2, fs. 222-25, 249-50 (late 1914).
57. Brunk, "Zapata and the City Boys," 35.
58. Most scholars date the creation of the Zapatista Ministry of Agriculture and Colonization to December 1914 or January 1915, as part of the Aguascalientes Convention. However, the "Decreto del 8 de septiembre de 1914" (AHUNAM, AGM, FLB, caja 69, exp. 2, f. 2; also reproduced in Espejel, Olivera de Bonfil, and Rueda Smithers, *Emiliano Zapata. Antología*, 238-39), and "A las comisiones agrarias del estado de Morelos of 10 September 1914" (reproduced in Espejel, Olivera de Bonfil, and Rueda Smithers, *Emiliano Zapata. Antología*, 240-42), show that Palafox had already created the ministry by early September 1914, before the Zapatistas had joined the convention. This government agency was sometimes called Ministerio (see the earliest example in AGN, FEZ, caja 2, exp. 4, fs. 51-52, 5 December 1914) and sometimes Secretaría (see the earliest example in AGN, FEZ, caja 17, exp. 9, f. 41, 11 December 1914).
59. Womack, *Zapata*, 166-67, quotation from 166.

60. Womack adds, "I believe that, without Palafox, zapatismo, as admirable as it was, would have never had the influence it gained in other regions of the country, not even in the south." See Womack, "Los estudios del zapatismo," 27.
61. On the Revolutionary Junta, see Magaña, *Emiliano Zapata*, 3:182–83. Although the Revolutionary Junta's constitution was signed in June 1913, it had already been in existence for several months. On the Aguascalientes Convention government, see Ávila Espinosa, *Las corrientes revolucionarias*, 392.
62. Womack, *Zapata*, 167.
63. Agronomy student Alfonso Cruz later said he had met Palafox in Tepic in 1910 and began collaborating with him from the time Palafox became General Headquarters secretary.
64. "Instrucciones para establecer la repartición de terrenos pertenecientes a los enemigos de la revolución" (11 February 1914), reproduced in Espejel López, Olivera de Bonfil, and Rueda, *Emiliano Zapata: antología*, 181–82.
65. Compare these requirements to circular 1, which stated, "The remainder of the lands will be divided and distributed among the chiefs or heads of family on the list, making every effort to do so as equitably as possible." Circular 1 (8 January 1912) in *DOF*, 16 January 1912; and Secretaría de Fomento, *Colección de leyes sobre tierras*, 172–74. On the concept of equality, see, for example, the 1851 Michoacán privatization law in Pérez Montesinos, "Geografía, política y economía," 2095.
66. Several Liberal laws for the privatization of communal village lands suggested distributing parcels by raffle. For Michoacán, see the "Reglamento de 15 febrero 1828 del Gobierno de Michoacán del decreto de 18 de enero de 1827" (reproducido en la ley 73 de 13 Dic 1851), in Coromina, *Recopilación de leyes, decretos, reglamentos y circulares expedidos en el Estado de Michoacán*, 3:29–35.
67. Madero's circular 1 (8 January 1912) mentioned a printed list of beneficiaries, with the number, location, and extent of the plots they received. In the nineteenth century, many state legislatures created village-elected distribution commissions to conduct censuses and manage the parceling and distribution of privatized communal lands. See Baitenmann "'El que parte y reparte.'" For examples of late nineteenth-century censuses conducted for the purpose of pueblo land privatization, see "Padrón que manifiesta el número de solteros del pueblo de Amatepec, con expresión de sus nombres, origen, vecin-

dad, edad, estado y profesión, formado conforme al Reglamento de 26 de junio de 1890," mentioned in AGA, Reconocimiento y Titulación de Bienes Comunales, exp. 276.1/765, leg. 10, fs. 2-5, Santiago Amatepec y Anexo Chinantequilla, Totontepec, Oaxaca (31 August 1890), and the 1895 "Lista de padres o cabezas de familia que se han presentado a la H. junta Municipal por tener derecho a un lote en el fraccionamiento de los ejidos de este pueblo," in AGA, Dotación de tierras, exp. 23/140, leg. 1, fs. 64-73 (Dzitbalché, Calkiní, Campeche).

68. Federal public lands laws were aimed at creating land plots that could satisfy the needs of a nuclear family. Ejido lands had to be divided into plots shared among heads of family. See, for example, the circular of 23 October 1889, in Secretaría de Fomento, *Colección de leyes*, 28-29. See also the 1901 "Lista de los vecinos del Barrio de San Martín que fueron agraciados en el fraccionamiento del fundo . . ." in Marino, *Huixquilucan*, 123n169. Marino also finds that it was *jefes de familia* who received land parcels during the repartos in Mexico State; *Huixquilucan*, 123-25.

69. Federal public lands laws also stipulated that after the distribution of the land in plots, the surveyor had to send to Fomento the *croquis* (sketch) of the divided lands and a list of all beneficiaries so that Fomento could issue the corresponding property titles. See, for example, "Resolución de 10 de diciembre de 1870," in de la Torre, *Legislación de Terrenos Baldíos*, 118-20.

70. Porfirian federal decrees also stipulated that privatized ejidos could only be rented out or sold after ten years. "Decreto [federal] del 18 de diciembre de 1909" reproduced in Pallares, *Leyes federales vigentes*, 362.

71. See photograph of title in Samponaro and Vanderwood, *War Scare on the Río Grande*, 49-50.

72. Womack adds that the "chief of Blanco's staff was a close childhood friend of [Zapatista General Gildardo] Magaña's, Francisco Múgica." Womack, *Zapata*, 196.

73. "Decreto del 8 de septiembre de 1914," AHUNAM, AGM, FLB, caja 69, exp. 2, f. 2; also reproduced in Espejel López, Olivera de Bonfil, and Rueda, *Emiliano Zapata. Antología*, 238-39, and "A las comisiones agrarias del estado de Morelos" (10 September 1914), reproduced in Espejel López, Olivera de Bonfil, and Rueda, *Emiliano Zapata. Antología*, 240-42. It was probably Cruz's idea to create agrarian commissions made up of agronomists to implement land reform. According to Cruz, once Palafox became secretary of General Headquarters,

Cruz suggested to Palafox the organization of field commissions be composed of students from the National Agricultural School to implement the promises made in the Plan de Ayala—an idea that civil engineers Ignacio Díaz Soto y Gama and Antonio Arguinzonis later claimed as their own. Díaz Soto y Gama, Arguinzonis, and Cruz met with Palafox, and according to Cruz, he was the one who persuaded them that the commissions had to be staffed with surveyors (agrónomos) rather than the civil engineers that Díaz Soto y Gama preferred. Once Palafox became the minister of agriculture and colonization in 1914, Cruz provided Palafox with a list of potential agronomists, and the groups he formed were called "agrarian commissions." Cruz, "Las primeras comisiones," 45-46. According to Womack, "Soto y Gama dated [the agrarian commissions'] inception at December 1914 because this was when Manuel Palafox had written a letter to Alfonso Cruz, a student at the National School of Agriculture in Mexico City." Womack, *Zapata*, 232.

74. See, for example, Zapata's instructions to General Suárez in Morelos: "You must allow that pueblos, on the basis of their titles, take possession of their lands and water resources, and, in case of difficulties, only the appropriate agrarian commission is competent to resolve them, not military chiefs." AGN, FEZ, caja 19, exp. 1, f. 75 (probably May or June 1915).
75. "A las comisiones agrarias del Estado de Morelos" (10 September 1914), reproduced in Espejel, Olivera de Bonfil, and Rueda Smithers, *Emiliano Zapata. Antología*, 240-42.
76. "A las comisiones agrarias del Estado de Morelos" (10 September 1914), reproduced in Espejel, Olivera de Bonfil, and Rueda Smithers, *Emiliano Zapata. Antología*, 240-42. On Molina Enríquez and the influence of his ideas in revolutionary Mexico, see Kourí, "Interpreting the Expropriation."
77. Crespo, "Introducción. Desde la violencia facciosa," 28.
78. Crespo, *Modernización*, 400-401.
79. Crespo, *Modernización*, 401-15, quotation from 415. See also Crespo, *Modernización*, 57-113, and Crespo, *Historia del azúcar*, 1:97-98.
80. Crespo, *Modernización*, 113.
81. In October and November 1914, revolutionary leaders Venustiano Carranza, Álvaro Obregón, Pancho Villa, and Emiliano Zapata (who had jointly defeated Huerta's federal army and forced his resignation) met in Aguascalientes to create a unified government. When these

meetings collapsed, a civil war broke out between the Conventionist forces (followers of Villa and Zapata), who seized control of Mexico City, and the Constitutionalist followers of Carranza, who set up a provisional government in Veracruz. On the Aguascalientes Convention, see, among others, Amaya, *La Soberana Convención Revolucionaria*, and Ávila Espinosa, *Las corrientes revolucionarias*.

82. Ervin, "Art of the Possible," 35–36; Womack, *Zapata*, 231.
83. Katz, *Life and Times of Pancho Villa*, 409–11; Ervin, "Art of the Possible," 46, 49.
84. Gómez, *Las comisiones agrarias del sur*, 18–21; Ervin, "Art of the Possible," 46; Womack, *Zapata*, 231.
85. See, for example, for the Federal District, AGN, FEZ, caja 7, exp. 6, f. 4; AGN, FEZ, caja 19, exp. 4, f. 66; for Guerrero, AGN, FEZ, caja 18, exp. 2, f. 258; AGN, FEZ, caja 19, exp. 3, f. 28; for Mexico State, AGN, FEZ, caja 18, exp. 4, f. 39; AGN, FEZ, caja 12, exp. 1, f. 27; for Puebla, AGN, FEZ, caja 10, exp. 6, f. 42; AGN, FEZ, caja 10, exp. 2, f. 5; and plans for Hidalgo AGN, FEZ, caja 15, exp. 5, fs. 50, 51 and Oaxaca AGN, FEZ, caja 10, exp. 9, fs. 2–4.
86. In Morelos, land conflicts between villages were common from the seventeenth century until 1910 because of the "ambiguous legal situation" that originated in colonial times. See von Mentz, *Pueblos de indios*, 77.
87. See also Ávila Espinosa, "Los conflictos internos," 334.
88. AGN, FGO, caja 1, exp. 7, f. 62 (17 April 1913). In fact, in Zapatista-controlled territories between 1914 and 1916 there were boundary conflicts involving at least 112 population centers within a state, and at least eight border disputes across state lines involving some eighteen villages. See Baitenmann, "Zapata's Justice." On boundary disputes, see also Ávila Espinosa, *Los orígenes del zapatismo*, 280; Ávila Sánchez, *Aspectos históricos*, 82; Brunk, *¡Emiliano Zapata!*, 148; and Herrera Sipriano, *La Revolución en la montaña*, 328–29.
89. AGN, FEZ, caja 19, exp. 6, fs. 42–43 (24 October 1915). Axochiapan is also across the border in Morelos.
90. Marino, "La fuerza de la ley," 207–8.
91. AGN, FEZ, caja 19, exp. 2, fs. 1–2 (June 1915).
92. AGN, FEZ, caja 17, exp. 8, f. 18 (5 November 1914).
93. AGN, FCR-EZ, caja 3, exp. 15, fs. 4–5 (27 May 1915).
94. Ayaquica to Zapata (10 May 1915), in Fabela, *Documentos históricos*, 21:218–19. Translation in Brunk, *¡Emiliano Zapata!*, 151–52.

95. Gómez, *Las comisiones agrarias del sur*, 69.
96. AGN, FEZ, caja 18, exp. 4, f. 119 (22 April 1915).
97. See, for example, the boundary dispute between Cacalutla (Guerrero) and Tlaltepexi (Puebla), where representatives signed an agreement not to cultivate disputed lands "until with the triumph of the Revolution [when] the one with most rights will receive the lands." AGN, FEZ, caja 19, exp. 2, f. 155 (28 May 1915).
98. AGN, FCR-EZ, caja 3, exp. 15, fs. 4–5 (27 May 1915).
99. AGN, FEZ, caja 9, exp. 1, f. 74 (8 July 1915).
100. AGN, FEZ, caja 8, exp. 4, f. 30 (2 June 1915).
101. Letter from Zapata to Sala (25 October 1914), in Sala, *Emiliano Zapata*, 49–50. It is difficult to tell whether it was Zapata or one of his advisers who wrote or signed a given document. In fact, Brunk believes that "the documents available for the study of Zapatismo were nearly all composed by an intellectual of one kind or another" (*¡Emiliano Zapata!*, 125). In this case, the letter states that Zapata had spoken to his "friend and colleague" Mr. Palafox.
102. AGN, FEZ, caja 17, exp. 2, f. 1 (13 February 1914).
103. AGN, FEZ, caja 18, exp. 1, fs. 29–30 (9 January 1915).
104. AGN, FEZ, caja 18, exp. 1, fs. 8–9 (5 January 1915).
105. AGN, FCR-EZ, caja 3, exp. 15, f. 7 (5 June 1915).
106. AGN, FEZ, caja 20, exp. 4, f. 19 (29 March 1916). San Lucas del Pulque is in Mexico State.
107. Brunk, *¡Emiliano Zapata!*, 197.
108. Cruz, "Las primeras comisiones agrarias," 50–51.
109. Birrichaga Gardida, citing *Gaceta del Gobierno* 20 December 1914, in "¿Ejidatarios o comuneros?," 339–40. The idea of a census probably came from Palafox, given that Baz deferred to Zapata when it came to land reform. For example, when Baz issued a decree in the summer of 1915 reestablishing the Superior Tribunal of Justice, he informed General Headquarters that he had limited the tribunal's powers to exclude "the agrarian promises." AGN, Fondo Soberana Convención Revolucionaria (FSCR), caja 8, exp. 2, f. 20 (2 July 1915).
110. See Palafox to Sala (8 January 1915), in Sala, *Emiliano Zapata*, 83, and Palafox to Zapata (11 January 1915), in Fabela, *Documentos históricos*, 21:149–52. Miguel Mendoza López Schwerdtfeger (minister of justice under the Convention government) later claimed to have been the author of this law, "cuyo articulado me encomendó el Sr. Gral. Manuel Palafox" (which Palafox had asked him to put in writing) (Villegas

Moreno, "Una legislación," 45). Although probably redacted by Mendoza, the main ideas echo Palafox's earlier thinking.

111. "Ley agraria del gobierno de la Convención de Aguascalientes," reproduced in Fabela, *Documentos históricos*, 21:246-53.

112. Díaz's decree of 18 December 1909, for instance, stated that ejido lands (considered terrenos baldíos) had to be divided and distributed, but the titles granted to these parcels had to state that the beneficiary or his or her offspring had to cultivate the parcel for ten years, during which time they could not rent, sell, or grant its use to a third party. Nor could the parcel be embargoed by a third party. Secretaría de Fomento, *Colección de leyes*, 149-52.

113. AGN, FEZ, caja 19, exp. 1, f. 78 (12 May 1915).

114. Baz's Office of Agriculture was part of the Secretaría de Estado y del Despacho de Agricultura y Colonización. AGN, FEZ, caja 19, exp. 3, f. 1 (14 June 1915). The Sección de Fraccionamiento of Palafox's Ministry of Agriculture and Colonization was also very active. By October 1915 it had already issued 539 instructions to various pueblos. AGA, Dotación de tierras, exp. 23/2979, leg. 1, f. 59, Metepec, Ocuituco, Morelos (4 October 1915).

115. Notices 538 and 539 of the Ministry of Agriculture. AGA, Dotación de tierras, 23/2979, leg. 1, fs. 59, 60, Metepec, Ocuituco, Morelos (4 October 1915). For more examples of Zapatistas employing population censuses, see Tlalancaleca (Puebla), AGN, FEZ, caja 19, exp. 1, f. 78 (12 May 1915); Huazulco (Morelos), AGN, FEZ, caja 19, exp. 1, fs. 76-77 (30 June 1915); and San Miguel Veladero (Mexico State), AGN, FEZ, caja 19, exp. 4, f. 64 (22 August 1915).

116. "Instrucciones a que deben sujetarse los representantes de los pueblos agregados a los ayuntamientos para el deslinde, fraccionamiento y reparto de tierras de los ejidos" (26 January 1917), CEHM-Carso, FJA, VIII-2 J.A.4.281.1.

117. AGN, FEZ, caja 18, exp. 2, fs. 128-31 (12 February 1915).

118. AGN, FEZ, caja 18, exp. 2, fs. 157-60 (14 February 1915).

119. AGN, FEZ, caja 19, exp. 4, fs. 46-48 (19 August 1915).

120. AGN, FEZ, caja 18, exp. 2, fs. 206-8 (16 February 1915).

121. AGN, FEZ, caja 19, exp. 4, fs. 46-48 (19 August 1915).

122. Villagers concerned about their montes who wrote to General Headquarters include those from Guerrero, San Gregorio (AGN, FEZ, caja 19, exp. 1, fs. 129-31) and Tecolapa (AGN, FEZ, caja 19, exp. 1, fs. 53-54); from Mexico State, Atlautla and San Juan Tehuixtitlán (AGN, FEZ, caja

19, exp. 8, f. 45); Azcapotzaltongo (AGN, FEZ, 19, exp. 2, f. 150), Chalma (AGN, FEZ, 19, exp. 3, fs. 42–43), Cuecuecuautitla (AGN, FEZ, caja 19, exp. 1, f. 7), Nepantla and Tlalamac (AGN, FEZ, caja 10, exp. 6, f. 11), San Juan Tilapa (AGN, FEZ, caja 19, exp. 5, f. 42–44), Santa María Nativitas (AGN, FEZ, caja 9, exp. 1, f. 57), Rancho San Juan (AGN, FEZ, caja 8, exp. 5: 53–54), and Tepetlixpa (AGN, FEZ, caja 19, exp. 2, f. 94); from Morelos, Hueyapan (AGN, FEZ, caja 17, exp. 8, f. 18) and Nepopualco (AGN, FEZ, caja 19, exp. 1, f. 75); and from Puebla, Atzala (AGN, FEZ, caja 6, exp. 2, f. 18), Los Ranchos (AGN, FEZ, caja 11, exp. 3, fs. 36–37), and Texcalapa (AGN, FEZ, caja 9, exp. 2, fs. 43–44).
123. AGN, FEZ, caja 5, exp. 1, f. 11 (6 February 1915).
124. AGN, FEZ, caja 19, exp. 1, f. 75 (probably May or June 1915).
125. AGA, Dotación de tierras, exp. 23/2979, leg. 1, f. 61, Metepec, Ocuituco, Morelos (15 October 1915).
126. "Ley agraria del gobierno de la Convención de Aguascalientes," reproduced in Fabela, *Documentos históricos*, 21:246–53.
127. Tortolero Villaseñor, "Water and Revolution in Morelos," 125. See also Valladares, *Cuando el agua se esfumó*.
128. Valladares, *Cuando el agua se esfumó*.
129. AGN, FEZ, caja 17, exp. 8, f. 55–56 (16 November 1914).
130. AGN, FGO, caja 15, exp. 3, fs. 92–94 (29 July 1914).
131. CEHM, FJA, VIII-2 J.A. 2.156.1 (3 August 1914).
132. AGN, FGO, caja 1, exp. 5, f. 48 (26 February 1913).
133. AGN, FEZ, caja 19, exp. 8, fs. 17–18 (9 December 1915).
134. AGN, FEZ, caja 19, exp. 8, fs. 17–18 (9 December 1915).
135. AGN, FEZ, caja 19, exp. 4, f. 86 (26 August 1915).
136. AGN, FEZ, caja 18, exp. 4, f. 96 (20 April 1915).
137. AGN, FEZ, caja 20, exp. 1, fs. 11–13 (15 January 1916). In this case, it was not clear which of the two pueblos had older rights to the water deposits.
138. AGN, FEZ, caja 17, exp. 8, f. 13 (3 November 1914).
139. AGA, Dotación de tierras, exp. 23/3008, leg. 2, f. 103 (9 February 1916), Atlatlahucan, Atlatlahucan, Morelos.
140. Palafox's nationalization of water resources went further than had Díaz's. The 1888 and 1894 Porfirian laws had granted the federal executive jurisdiction over major bodies of water, but they did not make them federal property until 1902 (and again in 1910). Only those major waterways (of which there were few in Mexico), and not smaller rivers, were considered to fall under federal jurisdiction. Aboites Aguilar, *El agua de la nación*, 83–88.

141. "Ley agraria del gobierno de la Convención de Aguascalientes," reproduced in Fabela, *Documentos históricos*, 21:246–53.

4. Constitutionalist Land Reform

1. Cabrera Acevedo, *La Suprema Corte de Justicia a principios del siglo XX*, 20. Between 1914 and 1917, state governors had jurisdiction over all three state branches of government. In Oaxaca from 1916 to at least 1920, the courts were in disarray and lacked independence from military authorities, who acted with great impunity (Garner, "Autoritarismo revolucionario," 254–56). As in Morelos (see chapter 3), however, many state-level civil and penal courts continued to function during the closure of the federal judiciary. See also Smith, *Gender and the Mexican Revolution*, 56.
2. See, for example, SJF, época 4, tomo 41, pp. 594–624, especially pp. 619–20 (9 December 1911).
3. For example, in Chihuahua in 1912 under the banner of "Land and Justice," Maderista provisional governor Braulio Hernández and other prominent signatories endorsed the nationalization of all lands for public utility (except for urban estates, hacienda manor houses, factories, ranches, and train lines). The plan was for the government to rent out national lands to petitioners, who would receive only as much land as they could personally cultivate with the help of their families. The lands would remain national property, but heads of family would have use rights (González Navarro, "El maderismo," 16). Also in Chihuahua in 1912, Pascual Orozco announced his rebellion against Madero with his Empacadora Plan. He not only proposed the distribution of national lands but also offered to expropriate the idle lands of large unproductive haciendas and distribute them as individual plots, compensating landowners in the form of agricultural bonds (Meyer, *El rebelde del norte*, 83). And in Colima in 1913, Governor J. Trinidad Alamillo (a Huerta supporter) granted the Cuyutlán *comisaría* (a type of rural settlement) pueblo status, thereby allowing villagers to receive a fundo legal taken from hacienda owner Francisco Santacruz. The owner filed an amparo, but he then allowed Cuyutlán villagers to keep the land in exchange for a pardon on back taxes (López Mestas Camberos, "Entre la desamortización y el reparto agrario," 260–62).
4. Knight, *Mexican Revolution* 2:49, 444; Sapia-Bosch, "Role of General Lucio Blanco," 50; Samponaro and Vanderwood, *War Scare on the Río Grande*, 49–50; and de María y Campos, *Múgica, crónica biográfica*,

65–70. A photograph of the land title is reproduced in Samponaro and Vanderwood, *War Scare*, 50.

Several Mexican federal laws had already been influenced by the homestead law exemptions, which were legislative provisions "to protect the family home from . . . creditors and to prevent alienation by the owner without consent of his spouse" (Haskins, "Homestead Exemptions," 1289–90). For instance, Fomento's November 1896 decree and its subsequent 1897 regulations authorized officials to grant titles to *labradores pobres* (poor laborers) who possessed terrenos baldíos or national lands worth less than two hundred pesos ("Decreto sobre cesión gratuita de terrenos baldíos o nacionales," 28 November 1896, in Secretaría de Fomento, *Colección de leyes sobre tierras*, 134–35, and "Reglamento de la ley sobre cesión gratuita de terrenos baldíos y nacionales," 6 September 1897, in Secretaría de Fomento, *Colección de leyes sobre tierras*, 135–41). Similarly, in November 1909, Fomento sent to the Chamber of Deputies an initiative for a new law on public lands that suspended all public land sales and claims to terrenos baldíos. This initiative continued to promote the granting of free national and terrenos baldíos to poor agricultural workers. The Fomento commission in charge of presenting the bill to Congress claimed that the proposed law aspired to protect Indians from large landholders by forbidding beneficiaries to rent or sell their land plots and by requiring them to cultivate their plots for ten consecutive years or risk losing them. At this hearing, Congressman Rosendo Pineda talked about creating "the homestead or agrarian family patrimony." Congress voted in favor of the new law and sent it to the Senate on the very eve of the Revolution of 1910. See González Navarro, *Historia moderna de México*, 194–95.

5. Rouaix had been an engineer in Durango in charge of terrenos baldíos surveys. Haciendas hired him and other engineers to survey their untitled lands, over which there were oftentimes disputes with neighboring villages. Together with his boss, topographical engineer Carlos Patoni (from a distinguished family of the Porfirian political class), Rouaix surveyed more than two million hectares in the state. Fernández de Castro, "Agrarian Reform from Below," 208.
6. Fernández de Castro, "Agrarian Reform from Below," 665–66.
7. Felicistas were followers of Félix Díaz, nephew of Porfirio Díaz, who opposed the revolutionary movements. Quotation from *Ley ejecutiva del reparto de tierras* (4 March 1913), reproduced in López Anaya, *Ge-*

neral Alberto Carrera Torres, 97–104. See also Ankerson, "Saturnino Cedillo," 144; Knight, *Mexican Revolution*, 2:188; and Cockcroft, "El maestro de primaria," 575–76, 578.

8. Archivo General del Estado de Veracruz (AGEV), Colección de Leyes, Decretos y Circulares (CLDC), Año 1914-15, 162:16-18.

9. Registro Agrario Nacional-Veracruz-Archivo del Cuerpo Consultivo Agrario (RAN-Ver-ACCA), exp. 23/12178, Xico; and Velasco Toro, *Reforma agraria y movilización*, 582. Around the same time, the president of "the Indian community of the Atzalan municipality" asked Veracruz Governor Aguilar "to return the lands seized during the dictatorship of [landowner] Benigno Ríos," owner of the Santa Cruz hacienda (CEHM-Carso, Manuscritos del Primer Jefe del Ejército Constitucionalista, 1889–1920, XXI. 2226. 23. 1 [19 December 1914]). See also Velasco Toro and García Ruiz, "Restitución de tierras," 67–68.

10. Knight, *Mexican Revolution*, 2:251.

11. "El proyecto de la nueva ley agraria formulada por la Secretaría de Fomento" (15 December 1914), reproduced as "Proyecto de ley agraria que expidió el C. Venustiano Carranza" in Fabila, *Cinco siglos*, 220–28. In August 1914 Rouaix became chief administrative officer (*oficial mayor*) in charge of the Office of Fomento, Colonization, and Industry; in January 1915 he became the undersecretary in charge of Fomento; and in September 1916 he became the minister of Fomento (Madrazo, "Pastor Rouaix," 370).

12. "El proyecto de la nueva ley agraria formulada por la Secretaría de Fomento" (15 December 1914), reproduced as "Proyecto de ley agraria que expidió el C. Venustiano Carranza" in Fabila, *Cinco siglos*, 220–28. The agrarian law project devoted an inordinate number of words to specifying inheritance laws—many more than, for example, those dedicated to the foundation of new pueblos—showing how important it was to protect future generations from land loss, a topic discussed further in chapter 5.

13. Richmond, *Venustiano Carranza's Nationalist Struggle*, 117.

14. Katz, *Life and Times of Pancho Villa*, 393.

15. "Acuerdo de la Primera Jefatura sobre la aplicación de la Ley Agraria de 6 de enero de 1915 y sobre jurisdicción de las comisiones agrarias" (26 January 1916), reproduced in Fabila, *Cinco siglos*, 236–38. In fact, President Álvaro Obregón (1920–24) understood that the 6 January 1915 law's restitutions and grants would not radically alter land distribution in Mexico. Therefore, on the day he became president, he sent

to Congress his "Ley de fraccionamiento de latifundios" (law to break up large properties). For details on this law, see Pedro Castro. *Álvaro Obregón*, 157–58.
16. Tannenbaum, *Mexican Agrarian Revolution*, 252–53.
17. "Proyecto de Ley Agraria y el discurso del Dip. Lic. Luis Cabrera" (*Diario de los Debates*, 3 December 1912), reproduced in Fabila, *Cinco siglos*, 184–205.
18. Chávez Padrón, *El proceso social agrario*, 45. The CNA, which opened on 19 January 1916 in Mexico City, comprised nine members, with the minister of fomento as its president; three lawyers representing the ministries of Gobernación (Interior), Justice, and Finance; and five officials from the various Fomento offices (usually engineers). See Acuerdo Número 2 (19 January 1916) in Silva Herzog, *La cuestión de la tierra*, 4:253–54.
19. These illegal practices included three possible scenarios: first, village land transfers by local political authorities or governors in violation of the Lerdo law; second, national and terrenos baldíos concessions and sales conducted by the ministries of Development and the Treasury from 1 December 1876 onward that had impinged on pueblo lands; and third, all illegal boundary surveys (juicios de apeo y deslinde) conducted by judges or political authorities. 6 January 1915 law reproduced in Fabila, *Cinco siglos*, 228–32. Sometimes documents mention not 1856 but federal acts from 1 December 1876 onward (see, for example, AGN, FSAF-CNA, caja 1, vol. 3, fs. 42–44).
20. "*Decreto de 6 de enero de 1915*," reproduced in Fabila, *Cinco siglos*, 229–31.
21. From March 1916 to January 1917, villagers sent 520 petitions for restituciones, 109 for dotaciones, and 357 others that did not specify a demand. Ulloa, *Historia de la Revolución Mexicana*, 368–70. In Michoacán's Purhépecha region alone, between 1915 and 1916 there were thirteen petitions. See Embriz Osorio, "Propiedad, propietarios, pueblos indios y reforma agraria en la región purhépecha," 242–52.
22. AGN, FCNA, caja 1, vol. 1, fs. 1–8 (31 October 1916). On Iztapalapa's Zapatista affiliation at the time, see Castillo Palma, "La revolución en la memoria."
23. According to Raymond Buve, despite formally allying with the Constitutionalists in 1914, several rebel factions continually challenged the authority of provisional governor Máximo Rojas. See Buve, "Agricultores, dominación política," 203–4.

24. AGN, FCNA, caja 1, vol. 1, fs. 17-19 (4 February 1917). This phrase came directly from judicial sentences following the Latin precept *Nemo plus juris ad alium transferre potest quam ipse habet*. For the citation in Latin, see AGN, FCNA, caja 1, vol. 1, fs. 80-82 (5 July 1917). This ruling also clarified that the 6 January 1915 law restituted to the pueblos their juridical standing.
25. AGN, FCNA, caja 1, vol. 1, fs. 80-82 (5 July 1917).
26. AGN, FCNA, caja 1, vol. 1, fs. 29-30 (4 February 1917). For the CNA acting as a quasi-legislature, see Baitenmann, "Popular Participation in State Formation," 21-22.
27. Circular 8 (29 July 1916), in Fabila, *Cinco siglos*, 248.
28. AGN, FCNA, caja 1, vol. 2, fs. 1-4 (20 September 1917).
29. AGN, FCNA, caja 1, vol. 1, fs. 52-55 (31 May 1917).
30. See, for example, Palacios, "Las restituciones." Santa Catarina Cuapiaxtla (Puebla) petitioned for a restitution in 1915 and mustered legitimate colonial titles, but agrarian officials saw no correspondence between the title's boundaries and the actual terrain. See AGN, FCNA, caja 1, vol. 3, fs. 86-87 (14 February 1918).
31. See, for example, Arrioja, "Conflictos por tierras."
32. AGA, Restitución de tierras, exp. 24/1495, leg. 3, fs. 14 (17 August 1916), 45 (26 September 1916), Huitexcalco de Morelos, Chilcuautla, Hidalgo.
33. Gómez Santana, "Ser indígena en la reforma agraria," 108-10.
34. AGA, Restitución de tierras, exp. 24/1773, leg. 1, f. 12, Jamay, Jamay, Jalisco (1917 case file "extract").
35. AGN, FCNA, caja 1, vol. 1, fs. 122-23 (30 August 1917).
36. AGN, FCNA, caja 1, vol. 1, fs. 52-55 (31 May 1917).
37. Many of these surveyors had previously worked at Fomento under Díaz, and later Madero. See, for example, Ervin, "Art of the Possible," 63.
38. AGN, FCNA, caja 1, vol. 5, fs. 55-58 (25 February 1919).
39. AGN, FCNA, caja 1, vol. 3, fs. 31-32 (31 January 1918).
40. AGN, FCNA, caja 1, vol. 6, fs. 1-4 (1 July 1919).
41. AGN, FCNA, caja 1, vol. 5, fs. 117-18 (6 June 1919). See also AGN, FCNA, caja 1, vol. 4, fs. 63-64 (22 August 1918), and AGN, FCNA, caja 1, vol. 6, fs. 77-78 (15 September 1919).
42. See, for example, the 17 February 1915 petition of San Luis Ajajalpan (Puebla) in AGN, FCNA, caja 1, vol. 1, fs. 96-97.
43. On pueblo representatives selling communal lands in the nineteenth century, see Acosta and Embriz, "Territorios indios en la región purhépecha," 156-57.

44. AGA, Restitución de tierras, exp. 24/1553, leg. 5, fs. 104-10 (Presidential resolution of 1924), La Estanzuela, Mineral del Chico, Hidalgo.
45. AGA, Dotación de tierras, exp. 23/4727, leg. 1, fs. 4-7, 25-27, 42, 48-49 (23 March 1916-28 November 1917), Villa de Tacotalpa, Tacotalpa, Tabasco.
46. AGA, Restitución de tierras, exp. 24/1508, leg. 4, fs. 21, 96, 172 (23 March 1916-21 October 1918), San Juan Tilcuautla, San Agustín Tlaxiaca, Hidalgo. See also the case of San Pablo Actipan, Puebla in AGN, FCNA, caja 1, vol. 1, fs. 23-28 (3 April 1917).
47. AGN, FCNA, caja 1, vol. 1, fs. 117-21 (August 1917).
48. AGA, Dotación de tierras, exp. 23/341, leg. 1, fs. 2-3 (1916), Suchitlán, Comala, Colima.
49. AGA, Dotación de tierras, exp. 23/5101, leg. 1, fs. 1, 3, 6-7, 9, 19, 81, 98-99 (1916), Acula, Acula municipality, Veracruz.
50. Circular 1 (24 March 1916), reproduced in Fabila, *Cinco siglos*, 241-42.
51. AGN, FCNA, caja 16, vol. 1, fs. 40-42 (29 April 1916).
52. Gómez, *Historia de la Comisión*, 101. The sitio originated in the nineteenth-century federal public lands laws that allowed pueblos to delimit four sitios de ganado mayor from terrenos baldíos for their ejidos. See Noyola, "Los juicios de apeos y deslindes," 352-53. The 25 March 1894 terrenos baldíos law granted pueblos without ejidos one square league (1,755.61 hectares) of terrenos baldíos for ejidos. Fabila, *Cinco siglos*, 171.
53. Carvajal, *Al margen de las resoluciones presidenciales*, 63-64.
54. Report of the Puebla Agrarian Commission (26 January 1916), in AGN, FGPR, caja 54, exp. 884, fs. 8-17.
55. AGN, FCNA, caja 1, vol. 1, fs. 110-12 (2 August 1917).
56. AGN, FCNA, caja 1, vol. 2, fs. 38-39 (15 November 1917).
57. AGN, FCNA, caja 1, vol. 2, fs. 94-95 (27 December 1917).
58. AGN, FCNA, caja 1, vol. 1, fs. 80-82 (5 July 1917). The CNA delegates also referred to a 1916 accord that limited the functions of state-level agrarian commissions to the implementation of the 6 January 1915 law. "Acuerdo de la Primera Jefatura sobre la aplicación de la ley agraria de 6 de enero de 1915 y sobre jurisdicción de las comisiones agrarias," reproduced in Fabila, *Cinco siglos*, 236-38.
59. AGN, FCNA, caja 1, vol. 1, fs. 83-85 (5 July 1917). Emphasis added.
60. AGA, Dotación de tierras, exp. 23/122, leg. 1, fs. 5-7 (21 November 1916), 50-51 (1 March 1918), San Antonio Sahcabchen, Calkiní, Campeche.

61. AGN, FCNA, caja 1, vol. 2, fs. 35-37 (11 October 1917) [Tolcayuca]; AGN, FCNA, caja 1, vol. 2, fs. 83-84 (27 December 1917) [Coquimatlán]; AGN, FCNA, caja 1, vol. 5, fs. 47-49 (4 February 1919) [Santa María Coatepec]; SJF, época 5, tomo 6, 476-80 (10 March 1920) [Santiago Tequixquiac]; AGN, FCNA, caja 1, vol. 3, fs. 101-3 (4 January 1918) [Erongarícuaro]; and AGN, FCNA, caja 1, vol. 5, fs. 26-28 (4 February 1919) [San Ildefonso Tultepec].

62. Baitenmann, "Popular Participation"; González Solano, "La lucha por la propiedad," 19, 21; Purnell, *Popular Movements*, 54; and Ulloa, *Historia de la Revolución Mexicana*, 374-81, 388, 390-403.

63. AGN, CNA, caja 1, vol. 5, fs. 34-36 (4 February 1919); AGN, FCNA, caja 1, vol. 5, f. 34 (4 February 1919).

64. Ulloa, *Historia de la Revolución Mexicana*, 376; AGN, FCNA, caja 16, vol. 1, fs. 26-27 (14 April 1916).

65. Landowners, in turn, could take their claims to court within one year and, if they did have rights to these lands, they would receive compensation for the assessed value of their lands as of 1913. See RAN-Ver-ACCA, exp. 24/797, Ayahualulco, "Manifiesto a los habitantes de los pueblos de Ayahualulco e Ixhuacán de los Reyes del Cantón de Coatepec," expedido por el Gobernador y Comandante Militar del Estado, Gral. C. Aguilar, en Veracruz (9 February 1915).

66. Departamento Agrario, telegrama (16 November 1916), published in *Gaceta Oficial del Estado de Veracruz* (23 November 1916), 2.

67. AGA, Restitución de tierras, exp. 24/1475, leg. 5, fs. 4-6 (11 January 1915), Tepenene, El Arenal, Hidalgo.

68. Purnell, *Popular Movements*, 125, citing Friedrich, *Agrarian Revolt*, 52-56.

69. See, for example, AGA, Restitución de tierras, exp. 24/2186, leg. 6, f. 16 (19 December 1916), Tepexpan, Acolman, Estado de México; and Castellano Suárez, *Empeño por una expectativa agraria*, 130.

70. AGA, Dotación de tierras, exp. 23/5101, leg. 1, f. 10 (11 April 1916), Acula, Acula, Veracruz.

71. AGA, Restitución de tierras, exp. 24/2321, leg. 3, fs. 2-5 (30 September 1914), 3 (7 October 1914), San Lucas Totolmaloya, Aculco, Mexico State.

72. AGA, Restitución de tierras, exp. 24/10926, leg. 3, fs. 5-8, Mayorazgo de la Concepción de León, Almoloya de Juárez, Mexico State (23 November 1916); AGA, Restitución de tierras, exp. 24/1474, leg. 8, fs. 39-40, Tlanalapa, Tlanalapa, Hidalgo (27 September 1915).

73. AGN, FCNA, caja 1, vol. 2, fs. 15-20 (26 September 1917).

74. AGN, FCNA, caja 1, vol. 2, fs. 29-32 (4 October 1917).
75. AGA, Documentos históricos, exp. 23/992, leg. 0, f. 2 (10 January 1916), San Bartolomé Aguascalientes, Apaseo, Guanajuato.
76. Like the Zapatistas, Arenas combined land restitution and grants by distributing fields to outlying towns as well as to resident workers—often from the same hacienda.
77. Buve, *El movimiento revolucionario*, 246; Buve, "'Neither Carranza nor Zapata!,'" 347, 350-56.
78. AGA, Restitución de tierras, exp. 24/1526, leg. 3, fs. 10, 11, 13, 15, 16 (12 January 1915-26 October 1915) and leg. 4, f. 22 (26 July 1917), Tetepango, Tetepango, Hidalgo.
79. AGA, Restitución de tierras, exp. 24/149, leg. 3, fs. 7-9 (12 June 1916-8 August 1916), Huitexcalco de Morelos, Chilcuautla, Hidalgo. See also the case of San Francisco Tlanalapa (Hidalgo) villagers, who had first petitioned for the restitution of their lands by hailing the Plan de Ayala and then, in March 1915, sent a petition to the governor of Hidalgo in which they acknowledged "our First Chief of the Constitutionalist Army, Señor General Don Venustiano Carranza, President of the United States of Mexico, in the Heroic City of Veracruz" and solicited land under the terms of Carranza's 6 January 1915 law. AGA, Restitución de tierras, exp. 24/1474, leg. 8, fs. 3-4 (9 January 1915); leg. 8, f. 20; leg. 8, fs. 39-40 (27 September 1915), Tlanalapa, Tlanalapa, Hidalgo.
80. AGA, Restitución de tierras exp. 24/2228, leg. 6, fs. 1-3, 22-25, 27, 47, 233-40 (17 February 1915-2 August 1922), Muitejé, Acambay, Mexico State. Also, in Mexico State, Agostadero ranch residents (who, citing the Plan de Ayala, had sent Governor Baz a petition seeking the restitution of woodlands allegedly seized by the de Solís hacienda) later sent a new petition to the recently established Mexico State Agrarian Commission. AGA, Restitución de tierras, exp. 24/2155, leg. 7, fs. 1-4, 22-27, 13, 30-32, 55, 60, 72, 74, 80 (8 January 1915), Agostadero, Acambay, Mexico State.

    For other examples of the same phenomenon in the Federal District and Mexico State, see AGN, FEZ, caja 19, exp. 1, fs. 113-14 (24 May 1915); AGA, Restitución de tierras, exp. 24/913, leg. 7, fs. 5-6, Santiago Atzacoalco, Gustavo A. Madero, Distrito Federal; AGA, Restitución de tierras, exp. 24/975, leg. 1, fs. 3-6, Santa Cruz Acalpixca, Xochimilco, Distrito Federal (22 May 1916); AGA, Dotación de tierras, exp. 23/2288, leg. 9, 1-115, Villa de Nicolás Romero (formerly San Pedro Atzcapotzalco), Villa de Nicolás Romero, Estado de México; AGA, Restitución de tierras, exp. 24/2155, leg. 7, fs. 1-4 (8 January 1915), fs. 264-66 (18 February 1918), leg. 8, fs. 83-87 (19 December 1918), Agostadero, Acambay, Estado de México; and Birrichaga Gardida, "¿Ejidatarios o comuneros?," 343-45. For Hidalgo, see Tepenene in AGN, FCNA, caja 1, vol. 2, fs. 10-14 (26 September 1917), and Tlanalapa in AGN, FCNA, caja 1, vol. 1, fs. 117-21 (30 August 1917).

81. A future review board under Coss's authority would issue titles, which would later be ratified by the First Chief of the Constitutionalist Army.
82. AGN, FCR-RRC, caja 3, exp. 68, f. 36 (2 February 1915).
83. AGN, FCNA, caja 1, vol. 1, fs. 72-75 (5 July 1917). Other early Puebla repartos in which villagers conformed to Constitutionalist laws include San Nicolás Zoyapetlayoca (AGN, FCNA, caja 1, vol. 2, fs. 91-93, 27 December 1917) and San Luis Ajajalpan (AGN, FCNA, caja 1, vol. 1, fs. 96-97, 19 July 1917).
84. Embriz Osorio, "Propiedad, propietarios, pueblos indios," 242-52.
85. "Reporte de la CNA" (21 August 1917), AGA, Restitución de tierras, exp. 2425/5818, leg. 5, fs. 19-20, Santo Tomás, Ojocaliente, Zacatecas.
86. AGA, Dotación de tierras, exp. 23/3311, leg. 1, f. 2 (15 January 1917), Nazareno Etla, Nazareno Etla, Oaxaca.
87. Garner, *La Revolución en la provincia*, 195-96.
88. AGA, Dotación de tierras, exp. 23/3313, leg. 1, f. 113 (23 January 1917), Santa María del Tule, Santa María del Tule, Oaxaca.

5. Return of the Judiciary

1. See also James, *Mexico's Supreme Court*, chapter 2.
2. Studies showing that the early amparo rulings favored agrarian reform efforts include Barrón, "La 'modernización' revolucionaria del discurso"; Cabrera Acevedo, *La Suprema Corte de Justicia durante los años constitucionalistas*, 1:42; James, *Mexico's Supreme Court*, chapter 2; and Kuntz Ficker, "Introducción."
3. Circular 22 (18 April 1917), reproduced in Fabila, *Cinco siglos*, 272-73. The quotation appears in the circular.
4. The debates surrounding article 27 have been extensively researched. See, for example, Kourí, "Interpreting the Expropriation," 107-10; Niemeyer, *Revolution at Querétaro*; Marván Laborde, *Nueva edición del diario*, vol. 1; Miranda Correa, "El artículo 27 en el Congreso Constituyente de Querétaro"; and Rouaix, *Génesis de los artículos 27 y 123*.
5. Supreme Court justices made this difference clear ("Siendo cosa distinta la restitución o dotación de ejidos y el fraccionamiento de los latifundios") in *SJF*, época 5, tomo 21, pp. 1085-94 (19 October 1927).

6. Some governors did take advantage of this right. See, for example, the "Ley agraria del Estado de Chihuahua" (25 May 1922) in Hall, "Álvaro Obregón," 235-37.
7. Translation of articles 14 and 16 by the Organization of American States (OAS), http://www.oas.org/juridico/mla/en/mex/en_mex-int-text-const.pdf.
8. District courts tended to side more with landowners than did the first two revolutionary Supreme Courts. See also *Amparo interpuesto por Carlos Markassuza contra actos del C. Presidente de la República y Comisión Nacional Agraria*.
9. *SJF*, época 5, tomo 1, pp. 400-403 (2 October 1917). This should have come as no surprise given that three of the justices (José María Truchuelo, Alberto M. González, and Enrique Colunga) had served as delegates to the 1916-17 Constitutional Congress (Cabrera Acevedo, "La Revolución Mexicana," 211).
10. *SJF*, época 5, tomo 4, pp. 402-7 (15 February 1919).
11. *SJF*, época 5, tomo 6, pp. 202-5 (26 January 1920).
12. *SJF*, época 5, tomo 6, pp. 476-80 (10 March 1920).
13. *SJF*, época 5, tomo 5, pp. 649-68 (15 October 1919); Cabrera Acevedo, *La Suprema Corte de Justicia durante los años constitucionalistas*, 1:40. La *cosa juzgada* is the "capacity to render binding decisions when deciding a contentious question of conflicting rights" (James, *Mexico's Supreme Court*, 71).
14. *SJF*, época 5, tomo 2, pp. 1049-68 (3 April 1918, Rafael G. de Salceda y Echave).
15. Herrera-Martin, "Judicial Review of Expropriation," 148-49.
16. AGN, FCNA, caja 1, vol. 1, fs. 104-6 (26 July 1917); *SJF*, época 5, tomo 1, pp. 945-46 (29 December 1917).
17. For example, when a month later Durango landowner Feliciano Cobián filed an amparo suit after part of his property was expropriated to grant a fundo legal to his former resident peons, he argued that the action violated his rights under articles 14, 16, and 27. In response, the second reinstated Supreme Court reiterated that "the precepts of the 6 January 1915 law are not only of general interest but are concerned with common prosperity and well-being. If the execution of the presidential resolution were to be suspended, the State would suffer grave damages [and] would violate the spirit of the 1917 Constitution, which concerns the adjudication or restitution of lands for the pueblos." *SJF*, época 5, tomo 2, pp. 271-76 (31 January 1918).

In another case from Durango, Julio F. Curbelo filed an amparo suit against the governor and legislature, arguing that the governor violated federal civil procedures when he granted former hacienda peons the political status of villa and expropriated Curbelo's lands to grant them a fundo legal. When the Durango District Court ruled in favor of Curbelo, the governor sought recourse with the Supreme Court. There the justices decided that "dotaciones for the pueblos' fundos legales and ejidos and all other matters related to the agrarian problem are of the highest national interest." Therefore "suspending acts of this nature would be contrary to the public interest and would cause severe damage to society." *SJF*, época 5, tomo 2, pp. 963-65 (21 March 1918).

18. *SJF*, época 5, tomo 3, pp. 1348-51 (24 December 1918). See also ACSCJN, Fondo SCJN, Sección Pleno, Serie Amparo, exp. 85-4 (1921), and Kuntz, "Introducción," 12. CNA delegates also talked about presidential resolutions creating jurisprudence. See, for example, AGN, FCNA, caja 1, vol. 5, fs. 23-25. More generally, as Suárez-Potts explains, "under the post-1917 governments, as well as intermittently before then, the federal judiciary adhered to a narrow policy of *stare decisis*. In general, five consistent, consecutive rulings by the Supreme Court on a legal point (*tesis*) established a controlling precedent, *jurisprudencia*, on lower federal courts and on its own subsequent decision making . . ." Suárez-Potts, *Making of Law*, 5-6.

19. *SJF*, época 5, tomo 2, pp. 829-33 (15 March 1918).

20. Gómez, *Historia de la Comisión*, 277.

21. Article 10 of the 6 January 1915 law, in Fabila, *Cinco siglos*, 231-32. Little is known about how many hacienda owners received compensation, but it is likely that very few did. We know, for example, that in the early 1920s the government expropriated parts of Morelos landowner Luis García Pimentel's Santa Clara and Jonacatepec haciendas, property valued at 232,000 pesos. Only in 1946 did the family receive compensation in the form of irrigated land in Tamaulipas, leaving them with "a credit" for 190,000 pesos. *DOF*, 27 August 1946, 5, and Barreto Zamudio, "La familia García Pimentel," 19.

22. *SJF*, época 5, tomo 3, pp. 539-43 (23 August 1918, Manuel Baigts).

23. Article 10 of the 6 January 1915 law, reproduced in Fabila, *Cinco siglos*, 231-32. See also the Iztapalapa dotación in AGN, FCNA, caja 1, vol. 1, fs. 1-8 (31 October 1916).

24. Cabrera Acevedo, *La Suprema Corte de Justicia de la Nación durante los años constitucionalistas*, 1:38.

25. AGN, FCNA, caja 1, vol. 4, fs. 92-95 (19 December 1918); AGA, Dotación de tierras, exp. 23/2155, leg. 4, fs. 5-12; Restitución de tierras, exp. 24/2155, leg. 7, fs. 97-99, 120-23, 138-50; Restitución de tierras, exp. 24/2155, leg. 8, fs. 290-95; all from Agostadero, Acambay, Mexico State. Similarly, as the Supreme Court justices explained to a Coahuila landowner in 1923, "In those cases in which an amparo is solicited against land restitutions and that person obtains judicial protection by declaring that the restitution of pueblo lands does not proceed [and officials should grant a dotación instead], the sentence will only give the owner the right to compensation" (ACSCJN exp. 656, 1923).
26. AGA, Restitución de tierras, 24/1533, leg. 1, f. 36 (22 January 1918), 24/1533, leg. 1, f. 71 (9 June 1920), El Puente, Atotonilco el Chico, Hidalgo.
27. AGA, Restitución de tierras, 24/10977, leg. 1, fs. 52, 53, 63 (February-April 1918), Almoloya del Río, Almoloya del Río, Mexico State.
28. AGA, Restitución de tierras, 24/735, leg. 10, f. 50, San Francisco del Malpaís, Nombre de Dios, Durango (11 November 1920).
29. Cuadros Caldas, *Catecismo agrario*, 453-56.
30. "Decree of 22 November 1921," cited by Mendieta y Núñez, *El problema agrario*, 178-79. See also the following cases: AGA, Restitución de tierras, 24/2268, leg. 2, f. 42 (8 April 1920), San Pedro Nexapa, Amecameca, Mexico State; AGA, Dotación de tierras, 23/4665, leg. 6, f. 18 (19 June 1923), Macoyahui, Álamos, Sonora; AGA, Dotación de tierras, 23/140, leg. 2, f. 165 (25 September 1923), Dzitbalché, Calkiní, Campeche; AGA, Dotación de tierras, 23/5130, leg. 3, f. 457 (30 July 1924), Ángel R. Cabada, Ángel R. Cabada, Veracruz; AGA, Restitución de tierras, 24/9840, leg. 3, f. 83 (19 March 1925), Petaquillas, Chilpancingo, Guerrero; AGA, Dotación de tierras, 23/1474, leg. 1, f. 85 (7 May 1925), Tlanalapa, Tlanalapa, Hidalgo; AGA, Restitución de tierras, 24/1384, leg. 6, f. 157 (30 September 1925), Chontalcoatlán, Tetipac, Guerrero; AGA, Restitución de tierras, 24/12228, leg. 2, f. 110 (3 September 1926), Santa María Huatulco, Santa María Huatulco, Oaxaca; AGA, Dotación de tierras, 23/11218, leg. 3, f. 11 (5 October 1926), Villa de Bustamante, Bustamante, Nuevo León; and AGA, Dotación de tierras, 23/13130, leg. 1, f. 69 (23 October 1928), Colima, Batopilas, Chihuahua.
31. See the CNA's circular 24 (8 June 1917), reproduced in Fabila, *Cinco siglos*, 275.
32. SJF, época 5, tomo 2, pp. 1049-68 (3 April 1918, Rafael G. de Salceda y Echave).

33. *SJF*, época 5, tomo 2, pp. 1110-13 (6 April 1918).
34. *SJF*, época 5, tomo 5, pp. 649-68 (15 October 1919); Cabrera Acevedo, *La Suprema Corte de Justicia de la Nación durante los años constitucionalistas*, 1:40. La cosa juzgada is the "capacity to render binding decisions when deciding a contentious question of conflicting rights" (James, *Mexico's Supreme Court*, 71).
35. ACSCJN, exp. 1872 (1922), reproduced in Kuntz, "Introducción," 117-24.
36. AGN, FCNA, caja 1, vol. 4, fs. 92-96 (19 December 1918); AGA, Dotación de tierras, 23/2155, leg. 4, fs. 5-12; Restitución de tierras, 24/2155, leg. 7, fs. 97-99, 120-23, 138-50; Restitución de tierras, 24/2155, leg. 8, fs. 108-10, 290-95; all from Agostadero, Acambay, Mexico State.
37. *SJF*, época 5, tomo 2, pp. 271-76 (31 January 1918).
38. Posseción y plena propiedad privada, *SJF*, época 5, tomo 3, pp. 1090-95 (21 October 1918).
39. AGN, FCNA, caja 1, vol. 2, fs. 99-100 (27 December 1917). Circular 1 (24 March 1916) is reproduced in Fabila, *Cinco siglos*, 241-42.
40. *DOF*, 28 May 1926, 408-12.
41. Circular 23 (1 June 1917), reproduced in Fabila, *Cinco siglos*, 274.
42. AGN, FCNA, caja 1, vol. 3, fs. 14-15 (24 January 1918). Article 27 included important environmental rights. On civil engineer and conservationist Miguel Ángel de Quevedo's influence on article 27, see Wolfe, *Watering the Revolution*, 56-57. On the conservationist movement in Mexico, see Simonian, *Defending the Land of the Jaguar*.
43. Gómez, *Historia de la Comisión*, 236-37 (23 April 1921 session).
44. Presidential resolution of 30 September 1921 in AGA, exp. Restitución de tierras, 24/1526, leg. 4, fs. 126-28, Tetepango, Tetepango, Hidalgo. See also AGA, exp. Dotación de tierras, 23/2984, leg. 2, fs. 46-49, Tetecalita, Jiutepec, Morelos (11 September 1924); AGA, Restitución de tierras, exp. 24/2268, leg. 1, fs. 117-23, San Pedro Nexapa, Amecameca, Estado de México (19 March 1925); and *SJF*, época 5, tomo 8, pp. 257-59 (8 February 1926).
45. *SJF*, época 5, tomo 8, pp. 270-72 (2 February 1921).
46. See, for example, chapter 1 and Mendoza García, *Agua y tierra en San Gabrial Chilac*, 66.
47. See, for example, *DOF*, 12 March 1920, 1137-39; Carvajal, *Al margen*, 75-77; and Sandré Osorio, "Reforma agraria," 184-89.
48. Wolfe, *Watering the Revolution*, 15.

49. *SJF*, época 5, tomo 1, pp. 616–19 (10 August 1920). See also the Cuautla River concession in Morelos, *DOF*, 19 January 1923, 306–8, and the San Jerónimo River concession in Colima in AGN, FCNA 4: 21: 107–8 (24 November 1924).
50. Aboites Aguilar, *El agua de la nación*, 135. See, also, AGN, FCNA, caja 3, vol. 18, fs. 100–101 (23 April 1924); AGN, FCNA, caja 4, vol. 21, fs. 99–100 (24 November 1924). On article 27 allowing the federal government to expand its role in overall water management, see Aboites Aguilar and Morales Cosme, "Amecameca, 1922," 55. For the history of the gradual federalization of water resources starting in the late nineteenth century, see, among others, Aboites Aguilar, *El agua de la nación*; Aboites Aguilar, Birrigchaga Gardida, and Garay Trejo, "El manejo de las aguas"; Escobar Ohmstede and Sánchez Rodríguez, "El agua y la tierra en México"; Lanz Cárdenas, *Legislación de aguas en México*; and Sandré Osorio and Sánchez, *El eslabón perdido*.
51. AGN, FCNA, caja 3, vol. 18, fs. 148–50 (26 June 1924).
52. For water granted for both domestic and agricultural needs, see the case of Ciudad Lerdo (Durango), which received a concession to water from the Nazas River for both domestic uses and irrigation. Ángel Carvajal, *Al margen de las resoluciones presidenciales*, 75–77. See also the cases of several Aculco (Mexico State) pueblos in AGN, FCNA, caja 4, vol. 19, fs. 182–84 (28 August 1924).
53. When Capultitlán (Mexico State) received land and access to the federally owned Los Jazmines springs, its residents had to share water with neighboring Tlacotepec, whose residents needed water for "public and domestic uses." AGN, FCNA, caja 4, vol. 21, fs. 121–22 (11 December 1924).
54. 6 January 1915 law, reproduced in Fabila, *Cinco siglos*, 228–32.
55. Article 27, reproduced in Fabila, *Cinco siglos*, 261–64. Quotation from 263. On the clarification that woodlands and water resources would remain communal property, see Francisco José Múgica's intervention in the Constitutional Convention debates, in Marván Laborde, *Nueva edición del Diario*, 1:1063.
56. *SJF*, época 5, tomo 2, pp. 1049–68 (3 April 1918).
57. *SJF*, época 5, tomo 8, pp. 273–79 (2 February 1921).
58. Kourí, "La promesa agraria del artículo 27," 37.
59. Kourí, "Interpreting the Expropriation."
60. For example, General Alberto Carrera Torres's 1913 "executive law for the distribution of land" granted farmers and soldiers provisional

but inalienable titles to ten-hectare plots (*Ley ejecutiva del reparto de tierras*, 4 March 1913, reproduced in López Anaya, *General Alberto Carrera Torres*, 97-104). Rouaix and Novelo's 1914 agrarian law project proposed granting land parcels on condition that beneficiaries not sell, mortgage, or transmit them except to legitimate heirs ("El proyecto de la nueva ley agraria formulada por la Secretaría de Fomento," 15 December 1914, reproduced as "Proyecto de ley agraria que expidió el C. Venustiano Carranza" in Fabila, *Cinco siglos*, 220-28). Lucio Blanco's 1913 Los Borregos expropriation forbade the embargo or taxation of the land, and beneficiaries could not sell or transfer their parcels to third parties—except to heirs (Samponaro and Vanderwood, *War Scare on the Río Grande*, 49-50). And San Luis Potosí governor Emilio G. Saravia issued a "decree for family patrimony" in April 1915 to grant citizens land parcels that when no larger than five hectares, could constitute family patrimony—meaning that the parcel could not be sold, divided, mortgaged, taxed, embargoed, occupied, or expropriated, not even by judicial authorities ("Decreto sobre patrimonio familiar," reproduced in Díaz, *Fuentes para la historia de la Revolución Mexicana*, 1:183-86).

61. Text reproduced in Villegas Moreno and Porrúa Venero, *De la crisis del modelo borbónico*, 334.
62. One reason why the idea of family patrimony was present in both articles is that eleven Convention delegates were part of both deliberation committees. For the numerical overlap, see Niemeyer, *Revolution at Querétaro*, 138.
63. See article 27 in Fabila, *Cinco siglos*, 264.
64. See the 1920 ejido law, reproduced in Fabila, *Cinco siglos*, 296-308, and the 1922 agrarian regulations, also in Fabila, *Cinco siglos*, 327-32.
65. See, for example, AGA, Dotación de tierras, exp. 23/5465, leg. 1, f. 44 (6 June 1924), Chavaxtla, Huatusco, Veracruz.
66. AGA, Restitución de tierras, exp. 24/12712, leg. 4, f. 3 (28 January 1922), Tepetlacingo, Olinalá, Guerrero.
67. Tinsman, *Partners in Conflict*, 4.
68. AGA, Restitución de tierras, 24/5004, leg. 3, fs. 10-13, 14-27 (12 September 1917), San Juan Quetzalcoapan, Tzompantepec, Tlaxcala; AGA, Dotación de tierras, exp. 23/380, leg. 4, fs. 2-12 (1922), San Juan, Balleza, Chihuahua.
69. AGA, Restitución de tierras, 24/1234, leg. 4, fs. 37-51 (12 September 1919), Tuliman, Huitzuco, Guerrero.

70. AGA, Restitución de tierras, exp. 24/1514, leg. 5, fs. 35-72 (December 1917), San Agustín Tlaxiaca, San Agustín Tlaxiaca, Hidalgo.
71. AGA, Restitución de tierras, 24/1489, leg. 5, fs. 289-90 (19 January 1918), San Jerónimo, El Arenal, Hidalgo. On women as beneficiaries in the privatization of communal lands, see Chassen-López, "¿Capitalismo o comunalismo?," 166-68. On women as beneficiaries in both privatization of communal lands and early agrarian reform, see Gómez Santana and Gómez Santana, "Mujeres y propiedad social en Jalisco, 1876-1924."

    Some censuses did exclude women. In Atasta (Campeche), the census listed ninety-four heads of family, all male. This was also the case in Pino Suárez (Hidalgo), San Antonio Sahcabchén (Campeche), San Juan Coyula (Oaxaca), and Zoquipan (Jalisco), where all potential land beneficiaries were male. In Cucurpe (Sonora), only one of 170 heads of family was female. In some cases, an initial agrarian census would include a few women, whereas a later version did not. In Mezquitlán (Guerrero), for example, the September 1921 restitution census listed thirty heads of family, including eight women, whereas the November 1921 census listed only men. AGA, Dotación de tierras, exp. 23/116, leg. 1, fs. 212-13, 208-11, Atasta, Municipio Libre del Carmen, Estado de Campeche; AGA, Restitución de tierras, exp. 24/1490, leg. 7, fs. 75-78 (February 1917), Pino Suárez, Tepetitlán, Hidalgo; AGA, Dotación de tierras, exp. 23/122, leg. 1, fs. 39-40 (13 August 1917), San Antonio Sahcabchén, Calkiní, Campeche; AGA, Restitución de tierras, exp. 24/12342, leg. 2, fs. 32-50, 51-54 (1918), San Juan Coyula, San Juan Cuicatlán, Oaxaca; AGA, Restitución de tierras, exp. 24/1846, leg. 2, fs. 124-26 (1923), Zoquipan, Zapopan, Jalisco; AGA, Restitución de tierras, exp. 24/15766, leg. 1, fs. 114-16 (1918), Cucurpe, Cucurpe, Sonora; AGA, Restitución de tierras, exp. 24/11130, leg. 4, fs. 27-28, 29-30 (1921), Mezquitlán, Copalillo, Guerrero.
72. On the effects of nineteenth-century civil codes on women in Mexico, see, for example, Arrom, "Changes in Mexican family law," and Deere and León, *Empowering Women*.
73. AGA, Restitución de tierras, exp. 24/1514, leg. 5, fs. 26-34 (December 1917), San Agustín Tlaxiaca, San Agustín Tlaxiaca, Hidalgo; AGA, Dotación de tierras, exp. 23/5689, leg. 1, f. 14; leg. 5, fs. 8-11, Xpechil, Peto, Yucatán; AGA, Restitución de tierras, exp. 24/15766, leg. 1, fs. 134-48 (9 April 1922), Cucurpe, Cucurpe, Sonora.

74. Fowler-Salamini, "Gender, Work, and Coffee in Córdoba, Veracruz," 60-61.
75. AGA, Dotación de tierras, exp. 23/942, leg. 1, fs. 20-29 (1923), Santa María Aztahuacan, Iztapalapa, D.F.; AGA, Dotación de tierras, exp. 23/4398, leg. 1, fs. 25-28 (August 1925), Santa Clara, Santo Domingo, San Luis Potosí.
76. AGA, Dotación de tierras, exp. 23/4727, leg. 1, fs. 51-54 (November 1917), Villa de Tacotalpa, Tacotalpa, Tabasco.
77. See, for example, AGA, Amplicación de tierras, exp. 25/3501, leg. 3, f. 151-59 (29 August 1922), San Nicolás Zoyapetlayoca, Tepeaca, Puebla; and article 22 of the 1922 agrarian regulation, reproduced in Fabila, *Cinco siglos*, 330.
78. AGEV-ACAM 208, El Chico, fs. 142-52, Dictamen CLA, 6 abril 1923; and Sánchez Gómez, "Afectación agraria y población beneficiada en la hacienda El Encero," 56.
79. AGA, Restitución de tierras, exp. 24/1234, leg. 4, fs. 37-51 (1919), Tuliman, Huitzuco, Guerrero.
80. AGA, Dotación de tierras, exp. 23/4394, leg. 1, fs. 35-37 (March 1925), Jesús María, Santo Domingo, San Luis Potosí.
81. AGA, Dotación de tierras, exp. 23/5197, leg. 1, fs. 50-64, 100-125, 176-200 (June 1922), Gabino Barreda, Cosamaloapan, Veracruz.
82. AGA, Restitución de tierras, exp. 24/943, leg. 6, fs. 10-17 (1916), San Juanico Nextipac, Iztapalapa, Distrito Federal.
83. AGA, Restitución de tierras, exp. 24/3320, leg. 5, fs. 25-36 (1917), Santo Domingo Jalieza, Santo Tomás Jalieza, Oaxaca; AGA, Restitución de tierras, exp. 24/12228, leg. 2, fs. 74-84 (1919), Santa María Huatulco, Santa María Huatulco, Oaxaca. The census used the masculine form for labrador, agricultor, and jornalero—even for women. Molendera, however, was considered a female profession.
84. Article 23 of the 1922 agrarian regulations; AGA, Dotación de tierras, exp. 23/4303, leg. 1, f. 7 (10 March 1923), Tanque Colorado, Villa de Guadalupe, SLP.
85. AGA, Restitución de tierras, exp. 24/605, leg. 6, fs. 18-34 (14 April 1928), Tuzantán, Tuzantán, Chiapas. We know, however, that it was often those who were better off in a village who promoted the land petition and then somehow managed to acquire land. The landowning farmers who became "revolutionaries" in Pisaflores (Hidalgo) are perhaps the best example of this phenomenon; see Schryer, *Rancheros of Pisaflores*.

86. CPAs should not be confused with the comités particulares ejecutivos, the supramunicipal committees under the state's local agrarian commissions, created by the 6 January 1915 law for land restitution and grant tasks. Even though women were generally not permitted to vote in municipal elections until 1947 (women briefly had suffrage rights in Yucatán, Chiapas, and Tabasco in the 1920s), agrarian laws allowed women to vote for all agrarian representatives. In Zoquipan (Jalisco), for example, eight women and fifteen men elected their land reform representative. AGA, Restitución de tierras, exp. 24/1846, leg. 2, f. 14 (20 July 1918), Zoquipan, Zapopan, Jalisco. In Tepozonalquillo (Guerrero) over 60 percent of the heads of household, males over eighteen years of age, widows, and single women elected officials. AGA, Restitución de tierras, exp. 24/1352, leg. 5, fs. 66–67 (18 October 1928), Tepozonalquillo, Teloloapan, Guerrero.
87. Circular 19 (20 March 1917), reproduced in Fabila, *Cinco siglos*, 267–69; circular 22 (18 April 1917), reproduced in Fabila, *Cinco siglos*, 272–73.
88. AGA, Restitución de tierras, exp. 24/2149, leg. 7, fs. 181–82 (June 1917), San Pedro Totoltepec, Toluca, Mexico State.
89. For example, when the San Simón Atzitzintla (Puebla) CPA petitioned agrarian authorities for access to nearby springs "to benefit small property owners and for the population's public use," the presidential resolution stated that "agrarian authorities created by the 6 January 1915 law . . . have the authority to review [*conocer de*] water petitions filed by the diverse pueblos of the Republic." AGN, FCNA, caja 4, vol. 21, pp. 1-3 (24 November 1924).
90. Circular 48 (1 September 1921), in Fabila, *Cinco siglos*, 314–25. Rural public schools were under municipal or state jurisdiction until 1921, when the federal Ministry of Public Education was established.
91. AGA, Amplicación de tierras, exp. 25/3501, leg. 3, fs. 198–200 (16 July 1925), San Nicolás Zoyapetlayoca, Tepeaca, Puebla.
92. AGA, Dotación de tierras, exp. 23/2149, leg. 1, f. 22 (19 January 1920), San Pedro Totoltepec, Toluca, Mexico State.
93. *Codificación de los decretos del C. Venustiano Carranza*, 144–47. For studies on the relationship between agrarian reform and the municipio, see (in order of publication date) Rincón Serrano, *El ejido mexicano*; Azuela, "Ciudadanía"; Baitenmann, "Las paradojas"; and Mendoza García, *Agua y Tierra*.
94. In contrast, Salvador Salinas sees CPAs in Morelos in the 1920s as "bastions of resistance against abusive state-level and municipal poli-

ticians and rural elites" (Salinas, *Land, Liberty, and Water*, 53). Archival material for this book rather points to systematic abuse of power.

95. AGA, Restitución de tierras, exp. 24/1384, leg. 7, fs. 100-101, Chontalcoatlán, Tetipac, Guerrero (1 December 1924). Agrarian officials told them to take their grievances to the *procurador de pueblos*.

96. See also Mendieta y Núñez, *El problema agrario*, 197-98. CPAs even became authorities whose actions could be suspended by the district courts and the Supreme Court. In 1919, for example, Tlaxcala landowners filed an amparo suit against the Tlaxcala Agrarian Commission and the Panotla CPA (*SJF*, época 5, tomo 4, pp. 402-7, 15 February 1919). Diego Moreno's lawyers claimed amparo suspension against the dotación for Guarachita (Michoacán), arguing that the participation of the *comité particular ejecutivo* (local committee in charge of implementing land reform) and CPA was illegal (*SJF*, época 5, tomo 7, pp. 965-69, 6 September 1920); and Victoriano Medina and the San Juan Ixtayopan (Xochimilco) CPA petitioned amparo suspension because the 1917 presidential restitution was granted to neighboring residents in 1920 (*SJF*, época 5, tomo 10, pp. 768-72, 6 April 1922).

97. AGA, Dotación de tierras, exp. 23/1474, leg. 1, f. 87 (12 November 1925); leg. 1, f. 85 (7 May 1925), Tlanalapa, Tlanalapa, Hidalgo. In Xochimilco (Federal District), for example, several residents took their grievances to the CNA, hoping to sidestep the CPA. AGA, Dotación de tierras, exp. 23/897, leg. 3, f. 96 (30 October 1924); f. 97 (31 October 1924); and f. 108 (3 December 1924), Xochimilco, Xochimilco, Federal District. And when some four hundred residents petitioned the CNA for the renewal of Xochimilco's CPA, the CPA president threatened those who signed the petition with the loss of their parcels. AGA, Dotación de tierras, exp. 23/897, leg. 3, f. 43 (August 1924) and f. 66 (10 September 1924), Xochimilco, Xochimilco, Federal District.

98. AGA, Dotación de tierras, exp. 23/3311, leg. 2, fs. 62-63, Nazareno Etla, Nazareno Etla municipality, Oaxaca.

99. Circular 48 (1 September 1921), reproduced in Fabila, *Cinco siglos*, 314-25.

100. Circular 51 (11 October 1922), reproduced in Fabila, *Cinco siglos*, 334-40. Simpson described the goals of circular 51 as being that "ejido lands were to be held and worked in common—all for one and one for all, and no questions raised concerning mine or thine" (Simpson, *Ejido*, 321). See also Eckstein, *El ejido colectivo en México*, 48, 50-51, and Velasco Toro, "De la ley de 6 de enero," 31-35.

101. "Ley reglamentaria sobre repartición de tierras ejidales y constitución del patrimonio parcelario ejidal," *DOF*, 31 December 1925, 881–85.
102. "Sesión ordinaria en la Cámara de Senadores" (23 November 1925), in *Recopilación de las principales leyes*, 240–41.
103. The 1934 agrarian code (reproduced in Fabila, *Cinco siglos*, 482–521) transformed the provisional ejido, as Azuela ("La jurisprudencia y la formación del régimen agrario," 351) calls it, into population centers with their own patrimony, juridical standing, and administrative and representative organs under the tutelage of the federal executive, operating parallel to the autonomous municipal governments.

6. The Morelos Laboratory

1. The state legislature confers political status (*categoría política*) on an urban entity, with the specific name varying according to its population size.
2. Womack found in the *Periódico Oficial del Estado de Morelos* 115 provisional grants by the end of 1923 (*Zapata*, 373). According to presidential resolutions reviewed at the AGN, FCNA, for this book, there were 114 provisional resolutions by the end of 1925. When it came to presidential resolutions, President Obregón signed forty between 1922 and 1924 (Salinas, *Land, Liberty, and Water*, 40).
3. Womack, *Zapata*, 369.
4. Warman, *"We Come to Object,"* chapter 4.
5. de la Peña, *Legacy of Promises*, 84–85.
6. See also Ávila Sánchez, *Aspectos históricos*, 78, and Salinas, *Land, Liberty, and Water*, 77, where the author argues that by 1929 "the agrarian reform had radically transformed land tenure in Morelos."
7. In many other states, governors and their state agrarian commissions were less supportive (Gómez, *Historia de la Comisión*, 194).
8. For Peralta's active involvement in the Morelos agrarian reform, see, for example, AGA, Dotación de tierras, exp. 23/2952, leg. 2, f. 34, Amacuzac, Amacuzac, Morelos; AGA, Dotación de tierras, exp. 23/2961, leg. 1, f. 26, Anenecuilco, Villa de Ayala, Morelos; AGA, Dotación de tierras, exp. 23/2953, leg. 1, fs. 44-47, Atlacholoaya, Xochitepec, Morelos; AGA, Dotación de tierras, exp. 23/2954, leg. 2, f. 23, Huazulco, Zacualpan, Morelos; AGA, Dotación de tierras, exp. 23/2981, leg. 1, f. 3, Huejotengo, Ocuituco, Morelos; AGA, Dotación de tierras, exp. 23/2956, leg. 3, f. 29, Popotlán, Zacualpan, Morelos; AGA, Dotación de tierras, exp. 23/2955, leg. 2, f. 38, Tecajec, Yecapixtla, Morelos; and

AGA, Dotación de tierras, exp. 23/3057, leg. 1, f. 1, Yautepec, Yautepec, Morelos. For the other figures, see, for example, Anaya Merchant, "Reconstrucción y modernidad," 29. Quote from Womack, *Zapata*, 367.

9. Villarreal was succeeded by Ramón P. Denegri (from May 1922 to November 1924), who, according to Marte R. Gómez, was a "spotless revolutionary" (Gómez, *Historia de la Comisión*, 205).

10. Mendoza also became CNA president for a brief period (Gómez, *Historia de la Comisión*, 310).

11. Gómez, *Historia de la Comisión*, 183. Other Zapatistas who played important supporting roles included Antonio Díaz Soto y Gama, who not only became head of the pro-agrarian Partido Nacional Agrarista but was also the legal representative for Huejotengo in the village's efforts to petition for a dotación. On Díaz Soto y Gama, see, for example, Castro Martínez, "Antonio Díaz Soto y Gama," 379-408. For his role as Huejotengo legal representative, see AGA, Dotación de tierras, exp. 23/2981, leg. 2, f. 102, Huejotengo, Ocuituco, Morelos. For an analysis of intra-Zapatista politics during this period, see, among others, Damián Rojano, *Las cenizas del zapatismo*, 89-134.

12. AGN, FGO, caja 26, exp. 2, f. 37 (11 September 1920).

13. Womack, *Zapata*, 369.

14. Parres decree no. 5, published in the *Periódico Oficial del Estado de Morelos*, 20 September and 1 October 1920, and reproduced in AGN, FGO, caja 26, exp. 2, fs. 50-53 (4 September 1920).

15. In his study of post-Zapatista land reform in Morelos, Salinas goes so far as to state that there is no "evidence to suggest that villagers considered the Zapatista agrarian reform more legitimate than the redistribution of the 1920s." Salinas, *Land, Liberty, and Water*, 61.

16. AGA, Dotación de tierras, exp. 23/2980, leg. 1, fs. 5-6, Tetelcingo, Cuautla, Morelos.

17. AGN, FCNA, caja 6, vol. 29, fs. 61-67 (Ocuituco); AGA, Restitución de tierras, exp. 24/2994, leg. 9, f. 215, Ocuituco, Ocuituco, Morelos; AGA, Dotación de tierras, exp.23/3052, leg. 1, f. 2-3, leg. 4, f. 2-3, San Miguel Huajintlán, Amacuzac, Morelos; AGN, FCNA, caja 10, vol. 40, fs. 177-82 (Huajintlán); and de la Peña, *Legacy of Promises*, 79, for Atlatlahucan and the unresolved nature of these petitions.

18. AGA, Dotación de tierras, exp. 23/2955, leg. 1, fs. 34-35 (26 January 1921), Tecajec, Yecapixtla, Morelos.

19. de la Peña, *Legacy of Promises*, 79.

20. In June 1922 Amacuzac became the first Morelos village to obtain a positive presidential resolution. AGN, FCNA, caja 2, vol. 11, fs. 3-5 (8 June 1922).
21. On returning landowners in the winter of 1919-20, see Womack, *Zapata*, 353-55. On Barrios being a Zapatista, see Gómez, *Historia de la Comisión*, 197. The accord can be found in AGN, FGO, caja 26, exp. 2, f. 36 (30 October 1920).
22. AGN, FGO, caja 26, exp. 2, fs. 50-53 (4 September 1920). A few examples of these certificates can be found in the Morelos government digital archive: http://marcojuridico.morelos.gob.mx/archivos/decretos_ejecutivo/pdf/DTENEXAYMO.pdf.
23. For the number of decrees issued by Parres giving population centers political status, see Ávila Sánchez, *Aspectos históricos*, 73. According to the Secretaría de Agricultura y Fomento, CNA presidential resolutions reviewed from caja 2, vol. 11 (1922), to caja 15, vol. 58 (1946), a total of 114 provisional possessions had been granted by 1925.
24. Circular 27 (24 July 1917), reproduced in Fabila, *Cinco siglos*, 278-79.
25. *SJF*, época 5, tomo 2, pp. 271-76 (31 January 1918); *SJF*, época 5, tomo 2, pp. 305-8 (2 February 1918); and *SJF*, época 5, tomo 2, pp. 963-65 (21 March 1918). See also the examples from San Luis Potosí in Escobar Ohmstede, "Cambios en el paisaje hidroagrario," 292-93.
26. Circular 40 (6 October 1920), reproduced in Fabila, *Cinco siglos*, 294-95.
27. AGN, FCNA, caja 10, vol. 39, fs. 294-300 (30 December 1926). Similarly, María Portillo de Diez de Sollano, owner of the El Puente hacienda, argued that the petitioners did not have political status because they were hacienda peons who lived on her property (AGN, FCNA, caja 2, vol. 12, fs. 34-36, 4 November 1922).
28. ACSCJN, exp. 1851 (1921) Viuda e Hijos de Manuel V. Vidal against San José Vista Hermosa's political recognition.
29. AGN, FCNA, caja 8, vol. 33, fs. 71-74 (11 November 1926).
30. See also the case of San Miguel Ixtlilco, a hamlet that received pueblo status in November 1921, then petitioned for a grant, and received a positive resolution only five months later (AGN, FCNA, caja 8, vol. 33, fs. 71-74); and the 22 December 1921 petition by Tlalayo (Axochiapan) appears in AGN, FCNA, caja 12, vol. 49, fs. 57-62 (6 October 1927) and AGN, FCNA, caja 11, vol. 43, fs. 52-57 (21 April 1927). Haciendas owned by Luis García Pimentel included Santa Clara, Tenango, and San Ignacio (Womack, *Zapata*, 391). The García Pimentel family maintained on separate occasions that neither Quebrantadero nor Tlalayo were pue-

blos; rather, they were merely ranchos created on their property. For Quebrantadero (Axochiapan), see AGN, FCNA, caja 12, vol. 49, fs. 183-88 (20 October 1927); for Ixtlilco (Tepalcingo), AGN, FCNA, caja 8, vol. 33, fs. 71-74 (11 November 1926); and for Tlalayo (Axochiapan), AGN, FCNA, caja 12, vol. 49, fs. 57-62 (6 October 1927).

31. "Decreto reformando los artículos 7°, 8° y 9° de la ley de 6 de enero de 1915" (19 September 1916), reproduced in Fabila, *Cinco siglos*, 250-52.
32. Circular 31 (8 October 1917), in Fabila, *Cinco siglos*, 282-83.
33. Circular 32 bis. (31 October 1917), in Fabila, *Cinco siglos*, 285.
34. Circular 39 (7 August 1920), in Fabila, *Cinco siglos*, 293-94.
35. For land grant expansions see, for instance, Cuautlixco (Cuautla), AGN, FCNA, caja 2, vol. 13, fs. 15-17; Tetelilla (Jonacatepec), AGN, FCNA, caja 3, vol. 16, fs. 45-46; Chapultepec (Cuernavaca), AGN, FCNA, caja 5, vol. 24, fs. 105-9; Huatecalco (Tlaltizapán), AGN, FCNA, caja 8, vol. 33, fs. 6-10; Tlaltizapán (Tlaltizapán), AGN, FCNA, caja 8, vol. 33, fs. 11-16; Ixtlilco (Tepalcingo), AGN, FCNA, caja 8, vol. 33, fs. 71-74; Huitchila (Tepalcingo), AGN, FCNA, caja 8, vol. 33, fs. 75-78; Xalostoc (Ayala); AGN, FCNA, caja 8, vol. 33, fs. 79-82; Amilcingo (Zacualpan de Amilpas), AGN, FCNA, caja 8, vol. 33, fs. 83-88; Chalcatzingo (Jantetelco), AGN, FCNA, caja 9, vol. 34, fs. 83-88; Jantetelco (Jantetelco), AGN, FCNA, caja 9, vol. 34, fs. 89-94; Jonacatepec (Jonacatepec), AGN, FCNA, caja 9, vol. 35, fs. 166-72; Xochitepec (Cuernavaca), AGN, FCNA, caja 9, vol. 35, fs. 247-52; Tlacotepec (Zacualpan de Amilpas), AGN, FCNA, caja 10, vol. 40, fs. 152-58; Chisco (Jojutla), AGN, FCNA, caja 10, vol. 40, fs. 189-94; Calderón (Cuautla), AGN, FCNA, caja 11, vol. 42, fs. 114-20; Atlatlahucan (Yautepec), AGN, FCNA, caja 11, vol. 43, fs. 38-42; San Miguel Ixtlilco (Tepalcingo), AGN, FCNA, caja 11, vol. 43, fs. 52-57; Totolapan (Yautepec), AGN, FCNA, caja 11, vol. 43, fs. 58-61; and Tilzapotla (Puente de Ixtla), AGN, FCNA, caja 11, vol. 45, fs. 217-22.
36. AGA, Dotación de tierras, exp. 23/2954, leg. 2, fs. 17-19 (8 February 1922), Huazulco, Zacualpan, Morelos. For Zacualpan (Jiutepec), see AGN, FCNA, caja 12, vol. 50, fs. 72-81 (10 November 1927).
37. Gómez, *Historia de la Comisión*, 257.
38. Gómez, *Historia de la Comisión*, 257.
39. Hernández Hernández, for example, argues that landowners obstructed justice, but she cannot identify a single case during this period in which the Supreme Court did not rule against landowners. See Hernández Hernández "La querella por la tierra y el agua."
40. Vélez et al., *Dos escritos dirigidos*, 51.

41. There are very few district court records from this period in the Casa de la Cultura in Morelos. Figures for the suits sent to the Supreme Court for review can be found in the digitized files of the ACSCJN. The Morelos district court denied the following amparos: ACSCJN, exp. 532, Ramón Álvarez against the provisional possession for Jiutepec, 6 January 1921; exp. 246, María Escandón de Bush against the survey for the Cuautla dotación, 7 October 1921; exp. 247, María Escandón de Bush against the provisional possession for the Cuautla dotación, 25 October 1921; exp. 252, Luis García Pimentel against the provisional possession for Tepalcingo, 12 November 1921; exp. 1851, Viuda e hijos de Manuel V. Vidal against the political status of San José Vista Hermosa, 13 May 1921; exp. 2499, Manuel Araoz against the Atlacholoaya dotación, 20 February 1923; exp. 1811, María Portillo de Diez de Sollano against the Xochitepec provisional possession, 31 May 1921; exp. 3080, Araoz against the San Miguel Treinta dotación, 21 September 1921; exp. 273, Santos Pérez Cortina against the Mazatepec dotación, 9 December 1921; exp. 333, María Escandón de Bush against the provisional possession of Cuautlixco, 28 January 1921; exp. 1660, María Portillo de Diez de Sollano against the provisional possession for Alpuyeca, 11 May 1921; exp. 1862, Viuda e hijos de Manuel Vidal against the provisional possession for Alpuyeca, 15 April 1921; exp. 2678, Cía. de las Fábricas de Papel de San Rafael against the provisional possession for Tlalmimilulpan, 30 August 1924; and exp. 1181, Luis García Pimentel against the provisional possession of Tetelilla 1924.

    The Morelos District Court granted the following amparos: ACSCJN, exp. 2546, María Portillo de Diez de de Sollano against the Atlacholoaya dotación, 27 and 29 June 1922; and exp. 1181, Luis García Pimentel against the Tetelilla dotación, (partially granted) 31 December 1925.
42. "Decreto abrogando la Ley de Ejidos de 28 de diciembre de 1920" (22 November 1921), reproduced in Fabila, *Cinco siglos*, 309-10.
43. ACSCJN, exp. 273 (1922).
44. ACSCJN, exp. 2499 (1922), Manuel Araoz against the provisional possession granted to Atlacholoaya. For other examples, see 1660 (1921), María Portillo de Diez de Sollano against the provisional possession granted to Alpuyeca; 7 (1923), Maurilio Fabre against the dotación for Totolapan; 729 (1924), Manuel Araoz against the dotación for Cuautla; 2546 (1922), María Portillo de Diez de Sollano against the Atlacholoaya grant; 1862 (1921), Viuda e hijos de Manuel V. Vidal against the provisional possession granted to Santa María Alpuyeca.

45. AGN, FSAF-CNA, caja 3, vol. 16, fs. 45-46 (24 December 1923); ACSCJN, exp. 1181 principal (1924) and exp. 1181 incidente (1924).
46. ACSCJN, exp. 1181 principal (1924) and exp. 1181 incidente (1924).
47. See also the María Escandón de Bush amparo against the provisional possessions granted to Cuautla and Santa Ana Cuautlixco, ACSCJN, exp. 333 (1921) and exp. 247 (1924), respectively; Luis García Pimentel against the Tepalcingo provisional possession, 252 (1924); María Portillo de Diez de Sollano against the Xochitepec provisional possession, 1811 (1921); and San Rafael paper factory against the Tlalmimilulpan provisional possession, 2678 (1924).
48. Hall, "Álvaro Obregón," 220, citing Warman, . . . *Y venimos a contradecir*, 151, 156-57.
49. These totals are from AGN, FCNA, presidential resolutions from caja 2, vol. 11 (1922), to caja 15, vol. 58 (1946).
50. AGN, FCNA, caja 9, vol. 36, fs. 138-49 (presidential resolution of 23 September 1926; petition in December 1921).
51. Villagers petitioned on 23 March 1923; the governor's resolution was on 28 September 1929; the presidential resolution was granted on 7 November 1929. See AGA, Restitución de tierras, exp. 24/10485, leg. 4, fs. 35, 70-73, 200, 163-72, 199, 229-31, and leg. 5, f. 148, Santa María Ahuacatitlán, Cuernavaca, Morelos.
52. de la Peña, *Legacy of Promises*, 79-82, 84.
53. AGA, Dotación de tierras, exp. 23/2981, leg. 2, fs. 63-65 (11 July 1924), Huejotengo, Ocuituco, Morelos.
54. See, for example, the case of San Andrés Cuauhtempan, AGN, FCNA, caja 12, vol. 49, fs. 11-16 (6 October 1927).
55. See, for example, the cases of San Miguel Ixtlilco (Tepalcingo) (AGN, FCNA, caja 11, vol. 43, fs. 52-57, 21, April 1927); Tecomalco (Villa de Ayala) (AGN, FCNA, caja 5, vol. 26, fs. 185-88, 9, July 1925); and Tenextepango (Villa de Ayala) (AGN, FCNA, caja 5, vol. 26, fs. 185-88, 9 July 1925).
56. Crespo, "Introducción," 28.
57. AGA, Restitución de tierras, exp. 24/2994, leg. 9, fs. 217-29 (14 November 1922), Ocuituco, Ocuituco, Morelos.
58. The Franco quote is from Brunk, *Posthumous Career*, 55. Most other villagers used exactly the same text. See, for example, the following petitions from Morelos: AGA, Restitución de tierras, exp. 24/3020, leg. 4, f. 11, Amayuca, Jantetelco; AGA, Dotación de tierras, exp. 23/3008, leg. 1, fs. 235-37, Atlatlahucan, Atlatlahucan; AGA, Restitución de tierras, exp. 24/14833, leg. 3, f. 7, Emiliano Zapata (formerly San Fran-

cisco Zacualpan), Emiliano Zapata (formerly Jiutepec); AGA, Dotación de tierras, exp. 23/2967, leg. 1, f. 7, Eusebio Jáuregui (formerly Santa Inés), Cuautla; AGA, Restitución de tierras, exp. 24/2994, leg. 9, f. 54, Ocuituco, Ocuituco; AGA, Restitución de tierras, exp. 24/3094, leg. 5, f. 7, Tlamomulco, Yecapixtla; and AGA, Dotación de tierras, exp. 23/3057, leg. 1, fs. 18-19, Yautepec, Yautepec. For José Robles's role in the 1915 boundary marking, see AGA, Dotación de tierras, exp. 23/2961, leg. 1, f. 285, Anenecuilco, Villa de Ayala, Morelos.

59. AGA, Dotación de tierras, exp. 23/2960, leg. 1, f.1 (11 September 1920), Villa de Ayala, Villa de Ayala, Morelos.
60. AGA, Restitución de tierras, 24/2961, leg. 8, fs. 20-21 (28 September 1920), Anenecuilco, Villa de Ayala, Morelos.
61. Report by CNA delegate Ing. Regino Guzmán, AGA, Dotación de tierras, exp. 23/2961, leg. 1, fs. 2-4 (28 October 1920), Anenecuilco, Villa de Ayala, Morelos; and report by CNA delegate José M. Nuñez, AGA, Dotación de tierras, exp. 23/2961, leg. 1, fs. 170-72 (11 May 1923). On Serafín Robles, see Valentín López González, *Los Compañeros de Zapata*, 214-16.
62. AGA, Restitución de tierras, exp. 24/2961, leg. 8, fs. 20-21, Anenecuilco, Villa de Ayala, Morelos. See also in Instituto Estatal de Documentación de Morelos (IEDM), Gobierno Tierras (GT), Villa de Ayala y Anenecuilco, ejidos, 1920, 11/021/97, caja 740, leg. 7.
63. See also Rojano, *Las cenizas*, 66.
64. Report by CNA delegate Ing. Regino Guzmán, AGA, Dotación de tierras, exp. 23/2961, leg. 1, fs. 2-4 (28 October 1920), Anenecuilco, Villa de Ayala, Morelos. On 30 November 1920 the district court declared that the procedural errors had not been substantive and denied the amparo; AGA, Dotación de tierras, exp. 23/2961, leg. 8, f. 31. Sometime before December 1920, Coahuixtla and El Hospital hacienda owner Julita Pagaza, widow of Vicente Alonso, also filed an amparo petition, which the district court denied as well. See Otero Muñoz, "La parcelación ejidal y sus efectos sociales," 139-40.
65. "Informe complementario sobre la tramitación del expediente San Miguel Anenecuilco," in AGA, Dotación de tierras, exp. 23/2961, leg. 1, fs. 37-39.
66. AGA, Dotación de tierras, exp. 23/2961, leg. 1, f. 88 (27 February 1923), Anenecuilco, Villa de Ayala, Morelos.
67. Womack, *Zapata*, 372. On the relationship between Sotelo Inclán and Franco and the Anenecuilco deeds, see Brunk, *Posthumous Career*, 119-21.

68. AGA, Restitución de tierras, exp. 24/2961, leg. 8, f. 7 (26 September 1920), Anenecuilco, Villa de Ayala, Morelos.
69. AGA, Restitución de tierras, exp. 24/2961, leg. 8, f. 2 (26 September 1920), Anenecuilco, Villa de Ayala, Morelos.
70. Sánchez Beltrán, *Anenecuilco, tierra de Zapata*, 35-36.
71. "Si los pierdes, compadre, te secas colgado de un casahuate [*sic*]" (Sotelo Inclán, *Raíz y razón*, 203). A cazahuate is a type of morning glory tree native to Mexico.
72. Sotelo Inclán, *Raíz y razón*, 203, and Womack, *Zapata*, 371-72.
73. Sotelo Inclán, *Raíz y razón*, 203; translation by Womack, *Zapata*, 372.
74. Zapata, before his death, allegedly told Franco that if he were to go missing one day, Franco should if necessary take the documents to the Carrancistas. Sotelo Inclán, *Raíz y razón*, 204, and Womack, *Zapata*, 372.
75. Gómez, *Historia de la Comisión*, 262. For Barrios's biography, see *Diccionario de generales de la revolución*, 1:120-22.
76. AGA, Dotación de tierras, exp. 23/2961, leg. 1, f. 67, Anenecuilco, Villa de Ayala, Morelos.
77. AGN, FCNA, caja 4, vol. 20, fs. 108-11 (9 October 1924), Santa Inés Oacalco, Yautepec. Had Franco and Robles delivered the titles before the agrarian commission sent the case to the CNA, they perhaps could have requested changing the petition from dotación to a restitution—as was the case with Santa Inés Oacalco, where the pueblo representatives first sought a dotación but later changed their petition to a restitution.
78. Gómez, *Historia de la Comisión*, 311-12, quote from 312.
79. AGA, Dotación de tierras, 23/2961, leg. 6, fs. 209-13, Anenecuilco, Villa de Ayala, Morelos.
80. Womack, *Zapata*, 373, citing Sotelo, *Raíz y razón*, 205-6.
81. AGA, Dotación de tierras, exp. 23/2961, leg. 1, f. 67 (29 January 1923), Anenecuilco, Villa de Ayala, Morelos.
82. AGA, Dotación de tierras, exp. 23/2961, leg. 1, f. 96 (28 February 1923), Anenecuilco, Villa de Ayala, Morelos.
83. AGA, Dotación de tierras, exp. 23/2961, leg. 1, f. 173, quote from leg. 5, fs. 15-16 (11 April 1923), Anenecuilco, Villa de Ayala, Morelos.
84. AGA, Dotación de tierras, exp. 23/2961, leg. 1, fs. 291-93; leg. 6, fs. 209-13 (7 January 1944), Anenecuilco, Villa de Ayala, Morelos.
85. AGA, Dotación de tierras, exp. 23/2961, leg. 1, fs. 223-24 (7 November 1929), Anenecuilco, Villa de Ayala, Morelos.

86. AGA, Dotación de tierras, exp. 23/2961, leg. 6, fs. 209-13 (7 January 1944), Anenecuilco, Villa de Ayala, Morelos.
87. AGA, Dotación de tierras, exp. 23/2961, leg. 2, fs. 62-63 (16 July 1954); leg. 2, fs. 69-71 (11 February 1956); and leg. 6, exp. 209-13 (7 January 1944), Anenecuilco, Villa de Ayala, Morelos.
88. Hernández Chávez, *Anenecuilco*, 25-26, 30.
89. Warman, *We Come to Object*, 136.
90. de la Peña, *Legacy of Promises*, 80, quote from 84. See also AGA, Dotación de tierras, exp. 23/3008, leg. 1, fs. 3, 8, 152, 158, 195, 197, 238-39, 323, 369, 437, Atlatlahucan, Atlatlahucan, Morelos. For a detailed account of intervillage conflicts during the Zapatista land reform, see Baitenmann, "Zapata's Justice."
91. AGA, Dotación de tierras, exp. 23/2954, leg. 2, fs. 5-9 (22 December 1922), Huazulco, Zacualpan, Morelos.
92. AGN, FCNA, caja 2, vol. 12, fs. 34-36 (4 November 1922).
93. AGN, FCNA, caja 3, vol. 15, fs. 33-35 (8 November 1923).
94. AGN, FCNA, caja 5, vol. 24, fs. 62-65 (7 May 1925).
95. AGA, Dotación de tierras, exp. 23/2952, leg. 1, f. 49 (20 December 1919); fs. 66-69 (10 January 1921); fs. 72-76 (18 May 1921); fs. 108-11 (16 December 1920); leg. 2, fs. 32-33 (2 June 1922), Amacuzac, Amacuzac, Morelos. Quote from AGA, Dotación de tierras, exp. 23/2952, leg. 2, fs. 32-33.
96. See also Salinas, *Land, Liberty, and Water*, 85.
97. Valladares, *Cuando el agua se esfumó*, 60-63. For conflicts among villages that aquired land and water rights, see also pages 87-110 in the same work.
98. See, for example, the hydrologic study for the state of Morelos done by the Geological Department (Departamento de Exploraciones y Estudios Geológicos) of the Ministry of Industry, Commerce, and Labor, in AHA, FAN, caja 491, exp. 5223, leg. 1, fs. 3-4 (26 September 1923).
99. See, for example, Valladares, *Cuando el agua se esfumó*.
100. Valladares, *Cuando el agua se esfumó*, 55-59.
101. Valladares, *Cuando el agua se esfumó*, 68, and AGA, Accesión y dotación de aguas, exp. 33/709, leg. 1, f. 1 (14 May 1924), San Mateo Tlaltenango, Cuajimalpa de Morelos, Federal District.
102. AGN, FSAF-CNA, caja 10, vol. 39, fs. 46-56 (2 December 1926). For the history of water distribution in the later part of the 1920s, see Ávila Sánchez, *Aspectos históricos*, 79-83; Salinas, *Land, Liberty, and Water*; and Valladares, *Cuando el agua se esfumó*.

103. For the different meanings of Zapata's legacy, see Brunk, *Posthumous Career* and "Remembering Emiliano Zapata."

7. Epilogue

1. Translation by Brunk, *Posthumous Career*, 66. See also Silva Herzog, *El agrarismo mexicano*, 309–10.
2. Brunk, "Remembering Emiliano Zapata," 464–65.
3. AGA, Dotación de tierras, exp. 23/4041, leg. 6, fs. 11-18 (19 May 1954), Buenavista de Zapata/Barrio de Ixcamilpa, Ixcamilpa de Guerrero, Puebla.
4. Marván Laborde, *Nueva edición del Diario de Debates*, 1:1004-5. The other four documents, according to Marván, were Francisco I. Madero's Plan de San Luis, Luis Cabrera's 1912 speech to Congress, Venustiano Carranza's additions to the Plan de Guadalupe, and the 6 January 1915 law.
5. Kourí, "Interpreting" and "La invención del ejido." For an interesting legal comparison of the Zapatista and Constitutionalist reforms, see Ruiz Massieu, "Principios agrarios."
6. Chávez Padrón, *El proceso social agrario*, 45.
7. Reprinted in Lemus, *Derecho agrario mexicano*, 227-33.
8. Translation and brackets in Womack, *Zapata*, 228-29, citing Magaña, *Emiliano Zapata*, 4:314.
9. For the Zapatista village representatives, see the "Ley relativa a los representantes de los pueblos en materia agraria" (3 February 1917) in AGN-FGO, caja 19, exp. 6, f. 54 (also reprinted in Espejel, Olivera, and Rueda, *Emiliano Zapata. Antología*, 369-72). For the Constitutionalist CPAs, see circular 19 (20 March 1917) and circular 22 (18 April 1917), both reprinted in Fabila, *Cinco siglos*, 267-69 and 272-73, respectively. See also Baitenmann, "'El que parte.'"
10. Zapatistas tried to reestablish the higher courts that had shut down during the revolutionary fighting. For example, when Mexico City was controlled by the Aguascalientes Convention, between December 1914 and May 1915, the Zapatistas in charge reestablished the Federal District's judicial system. See Hernández Chávez, *Breve historia de Morelos*, 176. And in the summer of 1915 Gustavo Baz, the provisional governor of Mexico State, issued a decree reestablishing the Superior Tribunal of Justice. See Colonel Gustavo Baz to the President of the Sovereign Revolutionary Convention, AGN, FCR, caja 8, exp. 2, f. 20 (2 July 1915). It was only later and only in

theory, when urban intellectuals—many with anarchist tendencies—took over the Zapatista leadership, that the purpose for these special tribunals shifted to their serving as municipal-level "people's tribunals" with the judicial authority to hear and resolve all land disputes.

11. In 1937, however, President Lázaro Cárdenas, responding to manifold village petitions, reformed Constitutional article 27 to make the executive responsible for boundary conflicts between pueblos with communal lands. See Baitenmann, "Ejerciendo la justicia fuera de los tribunales."

BIBLIOGRAPHY

Archives

Archivo Central de la Suprema Corte de Justicia de la Nación, Mexico City (ACSCJN).
    Fondo Suprema Corte de Justicia de la Nación (FSCJN)
Archivo General Agrario, Mexico City (AGA).
Archivo General de la Nación, Mexico City (AGN).
    Fondo Archivo de Buscas y Traslado de Tierras (FB)
    Fondo Colección Revolución, Sección Emiliano Zapata (FCR-EZ)
    Fondo Colección Revolución, Revolución y Régimen Constitucionalista (FCR-RRC)
    Fondo Genovevo de la O (FGO)
    Fondo Gobernación, Legajos (FG Leg)
    Fondo Gobernación, sin sección (FG s/s)
    Fondo Gobernación Período Revolucionario (FGPR)
    Fondo Junta Protectora de las Clases Menesterosas (FJPCM)
    Fondo Justicia (FJ)
    Fondo Leyes y Circulares de Fomento (FLCF)
    Fondo Nacionalización y Desamortización de Bienes (FNDB)
    Fondo Secretaría de Justicia (FSJ)
    Fondo Soberana Convención Revolucionaria (FSCR)
    Fondo Francisco I. Madero (FM)
    Fondo Secretaría de Agricultura y Fomento, Comisión Nacional Agraria (FSAF-CNA)
Archivo General del Estado de Veracruz, Xalapa (AGEV).
    Archivo de la Comisión Agraria Mixta (ACAM)
    Colección de Leyes, Decretos y Circulares (CLDC)
Archivo Histórico del Agua, Mexico City (AHA).
    Fondo Aguas Nacionales (FAN)

Fondo Aprovechamientos Superficiales (FAS)
Archivo Histórico de la Universidad Nacional Autónoma de México, Mexico City (AHUNAM).
Archivo Gildardo y Octavio Magaña Cerda (AGM)
Fondo León de la Barra (FLB)
Centro de Estudios de Historia de México Carso. Fundación Carlos Slim, Mexico City (CEHM-Carso).
Fondo Jenaro Amezcua (FJA)
Instituto Estatal de Documentación de Morelos, Cuernavaca (IEDM).
Gobierno Tierras (GT)
Registro Agrario Nacional-Veracruz, Xalapa (RAN-Ver).
Archivo del Cuerpo Consultivo Agrario (ACCA)
Universidad Iberoamericana-Biblioteca Francisco Xavier Clavijero, Acervos Históricos, Mexico City (UIA).
Colección Porfirio Díaz (CPD)

Periodicals and Serials

Diario de Debates de la Cámara de Diputados del Congreso de los Estados Unidos Mexicanos
Diario del Hogar
Diario Oficial de la Federación (DOF)
Gaceta del Gobierno (State of Mexico)
Gaceta Oficial del Estado de Veracruz
El Imparcial
El País
La Patria
Periódico Oficial del Estado de Morelos
Regeneración
Semanario Judicial de la Federación (SJF)

Published Works
Abbreviations

CIESAS	Centro de Investigaciones y Estudios Superiores en Antropología Social
FCE	Fondo de Cultura Económica
HAHR	*Hispanic American Historical Review*
INAH	Instituto Nacional de Antropología e Historia
INEHRM	Instituto Nacional de Estudios Históricos de la Revolución Mexicana

RAN   Registro Agrario Nacional
SCJN   Suprema Corte de Justicia de la Nación
SEP   Secretaría de Educación Pública
UAA   Universidad Autónoma de Aguascalientes
UABJO   Universidad Autónoma Benito Juárez de Oaxaca
UAEM   Universidad Autónoma del Estado de Morelos
UAM   Universidad Autónoma Metropolitana
UNAM   Universidad Nacional Autónoma de México

Aboites Aguilar, Luis. *El agua de la nación: una historia política de México (1888-1946)*. Mexico City: CIESAS, 1998.

Aboites Aguilar, Luis, and Alba Morales Cosme. "Amecameca, 1922: Ensayo sobre centralización política y Estado Nacional en México." *Historia Mexicana* 49, no. 1 (1999): 55-93.

Aboites Aguilar, Luis, Diana Birrichaga Gardida, and Jorge Alfredo Garay Trejo. "El manejo de las aguas mexicanas en el siglo XX." In *El agua de México: causes y encauses*, edited by Blanca Jiménez Cisneros, María Luisa Trejo Torregrosa y Armentia, and Luis Aboites Aguilar, 21-49. Mexico City: Academia Mexicana de Ciencias and Comisión Nacional del Agua, 2010.

Acosta, Gabriela, and Arnulfo Embriz. "Territorios indios en la región purhépecha, 1915-1940." In *Estudios campesinos en el Archivo General Agrario*, vol. 1, edited by Antonio Escobar Ohmstede, 119-95. Mexico City: CIESAS and RAN, 1998.

Actas del congreso constituyente del estado libre de México, revisadas por el mismo congreso e impresas de su orden. Mexico City: Imprenta Martín Rivera, 1824.

Alanís Boyzo, Rodolfo. *Historia de la revolución en el estado de México: los zapatistas en el poder*. Toluca: Gobierno del Estado de México, 1987.

Amaya, Luis Fernando. *La Soberana Convención Revolucionaria*. Mexico City: Trillas, 1966.

Amparo interpuesto por Carlos Markassuza contra actos del C. Presidente de la República y Comisión Nacional Agraria: sentencia dictada por el C. Juez Tercero Supernumerario de Distrito del Distrito Federal. Mexico City: Sobretiro de la Revista Jurídica de la Escuela Libre de Derecho, 1922.

Anaya Merchant, Luis. "Reconstrucción y modernidad: los límites de la transformación social en el Morelos posrevolucionario." In *Historia de Morelos: tierra, gente, tiempos del Sur*, vol. 8, *Política y sociedad en el Morelos posrevolucionario y contemporáneo*, edited by María Victoria Crespo and Luis Anaya Merchant, 25–54. Cuernavaca: Congreso del Estado de Morelos (LI Legislatura), Gobierno de Morelos, Instituto de Cultura de Morelos, UAEM, and Ayuntamiento de Cuernavaca, 2010.

Anaya Pérez, Marco Antonio. *Rebelión y revolución en Chalco-Amecameca, Estado de México, 1821-1921*, vol. 2. Mexico City: INEHRM and Universidad Autónoma de Chapingo, 1997.

Ankerson, Dudley. "Saturnino Cedillo: A Traditional Caudillo in San Luis Potosí." In Brading, *Caudillo and Peasant*, 140–68.

Anna, Timothy. *Forging Mexico, 1821-1835*. Lincoln: University of Nebraska Press, 2001.

Armienta Calderón, Gonzalo M. "Algunos aspectos relevantes de la competencia en materia agraria." *Revista de los Tribunales Agrarios* 3, no. 8 (1995): 7–42.

Arrioja Díaz Viruell, Luis Alberto. "Conflictos por tierras y pesquisas documentales en el Valle de Oaxaca, 1912." In *Conflictos por la tierra en Oaxaca: de las reformas borbónicas a la reforma agrarian*, edited by Luis Alberto Arrioja Díaz Viruell and Carlos Sánchez Silva, 185–213. Zamora: El Colegio de Michoacán and UABJO, 2012.

Arrom, Silvia Marina. "Changes in Mexican Family Law in the Nineteenth Century: The Civil Codes of 1870 and 1884." *Journal of Family History* 10, no. 3 (1985): 305–17.

Ávila Espinosa, Felipe Arturo. "La batalla por los símbolos. El uso oficial de Zapata." In *Historia de Morelos: tierra, gente, tiempos del Sur*, vol. 7, *El zapatismo*, edited by Felipe Ávila Espinosa, 405–40. Cuernavaca: Poder Ejecutivo del Estado de Morelos, Comisión de Colaboración de Festejos del Bicentenario de la Independencia de Nuestro País y Centenario de la Revolución Mexicana, Congreso del Estado de Morelos-L Legislatura, Universidad Autónoma del Estado de Morelos, Ayuntamiento de Cuernavaca, and Instituto Cultural Morelos, 2010.

———. "Los conflictos internos en el zapatismo." In *Los historiadores y la historia para el siglo XXI: homenaje a Eric J. Hobsbawm 25 años de la licenciatura de historia*, edited by Gumersindo Vera Hernández, et al., 401–25. Mexico City: Conaculta and INAH, 2006.

———. "El Consejo Ejecutivo de la República y el proyecto de legislación estatal zapatista." *Estudios de Historia Moderna y Contemporánea de México* 16 (1998): 53–77.

———. "El Consejo Ejecutivo de la República y el proyecto de legislación estatal zapatista." In *Historia de Morelos: tierra, gente, tiempos del Sur*, vol.

7, *El zapatismo*, edited by Felipe Ávila Espinosa, 249-71. Cuernavaca: Congreso del Estado de Morelos et. al., 2010.

———. *Las corrientes revolucionarias y la Soberana Convención*. Aguascalientes: H. Congreso del Estado de Aguascalientes (LXII Legislatura), Universidad Autónoma de Aguascalientes, El Colegio de México, INEHRM, and Secretaría de Educación Pública, 2014.

———. *La justicia durante el porfiriato y la revolución, 1898-1914*. Vol. 5, *El problema agrario a fines del Porfiriato y en los comienzos de la Revolución*. Mexico City: SCJN, 2010.

———. *Los orígenes del zapatismo*. Mexico City: El Colegio de México and UNAM, 2001.

Ávila Quijas, Aquiles Omar, Jesús Gómez Serrano, Antonio Escobar Ohmstede, and Martín Sánchez Rodríguez, eds. *Negociaciones, acuerdos y conflictos en México, siglos XIX y XX: agua y tierra*. Zamora: El Colegio de Michoacán, CIESAS, UAA, 2009.

Ávila Sánchez, Héctor. *Aspectos históricos de la formación de regiones en el estado de Morelos*. Mexico City: UNAM, 2002.

Avilés Fabila, René. *El gran solitario del palacio*. Buenos Aires: Compañía General Fabril Editora, 1971.

Azuela de la Cueva, Antonio. "Ciudadanía y gestión urbana en los poblados rurales de los Tuxtlas." *Estudios Sociológicos* 13, no. 39 (1995): 485-500.

———. "La jurisprudencia y la formación del régimen agrario en el siglo veinte mexicano." In *Los pueblos indígenas y la Constitución de 1917: una revisión del pasado hacia el presente*, 319-461. Mexico City: SCJN, 2015.

———. "El problema con las ideas que detrás." In Kourí, *En busca de Molina Enríquez*, 79-125.

Baitenmann, Helga. "Ejerciendo la justicia fuera de los tribunales: de las reivindicaciones decimonónicas a las restituciones de la reforma agraria." *Historia Mexicana* 66, no. 4 (2017): 2013-72.

———. "'El que parte y reparte...' Los arreglos institucionales locales a cargo de los repartos agrarios (siglo XIX-1927)." In *El mundo rural mexicano en la transición del siglo XIX al siglo XX*, edited by Antonio Escobar Ohmstede, Zulema Trejo Contreras, and José Alfredo Rangel Silva, 59-84. Mexico City: CIESAS, El Colegio de San Luis, and Institut de Recherche pour le Développement-México, 2017.

———. "Las paradojas de las conquistas revolucionarias: municipio y reforma agraria en el México contemporáneo." *Gestión y Política Pública* 10, no. 1 (2001): 103-23.

———. "Popular Participation in State Formation: Land Reform in Revolutionary Mexico." *Journal of Latin American Studies* 43 (2011): 1–31.

———. "Rural Agency and State Formation in Postrevolutionary Veracruz." PhD diss., New School of Social Research, 1997.

———. "Zapata's Justice: Land and Water Conflict Resolution in Revolutionary Mexico (1914–1916)." *Journal of Latin America Studies* 51, no. 4 (2019): 801–28.

Barrera, Florencio, and Claudio Barrera. "La falsificación de títulos de tierras a principios del siglo XX." *Historias* 72 (2009): 41–63.

Barreto Mark, Carlos. "Entre campesinos, arrendatarios y el Plan de Ayala: recuerdos y testimonios de una revolución." In *A cien años del Plan de Ayala*, edited by Edgar Castro Zapata and Francisco Pineda Gómez, 175–211. Mexico City: Ediciones Era and Colección Fundación Zapata y los Herederos de la Revolución, A.C., 2013.

Barreto Zamudio, Carlos. "La familia García Pimentel y los hacendados frente al reparto agrario." *Inventio* (UAEM) 13, no. 19 (2017): 13–19.

Barrón, Luis. "La 'modernización' revolucionaria del discurso político liberal: el problema agrario entre 1895 y 1929." In *La Revolución Mexicana, 1908–1932*, edited by Ignacio Marván, 102–65. Mexico City: Centro de Investigación y Docencia Económicas, INAH, Conaculta, and FCE, 2010.

Bartra, Armando. *Los herederos de Zapata: movimientos campesinos posrevolucionarios en México, 1920–1980*. Mexico City: Ediciones Era, 1985.

Bassols, Narciso. *La nueva ley agraria, antecedentes*. Mexico City: Editorial Cultura, 1927.

Benson, Nettie Lee. *The Provincial Deputation of Mexico: Harbinger of Provincial Autonomy, Independence, and Federalism*. Austin: University of Texas Press, 1992.

Berumen Félix, Claudia Serafina. "La legislación decimonónica y la Media Luna (San Luis Potosí)." In *Agua y tierra en México, siglos XIX y XX*, vol. 1, edited by Antonio Escobar Ohmstede, Martín Sánchez Rodríguez, and Ana Ma. Gutiérrez Rivas, 103–23. Zamora: El Colegio de Michoacán and El Colegio de San Luis, 2008.

Birrichaga Gardida, Diana. "Administración de tierras y bienes comunales: política, organización territorial y comunidad de los pueblos de Texcoco, 1812–1857." PhD diss., El Colegio de México, 2003.

———. "¿Ejidatarios o comuneros? Los proyectos de restitución de las tierras y aguas comunales en el Estado de México, 1914–1915." In Escobar Ohmstede and Butler, *Mexico in Transition*, 321–53.

———. "Lucha y defensa de los pueblos: el derecho al agua en el centro de México (1856–1868)." In *Formas de descontento y movimientos sociales, siglos XIX y XX*, edited by José Ronzón and Cármen Valdez, 255–81. Mexico City: UAM Azcapotzalco, 2005.

Birrichaga Gardida, Diana, and Alejandra Suárez Dottor. "Entre dos estados: derechos de propiedad y personalidad jurídica de las comunidades hidalguenses, 1856–1900." In *Agua y tierra en México, siglos XIX y XX*, vol. 1, edited by Antonio Escobar Ohmstede, Martín Sánchez Rodríguez, and Ana Ma. Gutiérrez Rivas, 245–67. Zamora: El Colegio de Michoacán and El Colegio de San Luis, 2008.

Blanco Martínez, Mireya, and José Omar Moncada Maya. "El Ministerio de Fomento, impulsor del estudio y el reconocimiento del territorio mexicano (1877–1898)." *Investigaciones Geográficas, Boletín del Instituto de Geografía*, no. 74 (2011): 74–91.

Borah, Woodrow. *Justice by Insurance: The General Indian Court of Colonial Mexico and the Legal Aides of the Half Real.* Berkeley: University of California Press, 1983.

———. "La justificación del Juzgado General de Indios (1595–1603)." In *Memoria del II Congreso de Historia del Derecho Mexicano (1980)*, 147–60. Mexico City: UNAM, 1981.

Brading, David A., ed. *Caudillo and Peasant in the Mexican Revolution.* Cambridge: Cambridge University Press, 1980.

Brunk, Samuel. *¡Emiliano Zapata! Revolution and Betrayal in Mexico.* Albuquerque NM: University of New Mexico Press, 1995.

———. *The Posthumous Career of Emiliano Zapata: Myth, Memory, and Mexico's Twentieth Century.* Austin: University of Texas Press, 2010.

———. "Remembering Emiliano Zapata: Three Moments in the Posthumous Career of the Martyr of Chinameca." *HAHR* 78, no. 3 (1998): 457–90.

———. "'The Sad Situation of Civilians and Soldiers': The Banditry of Zapatismo in the Mexican Revolution." *American Historical Review* 101, no. 2 (1996): 331–53.

———. "Zapata and the City Boys: In Search of a Piece of the Revolution." *HAHR* 73, no. 1 (1993): 33–65.

Buve, Raymundus Thomas Joseph. "Agricultores, dominación política y estructura agraria en la Revolución Mexicana: el caso de Tlaxcala (1910–1918)." *Revista Mexicana de Sociología* 51, no. 2 (1989): 181–236.

———. *El movimiento revolucionario en Tlaxcala.* Mexico City: Universidad Iberoamericana, 1994.

———. "'Neither Carranza nor Zapata!': The Rise and Fall of a Peasant Movement That Tried to Challenge Both, Tlaxcala, 1910–19." In *Riot,*

    Rebellion, and Revolution: Rural Social Conflict in Mexico, edited by Friedrich Katz, 338-75. Princeton: Princeton University Press, 1988.

Cabrera Acevedo, Lucio. "La Revolución Mexicana y la Suprema Corte de Justicia, 1910-1914." In *Diplomacia y revolución. Homenaje a Berta Ulloa*, edited by Anne Staples et al., 195-212. Mexico City: El Colegio de México, 2000.

———. *La Suprema Corte de Justicia en La República Restaurada (1867-1876)*. Mexico City: SCJN, 1989.

———. *La Suprema Corte de Justicia en el primer periodo del porfirismo (1877-1882)*. Mexico City: SCJN, 1990.

———. *La Suprema Corte de Justicia durante el fortalecimiento del porfirismo (1882-1888)*. Mexico City: SCJN, 1991.

———. *La Suprema Corte de Justicia a principios del siglo XX (1901-1914)*. Mexico City: SCJN, 1993.

———. *La Suprema Corte de Justicia durante los años constitucionalistas (1917-1920)*, vol. 1. Mexico City: SCJN, 1995.

Calderón Arozqueta, Rafael. "La formación de profesionales para el desarrollo rural: el caso de la agronomía en México." Master's thesis, UAM Xochimilco, 1993.

Camacho Altamirano, Hortensia. "Los derechos de la propiedad de la tierra y del agua." In *La propiedad rural en México en los siglos XIX y XX*, edited by José Alfredo Rangel Silva and Hortensia Camacho Altamirano, 103-28. San Luis Potosí: El Colegio de San Luis, 2012.

Camacho Pichardo, Gloria. "En pro de los privilegios 'sin excepciones': la desamortización del ejido decimonónico en los pueblos del Estado de México, 1889-1910." In Escobar Ohmstede, Falcón Vega, and Sánchez Rodríguez, *La desamortización*, 251-83.

Carregha Lamadrid, Luz. "En torno a los levantamientos armados en la Huasteca Potosina al inicio del porfiriato." In *El siglo XIX en las Huastecas*, edited by Antonio Escobar Ohmstede and Luz Carregha Lamadrid, 167-84. México City: CIESAS, and Colegio de San Luis, 2002.

Carrillo Cázares, Alberto. "'Chiquisnaquis' un indio escribano, artífice de 'títulos primordiales' (La Piedad siglo XVIII)." *Relaciones* 12, no. 48 (1991), 187-210.

———. *El debate sobre la Guerra Chichimeca, 1531-1585: derecho y política en Nueva España*. Zamora: El Colegio de Michoacán and El Colegio de San Luis, 2000.

Carvajal, Ángel. *Al margen de las resoluciones presidenciales sobre la cuestión agraria. Tesis que para optar al título de abogado presenta Ángel Carvajal, alumno de la facultad de derecho y ciencias sociales (28-11-1928), Universidad Nacional*. Mexico City: Talleres Gráficos de la Nación, 1929.

Casasola, Gustavo. *Historia gráfica de la Revolución Mexicana*, vol. 3. Mexico City: Archivo Casasola Ediciones, 1942.

Castellano Suárez, José Alfredo. *Empeño por una expectativa agraria: experiencia ejidal en el municipio de Acolman, 1915-1940*. Mexico City: INEHRM and Universidad Autónoma Chapingo, 1998.

Castañeda González, Rocío. *Las aguas de Atlixco. Estado, haciendas, fábricas y pueblos, 1880-1920*. Mexico City: Consejo Nacional del Agua, Archivo Histórico del Agua, CIESAS, and El Colegio de México, 2005.

Castillo Palma, Norma Angélica. "La revolución en la memoria: las haciendas y el general Herminio Chavarría en Iztapalapa." *Signos históricos* 11, no. 21 (2009): 170-81.

Castro, Pedro. *Álvaro Obregón: fuego y cenizas de la Revolución Mexicana*. Mexico City: Ediciones Era, 2009.

Castro Gutiérrez, Felipe. "Los ires y devenires del fundo legal de los pueblos de indios." In *De la historia económica a la historia social y cultural. Homenaje a Gisela von Wobeser*, edited by María del Pilar Martínez López-Cano, 69-104. Mexico City: UNAM, 2016.

Castro Martínez, Pedro. "Antonio Díaz Soto y Gama y las vicisitudes del Partido Nacional Agrarista." *Iztapalapa*, no. 50 (2001): 379-408.

Chance, John K. "Los Villagómez de Suchitepec, Oaxaca: un cacicazgo mixteco, 1701-1860." *Revista Española de Antropología Americana* 41, no. 2 (2011): 501-20.

Chassen-López, Francie R. "¿Capitalismo o comunalismo? Cambio y continuidad en la tenencia de la tierra en la Oaxaca porfirista." In *Don Porfirio presidente..., nunca omnipotente: hallazgos, reflexiones y debates, 1876-1911*, edited by Romana Falcón and Raymond Buve, 153-200. Mexico City: Universidad Iberoamericana, 1998.

———. *From Liberal to Revolutionary Oaxaca: The View from the South, Mexico, 1867-1911*. University Park: Pennsylvania State University Press, 2004.

Chávez Padrón, Martha. *El proceso social agrario y sus procedimientos*. Mexico City: Porrúa, 1971.

Cockcroft, James D. "El maestro de primaria en la Revolución Mexicana." *Historia Mexicana* 16, no. 4 (1967): 565-87.

Codificación de los decretos del C. Venustiano Carranza. Mexico City: Imprenta de la Secretaría de Gobernación, 1915.

Colección de acuerdos, órdenes y decretos, sobre tierras, casas y solares de los indígenas, bienes de sus comunidades y fundos legales de Jalisco, vol. 1. Guadalajara: Imprenta del Gobierno del Estado, 1849.

Colección de acuerdos, órdenes y decretos, sobre tierras, casas y solares de los indígenas, bienes de sus comunidades y fundos legales de Jalisco, vol. 3. Guadalajara: Tipografía de J. M. Brambila, 1868.

Congreso Nacional Agrario de Toluca: organización, funcionamiento y resoluciones. Mexico City: Talleres Gráficos de la Nación: 1959.

Córdova, Arnaldo. *La ideología de la Revolución Mexicana: la formación del nuevo régimen.* Mexico City: Ediciones Era, 1973.

Coromina, Amador, ed. *Recopilación de leyes, decretos, reglamentos y circulares expedidos en el Estado de Michoacán,* vol. 3. Morelia: Imprenta de los hijos de I. Arango, 1886.

Cortés I., María Eugenia, and Francisco Pablo Ramírez. "Rescate de antiguas medidas iberoamericanas." *Boletín de la Sociedad Mexicana de Física* 12, no. 1 (1998), n.p. https://www.smf.mx/boletin/Ene-98/articles/medidas.html (accessed 7 July 2019).

Craib, Raymond B. *Cartographic Mexico: A History of State Fixations and Fugitive Landscapes.* Durham: Duke University Press, 2004.

Crespo, Horacio. *Historia del azúcar en México,* vol. 1. Mexico City: FCE, 1988.

———. "Introducción. Desde la violencia facciosa a la ruptura del pacto de 'economía moral': el espejismo de la hacienda perfecta. Prolegómenos, auge y ocaso del orden porfirista en Morelos." In *Historia de Morelos: tierra, gente, tiempos del Sur,* vol. 6, *Creación del Estado: leyvismo y pofiritato,* edited by Horacio Crespo, 11-31. Cuernavaca: Congreso del Estado de Morelos et al., 2011.

———. *Modernización y conflicto social: la hacienda azucarera en el Estado de Morelos.* Mexico City: INEHRM, 2009.

Cruz, Alfonso. "Las primeras comisiones agrarias en el sur." In *Los agrónomos mexicanos: información histórica,* edited by Ateneo Nacional Agronómico, 43-52. Mexico City: Ediciones Atenagro, 1954.

Cuadros Caldas, Julio. *Catecismo agrario.* Mexico City: RAN, AGA, CIESAS, 1999.

Cuestión de ejidos y linderos. Documentos oficiales. Informe del Archivo General y Público de la Nación y de la Dirección Agraria sobre los linderos de la Hacienda de Gogorrón y los ejidos de Villa de Reyes. San Luis Potosí: Talleres Tipográficos de El Estandarte, 1912.

Cumberland, Charles C. *Mexican Revolution: The Constitutionalist Years*. Austin: University of Texas Press, 1972.

Cypher, James. "Reconstructing Community: Local Religion, Political Culture, and Rebellion in Mexico's Sierra Gorda, 1846-1880." PhD diss., Indiana University, 2007.

Deere, Carmen Diana, and Magdalena León. *Empowering Women: Land and Property Rights in Latin America*. Pittsburgh: University of Pittsburgh Press, 2001.

de Ibarrola, Antonio. *Derecho agrario: el campo, base de la patria*. Mexico City: Editorial Porrúa, 1975.

de la Peña, Guillermo. *A Legacy of Promises: Agriculture, Politics, and Ritual in the Morelos Highlands of Mexico*. Manchester: Manchester University Press, 1982.

de la Peña, Moisés T. *El pueblo y su tierra. Mito y realidad de la reforma agraria en México*. Mexico City: Cuadernos Americanos, 1964.

del Arenal, Jaime. "La protección del indígena en el segundo imperio mexicano: La Junta Protectora de las Clases Menesterosas." *Ars Iuris* 6 (1991): 1-35.

de la Torre, Juan, ed. *Legislación de Terrenos Baldíos. Colección completa de leyes, circulares y demás disposiciones vigentes en el ramo de baldíos, con un apéndice que contiene todas las disposiciones expedidas sobre designación y fraccionamiento de ejidos de los pueblos, compiladas, anotadas y concordadas por el Lic. Juan de la Torre, por acuerdo del Gobierno del Estado de Michoacán*. Morelia: Imprenta del Gobierno en la Escuela de Artes, 1892.

Delgado Aguilar, Francisco Javier. "La comunidad de riego del pueblo de indios de Jesús María." In Ávila Quijas, Gómez Serrano, Escobar Ohmstede, and Sánchez Rodríguez, *Negociaciones*, 211-23.

de María y Campos, Armando. *Múgica, crónica biográfica (aportación a la historia de la Revolución Mexicana)*. 1939. Reprint, Villahermosa: Universidad Juárez Autónoma de Tabasco, 1984.

Díaz, Lilia. *Fuentes para la historia de la Revolución Mexicana*. Vol. 1, *Planes políticos y otros documentos*. Mexico City: FCE, 1974.

Díaz González, D. Prisciliano María. *Sentencia del Tribunal de Circuito de México condenando a los denunciantes del pueblo de San Miguel Chapultepec. Estanislao Castellanos y socios a prestar la caución Judicatum Solvi en favor de los opositores a la demanda de baldíos*. Mexico City: Imprenta Popular de José Joaquín Terrazas, 1892.

Díaz Soto y Gama, Antonio. *Historia del agrarismo en México*. Mexico City: Ediciones Era 2002.

Diccionario de Generales de la Revolución, vols. 1 and 2. Mexico City: INEHRM, 2014.

La Diputación Provincial de México, vol. 2. Mexico City: Instituto Mora, 2007.

La Diputación Provincial de Nueva España: actas de sesiones, 1820-1821, vol. 1. Mexico City: Instituto Mora, 2007.

La Diputación Provincial de las Provincias Internas de Occidente (Nueva Vizcaya y Durango): actas de sesiones, 1821-1823. Mexico City: Instituto Mora, 2006.

La Diputación Provincial de San Luis Potosí: actas de sesiones, 1821-1824, vol. 1. San Luis Potosí: El Colegio de San Luis, 2012.

La Diputación Provincial de Zacatecas: actas de sesiones, 1822-1823. Mexico City: Instituto Mora, 2003.

Eckstein, Salomón. *El ejido colectivo en México*. Mexico City: FCE, 1966.

Ejecutivo de la XV Legislatura. *Proyecto de ley sobre repartición de terrenos comunales y formación de catastro del Estado de Hidalgo*. Pachuca: Imprenta del Estado, 1898.

Embriz Osorio, Arnulfo. "Propiedad, propietarios, pueblos indios y reforma agraria en la región purhépecha, 1915-1940." In *Estructuras y formas agrarias en México. Del pasado al presente*, edited by Antonio Escobar Ohmstede and Teresa Rojas, 231-71. Mexico City: RAN, CIESAS, 2001.

Ervin, Michael Andrew. "The Art of the Possible: Agronomists, Agrarian Reform, and the Middle Politics of the Mexican Revolution, 1908-1934." PhD diss., University of Pittsburgh, 2002.

Escalante Gonzalbo, Fernando. "El lenguaje del artículo 27 constitucional." In Kourí, *En busca de Molina Enríquez*, 229-51.

Escobar Ohmstede, Antonio. "Cambios en el paisaje hidroagrario. ¿La Revolución un detonante? El caso de San Luis Potosí (1910-1940)." *Relaciones* 34, no. 136 (2013): 265-315.

———. "Los pueblos indios huastecos frente a las tendencias modernizadoras decimonónicas." In *Pueblos, comunidades y municipios frente a los proyectos modernizadores en América Latina, siglo XIX*, edited by Antonio Escobar Ohmstede, Romana Falcón, and Raymond Buve, 169-88. Mexico City: El Colegio de San Luis and Centro de Estudios y Documentos Latinoamericanos, 2002.

———. "Tierra y agua en el oriente potosino de la segunda mitad del siglo XIX." In Ávila Quijas, Gómez Serrano, Escobar Ohmstede, and Sánchez Rodríguez, *Negociaciones*, 81-114.

Escobar Ohmstede, Antonio, and Matthew Butler, eds. *Mexico in Transition: New Perspectives on Mexican Agrarian History, Nineteenth and Twentieth Centuries = México y sus transiciones: reconsideraciones sobre la historia agraria mexicana, siglos XIX y XX*. Mexico City: CIESAS, 2013.

Escobar Ohmstede, Antonio, and Martín Sánchez Rodríguez. "El agua y la tierra en México, siglos XIX y XX. ¿Caminos separados, paralelos o entrecruzados?" In *Agua y tierra en México, siglos XIX y XX*, vol. 1., edited by Antonio Escobar Ohmstede, Martín Sánchez Rodríguez, and Ana Ma. Gutiérrez Rivas, 11–48. Zamora: El Colegio de Michoacán and El Colegio de San Luis, 2008.

Escobar Ohmstede, Antonio, Romana Falcón Vega, and Martín Sánchez Rodríguez, eds. *La desamortización civil desde perspectivas plurales*. Mexico City: El Colegio de México, El Colegio de Michoacán, and CIESAS, 2017.

———. "Introducción. En pos de las tierras civiles corporativas en México: la desamortización civil de la segunda mitad del siglo XIX." In Escobar Ohmstede, Falcón Vega, and Sánchez Rodríguez, *La desamortización*, 11–65.

Espejel López, Laura. "La organización del movimiento zapatista a través del Cuartel General en el Fondo Emiliano Zapata del Archivo General de la Nación." Bachelor's thesis, UNAM, 1984.

Espejel López, Laura, Alicia Olivera de Bonfil, and Salvador Rueda Smithers, eds. *Emiliano Zapata: antología*. Mexico City: INEHRM, 1988.

Fabela, Isidro, ed. *Documentos históricos de la Revolución Mexicana*. Vol. 6, *Revolución y Régimen Maderista*. Part 2. Mexico City: Editorial Jus, 1965.

———. *Documentos históricos de la Revolución Mexicana*. Vol. 21, *Emiliano Zapata, el Plan de Ayala y su política agraria*. Mexico City: Editorial Jus, 1970.

Fabila, Manuel. *Cinco siglos de legislación agraria (1493-1940)*. Mexico City: Secretaría de la Reforma Agraria and Centro de Estudios Históricos del Agrarismo en México, 1981; second edition, 1990.

Falcón Vega, Romana. "El arte de la petición: Rituales de obediencia y negociación, México, segunda mitad del siglo XIX." *HAHR* 86, no. 3 (2006): 467–500.

———. "Itinerarios de la negociación. Jefes políticos y campesinos comuneros ante las políticas agrarias liberales." In *Los efectos del liberalismo en México, siglo XIX*, edited by Antonio Escobar Ohmstede, José Marcos Medina Bustos, Zulema Trejo Contreras, 115–40. Hermosillo: El Colegio de Sonora and CIESAS, 2015.

———. *El jefe político: un dominio negociado en el mundo rural del Estado de México, 1856-1911*. Mexico City: El Colegio de México, El Colegio de Michoacán, and CIESAS, 2015.

———. "Litigios interminables. Indígenas y comuneros ante la justicia agraria liberal (1857-1928)." In *Sociedades en movimiento: los pueblos indígenas de América Latina en el siglo XIX*, edited by Antonio Escobar Ohmstede, Raúl J. Mandrini, and Sara Ortelli, 81-97. Tandil: Instituto de Estudios Históricos Sociales, 2007.

Fenner Bieling, Justus. "La defensa de las tierras colectivas en Chiapa, 1876-1900. Denuncios registrados en el Juzgado de Distrito de Chiapas." In *Historia judicial mexicana*, vol. 1, *Casas de la Cultura Jurídica*, edited by Poder Judicial de la Federación and SCJN, 867-98. Mexico City: SCJN, 2006.

Fernández de Castro, Patricia. "Agrarian Reform from Below: The Mexican Revolution in Durango, 1910-1915." PhD diss., University of Chicago, 2008.

Fix Zamudio, Héctor. "Lineamientos fundamentales del proceso social agrario en el derecho mexicano." *Revista de la Facultad de Derecho de México* 13, no. 52 (1963): 893-938.

Fowler-Salamini, Heather. "Gender, Work, and Coffee in Córdoba, Veracruz, 1850-1910." In *Women of the Mexican Countryside, 1850-1990: Creating Spaces, Shaping Transitions*, edited by Heather Fowler-Salamini and Mary Kay Vaughan, 51-73. Tucson: University of Arizona Press, 1994.

Fox, Jonathan, and Gustavo Gordillo. "Between State and Market: The Campesino's Quest for Autonomy." In *Mexico's Alternative Political Futures*, edited by Wayne Cornelious, Judith Gentleman, and Peter Smith, 131-72. La Jolla: Center for U.S.-Mexican Studies, University of California San Diego, 1989.

Friedrich, Paul. *Agrarian Revolt in a Mexican village*. Englewood Cliffs: Prentice Hall, 1970.

Galante, Miriam. "La historiografía reciente de la justicia en México, siglo XIX: perspectivas, temas y aportes." *Revista Complutense de Historia de América* 37 (2011): 104-5.

García, Alberto. *Informe a la vista, pronunciado por el Lic. Alberto García, en el insidente [sic] sobre falta de personalidad del apoderado, y del pueblo de San Pedro Tlaltizapan*. . . . Toluca: Imprenta de Atanasio Quijano, 1893.

García Castro, René, and Jesús Arzate Becerril. "Ilustración, justiciar y títulos de tierras. El caso del pueblo de La Asunción Malacatepec en el siglo XVIII." *Relaciones* 24, no. 95 (2003): 50-92.

García Castro, René, and Evelina Román Sevilla. "El amparo y la propiedad corporativa civil frente a la jurisdicción municipal en el Estado de México." In *La vida, el trabajo y la propiedad en el Estado de México: los primeros juicios de amparo en la segunda mitad del siglo XIX*, edited by César de Jesús Molina Suárez, René García Castro, and Ana Lidia García Peña, 191-246. Mexico City: SCJN, 2006.

García Ramírez, Sergio. "Establecimiento y horizonte de la jurisdicción agraria en México." *Revista de los Tribunales Agrarios* 57 (2012): 1-61.

Garner, Paul. "Autoritarismo revolucionario en el México provincial: el carrancismo y el gobierno preconstitucionalista en Oaxaca, 1915-1920." *Historia Mexicana* 34, no. 2 (1984): 238-99.

———. *La Revolución en la provincia: soberanía estatal y caudillismo serrano en Oaxaca, 1910-1920*. Mexico City: FCE, 2003.

Gilly, Adolfo. *La revolución interrumpida: México, 1910-1920; una guerra campesina por la tierra y el poder*. Mexico City: El Caballito, 1979.

Gledhill, John. "Introducción: pensando acerca del presente a través del pasado." In *Recursos contenciosos: ruralidad y reformas liberales en México*, edited by Andrew Roth Seneff, 15-39. Zamora: El Colegio de Michoacán, 2004.

Gobierno de los Estados Unidos Mexicanos. *Tercer Informe de Gobierno del Presidente Felipe Calderón Hinojosa*. Mexico City: Presidencia de la República, 2009.

Gómez Carpintero, Francisco Javier. "Comunidades de agua en el Nexapa: liberalismo y centralización en el control local de recursos hidráulicos." In *Paisajes mexicanos de la reforma agraria: homenaje a William Roseberry*, edited by Gómez Carpintero, 133-65. Morelia: El Colegio de Michoacán, Benemérita Universidad Autónoma de Puebla, and Instituto de Ciencias Sociales y Humanidades Alfonso Vélez Pliego, 2007.

Gómez Santana, Laura Guillermina. "Ser indígena en la reforma agraria: Jalisco, México, 1915-1924." *Sociedad Hoy* 17 (2009): 103-13.

Gómez Santana, Laura Guillermina, and Maricela Gómez Santana. "Mujeres y propiedad social en Jalisco, 1876-1924." In Escobar Ohmstede and Butler, *Mexico in Transition*, 545-63.

Gómez, Marte R. *Las comisiones agrarias del sur*. Mexico City: Miguel Ángel Purrúa, 1961.

———. *Historia de la Comisión Nacional Agraria*. Mexico City: Centro de Investigaciones Agrarias and Secretaría de Agricultura y Ganadería, 1975.

González Navarro, Moisés. "Indio y propiedad en Oaxaca." *Historia Mexicana* 8, no. 2 (1958): 175-91.

———. "El maderismo y la revolución agraria mexicana." *Historia Mexicana* 37, no. 1 (1987): 5-27.

———. *El Porfiriato: la vida social*. Vol. 4 of *Historia Moderna de México*, edited by Daniel Cosío Villegas. Mexico City: Editorial Hermes, 1957.

———. "Vallarta, indios y extranjeros en la Suprema Corte de Justicia de la Nación (1877-1887)." In Cabrera Acevedo, *La Suprema Corte de Justicia en el primer periodo del porfirismo*, 1075-90.

———. "Zapata y la revolución agraria mexicana." *Cahiers du Monde Hispanique et Luso-Brésilien*, no. 9 (1967): 5-31.

González Roa, Fernando. *Parte general de un informe sobre la aplicación de algunos preceptos de la Ley Agraria de 6 de enero de 1915*. Mexico City: Secretaría de Fomento, 1916.

González Solano, Martín. "La lucha por la propiedad de la tierra del rancho de la Concepción Villa Nicolás Romero, estado de México, 1915-1922." *Boletín del Archivo General Agrario* 12 (2000): 18-25.

González y González, Luis. *Obras completas de Luis González y González: el siglo de las luchas*. Mexico City: Clío, 1996.

Granados García, Aymer. "Comunidad indígena, imaginario monárquico, agravio y economía moral durante el segundo imperio mexicano." *Secuencia* 41 (1998): 45-73.

Guardino, Peter F. *Peasants, Politics, and the Formation of Mexico's National State: Guerrero, 1800-1857*. Stanford CA: Stanford University Press, 1996.

Hall, Linda B. "Álvaro Obregón and the Politics of Mexican Land Reform, 1920-1924." *HAHR* 60, no. 2 (1980): 213-38.

Hart, Paul. *Bitter Harvest: The Social Transformation of Morelos, Mexico, and the Origins of the Zapatista Revolution, 1840-1910*. Albuquerque: University of New Mexico Press, 2006.

Haskins, George L. "Homestead Exemptions." *Harvard Law Review* 63, no. 8 (1950): 1289-1320.

Henderson, Peter V. N. *In the Absence of Don Porfirio: Francisco León de la Barra and the Mexican Revolution*. Wilmington DE: SR Books, 2000.

Hernández Chávez, Alicia. *Anenecuilco: memoria y vida de un pueblo*. Mexico City: El Colegio de México, 1991.

———. *Breve historia de Morelos*. Mexico City: El Colegio de México and FCE, 2002.

Hernández Hernández, Aura. "La querella por la tierra y el agua en el Estado de Morelos posrevolucionario. Razonamientos de clase y argumentos históricos en la disputa por la tierra y el agua entre las haciendas y los pueblos de Morelos (1920-1924)." In *Historia Judicial Mexicana*, vol. 2, *La Propiedad*, edited by Poder Judicial de la Federación and SCJN, 77-125. Mexico City: SCJN.

Herrera Sipiriano, Francisco. *La revolución en la montaña de Guerrero: la lucha zapatista, 1910-1918*. Mexico City: INAH, 2009.

Herrera-Martin, Carlos R. "Judicial Review of Expropriation: The case of Mexico." PhD diss., University College London, 2014.

Herrera Sipriano, Francisco. *La revolución en la montaña de Guerrero: la lucha zapatista, 1910-1918*. Mexico City: INAH, 2009.

Holden, Robert H. *Mexico and the Surveys of Public Lands: The Management of Modernization, 1876-1911.* DeKalb: Northern Illinois University Press, 1994.

Huitrón Huitrón, Antonio. *El poder judicial en el Estado de México*, vol. 2. Toluca: H. Tribunal Superior de Justicia del Estado de México, 1992.

Huizer, Gerrit. "Emiliano Zapata and the Peasant Guerrillas in the Mexican Revolution." In *Agrarian Problems and Peasant Movements in Latin America*, edited by Rodolfo Stavenhagen, 375-406. New York: Doubleday.

James, Timothy M. *Mexico's Supreme Court: Between Liberal Individual and Revolutionary Social Rights, 1867-1934.* Albuquerque: University of New Mexico Press, 2013.

Karst, Kenneth I. "Latin American Land Reform: The Uses of Confiscation." *Michigan Law Review* 63, no. 2 (1964): 327-72.

Katz, Friedrich. "The Agrarian Policies and Ideas of the Revolutionary Mexican Factions Led by Emiliano Zapata, Pancho Villa, and Venustiano Carranza." In *Reforming Mexico's Agrarian Reform*, edited by Laura Randall, 21-34. Armonk NY: Sharpe, 1996.

———. *The Life and Times of Pancho Villa.* Stanford CA: Stanford University Press, 1998.

INEHRM. *Diccionario de generales de la revolución*, vol. 1. Mexico City: INEHRM, SEP, and Secretaría de la Defensa Nacional, 2014.

Jacobs, Ian. *Ranchero Revolt: The Mexican Revolution in Guerrero.* Austin: University of Texas Press, 1982.

Knight, Alan. "Land and Society in Revolutionary Mexico: The Destruction of the Great Haciendas." *Mexican Studies / Estudios Mexicanos* 7, no. 1 (1991): 73-104.

———. *The Mexican Revolution.* Vol. 2, *Counter-revolution and Reconstruction.* Lincoln: University of Nebraska Press, 1990.

Knowlton, Robert J. *Church Property and the Mexican Reform: 1856-1910.* DeKalb: Northern Illinois University Press, 1976.

———. "El ejido mexicano en el siglo XIX." *Historia Mexicana* 48, no. 1 (1998): 71-96.

———. "Tribunales federales y terrenos rurales en el México del siglo XIX: El Semanario judicial de la Federación." *Historia Mexicana* 46, no. 1 (1996): 71-98.

Kourí, Emilio, ed. *En busca de Molina Enríquez: cien años de Los grandes problemas nacionales.* Mexico City: El Colegio de México and Centro Katz, University of Chicago, 2009.

———. "Interpreting the Expropriation of Indian Pueblo Lands in Porfirian Mexico: The Unexamined Legacies of Andrés Molina Enríquez." *HAHR* 82, no. 1 (2002): 69-117.

———. "La invención del ejido." *Nexos*, no. 445 (January 2015): 54–61.
———. "La promesa agraria del artículo 27." *Nexos*, no. 470 (February 2017): 31–39.
———. *A Pueblo Divided: Business, Property, and Community in Papantla, Mexico*. Palo Alto: Stanford University Press, 2004.
———. "Los pueblos y sus tierras en el México porfiriano: un legado inexplorado de Andrés Molina Enríquez." In Kourí, *En busca de Molina Enríquez*, 253–333.
———. "Sobre la propiedad comunal de los pueblos, de la reforma a la revolución." *Historia Mexicana* 66, no. 4 (2017): 1923–60.
Kuntz Ficker, Sandra. "Introducción." In *La reforma agraria durante los años veinte en los expedientes de la Suprema Corte de Justicia de la Nación*, edited by Sandra Kuntz Ficker, 3–29. Mexico City: SCJN, 2012.
LaFrance, David G. *Revolution in Mexico's Heartland: Politics, War, and State Building in Puebla, 1913-1920*. Wilmington DE: SR Books, 2003.
Lanz Cárdenas, José Trinidad. *Legislación de aguas en México: estudio histórico legislativo de 1521 a 1981*, vol. 1. Villahermosa: Consejo Editorial del Gobierno del Estado de Tabasco, 1982.
Leal, Juan Felipe, and Mario Huacuja Roundtree. *Economía y sistema de haciendas en México: la hacienda pulquera en al cambio, siglos XVIII, XIX y XX*. Mexico City: Juan Pablos Editor, 2011.
Lemus García, Raúl. *Derecho agrario mexicano*. Mexico City: Porrúa, 1975.
Ley expedida por el Gobierno del Estado de Michoacán en 15 de setiembre [sic] de 1859, para terminar los negocios de indígenas sobre tierras. Morelia, 1859.
Ley y reglamento sobre reparto de las extinguidas comunidades de indígenas. Morelia: Talleres de la Escuela Industrial Militar Porfirio Díaz, 1902.
Lira González, Andrés. "Abogados, tinterillos y huizacheros en el México del siglo XIX." In *Memoria del III Congreso de Historia del Derecho Mexicano*, edited by José Luis Soberanes Fernández, 375–92. Mexico City: UNAM, 1983.
———. *El amparo colonial y el juicio de amparo mexicano: antecedentes novohispanos del juicio de amparo*. Mexico City: FCE, 1972.
———. "Extinción del Juzgado de Indios." *Revista de la Facultad de Derecho de México* 26, no. 101-2 (1976): 299–317.
Lockhart, James. *The Nahuas after Conquest: A Social and Cultural History of the Indians of Central Mexico, Sixteenth through Eighteenth Centuries*. Stanford: Stanford University Press, 1992.
López Anaya, Miguel, ed. *General Alberto Carrera Torres*. Ciudad Victoria: Gobierno del Estado de Tamaulipas, 1987.

López González, Valentín. *Los Compañeros de Zapata*. Mexico City: Ediciones del Gobierno del Estado Libre y Soberano de Morelos, 1980.

López Mestas Camberos, Martha Lorenza. "Entre la desamortización y el reparto agrario: una historia rural en las laderas del volcán, 1870-1920." Master's thesis, Universidad de Colima, 2006.

Luna Arroyo, Antonio, and Luis G. Alcérreca. *Derecho agrario mexicano*. Mexico City: Porrúa, 1982.

Lynch, John. *Caudillos in Spanish America: 1800-1850*. Oxford: Clarendon Press 1992.

Madrazo, Jorge. "Pastor Rouaix, 1874-1950." In *La Constitución mexicana de 1917: ideólogos, el núcleo fundador y otros constituyentes*, edited by Instituto de Investigaciones Jurídicas, 365-83. Mexico City: UNAM, 1990.

MacGregor, Josefina. *La XXVI Legislatura: Un episodio en la historia legislativo de México*. Mexico City: El Colegio de México, 2015.

Magaña, Gildardo. *Emiliano Zapata y el agrarismo en México*. 4 vols. Mexico City: Ruta, 1951-52.

Mallon, Florencia E. *Peasant and Nation: The Making of Postcolonial Mexico and Peru*. Berkeley: University of California Press, 1995.

Marino, Daniela. "Ahora que Dios nos ha dado padre [. . .] El segundo imperio y la cultura jurídico-política campesina en el centro de México." *Historia Mexicana* 55, no. 4 (2006): 1353-410.

———. "Buscando su lugar en el mundo del derecho: Actores colectivos, reforma y jurisprudencia." In *Historia de la justicia en México, siglos XIX y XX*, vol. 1, edited by Juan Pablo Pampillo Baliño and Francisco Wiechers Veloz, 235-62. Mexico City: SCJN, 2005.

———. "La fuerza de la ley: leyes, justicias y resistencias en la imposición de la propiedad privada en México, segunda mitad del siglo XIX." In *Sangre de ley. Justicia y violencia en la institucionalización del Estado en América Latina, siglo XIX*, edited by Marta Irurozqui and Mirian Galante, 203-34. Madrid: Ediciones Polifemo, 2011.

———. *Huixquilucan: ley y justicia en la modernización del espacio rural mexiquense, 1856-1910*. Madrid: Consejo Nacional de Investigaciones Científicas, 2016.

———. "'La medida de su existencia'. La abolición de las comunidades indígenas y el juicio de amparo en el contexto desamortizador (Centro de México, 1856-1910)." *Revista de Indias* 77, no. 266 (2016): 287-313.

———. "La modernidad a juicio: los pueblos de Huixquilucan en la transición jurídica (Estado de México, 1856-1911)." PhD dissertation, El Colegio de México, 2006.

———. "Tierras y aguas de Huixquilucan en la segunda mitad del siglo XIX: comunidades, vecinos y el ayuntamiento ante el desafío de la desamortización." In *Agua y tierra en México, siglos XIX y XX*, vol. 1, edited by Antonio Escobar Ohmstede, Martín Sánchez Rodríguez, and Ana Ma. Gutiérrez Rivas, 269-86. Zamora: El Colegio de Michoacán and El Colegio de San Luis, 2008.

Markiewicz, Dana. *The Mexican Revolution and the Limits of Agrarian Reform (1915-1946)*. Boulder CO: Lynne Rienner Publishers, 1993.

Marván Laborde, Ignacio. *Nueva edición del diario de debates del Congreso Constituyente de 1916-1917*, vol. 1. Mexico City: SCJN, 2005; reprint, 2013.

McCormick, Gladys. *The Logic of Compromise in Mexico: How the Countryside Was Key to the Emergence of Authoritarianism*. Chapel Hill: University of North Carolina Press, 2016.

Memoria de la Secretaría de Fomento presentada al Congreso de la Unión por el secretario de estado y del despacho del ramo Alberto Robles Gil, correspondiente al ejercicio fiscal 1911-1912. Mexico City: Secretaría de Fomento, 1913.

Méndez Martínez, Enrique, ed. *Límites, mapas y títulos primordiales de los pueblos del estado de Oaxaca: índice del Ramo de Tierras*. Mexico City: AGN, 1999.

Mendieta y Núñez, Lucio. *El problema agrario de México desde su origen hasta la época actual*. Mexico City, 1923.

Mendieta y Núñez, Lucio, and Luis G. Alcérreca. *Un anteproyecto de Nuevo Código Agrario*. Mexico City: Centro de Investigaciones Agrarias, 1964.

Mendoza García, J. Edgar. *Agua y tierra en San Gabrial Chilac, Puebla y San Juan Teotihuacán, Estado de México: el impacto de la reforma agraria sobre el gobierno local, 1917-1960*. Mexico City: Publicaciones de la Casa Chata, CIESAS, 2016.

———. "Desamortización y pequeños propietarios indígenas en el centro y sur de México, 1856-1915." In Escobar Ohmstede, Falcón Vega, and Sánchez Rodríguez, *La desamortización*, 217-48.

———. *Municipios, cofradías y tierras comunales: los pueblos chocholtecos de Oaxaca en el siglo XIX*. Oaxaca: UABJO, CIESAS, and UAM Azcapotzalco, 2011.

———. "Tierras de común repartimiento y pequeña propiedad en San Juan Teotihuacán, Estado de México, 1856-1940." *Historia Mexicana* 66, no. 4 (2017): 1961-2011.

Meyer, Eugenia. *Luis Cabrera*. Mexico City: SEP, 1972.

Meyer, Michael C. *El rebelde del norte. Pascual Orozco y la Revolución*. Mexico City: UNAM, 1984.

Middlebrook, Kevin J. "Caciquismo and Democracy: Mexico and Beyond." *Bulletin of Latin American Research* 28, no. 3 (2009): 411-27.

———. *The Paradox of Revolution: Labor, the State, and Authoritarianism in Mexico*. Baltimore: Johns Hopkins University Press, 1995.

Miranda Correa, Eduardo. "El artículo 27 en el Congreso Constituyente de Querétaro: un análisis social." In *Memoria del IV Congreso de Historia del Derecho Mexicano*, vol. 2, edited by Beatriz Bernal, 777-91. Mexico City: UNAM, Instituto de Investigaciones Jurídicas, 1986.

Molina Enríquez, Andrés. *Los grandes problemas nacionales*. Mexico City: Imprenta de A. Carranza e Hijos, 1909.

Muñoz Bravo, Pablo. "Los promotores de la desamortización eclesiástica en la Ciudad de México, 1856-1858." *Estudios de Historia Moderna y Contemporánea de México* 49 (2015): 19-32.

Neri Guarneros, Porfirio. "Sociedades agrícolas en resistencia: los pueblos de San Miguel, Santa Cruz y San Pedro, 1878-1883." *Historia Crítica* 51 (2013): 21-44.

Niemeyer, Eberhard Victor, Jr. *Revolution at Querétaro: The Mexican Constitutional Convention of 1916-1917*. Austin: University of Texas Press, 1974.

Noriega Elío, Cecilia. "Estudio introductorio." In *La Diputación Provincial de México*, edited by Cecilia Noriega Elío, 2:11-56. Mexico City: Instituto Mora, 2007.

Noyola, Inocencio. "Los juicios de apeos y deslindes en San Luis Potosí, 1883-1893." In *Agua y tierra en México, siglos XIX y XX*, vol. 1, edited by Antonio Escobar Ohmstede, Martín Sánchez Rodríguez, and Ana Ma. Gutiérrez Rivas, 331-57. Zamora: El Colegio de Michoacán and El Colegio de San Luis, 2008.

Nugent, Daniel. *Spent Cartridges of Revolution: An Anthropological History of Namiquipa, Chihuahua*. Chicago: University of Chicago Press, 1994.

Nugent, Daniel, and Ana María Alonso. "Multiple Selective Traditions in Agrarian Reform and Agrarian Struggle: Popular Culture and State Formation in the Ejido of Namiquipa, Chihuahua." In *Everyday Forms of State Formation: Revolution and the Negotiation of Rule in Modern Mexico*, edited by Gilbert M. Joseph and Daniel Nugent, 209-46. Durham: Duke University Press, 1994.

Ochoa Serrano, Álvaro. *Los agraristas de Atacheo*. Zamora: El Colegio de Michoacán, 1989.

———. "Revolución y liderazgo agrario en Atacheo: Miguel de la Trinidad Regalado y la Sociedad Unificadora de la Raza Indígena." In *Autoridad y gobierno indígena en Michoacán*, vol. 2, edited by Carlos Paredes Martínez and Marta Terán, 469–516. Zamora: El Colegio de Michoacán, CIESAS, INAH, and Universidad Michoacana de San Nicolás de Hidalgo, 2003.

Ordóñez Cifuentes, José Emilio Rolando. "Antecedentes y naturaleza del derecho social y la Revolución Mexicana." In *Impacto de la Revolución Mexicana*, edited by Patricia Galeana, 113–40. Mexico City: Siglo Veintiuno Editores and Senado de la República, 2010.

Orozco, Wistano Luis. *Legislación y jurisprudencia sobre terrenos baldíos*, vol. 1. Mexico City: Imprenta del Tiempo, 1895.

Otero, Luis G. *Asunto del pueblo de Tetelpa*. Mexico City: Antigua Casa "José María Mellado," 1906.

Otero Muñóz, Ignacio. "La parcelación ejidal y sus efectos sociales: análisis de los ejidos de Anenecuilco y Los Borregos." Law thesis, UNAM, 1971.

Ortiz Yam, Isaura Inés. "Formación de ejidos en los pueblos de Yucatán, 1870–1909." *Temas Antropológicos: Revista Científica de Investigaciones Regionales* 36, no. 2 (2014): 17–41.

Owensby, Brian P. "Comunidades indígenas y gobierno en la época de la independencia: reflexiones sobre antecedentes virreinales y transformaciones decimonónicas." In *Declaraciones de independencia. Los textos fundamentales de las independencias americanas*, edited by Alfredo Ávila, Jordana Dym, and Erika Pani, 81–110. Mexico City: El Colegio de México, 2013.

——. *Empire of Law and Indian Justice in Colonial Mexico*. Stanford CA: Stanford University Press, 2008.

Palacios, Guillermo. "Las restituciones de la Revolución." In *Estudios campesinos en el Archivo General Agrario*, vol. 3, edited by Ismael Maldonado Salazar, Guillermo Palacios, and Reyna María Silva Chacón, 119–61. Mexico City: CIESAS, RAN, Secretaría de la Reforma Agraria, SEP, and Consejo Nacional de Ciencia y Tecnología, 2001.

Palacios, Porfirio. *Emiliano Zapata. Datos histórico-biográficos*. Mexico City: Libro Mex Editores, 1960.

——. *El Plan de Ayala. Sus orígenes y su promulgación*. Mexico City: Frente Zapatista de la República, 1949.

Pallares, Eduardo. *Leyes federales vigentes sobre tierras, bosques, aguas, ejidos, colonización y el gran registro de la propiedad*. Mexico City: Herrero Hermanos Sucesores. 1922.

Pérez Montesinos, Fernando. "Geografía, política y economía del reparto liberal en la meseta purépecha, 1851–1914." *Historia Mexicana* 66, no. 4 (2017): 2073–149.

Pineda Gómez, Francisco. *Ejército Libertador. 1915*. Mexico City: Ediciones Era, 2011.

———. "La guerra zapatista, 1911-1915." In *Historia de Morelos: tierra, gente, tiempos del Sur*, vol. 7, *El zapatismo*, edited by Felipe Ávila Espinosa, 157-200. Cuernavaca: Congreso del Estado de Morelos et al., 2010.

———. *La irrupción zapatista. 1911*. Mexico City: Ediciones Era, 1997.

———. *La revolución del sur, 1912-1914*. Mexico City: Ediciones Era, 2005.

"Primer Informe de Gobierno del Presidente Constitucional de los Estados Unidos Mexicanos, Francisco I. Madero." In *200 años de administración pública en México*, tome 5, *La administración en los informes presidenciales*, vol. 1, *1824-1920, Guadalupe Victoria-Venustiano Carranza*, edited by José R. Castelazo, 431-40. Mexico City: Instituto Nacional de Administración Pública, 2011.

Purnell, Jennie. "Citizens and Sons of the Pueblo: National and Local Identities in the Making of the Mexican Nation." *Ethnic and Racial Studies* 25, no. 2 (2010): 213-37.

———. *Popular Movements and State Formation in Revolutionary Mexico: The Agraristas and Cristeros of Michoacán*. Durham NC: Duke University Press, 1999.

———. "'With All Due Respect': Popular Resistance to the Privatization of Communal Lands in Nineteenth-Century Michoacán." *Latin American Research Review* 34, no. 1 (1999): 85-121.

Recopilación de las principales leyes expedidas por conducto de la Secretaría de Agricultura y Fomento. Mexico City: Imprenta de la Dirección de Estudios Geográficos y Climatológicos, 1927.

Reyes Osorio, Sergio, Rodolfo Stavenhagen, Salomón Eckstein, Juan Ballesteros, Iván Restrepo, Jerjes Aguirre, Sergio Maturana, and José Sánchez. *Estructura agraria y desarrollo agrícola en México*. Mexico City: FCE, 1974.

Richmond, Douglas W. *Venustiano Carranza's Nationalist Struggle, 1893-1920*. Lincoln: University of Nebraska Press, 1983.

Rincón Serrano, Romeo. *El ejido mexicano*. Mexico City: Centro Nacional de Investigaciones Agrarias, 1980.

Rojano García, Edgar Damián. *Las cenizas del zapatismo*. Mexico City: INEHRM, 2010.

Rodríguez García, Martha. "Genovevo de la O: un jefe zapatista en el occidente de Morelos y sur del Estado de México." In *Emiliano Zapata y el movimiento zapatista*, edited by Rodríguez García, 7-98. Mexico City: SEP, INAH, 1980.

Romero Frizzi, María de los Ángeles. "Conflictos agrarios, historia y peritajes paleográficos: reflexionando desde Oaxaca." *Estudios Agrarios*, no. 47 (2011): 65-81.

Roseberry, William. "'El estricto apego a la ley.' La ley liberal y derechos comunales en el Pátzcuaro del Porfiriato." In *Recursos contenciosos: ruralidad y reformas liberales en México*, edited by Andrew Roth, 43-84. Zamora: El Colegio de Michoacán, 2004.

Rosoff, Rosalind, and Anita Aguilar. *Así firmaron el plan de Ayala*. Cuernavaca: Gobierno del Estado de Morelos, 2007.

Rouaix, Pastor. *Génesis de los artículos 27 y 123 de la Constitución Política de 1917*. Mexico City: INEHRM, 1959.

Rueda Smithers, Salvador. *El paraíso de la caña. Historia de una construcción imaginaria*. Mexico City: INAH, 1998.

Ruiz Massieu, Mario. "Principios agrarios del Plan de Ayala del 28 de noviembre de 1911." *Revista de la Facultad de Derecho de México*, no. 117 (1980): 937-46.

Ruiz Medrano, Ethelia. *Mexico's Indigenous Communities: Their Lands and Histories, 1500-2010*. Translated by Russ Davidson. Boulder: University Press of Colorado, 2011.

Ruiz Mondragón, Laura. "Los peones acasillados en la legislación agraria. Contratos de peones acasillados en el Archivo General Agrario." *Boletín del Archivo General Agrario* 15 (2001): 22-33.

Sala, Atenor. *Emiliano Zapata y el problema agrario*. Mexico City: Imprenta Franco-Mexicana, 1919.

Salinas, Salvador. *Land, Liberty, and Water: Morelos after Zapata, 1920-1940*. Albuquerque: University of Arizona Press, 2018.

Salinas Sandoval, María del Carmen. "Desamortización en Acambay, Estado de México: proceso articulador de conflictos por la tierra (1868-1910)." In Ávila Quijas, Gómez Serrano, Escobar Ohmstede, and Sánchez Rodríguez, *Negociaciones*, 143-75.

———. "Problemas por tierras de los pueblos de la municipalidad de Jilotepec. Siglo XIX." *Documentos de Investigación* (El Colegio Mexiquense), no. 54 (2001): 1-15.

Samponaro, Frank N., and Paul J. Vanderwood. *War Scare on the Río Grande: Robert Runyon's Photographs of the Border Conflict, 1913-1916*. Austin: Texas State Historical Association, 1992.

Sánchez, Evelyne. "Entre el caudillo y el presidente: el papel de los juristas en la implementación de la Reforma agraria. Estado de Tlaxcala, 1915-1923." *Nuevo Mundo, Mundos Nuevos*, 16 February 2018, https://journals.openedition.org/nuevomundo/71865.

Sánchez Beltrán, René. *Anenecuilco, tierra de Zapata*. Cuernavaca: Gobierno del Estado de Morelos, 1980.

Sánchez Gómez, Rosa Catalina. "Afectación agraria y población beneficiada en la hacienda El Encero." *Anuario* (Universidad Veracruzana) 2 (1979): 160–82.

Sanderson, Susan R. Walsh. *Land Reform in Mexico: 1910–1980*. Orlando: Academic Press, 1984.

Sandré Osorio, Israel. "Reforma agraria y distribución de aguas del río Tepotzotlán, Estado de México, 1898–1935." In Ávila Quilas, Gómez Serrano, Escobar Ohmstede, and Sánchez Rodríguez, *Negociaciones*, 177–209.

Sandré Osorio, Israel, and Martin Sánchez, eds. *El eslabón perdido. Acuerdos, convenios, reglamentos y leyes locales de agua en México (1593–1935)*. Mexico City: CIESAS, 2011.

Santos García, Lucía. "Élites e indígenas en disputa por la tierra, municipio de Huayacocotla, 1889–1921." In *La ley de 6 de enero de 1915: nueve estudios en el centenario de su promulgación*, edited by José Manuel Velasco Toro, Luis J. García Ruiz, and Olivia Domínguez Pérez, 101–30. Xalapa: Gobierno del Estado de Veracruz, 2015.

Sapia-Bosch, Alfonso F. "The Role of General Lucio Blanco in the Mexican Revolution, 1913–1922." PhD diss., Georgetown University, 1977.

Serrano Álvarez, Pablo. "Conflictos por el agua entre la hacienda de Nogueras y las comunidades indígenas de Comala, Colima 1912–1940." *Boletín del Archivo Histórico del Agua* 7 (2002): 21–29.

Schenk, Frank. "The *desamortización* in the Sultepec District: The Policy of Privatisation of Communal Landholdings in Mexico, 1856–1911." *Revista Complutense de Historia de América* 21 (1995): 209–29.

Schryer, Frans J. *The Rancheros of Pisaflores: The History of a Peasant Bourgeoisie in Mexico*. Toronto: University of Toronto Press, 1980.

Secretaría de Fomento. *Colección de leyes sobre tierras y disposiciones sobre ejidos*. Mexico City: Imprenta y Fototipia de la Secretaría de Fomento, 1913.

Secretaría de Fomento, Colonización e Industria de la República Mexicana. *Ley de aprovechamiento de aguas de jurisdicción federal*. Mexico City: Imprenta y Fototipia de la Secretaría de Fomento, 1911.

Serna de la Garza, José María. "The Concept of *Jurisprudencia* in Mexican Law." *Mexican Law Review*, n.s. 1, no. 2 (2009): 131–45.

Sedano P., Miguel A. *Revolucionarios surianos y memorias de Quintín González*. Mexico City: Editorial del Magisterio, 1974.

Schaefer, Timo H. *Liberalism as Utopia: The Rise and Fall of Legal Rule in Post-Colonial Mexico, 1820–1900*. New York: Cambridge University Press, 2017.

Shadle, Stanley F. *Andrés Molina Enríquez: Mexican Land Reformer of the Revolutionary Era*. Tucson: Univ. of Arizona Press, 1994.

Sierra Zavala, Fernando. "El juicio de amparo y las comunidades indígenas de Michoacán en el siglo XIX y XX: el caso de Tzitzio." In *El juicio de amparo a 160 años de la primera sentencia*, edited by Manuel González Oropeza and Eduardo Ferrer MacGregor, 2:415–28. Mexico City: UNAM, 2011.

Silva Herzog, Jesús. *El agrarismo mexicano y la reforma agraria: exposición y crítica*. Mexico City: FCE, 1959.

———. *Breve Historia de la Revolución Mexicana. La etapa constitucionalista y la lucha de facciones*. Mexico City: FCE, 1960.

———. *La cuestión de la tierra: 1911–1913*, vol. 2. Mexico City: Instituto Mexicano de Investigaciones Económicas, 1961.

———. *La cuestión de la tierra: 1915–1917*, vol. 4. Mexico City: Instituto Mexicano de Investigaciones Económicas, 1961.

Simonian, Lane. *Defending the Land of the Jaguar: A History of Conservation in Mexico*. Austin: Texas University Press, 1995.

Simpson, Eyler N. *The Ejido: Mexico's Way Out*. Chapel Hill: University of North Carolina Press, 1937.

Smith, Stephanie J. *Gender and the Mexican Revolution: Yucatán Women and the Realities of Patriarchy*. Chapel Hill: University of North Carolina Press, 2009.

Sotelo Inclán, Jesús. *Raíz y razón de Zapata*. Mexico City: Editorial Etnos, 1943.

Stevens, Donald Fithian. "Agrarian Policy and Instability in Porfirian Mexico." *Americas* 39, no. 2 (1982): 153–66.

Suárez-Potts, William J. *The Making of Law: The Supreme Court and Labor Legislation in Mexico, 1875–1931*. Stanford CA: Stanford University Press, 2013.

Tannenbaum, Frank. *The Mexican Agrarian Revolution*. New York: Macmillan, 1929; reprint, Archon Books, 1968.

Tinsman, Heidi. *Partners in Conflict: The Politics of Gender, Sexuality, and Labor in the Chilean Agrarian Reform, 1950–1973*. Durham NC: Duke University Press, 2002.

Tortolero Villaseñor, Alejandro. *Notarios y agricultores. Crecimiento y atraso en el campo mexicano, 1780–1920*. Mexico City: UAM Iztapalapa and Siglo Veintiuno Editores, 2008.

———. "Water and Revolution in Morelos, 1850–1915." In *A Land between Waters: Environmental Histories of Modern Mexico*, edited by Christopher R. Boyer, 124–49. University of Arizona Press, 2012.

Ulloa, Berta. *Historia de la Revolución Mexicana, 1914-1917. La Constitución de 1917*, vol. 6. Mexico City: El Colegio de México, 2005.

Valladares de la Cruz, Laura R. *Cuando el agua se esfumó: cambios y continuidades en los usos sociales del agua en Morelos, 1880-1940*. Mexico City: UNAM, Facultad de Estudios Superiores Cuautitlán, 2003.

Vaughan, Mary Kay. *The State, Education, and Social Class in Mexico, 1880-1928*. DeKalb: Northern Illinois University Press, 1982.

Velasco Toro, José Manuel. "De la ley de 6 de enero al Código Agrario de 1934." In *La ley de 6 de enero de 1915: nueve estudios en el centenario de su promulgación*, edited by José Manuel Velasco Toro, Luis J. García Ruiz, and Olivia Domínguez Pérez, 15-58. Xalapa: Gobierno del Estado de Veracruz, 2015.

———. *Reforma agraria y movilización campesina en Veracruz (México) durante el siglo XX*. Warsaw: CESLA, 2010.

Velasco Toro, José Manuel, and Luis J. García Ruiz. "Restitución de tierras e inicio de la reforma agraria en Atzalan, Veracruz, 1915-1950." *Ulúa. Revista de Historia, Sociedad y Cultura* 15 (2010): 59-96.

Velázquez Hernández, Emilia. *Territorios fragmentados: estado y comunidad indígena en el Istmo veracruzano*. Mexico City: CIESAS, 2006.

Vélez, Francisco A., Emmanuel Amor, Vda. de Vicente Alonso, Luis García Pimentel, Testamentaría Ignacio de la Torre y Mier, Reyna Hermanos, V. Salceda, Manuel Araoz, R. Pasquel, Vda. e Hijos de Manuel V. Vidal, María P. de Sollano, Hijos de Antonio Escandón, María Escandón de Buch, Francisca Campero de Pasquel, José Pagaza, and Sucesores de Arturo de la Cueva. *Dos escritos dirigidos a las autoridades por los hacendados de Morelos*. Mexico City: Antigua Imprenta de Murguía, 1921.

Villa-Flores, Javier. "Archivos y falsarios: producción y circulación de documentos apócrifos en el México borbónico." *Jahrbuch für Geschichte Lateinamerikas* 46 (2009): 19-41.

Villarreal Muñoz, Antonio. *Restitución y dotación de ejidos. El problema agrario en México; leyes, decretos, circulares y disposiciones expedidas últimamente en la materia*. Mexico City: Comisión Nacional Agraria, 1921.

Villegas Moreno, Gloria. "Una legislación para cimentar el 'Estado Social,'" *Boletín* (Archivo General de la Nación), no. 17 (2007): 36-65.

Villegas Moreno, Gloria, and Miguel Angel Porrúa Venero. *De la crisis del modelo borbónico al establecimiento de la República Federal*. Mexico City: México Instituto de Investigaciones Legislativas and M.A. Porrúa, 1997.

Von Mentz, Brígida. *Pueblos de indios, mulatos y mestizos, 1770-1870. Los campesinos y las transformaciones protoindustriales en el poniente de Morelos*. Mexico City: CIESAS, 1988.

Warman, Arturo. *"We Come to Object"*: *The Peasants of Morelos and the Nation State*. Baltimore: Johns Hopkins University Press, 1980.

———. *. . . Y venimos a contradecir: los campesinos del oriente de Morelos y el estado nacional*. Mexico City: Centro de Investigaciones Superiores del Instituto Nacional de Antropología e Historia, 1976.

Whetten, Nathan Laselle. *Rural Mexico*. 1948. Reprint, Chicago: University of Chicago Press, 1969.

Wolfe, Mikael D. *Watering the Revolution*: *An Environmental and Technological History of Agrarian Reform in Mexico*. Durham: Duke University Press, 2017.

Womack, John, Jr. "Los estudios del zapatismo: lo que se ha hecho y lo que hay que hacer." In *Estudios sobre el zapatismo*, edited by Laura Espejel López, 23–30. Mexico City: INAH, 2000.

———. "Prólogo: historias por estudiar sobre la Revolución del Sur (1911-1920); lo que aún no sabemos, lo que valdría la pena saber." In *Zapata y la Revolución Mexicana*, 15–44. Mexico City: FCE, 2017.

———. *Zapata and the Mexican Revolution*. New York: Alfred A. Knopf, 1968.

Wood, Stephanie. "Pedro Villafranca y Juan Gertrudis Navarrete: falsificador de títulos y su viuda, Nueva España, siglo XVIII." In *La lucha por la supervivencia en la América Colonial*, edited by David G. Sweet and Gary B. Nash, 472–85. Mexico City: FCE, 1987.

Yannakakis, Yanna. "Witnesses, Spatial Practices, and Land Dispute in Colonial Oaxaca." *Americas* 65, no. 2 (2008): 161–92.

Zamora, Stephen, José Ramón Cossío, Leonel Pereznieto, Jose Roldan-Xopa, and David Lopez. *Mexican Law*. Oxford: Oxford University Press, 2005.

Zárate H., J. Eduardo. "Comunidad, reformas liberales y emergencia del indígena moderno: pueblos de la Meseta Purépecha (1864–1904)." *Relaciones* 32, no. 115 (2011): 17–52.

Zuleta, María Cecilia. "La Secretaría de Fomento y el fomento agrícola en México, 1876–1910: la invención de una agricultura próspera que no fue." *Mundo Agrario* 1, no. 1 (2000), n.p.

INDEX

Page numbers in italics refer to illustrations.

agrarian commissions. *See* commissions, distribution and survey
Agrarian Congress (1923), 191
agrarian reform. *See* Constitutionalist agrarian reform; Morelos agrarian reform (1920-24); Zapatista agrarian reform
agronomists, engineers, and surveyors, 63, 76, 102, 187; Afonso Cruz, 98-99, 237n63, 238n73; in Constitutionalist agrarian reform, 20, 21, 120, 123, 124-26, 145, 163-64, 177, 179-80, 184, 186, 188, 192, 247n18, 248n37; in Madero's land surveys, 64-65, 67, 71, 248n37; in nineteenth and prerevolution twentieth century, 49, 245n5, 248n37, 256n42; in Zapatista agrarian reform, 19, 63, 76, 87, 88-91, 94, 99, 102-3, 106, 109, 237n63, 238n73. *See also* Gómez, Marte R.
Aguascalientes, haciendas in: San José las Trojes, 44
Aguascalientes, place names in: Jesús María, 42; San José de Gracia, 66
Aguascalientes Convention, 199, 232n3, 237n61, 239n81; and Zapatistas, 88, 91-93, 191, 236n58, 272n10
Aguayo, Manuel, 160
Aguilar, Cándido, 111-12, 128-29, 246n9
Alarcón, Manuel, 40
Alcérreca, Luis G., 215n65
Alonso, Ana María, 15
Álvarez, Juan, 37
Amezcua, Jenaro, 164
amparo (after 1917), 37, 131, 135, 149, 201; landowners' use of, 9, 10, 138-43, 168, 169; and Morelos agrarian reform (1920-24), 170-72, 179; and post-1917 Supreme Court rulings, 140-47, 149, 160, 170-72, 176, 179
amparo (before 1917), 30, 32, 38, 44, 47, 120; and intervillage conflicts, 30-31, 34, 39; used by villagers, 5, 32-36, 38-40, 42, 45, 49-51, 57, 59, 70, 72, 120
Araoz, Manuel, 170
arbitration, 74, 121, 231n69; in Madero's land surveys, 69, 193; in nineteenth and prerevolution twentieth century, 18, 26, 27-28, 30, 54, 217n21

303

Arenas, Domingo, 132, 251n76
Ariza, Carlos Víctor, 177
Arrioja Díaz Viruell, Luis Alberto, 44–45, 221n73
article 27 (1857 Constitution), 17, 31, 39, 48, 109, 196
article 27 (1917 Constitution), 135, 144, 151, 159; on communal versus private property, 150–51; on expropriation, 140–41, 143; 1992 reforms to, 12, 74; procedures under, 144–45, 159; on protection of woodlands, 150, 197, 256n42, 257n55; reforms to, 8, 273n11; scholarship on, 2–3, 209n6, 252n4; and 6 January 1915 law, 21, 135, 139, 145, 165, 168, 169; on water resources, 149, 150, 197, 256n42, 257n50, 257n55; and Zapatista agrarian reform, 21, 164, 165, 169, 190–92. *See also* family patrimony
Ávila Espinosa, Felipe, 38
Avilés Fabila, René, 191
Ayaquica, Fortino, 94, 105
Ayotuxco, San Lorenzo, San Francisco, and Santa Cruz (Mexico State), 34–35
Azuela de la Cueva, Antonio, 16, 203, 211n19, 214n53, 263n103

Baigts, Manuel, 142–43
Barrios, Ángel, 166, 181, 265n21
Barrios, Antonio, 61–62
Bassols, Narciso, 8
Baz, Gustavo, 99, 100, 132, 241n109, 242n114, 251n80, 272n10
Blanco, Lucio, 89, 110, 238n72, 258n60

Bonilla, Manuel, 91, 193
Borah, Woodrow, 26
Breña, Luis, 126
Brito, Manuel Castillo, 69
Brunk, Samuel, 19, 22–23, 85, 98, 241n101
burden of proof: in Constitutionalist agrarian reform, 14, 112, 113, 115, 117, 122, 194–95; in pre-1917 law suits, 25, 41–42, 194–95; in Santa Anna's 1854 decree, 41, 63; in Zapatista agrarian reform, 19, 54, 63–64, 93, 193, 194–95, 214n60, 229n36. *See also* Cabrera, Luis

Cabrera, Luis, 74–75, 151, 192, 231n70, 272n4; on burden of proof, 194–95; on restitutions and reconstitutions, 11, 74–75, 232n71; and 6 January 1915 law, 108, 113–15, 194
Cabrera Acevedo, Lucio, 4, 32–34, 36, 108, 143, 209n7
caciques, 2, 51, 57, 119, 201; and conflicts over land and water resources, 18, 52, 55–57, 224n9, 226n14; as landowners, 5, 42, 221n73; as Zapatista enemies, 63, 84, 86–87
Calles, Plutarco Elías, 159–60, 191
Campeche, haciendas in: Cerrillos, 127
Campeche, place names in: Atasta, 127, 259n71; Calkiní, 222n92; San Antonio Sahcabchén, 127, 259n71
Campos Mena, Francisco, 69–70
Cárdenas, Lázaro, 184, 273n11
Carranza Garza, Venustiano, 202, 239n81, 264n11; agrarian peti-

tions to, 109, 115, 132; agrarian policies of, 23, 109, *129*, 130, 200; government of, 5, 21, 75, 108–9, 112–13, 129, 132, 135, 158, 162, 168, 210n10, 232n70, 272n4; and judiciary, 7, 108, 117, 192; presidential agrarian resolutions by, 116, 146, 147; and 6 January 1915 law, 20, 109, 116, 129; and Zapatistas, 79, 192, 232n3. *See also* Constitutionalist agrarian reform; 6 January 1915 law

Carrera Torres, Alberto, 111, 257n60

Carvajal, Ricardo, 139

Castillo, Ambrosio, 37–38

Castillo C., Rafael, *177*

Castro, Jesús Agustín, 128

Castro, Santiago, 144

censuses, 152; commissions for, 152, 156; by Constitutionalists, 112, 152–56, 165, 259n71, 260n83; and Zapatista agrarian reform, 99–101, 111, 241n109

Cerro de Arévalo (Hidalgo), 144

Cervantes, José, 102

Cervantes Ahumada, Raúl, 11

Chávez Padrón, Martha, 10

Chiapas, haciendas in: El Sombreretillo, 34

Chiapas, place names in: Mazatán, 224n7; San Fernando, 34; Soyatitán, 58; Tuzantán, 156

Chihuahua, place names in: Namiquipa, 15; San Juan, 153

Church property, 31, 46, 84–85, 133, 229n32

Coahuila, place names in: Villa de Castaños, 148

Coahuila Agrarian Commission, 148

Cobián, Feliciano, 253n17

Colima, haciendas in: Nogueras, 123; San Antonio, 123

Colima, place names in: Coquimatlán, 127; Suchitlán, 123

Comisión Nacional Agraria (CNA). *See* National Agrarian Commission

commissions, distribution and survey, 110–12, 128, 133, 180, 237n67. *See also* local agrarian commissions; National Agrarian Commission; Zapatista agrarian reform

communal lands and water resources: in agrarian petitions to Madero, 55, 58, 67; Constitutionalist agrarian reform on, 1, 2, 20, 22, 115, 118–21, 123, 126–28, 134, 136, 144, 150–51, 156–57, 160, 196–98, 213n43, 257n55; in Madero's land surveys, 64, 88, 193, 231n63; in nineteenth and prerevolution twentieth century, 7, 16–17, 31, 33–35, 37, 41–44, 47, 50, 137, 144, 173, 205; in post-1934 agrarian reform, 16, 214n54, 273n11; privatization of, 5, 28, 47–48, 50, 58, 64–66, 193, 196, 226n14, 237nn66–67, 259n71; sale of, 73, 248n43; Zapatista agrarian reform on, 1, 22, 98, 101–2, 104, 193, 196–98, 235n44. See also *amparo* (after 1917); *amparo* (before 1917); *dotaciones*; *ejidos*; restitutions; village agrarian petitions

Constitutional Convention (1916–17), 23, 135–37, 258n62; scholarship on, 8, 168, 169, 192

Index 305

Constitutionalist agrarian reform, 1–7, 20, 21, 22, 128–29, 193–200; and agricultural lands, 98–101, 124–26, 140, 150–52, 159–60, 163, 187–88, 197–99; and *comités particulares administrativos* (CPAs), 6–7, 136, 156–60, 197–98, 261n86, 261n94, 262n96; and *comités particulares ejecutivos*, 261n86, 262n96; early versions of, 109–12, 244n3; *fundo legal* in, 111, 124, 132, 147–48, 167, 195, 253n17; and intervillage conflicts, 6, 12, 16, 22, 120–21, 163, 186, 190, 192–93, 200; and pasturelands, 126, 157, 175; *procurador de pueblos*, 145, 174, 204, 262n95; and restitutions, 116–21; scholarship on, 5, 210n10; and urban areas, 136, 147–48; village agency in, 130–34; and water resources, 22, 118, 131–32, 149–50, 157–59, 163, 165, 169, 171, 187–90, 197, 257n50, 257nn52–53, 257n55, 261n89, 271n97; and woodlands, 22, 118, 126, 136, 148–49, 157, 159, 196, 257n55. See also *dotaciones*; family patrimony; National Agrarian Commission; 6 January 1915 law

Constitution of 1824, 26–27

Constitution of 1857, 7, 31–32, 218n40; article 13 in, 51, 73; article 16 in, 30–31, 35–36, 40, 72; and expropriation, 84, 109, 140; and pueblos, 25, 68, 75, 219n49. *See also* article 27 (1857 Constitution)

Constitution of 1917, 4, 137, 140, 158, 160; article 13 in, 139; article 14 in, 9, 138, 139, 142, 212n25; article 16 in, 138, 143; article 123 in, 74, 151; and post-1917 Supreme Court justices, 141, 147. *See also* article 27 (1917 Constitution)

Córdova, Arnaldo, 12

corruption, 226; in Constitutionalist agrarian reform, 6, 12, 158–59, 197; in judiciary, 7, 17, 25, 36–40, 52; in Zapatista agrarian reform, 19, 22, 83, 87, 88, 191, 197, 199

Coss, Francisco, 133, 252n81

Craib, Raymond, 15

Crespo, Horacio, 90–91, 175

Cruz, Alfonso, 98–99, 237n63, 238n73

Curbelo, Julio F., 254n17

Damián, Dolores, 95

de Ibarrola, Antonio, 11

de la Barra y Quijano, Francisco León, 53, 55, 62; village agrarian petitions to, 53, 56–57, 59, 62, 76, 193, 223n1, 223n3, 225n9, 227n18

de la Cruz, Joaquín, 130

de la F. Regalado, Miguel, 92

de la Llave, Ignacio, 28

de la Luz Servín de Capetillo, María, 33

de la O, Genovevo, 93, 98, 103, 233n15; alliance with Obregón, 164, 177; village agrarian petitions to, 79, 80, 81–82, 85; and Zapatista agrarian reform, 79–80, 102, 103, 105, 233n18

de la Peña, Guillermo, 163, 175, 186, 213n43
de la Peña, Moisés T., 11
del Castillo, Arturo, 132
de los Ángeles Romero Frizzi, María, 45–46
de Luna, Paulín, 44
Department of Land, Water, and Colonization, 149–50, 188. *See also* National Agrarian Commission
de Salceda y Echave, Rafael G., 140, 145
de Velasco, Luis, 185
Diario del Hogar, 209n4, 229n31
Díaz, Félix, 51, 110, 111, 245n7
Díaz, F. Sabino, 100
Díaz, Miguel, 173
Díaz, Porfirio, 57, 118, 242n111; advisors and allies of, 59, 68, 70, 104, 111, 119, 131; and *científicos*, 2, 63, 84, 87, 131; and judiciary, 7–9, 36, 38; overthrow of, 4, 5–6, 53, 69, 78, 84, 91, 193, 204; village agrarian petitions to, 36–37, 49, 76, 77. *See also* Porfiriato
Díaz González, Prisciliano María, 31–32, 48–49
Díaz Soto y Gama, Antonio, 73–74, 191, 264n11
Díaz Soto y Gama, Ignacio, 239n73
disentailment, 48, 66, 82–83, 120, 123, 202. *See also* Lerdo law (1856); privatization of communal lands
district courts: and Constitutionalist agrarian reform, 131, 138–39, 141–42, 147, 253n8, 253–54n17, 262n96, 267n41, 269n64; and Madero's land surveys, 55, 57–59, 69–72, 231n64; and Morelos agrarian reform (1920–24), 170–71, 179, 267n41; in nineteenth and prerevolution twentieth century, 31–40, 44, 49–50, 120, 219n48, 223n101. *See also amparo* (after 1917); *amparo* (before 1917); judiciary
dotaciones, 20, 123–27, 152–56, 202; and *amparo*, 139–42, 146–47, 168, 170–71, 262n96; as compensation for failed restitutions, 20, 22, 115, 121–23, 152, 195; and expropriation, 140, 142; and Parres reforms, 172–84 *passim*; petitions for, 133–34, 152, 166; procedures regarding, 145, 166–67, 187, 214n54, 252n5; scholarship on, 9, 13–16, 185, 213n43, 214n55; and 6 January 1915 law, 23, 123, 140–42, 147, 150–51
Durán, Gustavo, 124
Durango, haciendas in: Casa Blanca, 144; Navacoyán, 224n7; San Gabriel, 111; San José Buenavista, 111; Santa Catalina Alamo, 56; Sombreretillo, 38; Tapona, 111
Durango, place names in: Arenal, 224n7; Cuencamé, 38; Guarisamey, 225n13; Nazas River, 257n52; Pasaje, 56; Peñón Blanco, 56; San Francisco del Malpaís, 144–45; San Pedro de Ocuila, 34, 38–39

Eckstein, Salomón, 11

ejidos, 34, 144, 170; in Constitutionalist agrarian reform, 20, 101, 118, 123-25, 127-28, 132, 145, 147-49, 158-60, 177, 195, 262n100; definitions of, 63-65, 74-75, 100, 115, 136, 145-49, 150-51, 202-3, 252n5, 254n17; Madero's land surveys of, 54, 65-69, 71-72, 222n92, 230n50, 231n64; in nineteenth and prerevolution twentieth century, 34, 111, 144, 183, 186, 211n11, 238n68, 249n52; organizational structure of, 159-60; in post-1934 agrarian reform, 1, 6-7, 22, 136, 160-61, 214n54, 263n103; prerevolutionary privatization of, 18, 47, 49, 64, 66, 238n70, 242n112; scholarship on, 11, 14-16, 211n19, 212n32, 214n55, 262n100. See also *dotaciones*; family patrimony

El Imparcial, 72

El País, 61, 68, 234n26

Escobar viuda de Alarcón, Eva, 167

ethnicity, 150, 196, 205, 211n11, 215n63

executive vs. judicial authority: Constitutionalists on, 4, 6, 8, 20-22, 75, 107, 108, 109, 111-21, 131, 135-43, 192-95, 198-200, 204; debates on, 72-75, 115; and 1857 Constitution, 51, 72-73; under Madero, 18-19, 53-54, 59, 65, 66, 68-71, 73, 75, 193, 222n92, 227n18, 231n63; and 1917 Constitution, 139, 212n25; in nineteenth and prerevolution twentieth century, 7, 17-18, 26-31, 35-36, 49-51, 55, 85, 193, 204, 217n13, 223n101; and post-1917 Supreme Court rulings, 20, 135-40, 142, 160, 196; scholarship on, 7-12, 212n40; villagers' role in, 5, 6, 18, 25-26, 49-52, 54-56, 64, 65, 69, 144; and Zapatista agrarian reform, 4, 19, 22, 64, 72, 75, 76, 79, 80, 83, 85, 89, 91, 107, 192-95, 198-99, 244n1, 272n10. See also judiciary; 6 January 1915 law; Supreme Court

expropriation, 74-75, 151, 244, 258n60; *amparo* against, 139, 140, 141, 142, 155, 253n17; Constitutionalists and, 2, 20, 22, 89, 108-13, 115, 122-23, 134, 135, 137, 139, 186, 195, 202, 254n21, 258n60; and post-1917 Supreme Court rulings, 140-43, 160, 196; scholarship on, 2, 9, 10, 14, 213n43; and Zapatista agrarian reform, 22, 84-89, 98, 99, 100, 107, 193, 195, 215n64, 229n32, 235n45. See also *dotaciones*; nationalization

Falcón, Romana, 45, 46, 217n21

family patrimony, 159-60, 242n112, 258n62; and Constitutionalists, 110, 197, 199, 258n60; as inalienable property rights, 111, 151-52, 197, 258n62; and 1917 Constitution, 151-52; and northern revolutionaries, 110, 113, 151-52, 246n12, 257n60; pre-1917 federal laws on, 242n112, 245n4; and U.S. Homestead Act, 110, 151. See also Zapatista agrarian reform

Federal District, haciendas in: Antonio Coapa, 227n18

Federal District, place names in: Iztapalapa, 116-17; San Andrés

Mixquic, 49-50; San Juanico Nextipac, 155-56; San Juan Ixtayopan, 118, 262n96; San Juan Xochimilco, 94, 119-20, 140, 146, 227n18, 262n97; San Lorenzo, 34-35; Santa María Aztahuacan, 155
federal public lands laws, 70, 75, 110, 238nn68-69, 245n4, 249n52; used by Madero, 18-19, 54, 64, 70; used by villagers, 18, 47-49, 52, 56, 70. *See also* Zapatista agrarian reform
female heads of household, 34, 152-56, 259n71, 261n86
Fenner Bieling, Justus, 38
Fix Zamudio, Héctor, 10
forgery of documents, 45-46, 118, 221n80
Fowler-Salamini, Heather, 155
Franco, Francisco, 77-78, 176-84, 269n67, 270n74, 270n77
Fuentes, Eduardo, 72-74
fundo legal, 44, 202, 203, 244n3; Madero's surveys of, 71, 230n50; in nineteenth and prerevolution twentieth century, 27, 32, 49, 225n11. *See also* Constitutionalist agrarian reform; Zapatista agrarian reform

Galeana, Crispín, 86
García, Genaro G., 141
García Pimentel, Luis, 168, 169, 171, 265n30
Gilly, Adolfo, 12
Gledhill, John, 15
Gómez, Marte R., 94, 142, 164, 169, 179, 182

Gómez Santana, Laura, 119
González, Pablo, 165
González, Zeferino, 147
González Garza, Roque, 91
González Roa, Fernando, 7-8
González y González, Luis, 36
Guanajuato, haciendas in: San Antonio Calichar, 131
Guanajuato, place names in: San Bartolomé Aguascalientes, 131; San Miguel Octopan, 224n6
Guerrero, Eligio, 69-70
Guerrero, place names in: Ahuatepec, 82; Ajuchitlán, 55; Cacalutla, 232n2; Chilacachapa, 225n11; Chilapa, 39; Chontalcoatlán, 158; Coachimalco, 82-83; Cochimalco, 83; Huamuxtitl, 98; Huixtac, 27, 219n48; Malinaltepec, 66, 224n9; Mezquitlán, 259n71; Olinalá, 82; San Miguel Totolapan, 83; Taxco, 27; Tecalpulco, 27; Tehuilotepec, 226n14; Temaxcalapa, 219n48; Tepetlacingo, 152; Tepozonalquillo, 261n86; Tlalixtaquilla, 101-2; Tlaquiltepec, 95; Tuliman, 153, 155
Gutiérrez, Eulalio, 91
Guzmán Vaca, Jesús, 171

haciendas. *See under individual states*
Hall, Linda, 13-14
Henderson, Peter V. N., 62
Hernández, Braulio, 244n3
Hernández, Juan, 59
Hernández, Rafael, 64-65, 69, 75, 229n37
Hernández Chávez, Alicia, 185
Herrera, Ezequiel, 87

Herrera-Martin, Carlos R., 140–41
Hidalgo, haciendas in: La Concepción, 122, 128; San Miguel Chingú, 149
Hidalgo, place names in: Ajacuba, 132; Atotonilco, 146; El Puente, 144; Huitexcalco, 132; La Estanzuela, 122; La Vega de Metztitlán, 59; San Agustín Tlaxiaca, 153; San Francisco Tlanalapa, 123, 131, 158, 251n79; San Jerónimo, 153; San Juan Tilcuautla, 123; Santiago Tlajomulco, 126; Tepeji River, 149; Tepenene, 130; Tetepango, 132, 148–49; Tlaxcoapan, 149; Tolcayuca, 127; Tulancingo, 226n14
Huerta, Epitacio, 29
Huerta, Victoriano, 75, 79, 108, 239n81

Indian courts. *See* judiciary
Indian litigation rights, 27–30
Indian Republic, 26
Institutional Revolutionary Party (PRI), 10, 12, 191–92
intervillage conflicts: and Constitutionalist agrarian reform, 6, 12, 16, 22, 120–21, 163, 186, 190, 192–93, 200; and Madero's land surveys, 18, 55, 57, 65, 67, 81, 163, 193; in nineteenth and prerevolution twentieth century, 5, 17, 28–31, 39, 40–52 *passim*, 240n85; and post-1934 agrarian reform, 12, 213n41, 273n11; and Zapatista agrarian reform, 6, 19, 77, 81, 93–95, 102, 105, 106–7, 192–93, 199–200, 232n1, 240n88, 241n97, 271n90

Islas viuda de Ramírez, Aurelia, 158
Isunza, Gonzalo, 63, 102

Jalisco, haciendas in: Guadalupe, 27; San Agustín, 119
Jalisco, place names in: Mascota, 57; San Gabriel, 27; Santa Cruz de la Soledad, 55; Sayula, 226n14; Villa de Zacoalco, 227n18; Zoquipan, 261n86
James, Timothy M., 20, 30
Jáuregui, José María, 27
jefes políticos, 203, 226n14; and judiciary, 17–18, 27–28; and Madero's land surveys, 230n49, 227n18; before 1910, 29–34, 38, 40, 41, 45, 47, 51, 59, 66, 69, 77, 144, 217n13, 217n21, 219n48, 227n18
Juárez, Benito, 30, 84, 235n47
judiciary: agrarian tribunals (1992), 12–13, 212n40, 213n41; and checks and balances, 7, 26–31, 49–50, 69, 72; and Constitutionalist agrarian reform, 3, 4, 6–13, 20–21, 108–9, 111, 114–17, 119–21, 128, 130–31, 134, 135–50 *passim*, 192–94, 198, 200, 218n40, 244n1, 250n65, 252n5, 253–54n17, 254n18, 255n25, 262n96, 266n39; corruption in, 8–9, 36–40; debates regarding, 73–75, 112–15; defending purview of, 26, 30, 31, 51, 223n101; Indian courts, 4, 26, 215n2; under Madero, 18–19, 54, 55, 58–59, 62, 65, 71–75 *passim*, 222n92, 227n18, 231nn63–64; and Morelos agrarian reform (1920–24), 21–22, 162–63, 168–72, 179, 190, 192–93, 195, 267n41; before

310 *Index*

1917, 17–18, 25–40, 44–45, 48–52, 54, 55, 57–59, 65–74, 77, 79, 85, 204, 218n40, 220n62, 223n101, 224n7, 230n50; and Plan de Ayala, 64, 83, 85, 198–99; scholarship on, 3, 4, 7–13, 45, 209n7; shutdown of (1914), 4, 75, 108, 134, 244n1; Superior or Supreme Tribunal, 29, 36, 48, 57, 109n241, 272n10; villagers sidestepping, 5, 18, 25, 49, 51, 53, 109, 130–31; and Zapatista agrarian reform, 63–64, 72–77, 79, 80–83, 85, 89, 91, 107, 192–95, 198–99, 241n109, 272n10. *See also* executive vs. judicial authority; jurisprudence; Supreme Court

juridical standing (pueblos), 66, 203; and Constitutionalist agrarian reform, 144, 160, 248n24; before 1917, 17–18, 25–27, 31–36, 39, 40, 48–52, 149, 217n21, 218n37, 220n62, 223n101

jurisprudence, 34, 203; after 1917, 116–18, 141, 254n18; before 1917, 30, 36, 218n40

Knight, Alan, 1, 17, 112, 210n10
Knowlton, Robert, 32, 38
Kourí, Emilio, 48, 151, 192, 202, 204, 214n62, 222n89

Laborde, Ignacio Marván, 192
Lagos Cházaro, Francisco, 91
La Patria, 65
"La Reforma" (1855–61), 31, 84, 202
latifundios, 108, 112, 215n65, 252n5
Lerdo de Tejada, Miguel, 214n61
Lerdo de Tejada, Sebastián, 30

Lerdo law (1856), 21–22, 31, 58, 116, 214n61; and 6 January 1915 law, 115, 175, 185, 247n19
Leyva, Francisco, 79–80, 174
Liberal privatization laws. *See* privatization of communal lands
local agrarian commissions, 9, 121, 129, 249n58; in Campeche, 127; in Coahuila, 148; in Federal District, 116, 119–20; in Guanajuato, 131; in Guerrero, 152; in Hidalgo, 93, 126, 144; in Mexico State, 131, 143, 144, 156–57; in Michoacán, 124, 126–27; in Morelos, 21, 163–90 *passim*, 270n77; in Oaxaca, 142, 146; in Puebla, 125, 128, *129*, 133; in Tlaxcala, 120, 131, 132, 138–39, 262n96; in Veracruz, 126, 129; in Zacatecas, 124
López de Santa Anna, Antonio, 37, 41, 63, 193, 221n68

Madero, Francisco I., 53, 75, 78, 204, 229n38; and executive vs. judicial authority, 18–19, 53–54, 59, 65, 66, 68–71, 73, 75, 193, 222n92, 227n18, 231n63; judiciary under, 18–19, 54, 55, 58–59, 62, 65, 71–75 *passim*, 222n92, 227n18, 231nn63–64; land surveys by, 18–19, 54, 55, 57–59, 64–72, 75, 88, 193, 222n92, 227n18, 230nn49–50, 231nn63–64, 237n67; and Plan de San Luis Potosí, 53–58, 61, 65, 224n6, 224n9, 228n18, 272n4; relations with Zapata, 1–2, 53–54, 79, 233n13; village agrarian petitions to, 53–61, *60*, 65–68, 193, 224nn6–7, 226n14, 227n18

Index 311

Madero land surveys: agronomists, engineers, and surveyors in, 64–65, 67, 71, 248n37; of communal lands and water resources, 64, 88, 193, 231n63; and district courts, 55, 57–59, 69–72, 231n64; of *ejidos*, 54, 65–69, 71–72, 222n92, 230n50, 231n64; and federal public lands laws, 18–19, 54, 64, 70; and *fundo legal*, 71, 230n50; and intervillage conflicts, 18, 55, 57, 65, 67, 81, 163, 193; and municipal governments, 66–69, 71–72, 230n50; and pre-1917 Supreme Court rulings, 70–72, 75; and primordial titles, 63, 67, 225n9; and private property, 54, 64, 71; and privatization of communal lands, 18, 64–65, 70, 193; and restitutions, 71, 72

Magaña, Gildardo, 164

Marino, Daniela, 32, 34, 39, 45, 238n68

Markiewicz, Dana, 14

Maximilian of Habsburg, 29, 30, 193

Medina, Antonio, 128

Mendieta y Núñez, Lucio, 9, 215n65

Mendiola Bringas, Alberto, 130

Mendoza, Rosalino, 87

Mendoza López Schwerdtfeger, Miguel, 164, 241n110, 263n10

Mercado viuda de Romano y Leopoldo, Leonor, 72

Mexican Liberal Party, 72–73, 84

Mexico State, haciendas in: Atenco, 121; Calpulalpan, 46; de Solís, 251n80; El Tular, 120; Gachopinco, 35; Guadalupe, 35; Jalmolonga, 79, 80; Jaltepec, 65, 82; San Juan de Guadalupe, 49; San Lucas, 98; San Pedro Mártir, 35; Santa Lucía, 120; Tenería, 82, 93; Tiacaque, 65, 68

Mexico State, place names in: Acatzingo, 82, 93; Agostadero, 147, 251n80; Almoloya del Río, 144; Amecameca, 35, 49; Atarasquillo, 34; Atlautla, 35; Cahuacán, 32; Calimaya, 216n5, 219n48; Capultitlán, 257n53; Huixquilucan, 34, 35; Jilotepec, 58; Jocotitlán, 65, 68; Mayorazgo de la Concepción de León, 131; Muitejé, 132; Nextipayac, 216n5; San Antonio Acahualco, 81; San Antonio la Isla, 102–3; San Antonio Pachuquilla, 65, 82; San Bartolomé Capulhuac, 47–48; San Francisco, 34–35; San Francisco Chejé, 68; San Juan de las Manzanas, 131; San Juan Tehuixtitlán, 35; San Juan Tezontla, 150; San Juan Xochiaca, 81; San Juan Zacazonapan, 216n2; San Lucas del Pulque, 95; San Lucas Totolmaloya, 130–31; San Martín Malinalco, 79, 80; San Miguel, 57; San Miguel Chapultepec, 121, 227n18; San Pedro Totoltepec, 140, 156–57, 225n9; San Simón de la Laguna, 57; San Simón el Alto, 81; San Simón Zozocoltepec, 226n14; Santa Cruz Ayotuxco, 34–35; Santiago Mamalhuazuca, 41; Santiago Tequixquiac, 127, 139; San Vicente Chimalhuacán Chalco, 41; Tepexoyuca, 95; Tepexpan, *154*; Tequisistlán, *154*; Texcoco, 130; Tlaltizapan, 47–48; Xaltocan, 120; Zumpahuacán, 83

Michoacán, haciendas in: Coapa, 33, 40; Porumbo, 126

Michoacán, place names in: Ahuirán, 52; Arocutín, 117, 126; Atacheo, 61, 68; Cherán Atzicuirín, 52; Coalcomán, 226; Ecuandureo, 68; Erongarícuaro, 127; La Ciénega, 133; Naranja, 130; Pamatácuaro, 120–21; Purhépecha region, 133, 247n21; San Juan Parangaricutiro, 225n9; San Miguel Guarachita, 71, 231n64, 262n96; Tanaco, 52; Tingambato, 35–36; Tiripetío, 33, 40; Tlazazalca, 68; Urapicho, 52; Urén, 52; Yurécuaro, 60; Zacapu, 68

Ministry of Agriculture and Colonization (Zapatista), 4, 6, 76–77, 199, 200, 236n58; and individual land titling, 99–100; judicial role of, 89, 193–94; *Sección de Fraccionamiento*, 100, 242n114; and temporary *repartos*, 94–95; and water resources, 106, 196; and woodland preservation, 103–4. *See also* agronomists, engineers, and surveyors

Ministry of Agriculture and Development (Constitutionalist), 135, 137, 164, 188, 200, 246nn11–12, 247n18; and 6 January 1915 law, 114, 116, 126, 128–29, 135; villagers' petitions to, 115, 166. *See also* agronomists, engineers, and surveyors

Ministry of Development (in nineteenth and prerevolution twentieth century), 51, 54–55, 214n61, 223n102; and federal public lands laws, 238n69, 245n4; villagers' petitions to, 221n68, 225n13, 226n14. *See also* agronomists, engineers, and surveyors

Ministry of Development, Colonization, and Industry (under Madero), 18, 64, 74; circulars issued by, 18, 54, 64–72, 74, 88, 230n50, 237n65, 237n67; and Rafael Hernández, 64–65, 69, 75, 229n37; role in land surveys, 18, 64–66, 68, 70–72, 74, 75, 230n50, 231nn63–64; villagers' petitions to, 54–55, 58, 65–66, 72, 130. *See also* agronomists, engineers, and surveyors

Ministry of Justice, 59, 227n18

Ministry of Public Education, 261n90

Ministry of the Interior, 51

Ministry of the Treasury, 51, 55, 71, 173, 230n50, 247n19

Molina Enríquez, Andrés, 36–37, 89, 90, 116, 151, 192, 239n76

Montaño, Otilio, 80, 83, 84, 235n47; and Plan de Ayala, 23, 53–54, 62, 63, 72, 79, 84, 193, 195, 198–99, 235

Morelos, haciendas in: Ahuacatitlán, 101, 121; Atlihuayán, 37; Chiconcuac, 83; Chiltepec, 79; Coahuixtla, 182, 269n64; Cuahuixtla, 177; Cuauchichinola, 61; El Hospital, 77–78, 82, 177, 182, 184–85, 186, 269n64; El Puente, 83, 265n27; Jonacatepec, 254n21; Miacatlán, 105; San Bernardo, 105; San Carlos, 188; San Gabriel, 61, 165, 187; San Gaspar, 61; San José Vista Hermosa, 167; Santa Clara, 82, 104, 165, 175, 187, 254n21; Santa Cruz Vista Alegre, 170; San Vicente, 61; Temixco, 174, 233n15; Tenango, 49, 87, 93, 168; Tenextepango, 177; Tizantes, 79

Index 313

Morelos, place names in: Alpuyeca, 186; Amayuca, 79; Amilcingo, 93; Atlacholoaya, 82, 170, 182, 186; Atlatlahucan, 106, 165, 186, 264n17; Atlihuayán, 105; Axochiapan, 93; Coatetelco, 83; Cocoyoc, 182; Coyotepec, 186; Cuauchichinola, 61; Cuautlixco, 182; Cuentepec, 106; El Hospital, 185, 186; El Puente, 186; Huazulco, 93, 104, 182, 187; Huejotango, 175; Itzamatitlán, 188; Ixtlilco, 168, 265n30; Jiutepec, 61–62, 267n41; Jonacatepec, 93, 186; Metepec, 82, 100, 103–4; Miacatlán, 104, 105–6; Moyotepec, 60; Nepantla, 106, 186; Oaxtepec, 94, 186; Ocotepec, 103; Ocuituco, 26, 82, 165, 175; Pazulco, 186; Popotlán, 182, 187; San Andrés Hueyapan, 93, 95; San Antonio Cuautzingo, 175; San Francisco Ocoxaltepec, 173–74, 176; San Francisco Zacualpan, 169; San Gabriel Amacuzac, 61, 165–66, 182, 187, *189*, 265n20; San Miguel Anenecuilco, 22, 77–78, 163, 176–85, *178*, 270n77; San Miguel Tlaltetelco, 104; Santa María Ahuacatitlán, 40, 79, 101–3, 174, 233n15; Tecajec, 165, 182, 187; Temilpa, 167; Temoac, 104; Tenextepango, 182; Tepalcingo, 186; Tepatitlán, 182; Tepoztlán, 29; Tetelcingo, 165, 186; Tetelilla, 171; Tetlama, 186; Ticumán, 105; Tlacotepec, 93–95, 187, 257n53; Tlaltetelco, 104; Tlatenchi, *92*, *96*, *97*; Villa de Ayala, 60, 78, 82, 176–77, 179, 182, 184–86; Xochitepec, 172, 186; Xoxocotla, 105; Yautepec, 37; Yautepec River, 188; Yecapixtla, 186; Zacualpan de Amilpas, 94, 187

Morelos agrarian reform (1920–24), 21–22, 174, 175; and Alfredo C. Ortega, 164, 165, 176, 181–82; and Álvaro Obregón, 162, 164, 170, 183; *amparos* against, 168–72, 179, 267n41; and Anenecuilco's failed restitution, 163, 176–85, 270n77; and Ángel Barrios, 166, 181; and Antonio I. Villarreal González, 164, 166–68, 172, 264n9; and article 27 (1917 Constitution), 164–65, 168, 169, 190; and Carlos M. Peralta, 164, 263n8; and Constitutionalist agrarian reform, 162–65, 168; *dotaciones* under, 163, 164, 166–68, 170–88; and El Hospital hacienda, 177, 182, 184–85, 186; and Francisco Franco Salazar, 176, 177–84, 270n74, 270n77; and Genovevo de la O, 164, 177; and José G. Parres, 166–69, 263n1, 265n30; and José Robles, 176, 180–84, 270n77; landowners' challenges to, 167–72, 265–66n30; and Lázaro Cárdenas, 184–85; and Marte R. Gómez, 164; and Miguel Mendoza López Schwerdtfeger, 164, 264n10; and Morelos Agrarian Commission, 163, 165–66, 168–70, 175–79, 181–84, 187, 190; and Morelos District Court, 170–72, 179, 267n41, 269n64; and National Agrarian

Commission, 162-75, 179-88, 190; and Plan de Ayala, 164, 177, 179, 185, 190; political status designation under, 162, 166-68, 175, 186, 204, 263n1, 265n27; and pre-1917 Supreme Court rulings, 162-63, 168-72, 185, 190, 267n41; and presidential agrarian resolutions, 163, 171-72, 182-84, 265n20; provisional possessions under, 162, 164, 166, 168-69, 172, 177, 179-80, 182, 186-87, 265n23; regional challenges to, 163, 186-90; restitutions under, 163, 164, 166, 172-76; and Ricardo Sarmiento, 181-83; scholarship on, 13-14, 162-64, 175, 179-82, 185, 263n6, 264n15, 266n39, 269n67; and Serafín M. Robles, 164, 177; and 6 January 1915 law, 21, 162-65, 168-75, 183-87, 190; Villa de Ayala *dotación* under, 176-77, 179, 182, 184-86; villagers' response to, 165-66, 264n15; and water resources, 163, 165, 171, 187-88, 190; and Zapatista agrarian reform, 165, 176, 177, 181, 184, 185. *See also* Morelos, place names in; Parres, José G.

Moreno Cora, Silvestre, 34-35

municipal governments, 41-42, 45, 47, 109, 261n90; accused of land grabbing, 5, 6, 17-18, 34-35, 45, 47, 50; *alcalde*, 27, 44, 201; *barrios*, 6, 45, 201, 204; *cabeceras*, 6, 54, 201, 204, 205, 210n11; and *comités particulares administrativos*, 156-60, 261n94; and Constitutionalist agrarian reform, 128-29, 133, 136, 147-48, 156-58, 159, 161, 166, 199-200; executive authority of, 17-18, 50-51; juridical standing of, 30-33, 217n21; and Madero's land surveys, 57-58, 66-69, 70-72, 230n50; in post-1934 agrarian reform, 1, 6-7, 203, 211n19, 261n93, 263n103; *síndico*, 48, 67, 99, 204, 210n11; *sujetos*, 6, 45, 204, 205; as village representatives, 5, 30, 40, 47, 48, 49, 55, 66-69, 71-72, 77, 210-11n11; in Zapatista agrarian reform, 77, 81, 86-87, 99, 100-6, 109, 199

Nájera, Enrique, 168
National Agrarian Commission, 21, 109, 145, 247n18, 248n26; and Anenecuilco (Morelos), 179-85, 270n77; and Department of Land, Water, and Colonization, 149-50, 188; *dotaciones* by, 122-29; judicial functions claimed by, 4, 7-8, 114, 134, 138; and Marte R. Gómez, 164, 169-70, 182; and Morelos agrarian reform (1920-24), 21, 162-69, 172-75, 179-88, 190, 264n10, 270n77; and presidential agrarian resolutions, 254n18, 265n23; publications by or for, 7, 209n6; resource policies of, 136, 147-50, 160, 188; restitutions by, 116-21, 160, 172-75, 179-85, 270n77; and village agrarian petitions, 130, 262n97. *See also* Constitutionalist agrarian reform; Ministry of Agriculture and Development (Constitutionalist)

Index 315

National Archives, 45, 67, 77, 122, 180, 194
nationalization, 46, 244n3; and Zapatista agrarian reform, 84-85, 86-89, 100, 101, 229n32, 235n45, 243n140. *See also* expropriation
National School of Agriculture, 91, 239n73
Nayarit, place names in: Ahuacatitlán, 57; Mexcaltitán, 56; San Blas, 71-72; Santa Cruz de Camotlán, 56; Sayamota, 227n18; Tepic Territory, 56-57, 71-72, 227n18
Novelo, José I., 112-13, 124, 258n60
Nugent, Daniel, 15

Oaxaca, place names in: Chalcatongo, 39; Nazareno Etla, 133, 141, 142, 159; San Agustín Etla, 44; San Gabriel Etla, 44; San Juan Guelache, 44-45, 221n73; San Lorenzo Cacaotepec, 133; San Miguel el Grande, 39; San Miguel Etla, 44; San Miguel Tequixtepec, 31, 51; Santa María del Tule, 134, 146; Santa María Huatulco, 156; Santo Domingo Jalieza, 156; Tamazulapan, 31, 51, 223n101; Tejúpam, 31, 51, 223n101; Teococuilco, 44-45; Tepelmeme, 31; Teposcolula, 31, 51, 223n101; Tlalixtac de Cabrera, 146
Obregón, Álvaro, 183, 239n81, 263n2; agrarian laws of, 136, 145, 159, 170, 246n15; and Plan de Agua Prieta, 162, 164; relation to Zapatistas, 21, 162, 164, 190, 191; scholarship on, 13-14, 23, 162-65. *See also* Morelos agrarian reform (1920-24)

Olivares, Facundo, 140, 146
Olvera Toro, Manuel, 59
Ortega, Alfredo C., 165, 176, 181-82
"Otero formula." *See* jurisprudence
Owensby, Brian P., 25, 45, 46

Palacios, Guillermo, 15-16
Palafox Ibarrola, Manuel, 63, 85, 87-88, 237n60; and agrarian commissions, 90-93, 238-39n73; and family patrimony, 88-89, 98-101, 197; laws authored by, 87-90; and Ministry of Agriculture, 89, 236n58; policies advocated by, 63, 88-91, 99-101, 103-4, 106, 196, 243n140; and Zapatista agrarian decrees, 88, 241n101, 241n110
Paniagua, Trinidad A., 83, 98
Parres, José G., 174, 184, 186; agrarian policies of, 21, 164-67, 175-77; as governor of Morelos, 21, 164, 172; landlords' challenges to, 167-68, 171-72; and political status for villages, 166-68, 175, 265n23; and provisional possessions, 162, 166, 168-69, 172, 177, 179, 180; and restitutions, 21-22, 172-73, 175-77. *See also* Morelos agrarian reform (1920-24)
Parrodi, Anastasio, 28
Peralta, Carlos M., 164, 263n8
Pérez, Romualdo, 67-68
Petriciolli viuda de Kennedy, Concepción, 139
Pineda, Rosendo, 245n4
Pinzón, Silvestre, 105
Plan de Agua Prieta, 162, 164
Plan de Ayala, 2, 22-23, 31, 62-63, 208n4; and article 27 (1917 Con-

stitution), 190, 192; burden of proof in, 53–54, 63, 194; and *caciques*, 86–87; and *científicos*, 2, 63, 84, 87, 131; on expropriations and nationalizations, 84, 86–87, 215n64, 235n45; and judiciary, 64, 83, 85, 198–99; and Morelos agrarian reform (1920–24), 164, 177, 179, 185, 190; provisions of, 63, 64, 81, 84, 88, 199, 234n24, 235n44, 235n46; and restitutions, 2, 53–54, 63, 80, 82, 85, 196; used by villagers, 86, 104, 132, 251nn79–80; and Zapatista revolutionary chiefs, 79–80, 86, 234n24

Plan de San Luis Potosí, 53, 58–59, 272n4; provisions of, 3, 54, 55–56, 65, 224n9; used by villagers, 55–56, 58, 60–61, 65, 224n6, 224n9, 228n18

political status designation, 167, 204, 263n1; in Constitutionalist agrarian reform, 254n17; in Morelos agrarian reform (1920–24), 162, 166–67, 168, 175, 186, 265n27

Ponciano, Florencio, 83

popular liberalism, 234n26

Porfiriato, 4, 9, 40, 90–91, 149, 204; legends about, 25, 38, 56. *See also* Díaz, Porfirio

Portillo de Diez de Sollano, María, 172, 265n27

primordial titles: and Madero's land surveys, 63, 67, 225n9; and *mercedes*, 42, 46, 124, 185, 204; and Morelos agrarian reform (1920–24), 183, 187; and nineteenth- and prerevolution twentieth-century court cases, 17, 36, 44–45; and Zapatista agrarian reform, 79, 89, 94, 95, 101–2

private property, 150–51, 197; and Constitutionalist agrarian reform, 8, 109–10, 112, 119–20, 123, 136, 140, 144, 150–52, 188, 197; debates regarding, 99–100, 151, 196; and judiciary, 54, 144, 150, 194; and landowners' rights, 14, 54, 71, 90, 120, 188, 217n13; and Madero's land surveys, 54, 64, 71; pueblos and, 42, 55; and water resources, 42, 149–50; and Zapatista land reform, 23, 84, 99–101, 195, 197, 215n64

privatization of communal lands, 31, 48; and Constitutionalist agrarian reform, 20, 120, 122, 123, 126, 152–53, 156; by disentailment commissions, 66, 237n67; and *ejidos*, 64, 238n70; and judiciary, 33, 35, 48, 50; and Madero's land surveys, 18, 64–65, 70, 193; nineteenth- and prerevolution twentieth-century federal laws on, 64, 202, 238n70; nineteenth- and prerevolution twentieth-century state laws on, 28, 44, 48–50, 70, 237n67; village requests for, 5, 18, 33, 44, 47–48, 52, 55, 58, 66, 82–83, 123, 130, 193, 226n14; women as beneficiaries of, 238n68, 259n71; and Zapatista agrarian reform, 77, 82–85, 88–100 *passim*, 196–97, 237n66. *See also* Lerdo law (1856); *repartos*

Index   317

provincial deputations, 26, 204, 216nn4-5
provisional possessions: and Constitutionalist agrarian reform, 98; and Morelos agrarian reform (1920-24), 166, 168-69, 172, 177-80, 186-87, 265n23. *See also* Parres, José G.
public lands laws. *See* federal public lands laws
public schools, 157, 167, 198, 230n50, 261n90
public utility, 9, 74; and Constitutionalist agrarian reform, 9, 109, 112, 140-43, 146, 160, 195-96, 244n3; and post-1917 Supreme Court rulings, 140-43, 146, 160; and Zapatista agrarian reform, 84, 195-96, 215n64, 235n44
Puebla, haciendas in: Atencingo, 49; Boquería, 95; Jaltepec, 49; La Concepción, 128; Santo Domingo, 57; Texcalapa, 85-86, 95
Puebla, place names in: Apapantilla, 225n13; Huilango, 105; Ixcamilpa, 80, 81, 191-92, 229n31; San Andrés Payuca, 128; San Antonio Cuautla, 105; San Felipe Cuapexco, 94; San Jerónimo Caleras, 57; San Juan Atzingo, 53; San Lorenzo Teotipilco, 148; San Lucas Tulcingo, 105; San Marcos Ayoxuxtla, 62; San Miguel, 105; San Nicolás Tetitzintla, 66; San Simón Atzitzintla, 261n89; Santa Catarina Cuapiaxtla, 248n30; Santa Catarina Ilamacingo, 224n9; Santa María Coatepec, 127; Santa María del Monte, 43; Santa María Ixtiyucan, 133; Santo Tomás Otlaltepec, 224n9; Tecomatlán, 85; Tehuacán, 43, 59, 66; Temoxtitla, 32; Tepexi el Viejo, 228n18; Texcalapa, 85-86, 95; Tlalancaleca, 116; Tlaltepexi, 232n2; Tzicatlán, 93; Xicotlán, 87; Zoyapetlayoca, 157
Purnell, Jennie, 14-15, 28, 45, 130

Querétaro, place names in: San Ildefonso Tultepec, 127
Quintanilla viuda de Orvañanos, Dolores, 143

Rangel, Modesto, 82, 83
Regalado, Miguel F., 61, 68
repartos, 204; in Constitutionalist agrarian reform, 128, 130, 133, 146, 158-59; and Madero's land surveys, 58, 65, 66-67; and Morelos agrarian reform (1920-24), 162, 164, 166, 190; and nineteenth- and prerevolution twentieth-century communal land privatization, 33, 130, 225n13, 226n14; village requests for, 225n13, 226n58; and Zapatista agrarian reform, 6, 19, 22, 77, 86-89, 94-95, 99-100, 102, 106-8, 111, 132, 133, 162, 164-65, 197-98
restitutions, 3, 204; in Anenecuilco (Morelos), 163, 176-85, 270n77; and Constitutionalist agrarian reform, 2, 4, 20-23, 108-9, 111-23 *passim*, 126-34, 137, 149-

50, 152, 156, 160, 186–88, 193–96, 199; debates regarding, 11, 72–75, 108, 193; and Madero's land surveys, 71, 72; and Morelos agrarian reform (1920–24), 22, 163, 164, 166, 168, 172–88, 270n77; in nineteenth and pre-revolution twentieth century, 4, 6, 17, 27, 35, 36, 40–46, 49, 216n4; and post-1917 Supreme Court rulings, 135–37, 140, 142–51, 160, 253n17, 255n25; in post-1934 agrarian reform, 202n4; scholarship on, 3, 7, 9, 11–16, 172, 213n42, 214n55; villagers' petitions for, 1, 56, 59, 61–62, 66, 130–34, 144–48, 152, 173–75, 224n9, 228n18, 247n21, 248n30, 251nn79–80; of water resources, 66, 149–50, 188; and Zapatista agrarian reform, 2, 4, 19, 54, 76, 80–83, 85, 87, 88–92, 94–98, *96–97*, 101–2, 105, 191–96, 232n3. *See also* executive vs. judicial authority; 6 January 1915 law
Restored Republic (1867–76), 29–30
Reyes Osorio, Sergio, 11
right to due process: landowners' demands for, 54, 62; in 1917 Constitution, 4, 9; villagers' rights to, 136, 142–47
Robles, José, 176, 180–84, 270n77
Robles, Serafín M., 164, 177
Rodríguez, Marcelino, 95
Rojas, Máximo, 247n23
Roseberry, William, 76
Rouaix Méndez, Pastor, 245n5; on agrarian reform, 112–13, 258n60; public offices held by, 110–12, 116, 124, 200, 246n11
Ruiz, Filiberto, 71, 231n64

Salazar, Eusebio, 100
Salinas, Salvador, 261n94, 264n15
Salinas de Gortari, Carlos, 12
Sánchez Beltrán, René, 180–81
Sánchez de Corona, Isabel, 61–62
Sánchez Galán, Luis, 177
Sanderson, Susan Walsh, 14
San Luis Potosí, place names in: Jesús María, 155; La Huasteca, 56; La Purísima Concepción Catorce, 56, 118; San Francisco de la Palma, 224n6; Santa Clara, 155; Tanque Colorado, 156; Villa de Reyes, 67
San Miguel Anenecuilco (Morelos), 77–78, 176–77; failed restitution to, 22, 163, 176–85, 270n77; *merced* of, *178*; and National Agrarian Commission, 179–85, 270n77
Santiago, Juan, 36, 219n51
Sarabia, Juan, 72–74
Saravia, Emilio G., 258n60
Schaefer, Timo, 38, 235n47
S. de Corona, Isabel, 169
Serna, Fermín, 61–62
Serralde, Francisco, 78
Serrano, José J., 102
Serrano, Jovito, 37–38
Sesma viuda de Ruiz, Elena, 117, 138
Sierra Zavala, Fernando, 38
Silva Herzog, Jesús, 11
Simpson, Eyler N., 10, 262n100
Sinaloa, place names in: Guasave, 57; Ocoroni, 58

Index 319

6 January 1915 law, 121, 128–29, 163, 209n5, 246n15; article 10 in, 143, 171–72, 199, 254n21; and article 27 (1917 Constitution), 21, 135, 139, 145, 165, 168, 169; contradictions in, 16–17; and *dotaciones*, 23, 123, 140–42, 147, 150–51; and executive vs. judicial authority, 7–8, 108, 136–43, 170–72, 253n17; and landowners, 142–43; and Lerdo law (1856), 115, 175, 185, 247n19; and Luis Cabrera, 108, 113–15, 194; and Ministry of Agriculture and Development (Constitutionalist), 114, 116, 126, 128–29, 135; and Morelos agrarian reform (1920–24), 21, 162–65, 168–72, 174–75, 183–87, 190; and post-1917 Supreme Court rulings, 136–45, 170–72, 253n17; provisions of, 115, 120, 122, 150–51, 168, 248n24, 261n89; on restitutions, 2–3, 23, 117, 119–20, 247n19; scholarship on, 8, 11, 143, 209n6, 272n4; used by villagers, 120, 122, 130–33, 144–45, 251n79, 253n17; and Venustiano Carranza, 20, 109, 116, 129; and Zapatista agrarian reform, 162, 164, 185, 191–200
Sonora, place names in: Cucurpe, 155, 259n71; Natora, 225n13
state agrarian commissions. *See* local agrarian commissions
Stavenhagen, Rodolfo, 11
Suchiquiltongo (Oaxaca), 47
Supreme Court: closure of (1914), 4, 75, 108, 134, 244n1; justices, 33–36, 59, 171; and Madero's land surveys, 70–72, 75; and Morelos agrarian reform (1920–24), 21, 162–63, 168–72, 190, 267n41; post-1917 rulings of, 4, 12, 20–21, 109, 117, 120, 134–43, 145–47, 149–50, 160, 170–72, 190, 196, 201, 252n5, 253n8, 253–54n17, 254n18, 255n25, 262n96, 266n39; pre-1917 rulings of, 17, 26, 30–42 *passim*, 49–51, 54, 55, 57, 59, 70–72, 74, 219n48, 223n101, 252n5, 253–54n17, 255n25; scholarship on, 4, 8, 10–11, 209n7. *See also amparo* (after 1917); *amparo* (before 1917); executive vs. judicial authority; judiciary; jurisprudence

Tabasco, place names in: Huimanguillo, 50; Villa de Tacotalpa, 122–23, 155
Tamaulipas, haciendas in: Los Borregos, 89, 110, 258n60
Tamaulipas, place names in: San Joaquín del Monte Mission, 223n3
Tannenbaum, Frank, 2–3, 9, 114, 209n6
Tapia, José L., 82, 87, 101, 102
terrenos baldíos, 73, 193, 205, 223n3, 247n19. *See also* federal public lands laws
Tinsman, Heidi, 152
Tlaxcala, haciendas in: Santa Ana Portales, 120
Tlaxcala, place names in: Calpulalpan, 39, 46; Cuecillos Ranch, *114*; La Concordia, 120; La Trinidad Chimalpa, 121; Panotla, 139; Quiahuixtlán, 121; San Cosme Xaloztoc, 117, 138; San Jerónimo Zacualpan, 120; San Juan Quetzalcoapan, 153; San Lorenzo

Axocomanitla, 118, 119, 120, 131;
San Pablo Zitlaltepec, 227n18;
Santa Inés Tecuexcomac, 139;
Teacalco, 120; Zacatelco, 120
Torres Burgos, Pablo, 78

Ulloa, Berta, 5
Urbina, Miguel, 37
use rights, 31, 42, 56; and Constitutionalist agrarian reform, 150, 152, 153; and other agrarian reform projects, 16, 77, 129, 244n3
U.S. Homestead Act (1862). *See* family patrimony

Vaca, Guzmán, 171
Valladares de la Cruz, Laura R., 187
Vallarta, Ignacio L., 33–34, 36
Velasco, Ismael, 174
Veracruz, haciendas in: El Encero, 155; Paso de San Juan, 47; San Marcos de León, 112; Santa Cruz, 246n9; Tenextepec, 128
Veracruz, place names in: Acula, 123, 130; Altotonga, 50; Ayahualulco, 128–29; Chicontepec, 33; Chiltoyac, 47; El Chico, 155; Ixhuacán de los Reyes, 128; Papantla, 48; San Andrés Tuxtla, 66; Santa Cruz, 155; Santa María Magdalena de Xico, 112
Villa, Francisco (Pancho), 106, 151, 208n1, 239n81
Villa de Ayala (Morelos): and Morelos agrarian reform (1920-24), 176–77, 179, 182, 184–86; and Zapatista agrarian reform, 60, 78, 82
village agency: and executive vs. judicial authority, 5, 18, 25–26, 49–56, 64, 65, 69, 109, 130–31, 144; in Morelos agrarian reform (1920-24), 186–90, 264n15; and use of National Archives, 45, 67, 77, 122, 180, 194, 221n68, 221n73, 228n25; in privatization of communal lands, 5, 18, 33, 47, 48, 52, 55, 58, 66, 82–83, 193, 226n14; in *repartos*, 225n13, 226n14, 226n58. *See also* intervillage conflicts; village agrarian petitions
village agrarian petitions, 54–64; via *amparo*, 5, 32–36, 38–40, 42, 45, 49–51, 57, 59, 70, 72, 120; to de la Barra, 53, 56–57, 59, 62, 76, 193, 223n1, 223n3, 224n9, 227n18; to Madero, 53–61, 60, 65–68, 72, 130, 193, 224nn6-7, 226n14, 227n18; to Ministry of Agriculture and Development (Constitutionalist), 115, 166; to Ministry of Development, 221n68, 225n13, 226n14; and Morelos agrarian reform (1920-24), 165–66, 268n58; and privatization of communal lands laws, 5, 18, 44, 47–48, 52, 130; for restitutions, 1, 56, 59, 61–62, 66, 130–34, 144–48, 152, 173–75, 224n9, 228n18, 247n21, 248n30, 251nn79-80; using federal public lands laws, 18, 47–49, 52, 56, 70; using Lerdo law (1856), 58; using Plan de Ayala, 86, 104, 132, 251nn79-80; using Plan de San Luis Potosí, 55–56, 58, 60–61, 65, 224n6, 224n9, 228n18; using 6 January 1915 law, 120, 122, 130–33, 144–45, 251n79, 253n17; to Zapatista General Headquarters, 6, 242n122

Index 321

village representatives, 210n11; forming commissions, 55, 57, 77, 133, 194, 226n14; and municipal governments, 5, 47, 48, 49, 55, 66–69, 71–72, 77, 210–11n11
Villamil, José Ignacio, 139
Villarreal González, Antonio I., 164, 166–68, 172, 264n9
Villarreal Muñoz, Antonio, 135
Villaseñor, Cástulo, 191–92
Villaseñor Tortolero, Alejandro, 104

Warman, Arturo, 13–16, 162–63, 172, 184–85
Whetten, Nathan L., 10
Wolfe, Michael D., 149
Womack, John, Jr., 162, 209n9, 215n63, 235n46

Yáñez, Agustín, 173–74
Yucatán, place names in: Hampolol, 69–71; Tekit, 47; Ticul, 34; Xpechil, 155

Zacatecas, haciendas in: Griegos, 133
Zacatecas, place names in: Santo Tomás, 133; Susticacán, 56; Valparaíso, 59
Zapata Salazar, Emiliano, 62–64, 77–78, 101n241, 215n63; and Aguascalientes Convention, 91, 239n81; assassination of, 162, 191; on autonomy for pueblos and municipalities, 83, 103; and early hacienda invasions, 19, 60–61, 78, 184; followers of, 205, 234n26; leadership by, 77–80, 205, 234n26; relations with Madero, 1–2, 53, 62; scholarship on, 22–23, 62. *See also* Plan de Ayala; Zapatista agrarian reform; Zapatista General Headquarters
Zapata Salazar, Eufemio, 80
Zapatista agrarian reform: and agrarian commissions, 76, 89, 93, 98, 100, 164–66, 194, 199, 238n73; agricultural lands in, 19, 77, 98–102, 196–99; agronomists, engineers, and surveyors in, 9, 63, 76, 87–91, 94, 99, 102–3, 106, 109, 237n63, 238n73; and burden of proof, 19, 54, 63–64, 93, 193, 194–95, 214n60, 229n36; censuses in, 99–101, 111, 241n109; and communal lands and water resources, 1, 22, 98, 101–2, 104, 193, 196–98, 235n44; corruption in, 19, 22, 83, 87, 88, 191, 197, 199; *ejidos* in, 63, 100; and executive vs. judicial authority, 4, 19, 22, 64, 72, 75, 76, 79, 80, 83, 85, 89, 91, 107, 192–95, 198–99, 244n1, 272n10; expropriation in, 22, 84–89, 98–100, 107, 193, 195, 215n64, 229n32, 235n45; family patrimony in, 88–89, 98–101, 197; and federal public lands laws, 77, 88, 98–100, 196; *fundo legal* in, 81–82, 85, 102, 198; and intervillage conflicts, 6, 19, 77, 81, 93–95, 102, 105, 106–7, 192–93, 199–200, 232n1, 240n88, 241n97, 271n90; and judiciary, 63–64, 72–77, 79, 80–83, 85, 89, 91, 107, 192–95, 198–99, 241n109, 272–73n10; laws concerning, 80–81, 85, 87–

90, 98–99, 233n22, 233n24; and municipal authorities, 77, 81, 86–87, 99, 100–106, 109, 199; and nationalization, 84–89, 100, 101, 229n32, 235n45, 243n140; and pasturelands, 19, 77, 101–2, 198; and primordial titles, 79, 89, 94, 95, 101–2; and private property, 23, 84, 99–101, 195, 197, 215n64; and privatization of communal lands laws, 77, 82–85, 88–90, 98–100, 196–97, 237n66; and public utility, 84, 195–96, 215n64, 235n44; *repartos* in, 6, 19, 22, 77, 86–89, 94–95, 99–100, 102, 106–8, 111, 132, 133, 162, 164–65, 197–98; restitutions in, 4, 19, 54, 76, 80–83, 85, 87, 88–91, 94–98, 96–97, 101–2, 105, 193–96, 232n3; and urban areas, 102–3; use rights in, 77; and water resources, 104–6, 118, 131–32, 149–50, 157–59, 163, 165, 169, 171, 187–90, 243n140, 257n50, 257nn52–53, 257n55, 261n89, 271n97; and woodlands, 77, 99, 101, 103–4, 198, 251n80; and Zapatista General Headquarters, 83, 86, 88, 100, 103, 197, 232n3, 241n109. *See also* Ministry of Agriculture and Colonization (Zapatista); Palafox Ibarrola, Manuel

Zapatista General Headquarters, 83, 88, 237n61; and agrarian reform, 83, 86, 88, 100, 103, 197, 232n3, 241n109; and inter-village conflicts, 94, 105, 106, 199–200; as judicial authority, 76, 194; and Revolutionary Junta of the Center and South of the Republic, 80; and Revolutionary Junta of the State of Morelos, 80; village agrarian petitions to, 6, 242n122. *See also* Palafox Ibarrola, Manuel

Zúñiga y Acevedo, Gaspar de, 117

In the Mexican Experience Series

Women Made Visible: Feminist Art and Media in Post-1968 Mexico City
Gabriela Aceves Sepúlveda

From Idols to Antiquity: Forging the National Museum of Mexico
Miruna Achim

Seen and Heard in Mexico: Children and Revolutionary Cultural Nationalism
Elena Jackson Albarrán

Railroad Radicals in Cold War Mexico: Gender, Class, and Memory
Robert F. Alegre
Foreword by Elena Poniatowska

The Mysterious Sofía: One Woman's Mission to Save Catholicism in Twentieth-Century Mexico
Stephen J. C. Andes

Matters of Justice: Pueblos, the Judiciary, and Agrarian Reform in Revolutionary Mexico
Helga Baitenmann

Mexicans in Revolution, 1910–1946: An Introduction
William H. Beezley and Colin M. MacLachlan

Routes of Compromise: Building Roads and Shaping the Nation in Mexico, 1917–1952
Michael K. Bess

Apostle of Progress: Modesto C. Rolland, Global Progressivism, and the Engineering of Revolutionary Mexico
J. Justin Castro

Radio in Revolution: Wireless Technology and State Power in Mexico, 1897–1938
J. Justin Castro

San Miguel de Allende: Mexicans, Foreigners, and the Making of a World Heritage Site
Lisa Pinley Covert

Celebrating Insurrection: The Commemoration and Representation of the Nineteenth-Century Mexican Pronunciamiento
Edited and with an introduction by Will Fowler

Forceful Negotiations: The Origins of the Pronunciamiento *in Nineteenth-Century Mexico*
Edited and with an introduction by Will Fowler

Independent Mexico: The Pronunciamiento *in the Age of Santa Anna, 1821–1858*
Will Fowler

Malcontents, Rebels, and Pronunciados: *The Politics of Insurrection in Nineteenth-Century Mexico*
Edited and with an introduction by Will Fowler

Working Women, Entrepreneurs, and the Mexican Revolution: The Coffee Culture of Córdoba, Veracruz
Heather Fowler-Salamini

The Heart in the Glass Jar: Love Letters, Bodies, and the Law in Mexico
William E. French

Silver Veins, Dusty Lungs: Mining, Water, and Public Health in Zacatecas, 1835–1946
Rocio Gomez

"Muy buenas noches": Mexico, Television, and the Cold War
Celeste González de Bustamante
Foreword by Richard Cole

The Plan de San Diego: Tejano Rebellion, Mexican Intrigue
Charles H. Harris III and Louis R. Sadler

The Inevitable Bandstand: The State Band of Oaxaca and the Politics of Sound
Charles V. Heath

Redeeming the Revolution: The State and Organized Labor in Post-Tlatelolco Mexico
Joseph U. Lenti

Gender and the Negotiation of Daily Life in Mexico, 1750–1856
Sonya Lipsett-Rivera

Mexico's Crucial Century, 1810–1910: An Introduction
Colin M. MacLachlan and William H. Beezley

The Civilizing Machine: A Cultural History of Mexican Railroads, 1876–1910
Michael Matthews

Street Democracy: Vendors, Violence, and Public Space in Late Twentieth-Century Mexico
Sandra C. Mendiola García

The Lawyer of the Church: Bishop Clemente de Jesús Munguía and the Clerical Response to the Mexican Liberal Reforma
Pablo Mijangos y González

From Angel to Office Worker: Middle-Class Identity and Female Consciousness in Mexico, 1890–1950
Susie S. Porter

¡México, la patria! Propaganda and Production during World War II
Monica A. Rankin

A Revolution Unfinished: The Chegomista Rebellion and the Limits of Revolutionary Democracy in Juchitán, Oaxaca
Colby Ristow

Murder and Counterrevolution in Mexico: The Eyewitness Account of German Ambassador Paul von Hintze, 1912–1914
Edited and with an introduction by Friedrich E. Schuler

Deco Body, Deco City: Female Spectacle and Modernity in Mexico City, 1900–1939
Ageeth Sluis

Pistoleros and Popular Movements: The Politics of State Formation in Postrevolutionary Oaxaca
Benjamin T. Smith

Alcohol and Nationhood in Nineteenth-Century Mexico
Deborah Toner

Death Is All around Us: Corpses, Chaos, and Public Health in Porfirian Mexico City
Jonathan M. Weber

To order or obtain more information on these or other University of Nebraska Press titles, visit nebraskapress.unl.edu.

www.ingramcontent.com/pod-product-compliance
Lightning Source LLC
Chambersburg PA
CBHW030333240426
43661CB00052B/1621